PLAINS HISTORIES

To Jane,
thanks for
being the high
bidder!

John R. Wunder, *Series Editor*

ALSO IN PLAINS HISTORIES

America's 100th Meridian:
A Plains Journey,
by Monte Hartman

American Outback:
The Oklahoma Panhandle in the Twentieth Century,
by Richard Lowitt

Children of the Dust
by Betty Grant Henshaw; edited by Sandra Scofield

From Syria to Seminole:
Memoir of a High Plains Merchant,
by Ed Aryain; edited by J'Nell Pate

Railwayman's Son:
A Plains Family Memoir,
by Hugh Hawkins

Rights in the Balance:
Free Press, Fair Trial, and the *Nebraska Press Association v. Stuart,*
by Mark R. Scherer

Ruling Pine Ridge:
Oglala Lakota Politics from the IRA to Wounded Knee,
by Akim D. Reinhardt

The Death of
Raymond Yellow Thunder

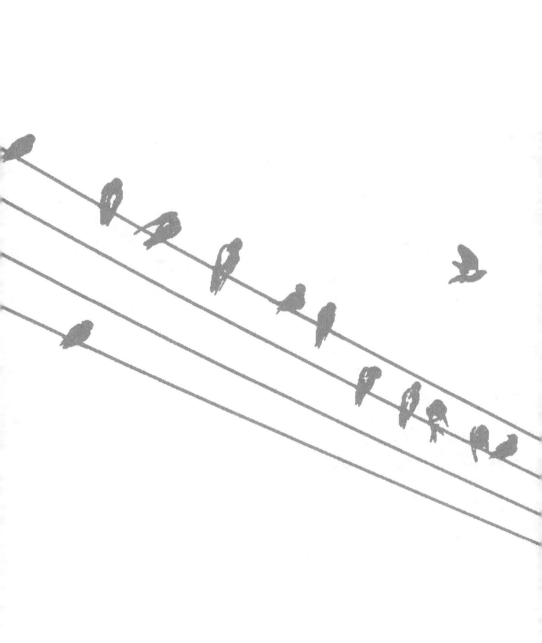

The Death of
RAYMOND
YELLOW
THUNDER

And Other True Stories from the
Nebraska–Pine Ridge Border Towns

STEW MAGNUSON
Foreword by Pekka Hämäläinen

TEXAS TECH UNIVERSITY PRESS

This book is typeset in Monotype Bodoni. The paper used in this book meets the minimum requirements of ANSI/NISO Z39.48-1992 (R1997). ∞

Designed by Lindsay Starr

LIBRARY OF CONGRESS CATALOGING-IN-PUBLICATION DATA
Magnuson, Stew.
    The death of Raymond Yellow Thunder : and other true stories of the Nebraska-Pine Ridge border towns / Stew Magnuson ; foreword by Pekka Hamalainen.
      p. cm. — (Plains histories)
    Summary: "A nonfiction account of the Oglala of Pine Ridge, South Dakota, and the white settler towns of Sheridan County, Nebraska. Explores the repercussions of Raymond Yellow Thunder's death at the hands of four white men in 1972 and the struggle of American Indian Movement Nebraska Coordinator Bob Yellow Bird Steele"—Provided by publisher.
    Includes bibliographical references.
    ISBN-13: 978-0-89672-634-5 (hardcover : alk. paper)
    ISBN-10: 0-89672-634-7 (hardcover : alk. paper) 1. Oglala Indians—South Dakota—Pine Ridge—History—20th century. 2. Ethnic conflict—South Dakota—Pine Ridge—History—20th century. 3. Ethnic conflict—Nebraska—Sheridan County—History—20th century. 4. Borderlands—South Dakota—Pine Ridge—History—20th century. 5. Borderlands—Nebraska—Sheridan County—History—20th century. 6. Pine Ridge (S.D.)—Ethnic relations. 7. Sheridan County (Neb.)—Ethnic relations. I. Title.
    E99.O3M34 2008
    978.004'975244—dc22   2008014712

Page ii photo by John Vachon of Whiteclay, Nebraska, in November 1940. (Courtesy of Library of Congress.)

Printed in the United States of America
08 09 10 11 12 13 14 15 16 / 9 8 7 6 5 4 3 2

TEXAS TECH UNIVERSITY PRESS
Box 41037, Lubbock, Texas 79409-1037 USA
800.832.4042 | ttup@ttu.edu | www.ttup.ttu.edu

For my mother, Julie Strnad,

and stepdad Charley

" I hope that all your children and our children

will treat each other like brothers—and also

our children of the future—as if we were

children of one family. **"**

CHIEF RED CLOUD
of the Oglalas to citizens of Nebraska,
Independence Day, 1889

CONTENTS

Illustrations xiii
Foreword xv
A Brief Note from the Author xix

Prologue.. 3

A Cold Night in Gordon...................................... 11

The Story of John Gordon.................................. 25

Where Is Uncle Raymond?.................................. 37

The Oglalas' Long Journey to Pine Ridge............. 63

The White Folks' Journey to Sheridan County........ 87

A New World.. 105

Indian Scare.. 129

Two Paths... 157

Thunder in the Courthouse................................ 185

Billy Jack Goes to Gordon.................................. 215

Little Skid Row on the Prairie............................ 257

The Battle of Whiteclay..................................... 287

Another Saturday Night in Gordon...................... 305

Acknowledgments 321
Notes 325
Sources 341
Index 349

ILLUSTRATIONS

ii........ Whiteclay, Nebraska

xiv........ Map of Pine Ridge area and Sheridan County

2........ Tom Poor Bear's march to Whiteclay

12........ Raymond Yellow Thunder

27........ Camp Sheridan, Nebraska

39........ Sheridan County Attorney Michael Smith

62........ Chief Red Cloud

88–89........ Oglalas and Sheridan County residents

104........ Sheridan County settlers in front of Fort Nendle,
circa 1890

131........ Protesters at the Gordon City Auditorium

159........ Sam Hinn and unidentified bartender at the
Barrelhouse Tavern

184........ Native American activists marching through
downtown Alliance

214........ Bob Yellow Bird at the Gordon City Council meeting

256........ Storeowner John David's car on Whiteclay's main
street

286........ Protesting against the Oglala Tribal Police and
Nebraska State Patrol

304........ Dennis Yellow Thunder at the resting place of his
uncle Raymond Yellow Thunder

323........ Pat Shald at the site of Camp Sheridan

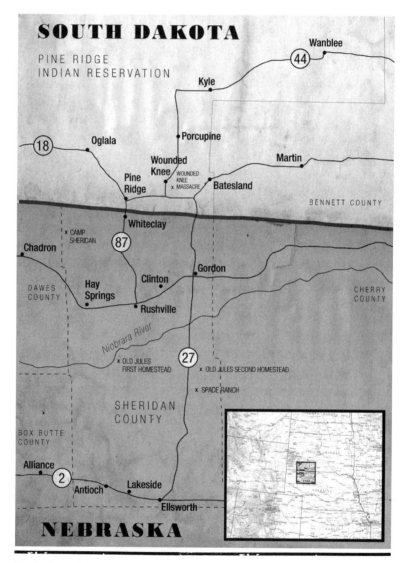

Map by Brian Taylor.

For most Americans, border towns represent the storied urban places that dot the desert landscapes where the United States becomes Mexico. The associations may be positive at first, but soon darker images interfere. The U.S.-Mexico border towns of American imagination are a netherworld of *narcotraficantes*, primal racial violence, and corrupt, callous state authorities; they are scarred places where the legacy of conquest takes on concrete form in the vast income gap that segregates the North from the South. These border towns impart mixed emotions of fear, frustration, anger, and shame, but they may not be North America's most troubled border communities. The border towns that edge Indian reservations in places like Arizona or Nebraska are plagued by many of the same problems that haunt Tijuana or Matamoros. But while U.S-Mexico border towns figure prominently in popular culture, their reservation counterparts rarely enter the picture. Although quintessential American places, they are largely forgotten.

In his book, Stew Magnuson recovers the deep, loaded, often disturbing history of these shadowy border towns by taking us into Sheridan County, Nebraska, where a host of white settlements serve, largely as alcohol depots, the Pine Ridge Lakota Reservation in South Dakota. Told through layered stories that move back and forth in time and across the physical and mental borders separating Native and white communities, *The Death of Raymond Yellow Thunder* is not conventional academic history. It is instead about the people—drunks and petty criminals, Indian militants and exasperated state officials, journalists and shopkeepers, men, women, and children—who occupy these peculiar American places and whose lives and histories have become irrevocably entwined. Magnuson's mission is to reveal the full spectrum of human experience in the border towns' charged cross-cultural spaces, and in that he succeeds beautifully.

The cumulative effect of the numerous individual stories Magnuson tells us is devastating: they evoke a deep sense of sadness over the destitution, exploitation, fraud, racial hatred, sheer boredom, and alcohol-fueled aggression that permeate the lives of these border peoples. The book's broken temporal composition compellingly underlines its author's notion that violence in the Nebraska–Pine Ridge border towns is historically conditioned and structural: the past, and peoples' inability to let go of the past, fuels an endless cycle of violence between Indians and whites even as the social space between the two groups grows narrower. Although the topic is controversial and veiled by distorting layers of historical memory, Magnuson's approach is remarkably balanced. His sympathies certainly lie with the Lakotas, but he resists the all too common scholarly tendency to demonize the whites and absolve the Indians as innocent victims or freedom fighters. In these stories all the protagonists are multifaceted, flawed, and profoundly human; whether Indians or whites, they all struggle—and repeatedly fail—to come to terms with each other's presence in their lives.

But there is more to the book; like all good stories, *The Death of Raymond Yellow Thunder* spins against the way it drives. Even as the peoples of Sheridan County despise, scorn, exploit, assault, and kill one another, their lives, like objects slipping out of control, become more and more inseparable. Indians and whites coexist and, against all odds, somehow get along, sharing space they really don't want to share. This countercurrent is the source of the many unexpected stories Magnuson brings forth—like that of a policeman who cares for a town drunk, an Indian, by regularly locking him up on freezing nights. I read *The Death of Raymond Yellow Thunder*—and mine is only one of many readings this open-ended book yields—as a story of a borderland where peoples from two seemingly incompatible cultural systems forge a new mutual world of tenuous accommodation. A deepening interdependency marks the relations between Lakotas and white Nebraskans, and *The Death of Raymond Yellow Thunder* draws much of its dramatic thrust from the failure of so many from both sides to accept that fact.

While fixing its focus on the local, *The Death of Raymond Yellow Thunder* does not ignore the larger developments influencing the history of Nebraska–Pine Ridge border towns. The U.S. government's repeated attempts to dismantle Lakota culture, the shock of the Wounded Knee Massacre in 1890, the crushing poverty and hopelessness of Pine Ridge, the ascendancy of the American Indian Movement in reservations, the climactic 1973 occupation of Wounded Knee, and the post–Wounded

Knee dirty war between AIM and Indian activists on the one side and the FBI and U.S. government on the other are all here. Other historians have discussed these events, but *The Death of Raymond Yellow Thunder* provides a rare look into the ways in which they played out at the grass-roots level. The scale of this book is the human scale. *The Death of Raymond Yellow Thunder* also breaks new ground by bringing the story to the twenty-first century. By doing so, it reminds us that although it rarely makes headlines, racial violence between Indians and whites is still here. Deep in America's heartland, Magnuson suggests, a slow-burning conflict smolders: Nebraska–Pine Ridge border towns are battle zones, where the meaning of sovereignty and peoples' right to defend themselves against external exploitation remain undetermined.

The book's lucid story-centered approach deceives, for underneath it lies a serious core. Magnuson's unflinching focus on individuals and their fates reveals things that often are lost in more self-consciously scholarly histories. One is the complexity of the two ethnic groups that collide and constantly redefine themselves in interaction. Neither Indians nor whites emerge as monoliths but rather as diverse collections of individuals with often clashing personalities, aspirations, and allegiances. Magnuson reconstructs several instances of white violence toward Indians, but unlike many other histories that take white aggression and racism as givens, he shows the historical forces and personal burdens that pushed individuals to violence. Magnuson deepens our understanding of border towns by showing how many white Nebraskans (including state authorities) were disturbed by racial violence and how they fought to suppress it. In a similar vein, he shows how the actions of Indian activists sometimes stemmed less from genuine concerns for their people than from power rivalries, personal tragedies, and impulses toward self-aggrandizement. More broadly, *The Death of Raymond Yellow Thunder* engages a number of key themes of current scholarship—racism, masculinity, construction of cross-cultural spaces, historical memory—without the interference of a heavy theoretical apparatus. Refreshingly, Magnuson doesn't place anything between his words and readers. His stories lie bare and thoroughly accessible.

Pekka Hämäläinen
Santa Barbara, California, 2008

A BRIEF NOTE FROM THE AUTHOR

This is a collection of stories and vignettes about two peoples, the Oglala Lakotas of the Pine Ridge Reservation in South Dakota and the border town residents of Sheridan County, Nebraska.

The stories within are true. They are written in narrative nonfiction style, meaning they are not presented in the manner of an analytical scholarly history book or as a piece of journalism where all versions of a story are considered. They are written much like a novel or short story. Choosing this style places a great burden on the author because he is saying that "this is the way it happened."

This burden was not taken lightly and resulted in many sleepless nights. Memories are faulty, conflicting versions of the same story are common, loose ends can't always be tied up, and facts don't always jibe with each other. In these cases, the author followed the "when in doubt, leave it out" axiom.

Nevertheless, the stories are constructed from the same sources a history professor might employ: memoirs, FBI files, local law enforcement and court documents, newspaper articles, scholarly works, photos, videotapes, the author's own observations, and more than seventy interviews. And as a conscientious journalist would do, the author made every effort to interview those still living who had direct knowledge of an event. Those who agreed to an interview had their points of view represented fairly and accurately in the book. Only four subjects asked that they not be named.

Those wishing to discover how a particular scene or story was constructed may refer to the sources cited in the endnotes.

—SM

The Death of
Raymond Yellow Thunder

Tom Poor Bear marches to Whiteclay, July 3, 1999.
(Photo by author.)

hey gathered under the blistering July sun to march on the town of Whiteclay, Nebraska.

Population twenty-two.

Unincorporated.

Two thousand Oglala Lakotas waited on the edge of the Pine Ridge Reservation. Women, children, the elderly. Some were pushing baby carriages. Old men walked with canes. A few were riding horses. Others were American Indian Movement activists—middle-aged men and women—wearing T-shirts commemorating their glory days. Some were angry young men hoping for a fight. Reporters and TV crews tagged along, wondering if there would be any violence again.

They stood at the beginning of a two-mile stretch of highway in South Dakota that led south to the nearby Nebraska border. Ahead of the marchers, Route 87 passed through Whiteclay, a blink-and-you-miss-it town, and continued into the farmland and ranches of Sheridan County, Nebraska. The road passed over the pine-covered ridge that gave the reservation its name, until it ended twenty-eight miles later, just west of Rushville, another Nebraska border town. But they wouldn't be marching that far. Their destination was Whiteclay—a town of two restaurants, one pawnshop, two grocery stores, and four off-sale beer stores. Combined, the beer merchants sold four million cans of beer per year to customers from the reservation, where alcohol was prohibited.

The marchers assembled between Billy Mills Hall—a multipurpose community building that had seen better days—and the much newer Big Bat's gas station/convenience store. It was just after noon, the day before Independence Day, July 3, 1999. The asphalt soaked up the sun's heat, sending the excess energy up in shimmering waves. A few dashed into Big Bat's to grab some last-minute bottles of water or soda.

The marchers unfurled the red and white Oglala Pine Ridge tribal flag and raised their protest signs.

Justice For Hard Heart
Remember Crazy Horse
Metcalf Lakota Killer!

After a spiritual leader led them in prayer, they turned south and began to walk. Two protesters rolled out a yellow AIM banner with a warrior wearing an eagle feather holding an M-16 rifle.

American Indian Movement
Free Leonard Peltier
Lakota Nation
Remember Wounded Knee 1890–1973

The words recalled both AIM's heyday in the 1970s and the disastrous December morning eleven decades earlier when so many died.

They could hear the Nebraska State Patrol helicopter thumping two miles ahead, circling Whiteclay like a red-tailed hawk. Below it, 109 state patrolmen and 40 tribal police officers, dressed from head to toe in black, began to mobilize. The tribal police, there to reinforce the Nebraskans, picked up their riot shields and batons, then marched in military formation to the state line. They wouldn't put on their teargas masks until the last minute. It was just too damn hot.

Everyone feared the angry young men. What would they do in Whiteclay that day? The leaders pleaded that morning in Billy Mills Hall for a peaceful, prayerful march. One week before, the same angry young men had run into the ramshackle town of twenty or so buildings, set a grocery store on fire, stole a fire truck when it came to put out the flames, and relocated the "Welcome to Nebraska" sign to the other end of town where they thought it belonged. They were fueled by righteous anger, hopelessness, and the rare opportunity to add some excitement to the soul-crushing boredom on "the rez." This week, the state patrol was determined not to let that happen again.

"Walk slowly for the elders," a leader called through a bullhorn as they started the slow procession to Whiteclay.

Onetime AIM leader Russell Means led the march. He wore long braids and a black T-shirt with a round Wile E. Coyote cartoon bomb with its fuse lit, ready to explode, and the words "Talk is Cheap" written across his chest. He had a long, striking face and wore dark sunglasses.

He looked like a damn movie star. Hell, he was a damn movie star. Or a movie actor, at least.

Walking alongside Means was the portly Clyde Bellecourt, his gray hair tied back in a ponytail. Next to him, the gaunt-looking Dennis Banks. Both he and Bellecourt were longtime AIM activists from the Ojibwa nation in Minnesota.

Twenty-seven years ago, Banks, Bellecourt, and Means were angry young men themselves when they led a march into nearby Gordon, Nebraska, to protest the death of a Lakota ranch worker at the hands of four white men. They were little-known leaders from a little-known organization. But after Gordon, everyone on the reservations knew their names. The three would go on to occupy the village of Wounded Knee for seventy-one days and fight a small-scale war with the FBI and tribal authorities for the remainder of the decade. They were no longer angry young agitators and hadn't worked together in two decades, but now they were marching into Sheridan County again to demand justice for two more deaths.

On the other side of Means, Tom Poor Bear strode down the highway wearing a black mustache, a black vest, and a white T-shirt commemorating AIM's occupation of Wounded Knee. Poor Bear was no longer a young man, but he was certainly angry. His half brother, Wilson "Wally" Black Elk, Jr., and cousin Ronnie Hard Heart had been found one month earlier beaten to death on the South Dakota side of the border in a ditch a few yards from Whiteclay. Poor Bear was a sixteen-year-old student back in 1972 when he heard Means, Bellecourt, and Banks speak in Gordon. The next day he dropped out of the reservation boarding school and devoted his life to the cause.

It was Poor Bear who two weeks ago had called the Minnesota-based AIM leaders to help him demand justice. He didn't call Russell Means, though. He showed up anyway. And then a riot broke out.

A reporter sidled up to Means to ask him what it was like working with director Oliver Stone in the movie *Natural Born Killers*.

A smile lit up his face.

It was a great time, he replied, clearly glad to be talking about his Hollywood experiences.

Means didn't trust "the white media," but he was glad they were there. Without the cameras, the state patrol would probably beat the crap out of them, he thought.

On top of the soil, mingled among the dry summer grass in the ditches where the marchers pass by, lie thousands of aluminum cans. Budweiser, Miller, Coors—lager, light beers, and malt liquor. Some are covered by weeds; others lie glistening in the sun. In the middle of night, drinkers toss the cans out their car windows. They hit the pavement and roll around in the cool air until the front wheel of a second car smashes them flatter than fry bread. And there they sit for weeks until sheer physics—wind, rain, gravity—budges them over to the shoulder. Some of the cans make it into the ditch, there until the mower makes his monthly pass and shreds them into twisted, jagged pieces. Dark amber bottles find their way into the ditch, too. Some shatter on the asphalt, the paper label holding the fragments together until rotting away, scattering the glass chunks like rocks in a stream.

Underneath the grass lies the litter of 120 years. Dig beneath the cans, and dark amber forty-ounce bottles appear, some still wrapped in their decaying brown paper bags; deeper still, the pull tabs from steel cans, rusting away. Next come the pints of fortified wine—Mad Dog 20/20, muscatel—sold for decades by a legendary Whiteclay bootlegger from her back window. Several feet down, back when the road was gravel and curvy, the drinkers tossed clear glass whiskey flasks from their horse-drawn wagons. For as long as the Oglalas have been here, Nebraska merchants across the border have sold alcohol to the dry reservation. Four million cans per year from the tiny hamlet. Would anyone ever adopt this stretch of highway for litter control? The troubled two miles of pavement is an unwanted orphan.

The marchers stopped a few hundred yards outside the town where the bodies of Black Elk and Hard Heart were found. The victims' families walked down into the tall grass among the thistles and grasshoppers to pray. The state patrol helicopter thumped overhead as nonfamily members stood along the highway and eyed the line of one hundred men dressed in riot gear.

The elders didn't want any trouble. President Bill Clinton was due to arrive within four days. He would be the first sitting president to visit an

Indian reservation in sixty-three years. Proof indeed that Native Americans were the country's most ignored minority.

Clyde Bellecourt spoke on the reservation's public access station, KILI radio, the day before and told listeners that AIM didn't want any violence in Whiteclay. AIM wanted the president to come and see the poverty for himself. He wanted Clinton to hear their grievances. Bellecourt had organized a security team of AIM members to make sure the angry young men didn't get out of hand as they had a week ago. He'd met with the state patrol and other Nebraska officials the previous night in Whiteclay and assured them that they were going to pray at a designated spot north of the police line, make some speeches, and return to the reservation. Bellecourt even agreed to let the patrol plant undercover officers among the marchers so they could monitor the angry young men. Nobody wanted to scare Clinton away, he insisted.

Except Russell Means.

Means and the other AIM leaders had been butting heads for the past thirty years. Earlier that year, the organization's Web site proclaimed him an ex-member. He was an avowed libertarian and had nothing but contempt for Democrats and Republicans alike. He didn't give a damn if the "sleaze of all sleazes," as he called Clinton, came to Pine Ridge or not. He actually didn't care how many cans of beer Whiteclay sold to the reservation per year. He didn't want to see the four package stores shut down. It was everyone's right to drink if they wanted. But Whiteclay once sat on the Extension, a ten-mile buffer zone created by treaty to keep the whiskey away from the Oglalas. President Theodore Roosevelt took it away by executive order in 1904. Unjustly, Means believed. Whiteclay was sitting on Indian land as far as he was concerned, and the Oglalas should take it back.

Means was the one who told the protesters to tear down the "Welcome to Nebraska" sign the previous week, kicking off the riot. And he didn't intend to stand around for speeches and prayers this week.

The marchers set out for the final time.

Bellecourt, yelling through a bullhorn, led the chant every protester knew:

"What do we want?"

"JUSTICE!"

"When do we want it?"

"NOW!"

The sun was already cooking the troopers inside their riot gear when their captains ordered them to put on their gas masks. German shepherds panted in the waist-high grass. Four snipers deployed on four rooftops aimed their scopes on the mounted protesters, ready to take out a horse or shoot a car wheel if they tried to bust through the lines.

The head of the state patrol, Colonel Tom Nesbitt, stood behind the phalanx of men in black monitoring the situation. The short, muscular Nebraskan had two undercover officers marching with the crowd. Already things weren't going as planned. Bellecourt promised the night before that there wouldn't be any civil disobedience. But Nesbitt, monitoring speeches broadcast over KILI from Billy Mills Hall late that morning, heard some leaders threaten to bust through the police line. Now, the undercover officers were radioing in a report of protesters picking up rocks and carrying fireworks. They reported that the women and children were falling to the back of the crowd and the young men moving up front. Some intended to splinter off and attack the town from the west. One of Nesbitt's lieutenants ordered the bulk of the troopers to the dirt road that skirted the west side of town, leaving mostly Pine Ridge officers on the highway.

Nesbitt had spent most of his career in the east side of the state as a narcotics investigator. He knew little about Whiteclay until the governor appointed him to lead the state patrol four months earlier. Now, the town and its twenty-two inhabitants were his number-one headache. The Pine Ridge police department had told him that AIM had been losing support on the reservation for years and might be looking to pull off an occupation, or some other big event, before the president arrived. Nesbitt had met that week with Governor Mike Johanns in Lincoln. Some of the governor's advisors wanted to call up the Nebraska National Guard. The colonel convinced them that the patrol could handle the situation. Now it was time to prove it.

Allen Sheppard, a twenty-three-year-old AIM member from Granite Falls, Minnesota, jogged up to the line wearing a red T-shirt, green camouflage pants, and an eagle feather in his hair. A graying Justice Department observer carrying a walkie-talkie followed.

Sheppard stopped in front of the riot police, puffing furiously on a cigarette.

"You're all on Indian land and you gotta move to the other side of town," he declared. "We're gonna be coming down and we're gonna pray between those buildings."

"That's not what Mr. Bellecourt agreed to last night," a lieutenant replied. The line would stay where it was.

"I'll be back," he said, and turned to rejoin the march.

When the marchers came over the ridge they could see the long, black line of state troopers and tribal police blocking the road. A thin yellow plastic ribbon with the word "caution" was strung knee-high to mark the line that they were forbidden to cross.

"This is the Nebraska State Patrol," a voice droned through a bullhorn from inside Whiteclay. "You are welcome to this portion of Nebraska. You may not cross the yellow-taped line. If you cross the line, you will be in violation of Nebraska statutes and enforcement action will be taken."

The yellow tape separating the two sides marked a divide that had persisted for more than a century. The Pine Ridge Reservation in South Dakota spreads out from the last fingers of the Sand Hills in the south, to the pasty-colored Badlands to the north. Just beyond its border are the silhouettes of the Black Hills, the Lakotas' sacred land, lost to them forever after a bitter and bloody war. The reservation, home of the proud Oglala Lakotas, part of a nation better known as the Sioux, is a land of stark and remarkable beauty and crushing poverty.

South of the reservation's border lies Sheridan County, Nebraska, forty miles wide and seventy-five miles long. This is Sand Hills country, where gently rolling sand dunes are held in place by a thin layer of grass. The county is the home of proud ranchers, farmers, and three border towns serving the reservation. The residents—some poor, some middle class, and some wealthy—are largely the descendants of European immigrants. For more than 130 years, the Oglalas and the people of Sheridan County have lived next to and among each other. Like Highway 87, the fear, hatred, and misunderstandings run both ways. That hot day in Whiteclay would be only one more chapter in their intertwined, tumultuous history.

The tinny bullhorn crackled again. "This is the Nebraska State Patrol . . ."

Fifty yards in front of the line, Tom Poor Bear told the crowd to stop. This was as far as they were supposed to go. He knew this was a dangerous situation. Despite all his bravado quoted in the newspapers that week, he didn't want anyone to get hurt.

"What are you doing?" Means shouted at him loud enough for everyone to hear. "Let them through! Never negotiate away their rights!"

And with that the Oglalas let out the war whoops of their ancestors and surged toward the police line.

A Cold Night in Gordon

They began to crisscross downtown in the light blue Ford Custom looking for the old Indian. It had been a while since Les had jumped him on the sidewalk, but maybe he was still hanging around. They hunted between the brick and stucco buildings, systematically searching each block, creeping down the alleyways where a drunken Indian might hang out.

The passengers were drinking their way through a case of beer and a quart of cheap wine. They drained the containers, rolled down the windows, and tossed the empties into the yards of the respectable townies where they would be found the next day in the brown grass as the homeowners made their way to church.

Country-western twang cried from the scratchy AM radio as the heater filled the car with warm air. The temperature was quickly dipping down into the twenties since there was no cloud cover to insulate the town.

It was February 12, 1972. A USO benefit dance was under way at the American Legion Hall out on Highway 20. Just about everyone was there—everyone who liked to drink and dance anyway. But two of the car's five passengers, brothers Les and Pat Hare, had been banned from the club, so they decided to cruise the streets as they had when they were teenagers. But none of them were teenagers anymore.

The oldest of the men, twenty-seven-year-old Les Hare, had his left arm around his much younger girlfriend, Jeannette Thompson, who sat up front between him and the car's owner, Robert Bayliss, known to everyone as "Toby."

The tall and raw-boned Toby drank from a can of Budweiser nestled in his lap as he drove through quiet neighborhoods with single-frame houses sitting under leafless trees. Toby was a mechanic and a body man at a local dealership. He knew how to paint a car, and the Custom two-door was his pride and joy.

Raymond Yellow Thunder, date unknown. (Courtesy of Dennis Yellow Thunder.)

In the back seat with Les's younger brother Pat was their buddy, Bernard "Butch" Lutter. The two were knocking back beers as well. Only Jeannette refrained from drinking.

Where was that god-damned Indian?

They drove north toward South Dakota and the Pine Ridge Reservation, but stopped at the edge of town when they reached Shald's Jack and Jill grocery. The flat metal-framed building was the last chance for Oglala shoppers to buy supplies before heading north. Toby made a U-turn at the store's parking lot and headed back south toward Main Street, passing silent houses with living room lights seeping out of closed curtains. Empties clanked into the gutters. Les liked Schlitz and Toby was a Bud man, so they'd bought a twelve-pack of each. The Schlitz came in amber bottles, and they hit the pavement with sharp "clinks." The containers marked their path like Hansel and Gretel's breadcrumbs. Les blew a stream of smoke out the cracked-open window.

The brown-brick movie theater, still under construction, marked the beginning of downtown. Next to it was Messenger and Milburn's used-car lot and garage where Toby had worked with his dad until the elder Bayliss was killed in a car wreck the year before. They passed the storefronts of Gordon's downtown businesses, most of them closed for the evening: Saub's clothing store, Saults and Son Drug, the Coast to Coast, Gordon Cleaners, Strong Insurance Agency, the Gordon State Bank, J. C. Penney, the First National Bank, Stockman's Rexall Drugs, Borman Chevrolet, and the office of the *Gordon Journal*.

Only the Z-K and Western bars showed any signs of life.

Wagon Wheel Liquors stood to the east, beside the Chicago & North Western railroad tracks. The package store had opened just the month before where the train depot used to sit, and Toby and Les were already giving the owner plenty of business.

The car rumbled over three sets of railroad tracks and passed the two massive grain elevators, which stood like two sentinels on either side of the road. The white 150-foot monoliths were the closest western Nebraska would ever come to having a skyscraper. They passed the Bowl-Mor Lanes on their left, then reached the end of Main Street, which continued south as Highway 27 into the depths of the Sand Hills. The townies called the county below them the South Hills and the insular residents Southhillers. They'd tell you that the folks down there were "a different breed of cat."

Highway 20 ran east and west, stretching from Chicago to the Oregon coast. It used to be an important road back in the 1950s. Then Interstate 80 opened one hundred miles to the south, and Interstate 90 one hundred miles to the north. Now, only a few scattered eighteen-wheelers rumbled by.

The slickly painted Ford sped across the intersection and pulled into the Ideal Supermarket parking lot. From the grocery store, they could see the Legion Hall a half block east just past the Enco service station and Otto and Mickey's Cafe. The club's parking lot was already full of cars and pickups. Toby turned around and headed back north, more empties sailing out the window.

Now, where was that god-damned Indian?

Les, Butch, and Pat started talking about flying. All three were pilots. Toby, who didn't fly, perhaps feeling left out of the conversation, took a sharp turn past the railroad tracks, steering the car into the southeast corner of town where the impoverished Oglalas lived. They drove past rundown mobile homes and houses that were nice fifty years ago. Rusty old cars parked in front; trees and weeds brown from winter. Toys, doghouses, old bicycles were strewn on the lawns. This was "Indian town," where most of Gordon's two hundred Oglalas lived.

Jeannette didn't know much about flying, either. She was just happy to be with Les. The twenty-year-old brunette was content to sit quietly between the two longtime friends. It was an anniversary of sorts for Les and Jeannette. Nearly one year ago, they'd both abandoned their spouses and children and run off to Colorado together.

Les's wife, Jerene, still lived in Gordon with their nine- and four-year-old daughters. Jerene Schmidt, a pretty blonde from Gordon, married Les while he was in the service in Texas ten years earlier. The match came as a shock to their Gordon High School classmates. Jerene came from a well-respected farming family. She and her twin brother were smart, and most expected her to do well. Les was about as different as they came. He had little use for school and didn't participate in any activities. He was a wild boy from the depths of the South Hills. He could be charming and funny when not drinking, but he wasn't much for formal schooling. Unlike Jerene, no one expected a damn thing from Les—except an early death.

Many South Hills ranchers kept light aircraft in their barns so they could check on their vast holdings or make quick trips to town. Les borrowed one and taught himself how to fly. He ran the single-prop plane along the grass runway, lifting off and setting it down little by little until he felt comfortable enough to fly around a bit. It was just the sort of crazy thing he did. Soon he was flying over the ranchlands without a license. He delighted in bringing unsuspecting classmates up in the air with him, and laughed as he buzzed a few feet above the Niobrara River's cottonwood treetops, snapping off branches, watching with pleasure as his victims' faces contorted in terror. A drive home in one of his fixed-up jalopies was no different. Accepting a ride home from him was to court death. Get him on a gravel road where no law enforcement lurked, and he really let loose. A mutual love of cars was how he buddied up with Toby when they were in their early teens. Les never finished high school. He went into the army and married Jerene. But that was over now. He hadn't lived with her for a year, preferring the company of Jeannette instead. The brunette was a farmer's daughter with average looks and a medium build.

Jeannette Hartwig had married her high school classmate John Thompson in the summer after their junior year. Seven months later their son Michael was born, so Jeannette never returned to school. From the beginning, she showed little interest in her child or the marriage. Two weeks after the boy's second birthday, she dropped the toddler off at her mother-in-law's house without saying where she was going, then disappeared for six months. Her husband, John, filed for divorce, claiming child neglect, abandonment, and adultery. He ran an ad in the *Gordon Journal* for three weeks proclaiming his intention to divorce his wife. By that time, Jeannette was shacking up with Les in Colorado. She did not appear in court.

Toby was married, too. His wife, Sharan, and their two boys were back at the farmhouse eight miles west of town. It hadn't been a good year for the twenty-six-year-old. On a Saturday afternoon the previous August, his father Robert, Sr., had pulled out onto Highway 20 and collided with an oncoming car, dying instantly.

His dad had taught Toby everything he knew about fixing cars, and he was now considered one of the best mechanics in town. He was still smarting from his father's death and his mother Harriet's quick remarriage to a welder in Scottsbluff, Nebraska.

In the backseat sat Les's twenty-four-year-old brother Melvin. But no one called him that. He went by his middle name, Pat. The younger

Hare was a tall drink of water, and looked nothing like his brother, who had a rather long, dour face. Pat wore a handsome, wide-open expression. He wasn't as wild, either. Pat was the quiet one, but like Les, he wasn't much for book learning. Although they were opposites in many ways, Pat looked up to his slightly shorter older brother. Les quit school and joined the army in his senior year. Pat later did the same. Les learned how to fly, and Pat did as well (although he took formal lessons and earned a license). And Pat had followed his brother to Colorado where they took jobs driving trucks. The only thing Pat wouldn't take up was Les's smoking habit. He hated the smell of tobacco.

Bernard "Butch" Lutter sat next to Pat. The twenty-five-year-old brown-eyed, brown-haired carpenter was the only one without Gordon roots. He came from Gannvalley, South Dakota, and traveled the region, going from job to job as a carpenter. He met Pat a couple years before at the Chadron, Nebraska, airport where they were both studying for their pilot's license. A year later, he arrived in Gordon to work on a housing project. Pat introduced him to Les, and they hit it off immediately. They both liked to fly, and they both liked to drink beer. Butch fixed Les up with a job at the construction site, which was the latest in a series of low-skill, low-wage jobs for him. After Les's discharge from the army, he'd worked as a ranch hand, a carpenter, and a mechanic. After running off with Jeannette, he landed the truck-driving job in Longmont, Colorado.

Toby drove the car back north on Main and turned left onto Second, where they'd encountered the Indian earlier in the evening. They'd been heading east toward the rodeo grounds when Les had spotted the man walking on the sidewalk. He was tall but lanky, with a sharp face and dark brown skin. He was neatly dressed, wearing a pair of new blue jeans and a red plaid shirt he'd bought that day. His hair was freshly cut and combed back with a dab of cream. He seemed to be all legs.

"Pull over," Les had hollered.

Les jumped out of the car, called the man a few names, and shoved him. He got back in the car, grinning as the old man, stunned by the sudden attack, stood on the sidewalk.

"I really got him good!" Les said, laughing. Toby took off, leaving the old Indian behind. They drove around the corner to the Wagon Wheel and bought another case of Schlitz and Bud. A little while later, Les came up with the plan and they began searching for the Indian.

Les, Pat, and their father, Dean, had spent the day crisscrossing the Sand Hills hunting for coyotes. Toby had to work Saturdays, but Butch was there up in the sky, flying patterns over the winter brown hills, looking for their prey. Les had phoned Butch earlier in the week, inviting him up for a weekend of drinking and hunting. Butch was on the fence as to whether he should go—he couldn't leave the construction site in Colorado until late Friday afternoon—but in the end, he decided to fly up.

Dallas Dean Hare was in charge of the hunt. He rode in the front of the pickup while his pack of greyhounds stuck their long noses out the back, sniffing the cool air for any sign of their canine cousins. Dean wore a white cowboy hat and peered out into the prairie through rectangular wire-rimmed glasses. He had a square jaw, like his son Les, and a grim expression put there by decades of eking a living out of the Sand Hills.

Dean was a legend in Sheridan County. Legendary for his temper and outright meanness, some said. He was a tough Sandhiller and an old-fashioned horse trader. He traveled the region exchanging incorrigible horses for tamer ones. He sold the hard-to-break horses as "killers" for slaughter. Some didn't make it to the slaughterhouse. They became bucking broncos for his side business raising rodeo livestock. Dean's livelihood depended on him coming out on top in every deal—and he always came out on top. He could be a charming storyteller when he wanted. Ranch hands in bunkhouses would gather around to hear him spin his yarns, but he was equally well known for being cruel to animals. He beat uppity horses with whatever he had handy. He had to show them who was boss.

He felt the same way about his wives.

Les and Pat's mother, Norma Hooper, lived on her deceased father's horse ranch in the South Hills where she was caring for her elderly mother. She'd divorced Dean when the boys were toddlers because she couldn't take his violence and temper. Despite the mean streak, Norma let Les visit his father in the summers, and her eldest cherished his time with Dean, who'd remarried twice by the time Les had reached his teens. Dean's first home sat on the banks of the Niobrara in a V-shaped valley, covered in the shade of tall cottonwoods. The Niobrara was flat and shallow, just knee-deep in the summer and narrow enough for Les to toss a rock to the opposite bank. He lived on the border of Sheridan County's two societies. South of the river, the Sand Hills ranching country stretched down an arduous gravel road forty miles to the county line. To the north, the land was flat enough for farming. Until the 1950s, the Niobrara was as far as the paved road went. The insular people of the South Hills rarely mingled with the townies and farmers to the north. They took few trips to Gordon, preferring to head west to the larger town of Alliance.

While the paved road north of Dean's home meant easy access to town, Les's interests remained in the stark but beautiful Sand Hills, where he could fish, hunt, and drive at breakneck speeds on the back roads. His knack for resurrecting scrap-heap cars was as legendary in the South Hills as his reckless driving. But he loved coyote hunting best. Ranchers considered the coyotes that roamed the grasslands a threat to their cattle, but the Hares didn't hunt them out of concern for their meager livestock holdings, or the small bounty the county paid for ears. This was a blood sport, and Les took to it with fervor. Once he got on the trail of a coyote, there was nothing he wouldn't do to make the kill. He once fixed up an old truck and attached a wedge to the front so he could slice through barbed-wired fences. Often he wouldn't return to fix them, which infuriated the local ranchers.

By 1972, Dean had moved closer to Gordon, taking up residence with his third wife, Charlotte, in a small brick house next to the cemetery and golf course, which was within sight of the grain elevators and water tower to the north. He started a second family and had three more boys, Scott, Miles, and Vernon.

Hunting coyotes was serious business for the Hares. It was widely rumored that Dean snatched stray dogs and cats off the street and used them to train his greyhounds. When his notorious pack caught up with a target, each hound had a role. One would grab the prey by the hind leg and twist the unfortunate animal over, flipping it on its back to expose the neck. A second hound went for the jugular. If the dogs couldn't finish the job, Dean would step in with a mallet and do it himself.

Pat went along for the hunt that day even though Dean and he had never been close. Pat arrived at the end of his parents' rocky marriage when Dean was consumed with jealousy and suspicion. He did not believe that Pat was his son. Norma's second husband felt the same way about the boy. Pat still came through Gordon with Les to visit their mother, but even if Norma weren't living there, he would have still gone along for the ride. Rejected by two father figures, Pat worshiped his older brother. He would do anything for him.

It wasn't such a bad day for February, clear in the midforties with no snow on the ground. With Dean's specially trained greyhounds, two generations of accumulated knowledge in the pickup, and Butch's keen eyes spotting their prey from the air, the coyotes didn't stand a chance.

Now, where the hell was that Indian?

There were other cars cruising the streets of Gordon that night. Pickups and sedans full of teens drinking beer bought for them by sympathetic elders passed by Toby's Ford Custom. As in many small towns where there wasn't anything to do, the cruising tradition went back decades. Toby and Les used to cruise these same streets as teenagers. Now they were doing it again, and growing drunker as the night went on. This wasn't a nostalgia trip for them, though. Earlier in the year, Bernard Sandage, the cantankerous American Legion Hall manager, had kicked Les and Pat out for harassing a waitress and refusing to take off their hats.

"Our hats are off," Les said, doffing his cap, then using it to swat the waitress's behind. Pat snapped her butt with a handkerchief. The "no hats" rule was always a source of tension between the ranch hands and townies.

Just as Sandage asked them to leave, Bob Case, the chief of police, coincidentally showed up.

"Are you boys leaving on your own or with him?" said Sandage, who was a World War II vet and D-Day survivor. He knew how to handle himself.

They decided to leave, but not without tossing a few threats Sandage's way.

Les was still steamed about the incident. After all, they were only having a few beers and a bit of fun.

So he cooked up the plan.

"There he is," Les shouted, finally spotting the Indian walking with a bottle of wine into a lot full of unwanted junkers in the back of the Borman Chevrolet dealership.

Like the coyotes, the old man didn't have a chance.

Toby turned the car around and headed down the side street. By the time he pulled up to the east end of the lot, across the street from Morsett's Laundromat, the Indian had disappeared into the rows of rusting heaps. The four men left Jeannette in the car and spread out to look for their prey. Les quickly found him in the front of an old light blue pickup with wood side panels. The Indian was just settling in to sleep when Les opened the door and yanked him out.

"I got him!" he yelled to the others.

As Butch came running, he saw Les on the other side of the truck, hopping up and down, grabbing the panels for leverage.

"I'm really stomping him!" Les said.

Toby arrived next, with Pat on his heels. Toby grabbed the old man by his hair, lifted his head, and punched him in the mouth twice.

"Come on, Butch, this is a lot of fun," Toby said.

The beating shocked Butch. In the car, Les and Toby had talked about "busting Indians" when they were younger, but he'd never witnessed anything like this.

Pat stood watching, just as surprised as Butch was. He hadn't grown up in the border town or inherited any of Dean Hare's meanness.

"C'mon. Let's get his pants off," Les said.

Pat did as his brother asked and helped him strip the old man of his shoes, underwear, and pants, leaving him only his socks from the waist down. The brothers carried the half-naked man between them as Toby jogged ahead to open the trunk.

"That stinkin' Indian ain't riding in front!" Toby declared.

Les shoved him in the trunk as Jeannette watched passively from the front seat. Toby slammed the lid shut and the four piled back in the car, leaving the old man's shoes and pants in a heap in the car lot.

They raced out to the Legion Hall, where the dance was still under way, the car rumbling over the rough railroad tracks. They drove back and forth along the highway casing out the club, just a simple red building with a log exterior. Customers kept going in and out, so it was always too busy when they passed. They kept circling, arguing whether or not they should pull off the prank.

"Come on. Let's just do it," Butch finally said. He was worried about the man freezing back there. And what about the exhaust fumes? "Let's just get rid of him."

After they drove around for an hour, the parking lot looked still and Les finally decided to put his plan into action. As Toby eased the car into the lot, they saw a teenager sitting in a pickup. He had his motor running and his headlights on, pointing at the front of the building. That wouldn't do. They needed darkness. Les and Jeannette knew him, though.

Max Anderson was a skinny kid—about her age—who worked at the meat-packing plant.

Les walked over to the truck as the muffled sounds of the Bud Paul Band's accordion seeped through the building. Max rolled down his window, allowing the chilly air to fill the cab. Les said "hi" and asked Max what he was up to. A couple of his older buddies were inside, and he was waiting for them to come out since he was too young to drink.

"Hey, Max. Ain't I your friend?"

"You always have been," Max said.

"Can you turn your lights off? We got a drunk Indian in the trunk with his pants off. We're gonna throw him in the Legion."

Max switched off the lights and watched as Pat and Butch guided the half-naked man between them to the front door. Meanwhile, Toby drove off with Les and Jeannette to the highway intersection to wait.

The old man could walk on his own, but he seemed resigned to his fate. He didn't say a word as Butch opened the door. Warm air and a country waltz rushed through in a wave as Pat shoved the old man inside. Butch slammed the door shut, held it a few seconds to make sure he couldn't escape, then sprinted away with Pat to meet the others.

Inside, the drinkers and dancers heard the door slam shut with a startling bang. They craned their heads over the booths and saw an Indian man standing near the edge of the dance floor, one hand pulling his shirttail over his groin, the other covering his face in shame. A few women near the dance floor gasped. Marvin Wheeler was sitting closest. He left his shocked wife Virginia in the booth next to the door and grabbed his suit coat to cover up the old man.

Sandage was on the other side of the dance floor tending bar with the portly Bob Buchan when a young man darted up. "You got trouble!" he said.

The two men went over to see what the commotion was all about. They saw the old Indian—disheveled, his forehead bruised, his hair out of place, dirt caked into his hair cream. Dancers stopped and stared. Sandage and Buchan, leaving Wheeler and his suit coat behind, guided him out the front door into the freezing air.

"What's going on here?" Sandage asked.

"Some boys roughed me up," the Indian said, still pulling his shirt-tail down.

Sandage knew the Indian. He'd hired him a few times to put up hay on his farm. He already suspected that the Hares were part of this.

"You want us to call the police?" Buchan asked.

The old man shook his head, said he wanted to leave.

He trotted back toward the highway into the bitterly cold night, stepping over the gravel parking lot with only socks between his feet and the frozen ground.

If he doesn't want any help, then he doesn't want any help, the two men thought. They went back inside. Neither of them called an ambulance or the police.

After picking up Pat and Butch, Toby drove around for a few minutes until Les told him to swing back to the Legion Hall. He wondered what kind of mayhem they'd sprung on the Legionnaires. They cruised past the building, but it was quiet. Les was disappointed. No mayhem. No brouhaha. No commotion at all. Toby pulled up next to Max's pickup as Les rolled down his window.

What happened?

Not much, the teenager said. The old Indian and some fellows came out the door right away, then he ran off.

A car pulling in behind them interrupted their conversation.

"Come on with us," Les said. Max left his truck and squeezed into the backseat with Pat and Butch. Someone passed him a can of beer as Toby sped out of the parking lot. They drove north again past the railroad tracks, east of the grain elevators. The Indian emerged in the headlights, gingerly walking along the side of the road, heading toward the used-car lot.

"Ah hell, it's too damn cold out for him to be walking with no pants," Les said. Toby stopped.

Les fetched the man again as Toby stepped out to pop open the trunk.

The Indian found himself back in the dark, cold hole. Toby slammed the lid shut, and they drove off, passing the used-car lot, heading north to where the houses ended and the prairie began. They took a right, going east for a mile on a gravel road—more empties flying into the ditch—until they came to the end of the mile section. They stopped to relieve themselves by the side of the road.

"What are we gonna do with the Indian in back?" Toby asked after they got back in the car and drove off again.

"Let's take him back to his clothes and give him a beer for being a good sport," Les said as they hooked south toward the airport.

Pat, always a lightweight despite his size, started feeling the effects of the beer. He felt sick and wanted to go back to Dean Hare's. They passed the airport and emerged from the country road back onto Highway 20.

Max wanted out, too. He'd left his pickup idling; plus the local cops had arrested him the previous summer for being a minor in possession. Maybe it wasn't such a good idea to be driving around with the Hares. But Pat wasn't looking good, so they passed the Legion Hall, continued for another mile, and took a left up another gravel road. After guiding the stumbling Pat into the small brick house, Toby turned around and drove back to the Legion. By the time they dropped Max off and made it back to the used-car lot, the old man had spent another forty-five minutes in the trunk.

They parked in front of Morsett's Laundromat across the street from Borman's. It was still open, but no one was around.

Les pulled the half-naked old man out of the trunk and brought him into the laundry. He told Butch to fetch the man's clothes across the street. Butch found the pants, shoes, and long underwear spread out on the ground. He went through the pants and found three dimes and a nickel and pocketed the change before walking across the street. Les tossed the clothes to the old man. They left him there, forgetting to give him a beer for being "a good sport."

Les, Jeannette, Butch, and Toby drove off to get some breakfast at Seger's Cafe, the twenty-four-hour greasy spoon just past the outskirts of town.

The man slowly put on his pants. He tied his shoes and shuffled quietly out of the laundromat. He wasn't going back to the used-car lot. He'd had enough of the white men. His sister and a niece lived in town, but it was late, he'd been drinking, and he was too ashamed to go there. He would ask the police if he could do a voluntary sleepover in the city jail. Only then could he be certain his tormentors wouldn't be back to rough him up again. His face was scuffed up. It hurt, but it wasn't so bad. He broke horses when he was younger, and he'd had worse knocks than that. It was the shame he felt most. All those people looking at him . . .

The old Indian's name was Raymond Yellow Thunder. Eight days later, he would be found dead in the front seat of a truck behind Borman's Chevrolet.

The Story of John Gordon

In the fading evening light, John Gordon watched the soldiers on the hill overlooking his encampment with more than a little trepidation. He could see the shadow of a sentry outlined against their campfires. A spring breeze, cool enough to make the men in his party huddle around their fires, carried the smell of burning wood down the hill to where he paced nervously. There was an uneasy truce between the thirty U.S. Cavalry men and his wagon train of 150 determined miners. Gordon wondered how long it would last.

The smell of stewed venison from black cooking pots wafted through his own camp. The fires were fueled by pine and cottonwood found in the ravine. The Niobrara River, "Running Water" in the Lakota language, gurgled below them. This was a good spot to camp, close to water, with an abundance of firewood in an otherwise treeless land. Deer were plentiful in the Sand Hills to the south, and it was a good spot for the wagons to cross the river should the troops ever stop shadowing them, or the treaty preventing his men from traveling to the Black Hills cease to be.

For the past five weeks, resolute men and one equally determined woman had traveled hundreds of miles under Gordon's leadership. They were from every walk of life: merchants, blacksmiths, cowboys, railroad workers. Iowans and Hoosiers. Young and old. Immigrants who could barely speak the English language; Civil War veterans looking to recapture some of the adventure they'd experienced ten years before. A few were even experienced miners. Every one of them was a dreamer. Every one of them had caught gold fever. Every one of them had scraped up the hundreds of dollars needed to outfit themselves for the long journey from Sioux City, Iowa, to the Black Hills where the newspapers said the precious metal was found "from the roots on down." Many had handed their last penny over to Gordon's bosses at the Sioux City and Black Hills Transportation Company, and it was his job as captain of the wagon train to deliver them to the "new El Dorado."

But now the damnable army was standing in their way.

Gordon wasn't certain if the hills had paying quantities of gold. There was some gold there, however. He'd been to the hills once and found some himself. Lt. Colonel George Armstrong Custer had led one thousand men the previous year, the summer of 1874, into the mysterious hills that jutted out of the vast prairie. The expedition's geologists had found traces of gold. Not much, but by the time the newspapers exaggerated the general's claims, you would have thought the mountains were made of the stuff.

The Sioux City merchants knew the real gold mine was in supplying the hundreds of dreamers who were flocking to the area. The frontier economy had soured the past few years. A three-year drought had turned crops into dust. Banks were forcing homesteaders to abandon their farms. A dose of gold fever was just what the people needed. America had experienced several gold rushes, and the smart merchants knew—poor economy or not—that merchants in the city that supplied the prospectors would profit handsomely. And Sioux City, Iowa, although it was five hundred miles from the Black Hills, was the front-runner. Yankton, South Dakota, was closer. Cheyenne, Wyoming, and Sidney, Nebraska, were closer still. But Sioux City had something the other hopeful towns did not: namely John Gordon.

Gordon had led the first successful expedition to the Black Hills the previous year. The trip had gone much more smoothly then, although there were several complications. Charles Collins, editor of the *Sioux City Journal*, and his partner T. H. Russell went to Chicago and signed up eleven hundred men willing to invade the hills. And it would be an invasion. Because the Black Hills belonged by treaty forever to the Sioux.

But this was gold. And gold-crazed white men wouldn't allow a treaty with the savages to stand in their way. Collins and Russell made no secret of their intentions. Yes, there was a treaty with the Sioux. But that was made before the discovery of gold, wasn't it? What use did the red men have for gold?

The army, foreseeing trouble with the Sioux on the horizon, had other thoughts. General William Tecumseh Sherman declared the hills "off-limits" to gold seekers. The army brass knew the Lakota Sioux considered the Black Hills sacred. The generals had already fought one war seven years ago with their leader, Chief Red Cloud, on the "bloody" Bozeman Trail—a war the U.S. Army lost. They didn't want to tangle with the most powerful tribe on the Plains again.

Camp Sheridan, Nebraska, circa 1875.
(Courtesy of Nebraska State Historical Society.)

Collins and Russell proclaimed in the press that they were abandoning the expedition. Privately, they sent letters to a select few, inviting them to come to Sioux City in September with three hundred dollars. Among the twenty-six men, one woman, and one boy to answer the call was John Gordon.

They secretly assembled their wagons and supplies three miles west of town, then lit out west across the prairie. While the newspaperman Collins stayed behind, his partner Russell left with the party. But Russell didn't know the territory. Gordon claimed to know the area well (a lie) and that he had experience driving ox teams (the truth). The others, mostly tenderfoots with little frontier experience, took him at his word and voted him the captain.

They painted "O'Neill or Bust" on the sides of their wagons as a bit of subterfuge. The Irish settlement on the Elkhorn River was the last outpost on their way to the hills. The townsfolk along the trail took one look at the wagons full of mining equipment and had a good laugh. Maybe that ploy didn't work, but the rest of Gordon's strategies did.

After leaving O'Neill, Gordon made the wagon train circle back and zigzag through the Sand Hills to confuse any Sioux warriors or army regulars hunting for them. He made the tenderfoots extinguish their fires at sunset even though the autumn air grew more brisk with each passing day. He insisted on vigilance during the long, cold nights and posted sentries. Oh, how the men complained about waking up in the middle of the chilly nights to stand watch. The others, including the only woman in the party, Annie Tallent, didn't care for sleeping on the frozen ground without a fire. They grumbled, threatened mutiny, but in the end he got them there, didn't he? Maybe it was the relatively small size of the party. Maybe it was the discipline. Maybe it was just plain luck. For whatever reason, they made it to the Black Hills without seeing a single bluecoat or Sioux warrior. Gordon later found out that two army details had been dispatched to intercept them, and a second party of seven would-be miners leaving from Yankton had encountered a band of angry Brulé Sioux. Only six made it back alive.

The Gordon party built a stockade on French Creek, only a mile from where Colonel Custer had camped that summer. It was already winter, not the best season for mining since the ground was frozen, but after a month of prospecting, they'd found forty dollars worth of gold. Not much, but enough to convince the dreamers back in Sioux City that it was there.

Gordon and Eph Witcher left the stockade in February with a packet of letters encouraging others to follow and a small sack of gold to prove their claim. But Gordon's horse had drawn up lame just a day out of Yankton. The scoundrel Witcher rode out ahead of him and was wined, dined, and toasted in every saloon in town before Gordon arrived. The news of their discovery was front-page news as far away as New York City. But everyone would soon know that Gordon was the man who'd led the party. When the new company was formed in April, it was Gordon who was hired to lead the new party, not Witcher. And for the princely sum of one thousand dollars!

But this time it was 149 men, 1 woman, 47 wagons, and 80 ox teams heading west in mid-April 1875. Their plans were hardly a secret. Journalists sent dispatches about the trip to every corner of the nation. It didn't take long for the army to find them.

Gordon walked through the camp, passing scores of angry men eating their supper, smoking their pipes, playing cards, or just sitting around fires grumbling about their misfortune. He glanced back up at the cavalrymen on the ridge and thought about his predicament.

Captain Fergus Walker, leading his men out of Fort Randall in Dakota Territory, had already captured another expedition leaving Sioux City. Fortunately for the Gordon party, most of Walker's troops had to escort the other party back, which left the Irish-born captain with only thirty men. Walker's weakened force had confronted the Gordon party a few days before. The cavalrymen lined the miners up and insisted that they hand over their arms. Some did, but most refused. Gordon stayed in the background and kept his mouth shut. Only he could guide them to the Black Hills, and Walker undoubtedly read the newspapers and knew this. The Irishman, perched up on his horse, offered a fifty-dollar reward to any man who would reveal Gordon's identity, but no one took him up on the offer. Gordon looked like the rest of the men—scruffy and with a monthlong growth of beard. Each man knew if they lost their guide, they lost everything. Who would take fifty bucks when untold riches awaited them on the other side of the Badlands?

After Walker followed them from camp to camp for several days, the men decided that the army couldn't legally arrest them if they weren't on Sioux territory. Where the Sioux territory began was a matter of debate. But it certainly wasn't south of the Niobrara River. So as long as they camped on the south side of the river, in the free state of Nebraska, there wasn't a damn thing Captain Walker could do, they reasoned. They told the captain that they had the right to camp there until the treaty was renegotiated. The captain extracted a promise from the men not to cross into Sioux territory, although Gordon knew some of the would-be miners intended to break that promise at the earliest possible opportunity. The men who'd voluntarily given up their firearms demanded that the army return what was rightfully theirs. Walker said the weapons had already been sent back to Fort Randall, which was probably a bald-faced lie. He also claimed he was only camping nearby to protect the party from angry Sioux. Gordon doubted that.

A handful of men had decided not to wait and started back for Sioux City, but Gordon knew the remaining ones were angry and desperate. Some of them were farmers who'd given up tilling the soil after watching the grasshoppers eat three straight seasons of crops. But some were experienced outdoorsmen, men hardened by years in the wilderness and rough towns out west. And the Civil War veterans knew how to handle guns. The men had nothing to lose by remaining.

It had all been going so well, Gordon thought. They had nearly made it through the empty prairie. They would have crossed the river and made their way up Antelope Creek. From then on, it would be hard ground; no more of these cursed Sand Hills with soil so soft the wagon wheels sunk in like mud. In a couple days, they would have seen the outlines of the Black Hills to the north. The Badlands were rugged and dry, and the Sioux could be anywhere, but with some luck they would have made it.

Gordon threw his blanket next to his wagon and settled in to sleep, taking one last, suspicious look at the infernal cavalrymen and their pickets surrounding them to the south. He cursed his luck. He cursed the U.S. Army. He cursed Captain Walker. Everyone was afraid of the Sioux. Hell, it was his own people keeping him from his just reward. What use did the Indians have for gold? If the federal government didn't want them to mine the Black Hills, why did they send Colonel Custer up there in the first place? Why was the army protecting savages when it should be fighting them? And the men were right. They weren't on Indian land. So the army could be damned for all he cared.

Gordon pulled a musty wool blanket over his head and fell asleep.

Captain Anson Mills rode with his men past hundreds of tipis lined along a creek bed a few miles south of Camp Sheridan. Trailing behind him were two companies of mounted cavalry, an ambulance wagon, and a battery of Gatling guns. There were nearly five thousand Sioux in the camp nestled in the valley between two pine-covered ridges. They were mostly of the Brulé band, with a few Oglalas as well. It was midafternoon. Everything looked peaceful—children were laughing and playing, dogs were lying in the shade, women were going about their chores—but Mills wondered if all was as it appeared.

There was trouble to the east. Trouble he had to deal with, or the peaceful scene before him could change quicker than prairie weather on an April day. The Natives at the Spotted Tail Agency looked calm enough. And that was a small miracle. When Captain Mills arrived a few weeks before to take command, the agency was in turmoil. It had been a tough winter for Chief Spotted Tail's people. The snow was deep, the temperatures cold, and the civilian put in charge of the agency was both incompetent and corrupt—typical of the greedy dunderheads the Office of Indian Affairs appointed to watch over its wards. To start, the beef rations the agent was charged with delivering were insufficient, which caused the Sioux to complain bitterly. The wholesaler contracted to provide flour, and the federal inspector in Cheyenne responsible for ensuring that he fulfilled his orders, had conspired to defraud the federal government. Only one-third of the flour intended for the agency Indians had been delivered. Mills put a stop to that. When the contractor and his wagons arrived with a load of flour, he was quite surprised to find the new commanding officer greeting him instead of the corrupt agent. After proving beyond a doubt that the man was shorting the flour ration by two-thirds, Mills sent the thief to the stockade. Only the army could be trusted to deal with the red man, Mills, and many of his fellow officers, believed. The civilian agents were always mucking things up. They cheated the Indians, and when the Indians went on the warpath the army had to come in and clean up the mess.

Mills was army through and through. He sported a bushy mustache and a goatee—practically part of an officer's uniform. He was a native of Indiana, and a West Point dropout, who had to quit the academy when he failed a mathematics exam. He and his two brothers spent their early years as pioneers in Texas helping to found the town of El Paso, until the Civil War ripped their lives apart. They were well-known Unionists living in rebel territory, and all three had to escape when hostilities broke out. One of his brothers was captured by the rebs and taken prisoner. Another was killed when Apaches attacked his stagecoach as he fled to California. Mills made his way to Washington DC, where the War Department desperately needed officers. After he served in the war with distinction, the army kept him in the service and sent him to the cavalry.

Captain Mills took one last look at the tipis before leaving the valley. He felt he could trust Chief Spotted Tail. In his early years, the tall, handsome chief had been sent to the prison at Leavenworth, Kansas, for attacking a stagecoach. The experience convinced him that it was useless to fight the whites. The chief was a peacemaker and a diplomat now. Mills and his wife, Nannie, had invited Spotted Tail for dinner at their rustic home inside the camp, and they found him to be a man of reason. The chief was impressed when Mills replaced the corrupt agent, and quite pleased when he ordered extra rations of bacon and hard bread delivered to the camp.

But Mills couldn't be completely at ease. Ever since Colonel Custer had led the expedition into the Black Hills the previous year, the Sioux bands, including many of Spotted Tail's young, excitable warriors, were infuriated over the encroachment on their sacred ground, their rights to it acknowledged in the Treaty of 1868. The press was sensationalizing the discovery of gold, and now that winter was over, miners were swarming to the hills like a trail of ants on a pile of sugar. One party, led by John Gordon, had set up a mining camp that winter. It took some doing, but soldiers forty miles to the west stationed at Fort Robinson near the Red Cloud Agency managed to expel the party Gordon had left behind. The lawbreakers were fortunate that the U.S. Army found them before Red Cloud's Oglala warriors. They may not have been treated so well.

But Gordon was back. This time the muleskinner would not be so lucky. An Indian scout in the employ of the army had arrived that day with word from a Captain Walker. The officer had been following Gordon's wagon train for several days, but he didn't have a sufficient force to confront the lawbreakers. He wondered if Camp Sheridan had received any change of orders concerning the expulsion of miners. (They had not.) If not, could the captain send reinforcements? (He could indeed.)

Camp Sheridan had no telegraph, and as far as Mills knew the orders to expel miners had not been rescinded. Lieutenant General Philip Sheridan, the very man whom the fort was named after, had reinforced the order himself. General Order No. 2 stated that any force encountering miners headed for the Black Hills was to "burn the wagon trains, destroy the outfits and arrest the leaders, confining them to the nearest military post." The army intended to enforce the treaty. If it didn't, the soldiers would have to deal with the angry Sioux. History would repeat itself, as it had dozens of times in recent memory. Settlers—in this case miners—would encroach on treaty lands, infuriating the Indians and sending them on the warpath. The squatters would beg the Washington politicians for military protection. Soon enough, the Washington bigwigs would order the army to take care of the "Indian problem." The Treaty of 1868 placed the Black Hills within Sioux territory and stipulated that no white persons could settle there "without the consent of the Indians." But few of the gold-crazed frontiersmen cared about treaties with Indians. Now, the army had to show these desperate men that they were serious about enforcement. As for General Sheridan, he probably didn't care one whit what happened to the Sioux's sacred land. In fact, he thought the Black Hills should be scouted for a possible fort. After all, he was the man who had infamously said "the only good Indian was a dead Indian."

Gold or no gold, sacred land or not, Captain Mills had his orders.

And so the scout led him and his men past the tipis, off the Pine Ridge, and along a stretch of hard land on the northern edge of the Sand Hills. For most of the journey, at least, they wouldn't have to travel through the soft soil.

What forces had created these frozen dunes, Captain Mills had to wonder as he looked to the south. Only a thin layer of grass stopped them from turning into rolling waves of sand. Early explorers called the hills the "Great American Desert," although this was not completely barren land. There were numerous creeks to cross, most of them full from the winter runoff. They passed alkaline lakes, as flat and shiny as mirrors. And despite the reports, there was life here. As the column rode east, elk, antelope, and deer darted over the hills. They passed prairie dog towns that seemed to stretch for miles. The critters poked their heads up from their holes, looked at them curiously, and barked while searching the sky for red-tailed hawks.

A spring thunderstorm from the west crept up behind the column. A bulbous black cloud followed them, while the skies to the south and north were clear. The rain came in thick drops, soaking Mills and his men. Lightning struck a nearby hill, sending dust into the air, cracking like an artillery shell, alarming Mills and his men because there was no cover to protect them from God's wrath.

The first Americans hunted this land for aeons. Ten thousand years, maybe longer. Back when Europeans were still living in caves, Native Americans chased the buffalo across the treeless plain, and the evidence of their hunts littered the ground beneath Captain Mills and his men. When warm gusts from the south cut through the hills in the summer, and the grass lost out to the sand, the wind exposed the hard ground beneath. In these blowouts, arrowheads lay scattered among rocks and pebbles carried there by the glaciers and ancient riverbeds. There were rusty arrowheads, fashioned from scrap metal and traded to the Lakotas over the last century. Round musket balls and flints poked out of the dust. The Lakotas had ruled the High Plains ever since horses and guns arrived a century before. Beneath the metal ammunition were the leavings of the peoples who'd hunted these hills for centuries: stone arrowheads, carefully crafted from brown flint mined in the mountains hundreds of miles away; knives to cut the game; scrapers to peel the flesh away from the hides. These were the tools of the Kiowas, Crows, Cheyennes, Arapahos, those who followed the buffalo herds, before the whites began to wipe the Indian's food source from the face of the prairie. Next to their arrowheads, hidden among the grass roots, were the points of sedentary villagers from the east—the Pawnees, Omahas, Poncas—who made annual excursions to the hills to hunt for game. Deeper still, the Plains Apaches, and tribes whose names were long forgotten, left their arrowheads, campfire charcoal, bison bones, and pottery shards along the rivers and streams.

Lying several feet beneath the soil where the cavalry horse hooves trod were the bones and tusks of mammoths, the extinct beasts hunted by nomads ten millennia earlier. Their exquisitely chipped spear points made of clear, black obsidian were all these people left behind.

Over the centuries, the sand dunes rolled over the plains, stopping when the weather was wet and the grass grew high. The hills migrated again in times of drought, covering some arrowheads, spear points, and fossilized bones while exposing others. The detritus of these ancient peoples were lying in the sandy blowouts and washed-out gullies. The bones of the vanished animals stuck out from stream banks as the cavalry passed by.

This land had once belonged to the Sioux by treaty—all the way down to the Platte River. Now that line had moved north. Their territory was shrinking. Few of them would be able to hunt the Sand Hills now that whites had come.

As night fell and coyotes howled at the moon, Mills ordered his men to push on. His column arrived in the middle of the night, but stopped short of the miners' camp. The men from Fort Randall were camped on the other side of the lawbreakers, who were all fast asleep. From the ridge to the west, Mills cautiously looked over the moonlit camp. Gordon had chosen a poor spot. The miners were camped on the banks above a river bend, with high bluffs on either side. They couldn't escape. He dispatched two of his men in plain clothes to tell Captain Walker that they would attack as soon as the sun broke in the east. He set up the Gatling guns on top of the ridges and ordered the ambulance wagon to be at the ready.

Just before daybreak, Mills looked down from the ridge at the embers of the miners' dying fires. Some of the men were beginning to stir. As soon as the sun peaked over the hills, he ordered the charge.

John Gordon woke to the sound of thunderous hoofbeats. Before he could arise, the miners were completely surrounded. The men went from groggy to angry within seconds. Captain Walker, that vile snake, had promised to leave them alone. What was this?

They hurled curses at the bluecoats.

One man's gun went off by accident.

"You may get the first shot off, but by God we'll get the last!" Mills shouted down at them from atop his horse. However, the men, seeing the menacing Gatling guns trained at them, threw down their weapons.

Gordon was put under arrest. The captain carried out his orders to the letter. To burn the wagons, he sent a few down the ravine and had them set ablaze. As soon as the flames reduced the pile to ash, the soldiers pushed another wagon on top. The giant bonfire sent a black plume soaring into the blue sky. The miners never stopped cursing the soldiers. They weren't on Indian land! They had no right!

Mills took Gordon in shackles to Camp Sheridan. Later, the muleskinner would be tried in Omaha and given a slap on the wrist. The army officers became pariahs in the Sioux City newspapers. Captain Walker and Captain Mills were the real criminals, or so said the men who wanted the Black Hills all to themselves. News of the Gordon party's fate reached the East and caused a sensation, but that did nothing to discourage would-be gold seekers. They invaded the Lakotas' sacred land by the thousands—burrowing, digging, panning. The army caught a few and handed them over to civilian courts, but as soon as they were freed, they went right back to their claims.

By the end of 1875, the army quit trying.

Ten years later, a group of churchgoing settlers from Indiana led by a Methodist minister would arrive to build a town twenty miles northwest of where Captain Mills burned the wagon train. They would name the settlement "Gordon" in tribute to the "resolute sooner." It was a rare honor to bestow upon a lawbreaker. John Gordon, by that time, had been lost to history and may have never known that his fleeting fame inspired a town's name a decade later.

But before the Hoosiers could settle the town, the prairie and the Black Hills would have to be made safe for pioneers. And for that to happen, the U.S. Army and the Lakotas would spill a river of blood onto the grasslands.

Where Is Uncle Raymond?

id you hear what happened at the Legion club Saturday night?" one of Arlene Lamont's volunteers at the new Head Start school asked Monday morning.

"No, what happened?" she said as the kids hollered around her.

"Someone pushed an Indian man through the front door with his pants off."

Arlene was shocked. The shame and humiliation the man must have felt. To the Lakotas, nudity was taboo. They didn't even like undressing in front of their doctors.

"Who pushed him?"

She didn't know. It happened so fast. A member covered him up with his coat, and then the manager and a bartender escorted him outside.

Arlene couldn't believe that anyone would do such a thing. Petite, with black-rimmed glasses and a dark complexion, she was Oglala herself and had lived in Gordon since she was two years old. Her father, Albert Crazy Bear, was a mechanic at Borman Chevrolet. She was a full blood, the third generation in her family to live in the border town. She graduated from Gordon High and planned on living in the town the rest of her life. She was married to an Oglala mixed blood, Ray Lamont, and they had four children. Now, thirty-three years old, she'd just been named the director of the Head Start program the previous fall—a source of pride for her.

Her folks had raised Arlene, her brother, and sister in the "nice" part of town, not over in the southeast section with its shabby houses and reservation refugees. When she was a girl, her grandfather had taken her over to the tent city next to the sale barn, where a year-round settlement had sprung up next to the animal stockades. The smell of manure permeated the air. She couldn't believe people could live like that. Before she was born, most of Gordon's Oglala population lived in government-issued canvas tents. At first, the tent city only sprang up in the late summer and fall when the reservation residents came down for the county fair and the potato harvest. But some of them ended up staying, and the tent city became permanent. Eventually, the families moved into the nearby turn-of-the-century houses or mobile homes.

Then there were the men who'd stepped off the train at Gordon after coming back from the military and never resettled on the rez. For Oglala men like her father who wanted to work, who wanted to escape the cycle of poverty on the reservation, Gordon had jobs. It was menial labor—construction work for building contractors, dock loaders at the grain elevator, or ranch and farm work—but there were jobs to be had, unlike on the reservation where you had to know somebody in the tribal government. The American Horses, the Red Owls, the Hollow Horns, the No Leafs, and the Crazy Bears. They showed up to work on time. They sent their kids to school, made sure they were washed and fed, and wore nice clothes for Sunday services.

There were other families, those from the reservation who ended up in Gordon because they just wanted to be closer to town or needed a place to live. They had brought the cycle of poverty with them. Their kids were rarely seen in school. When her grandfather had taken her over to the tent city, Arlene was shocked at how these other Indians lived. The tent city was long gone, but the poverty remained. Her attitudes had softened since she was a child. Now, she had a job with Head Start where she could help these kids. She also attended night classes at Chadron State College twice a week. Her husband, Ray, wasn't crazy about her efforts at self-improvement. They married when she was nineteen and Ray thirty-one. He worked doing menial labor at nearby farms and felt threatened. He had a temper and sometimes became violent, but she was determined to get her degree and make something of herself. She had filed for divorce the previous summer, but they patched things up for the sake of the kids.

She remembered how cold it was Saturday night. The more she thought about the man being pushed into the club, the more incensed she became. The humiliation. What kind of person would do such a thing? She'd never felt prejudice or racism in Gordon—not in school when she was a kid, and not at work.

She asked one of the assistant teachers to take over. She jumped in her car and drove downtown to see Mike Smith, the county attorney,

Sheridan County Attorney
Michael Smith. (Courtesy
of *Sheridan County
Journal Star.*)

who also sat on Head Start's board of directors. She would demand an
investigation. As Arlene drove to Smith's Main Street office, she had no
idea that the man who'd been pushed half-naked inside the dance was her
Uncle Raymond.

Pat Shald was stocking shelves at the Jack and Jill grocery store on the
north edge of town when one of his customers told him about Saturday
night. He stopped stacking the cans.

He too was incensed. What did the Legion do about it?

"Nothing," said the man who'd witnessed the event.

"What do you mean nothing?"

"Nothing."

"They didn't call the police?"

"Nothing."

That was typical of the old guard down at the Legion, Shald thought. He'd been in the army and was a member, but he didn't hang out there much. He had strong opinions about the Vietnam War, and every once in a while he'd go down to the club and provoke an argument with the America-love-it-or-leave-it types like the manager, Bernard Sandage. Pat was the town gadfly. He loved a good verbal spat and was proud to be Gordon's most resolute liberal. There had to be at least one in every town in western Nebraska.

Pat came from a large Catholic family that had a dollop of Indian blood running through their veins. He was one-sixteenth Indian, but you'd never know it by looking at him with his light complexion and pale blue eyes. His mother, Gladys Shald, grew up on a ranch on the reservation just north of Gordon near Lake Wakpamni and was one-eighth Lakota. Her grandmother was part of Chief Red Cloud's Bad Face band, and two of Pat's uncles had married Oglala women, so he had first cousins all over the reservation. Some thought his mother's maiden name, Trueblood, was Indian, but it was Anglo-Saxon. The Truebloods were among the original founders of Gordon in 1885. Pat's father, Ferd, was a grocer of German stock. Like many Gordon merchants, he started as an itinerant peddler, traveling the countryside by wagon, offering his butchering services to remote farms and ranches until he saved enough money to open a grocery store on Main Street. His father was a big man, every muscle built by hauling slabs of meat around the locker. Pat and his brother, Mike, inherited their late father's blue eyes, hawkish nose, and business sense.

Now the Shald brothers ran the Jack and Jill on the north end of town, the last stop before heading up Highway 27 to the reservation.

His mother, despite moving to Gordon as a young wife, had always stayed involved in reservation matters, and tried to instill in her children a sense of their Oglala roots. She took her kids to powwows every summer to show them the culture. Her love of the Oglalas had stuck with her daughters, but her two boys were indifferent. Pat was too busy at the store to go to powwows, although he dealt with Indian customers every day.

"Is the Legion going to press charges?" Pat asked.

The customer didn't know. He only knew that Sandage didn't do a thing after he escorted the old Indian out the door.

Rumor had it that the Hares were behind it, he said. That made sense to Pat. He was a townie. Only some stupid Southhiller or dumbass redneck would toss an Indian half-naked into a dance, he thought. Pat knew Les Hare's reputation. Once, Les had been hunting without permission on the Shald ranch south of town on his motorcycle, chewing up the pasture. Pat's father and the ranch foreman asked Pat to go to the truck stop next to Seger's Cafe where Les worked to tell him to knock it off, which he did. Les was a fairly big guy, but Pat was bigger, having inherited a bit of his father's size. Les just stood there and nodded.

"Someone should have called the police or an ambulance," Pat told the customer. To use another human being like that. Not only was it a horrendous thing to do, it was an affront to the people in the club that night. Why weren't they as upset as he was? Pat fumed about the incident for the rest of the day. He thought about going down to the Legion and giving Sandage a piece of his mind, but he was just too busy.

By the beginning of the week, the story had reached the ears of many in the town of twenty-two hundred. Even Raymond Yellow Thunder's employer, Harold Rucker, on an isolated ranch fifteen miles north of town, had heard the story. His teenage son, Bucky, and his buddy Jerry Matula had given Raymond a ride to Gordon on Saturday, his payday, so he could buy new clothes at Saub's and get a haircut. They'd brought him back to the ranch, but that evening Raymond grew restless and asked the boys for a lift back to town. They didn't want to make a second trip, but Raymond promised them a half-case of beer if they'd do it. They dropped him off on Main Street and never saw him again. By Sunday night, the boys had heard the Legion Hall story.

Les Hare had done more to spread the news than anyone. He, Butch, Toby, and Jeannette met with Max Anderson on the edge of town at Seger's Cafe. They crowded into a booth upholstered in vinyl; everyone but Jeannette was so drunk they couldn't see straight.

Les began crowing for all to hear.

"We pushed that naked Indian in the Legion Hall full of all them people!" he said once, then twice, then three times in case the other late-night diners had failed to hear him. Many of them were stopping for coffee on the way back from the dance and had witnessed the cruel act.

Toby thought Les was hilarious. He couldn't stop laughing.

"Why would you do such a thing?" one disgusted woman asked.

"Look. Here's where he shit on my hands," Les said, holding up his fingers.

"So go wash them, then!" Jeannette said, rolling her eyes. Les weaved over to the restroom.

They stayed about an hour; acquaintances joined them, then left. Les told the newcomers the story again. The effects of the beer weren't diminishing one bit. Butch kept demanding coffee as Toby laughed at every word slurring out of Les's mouth. Finally, the waitress had taken enough. She refused to serve them, and they left without paying their bill.

Where was Uncle Raymond?

Arlene Lamont was worried. His boss, Harold Rucker, had come by her mother's house Monday morning to pick him up and take him back to the ranch, but Raymond hadn't spent the night there. Sometimes he would hitchhike up to the reservation town of Porcupine to see his two oldest sisters, Amelia and Annie. Arlene called them, but he hadn't been there in weeks. Raymond liked to go on a bender on Saturday nights, but he would have made it back to her mother's place before Rucker showed up. The Crazy Bears lived on the west side near the railroad tracks. Raymond would sometimes sleep on the sofa and drink with Albert and Winnie, but he hadn't done so that weekend.

Raymond and his brothers and sisters were all born near Kyle on the reservation in a log cabin in the countryside. Their mother's father was the legendary Chief American Horse, a so-called progressive Indian who advocated taking the white path. But American Horse's descendants didn't benefit much from the chief embracing "progress." They lived in poverty ten miles south of Kyle along American Horse Creek. Their father, Andrew Yellow Thunder, was hard working and strict. He made sure everyone did their chores on the meager farm and horse ranch. Unlike the "traditionals," Andrew and the boys wore their hair short. Their mother, Jennie, sent all seven children to the one-room schoolhouse in the morning, and made sure they were all scrubbed and wearing their nicest clothes for Sunday services at the Episcopal church.

Raymond didn't take to school. He wasn't interested in reading, writing, and arithmetic. He was a good athlete—tall and lanky enough to excel at basketball and track. He did have an innate talent for drawing and was the best artist in school. He could produce perfectly rendered pictures of the empty but beautiful countryside around him. His favorite subject was horses. His father raised horses, and he drew pictures of them running through the Badlands, or in rodeos, with cowboys riding bareback. After the federal government built a better schoolhouse in Kyle, Raymond and his siblings rode their horses there ten miles each way.

He left school as soon as the law allowed, only finishing the ninth grade. He had a way with animals. He could calm all but the most obstinate broncos, so he started making money breaking horses on the ranches around the reservation. He was good enough to be in rodeos, but he never had the itchy feet to travel on the circuit. Raymond grew up to be a quiet young man. The frenzied competition of a rodeo wasn't for him.

He married Dora Cutgrass in his early twenties. He knew her from grade school, and she shared his love of horses. When they rode around Kyle, the kids would call them "Roy Rogers and Dale Evans." But the marriage didn't last. Raymond discovered the bottle, and when he started drinking, he couldn't stop. He was the opposite of a belligerent drunk. In fact, the more wine he downed, the quieter he became. He was generous to a fault as far as Dora was concerned. He would buy everyone drinks, so they never had any money for food. The drinking became too much for her, and she left him after a few years.

Raymond, heartbroken, started drinking more. There was work for cowboys near Gordon, so he wandered south in the early 1950s, hiring on at nearby ranches where his talent for working with livestock was in demand. There wasn't a job on a farm or ranch he couldn't do, and he was dependable. After bouncing from ranch to ranch for a couple years, he landed with Harold Rucker. He lived there for eighteen years in a simple room in the bunkhouse. Raymond never needed much—just a few extra changes of clothes and enough money to buy himself some cheap wine on the weekend. All his spare money went toward buying groceries for his sisters' families or gifts for his nieces and nephews.

All the kids loved Uncle Raymond. Whenever he came through the door they ran up and grabbed him around his bony legs. He always had a small toy or some candy to share.

His favorite nephew was his brother Russell's youngest boy, Dennis. He had a real talent for art, and Raymond always arrived at his brother's house across the road from Lake Wakpamni with some watercolors, crayons, colored pencils, or sketch pads he'd bought at Saults and Son

Drug in Gordon. He would stretch out alongside the boy on the floor and teach him how to draw.

So where did Uncle Raymond go?

Arlene checked at her Uncle Russell's house at Lake Wakpamni, too. He wasn't there.

His boss had checked the jail to see if he'd been tossed in for intoxication. The police chief, Bob Case, said he was there for a sleepover Saturday night, but he'd left early Sunday morning.

Where did he go after that?

She called the city jail again to see if he'd turned up. She called her aunties to see if they would drive down and help her look. Raymond's world was the ranch, Gordon, the city jail, and the reservation. If he wasn't at one of these four places, where could he be?

Neither Rucker nor the city cops told Arlene or her family about the Legion Hall incident. Perhaps they were too embarrassed. However, the conspiracy of silence wouldn't last long.

The day after the attack, George Ghost Dog left his home on the southwest side of town and made his way to the Neighborhood Center. The skinny fifteen-year-old had a part-time job there sweeping up, a welcome respite from his ramshackle house full of screaming brothers and sisters. George's mother, Virginia, did her best to raise nine kids on her own. She worked cleaning the white folks' houses and occasionally clerked at a small grocery store.

George's attitude about Gordon differed from Arlene Lamont's. There was plenty of prejudice toward Indians here. He had such a hard time at Gordon High that he was forced to enroll in an alternative school on the reservation. Some Gordon boys in a snazzy car once caught him hitchhiking north of town. They pulled over and surrounded him. The biggest one challenged him to a fight, and they ended up wrestling on the grassy shoulder until a cop drove by and told the white boys to beat it. What would the cop have done if it were a gang of Indians beating up a lone white boy, he wondered.

It was a chilly February morning, and he wanted to make it to the office as soon as possible, so George cut through Borman's back lot where they kept the junkers. He caught a glimpse of a head poking up over the

window in a panel truck, one of the many broken-down heaps they kept 45
back there hoping to sell before they rusted away. It was Raymond Yellow
Thunder, one of his mother's cousins. He was a nice old guy. When he was
drunk, he would hand out quarters to the Indian kids. George thought
he would give him a little surprise. He crept up to the passenger door and
flung it open.

"Hey, wake up, man!"

But Yellow Thunder didn't jump out of his skin like he thought he
would. He slowly stirred awake. It looked like someone had worked him
over pretty bad. He had a fat lip, a black eye, and specks of blood on his
shirt.

"Hey, what happened to you?"

"Four white guys beat me up. They tried to steal my wine."

"What? They tried to steal your wine? They don't drink wine, do
they?"

"They beat me up."

"Are you okay?"

"Yeah. I'm all right."

"All right."

George closed the door and left Raymond alone so he could go back to
sleep. Later, he told his boss at the Neighborhood Center that he'd seen a
man he knew beaten up in the back of a truck at Borman's. She asked if he
was all right. He said he thought so. Then they both forgot about him.

John Paul was a big man: six foot five, over two hundred pounds. Plenty of
it muscle. Despite his size, the young policeman had a baby face. It didn't
take much to be a small-town cop in those days. A high school education
was enough. As for training, it was minimal.

Paul had a reputation as a bully in high school, and that did not disappear after he joined the Gordon Police Department. Oglalas staggering
down the sidewalk learned to steer clear of big bad John Paul. Some witnessed him grabbing drunks none too gently, thwacking them a few times
with his billy club if they smarted off, before shoving them in the back of
the patrol car. He would never do this to a white man, of course. If white
men were ever arrested for public intoxication in Gordon, it never showed
up in the court record, which was published every week without fail by

Reva Evans, the owner and editor of the *Gordon Journal*. Paul was only the latest in a long line of cops who roughed up intoxicated Indians in the border town. While not every policeman did so—the police chief Bob Case was a decent guy by all accounts—keeping downtown from turning into a skid row with chronic alcoholics passed out in the gutter was a policy tacitly approved by most downtown businessmen. Gordon wasn't White-clay after all.

Once again, Yellow Thunder's niece Arlene stood before Paul in front of the counter at the police station inquiring about her uncle. And once again, Paul told her he didn't know where he was. Yellow Thunder's employer, Rucker, had been around once asking the same questions. The city jail was a logical place to look. Since 1951, Yellow Thunder had stayed there hundreds of times, mostly on intoxication charges. The rest were sleepovers.

Paul was out on patrol Saturday night when the dispatcher and magistrate, Kay Lou Peterson, radioed him so he could check in Yellow Thunder for a voluntary sleepover. When he arrived, Raymond was standing by the counter. Paul smelled liquor on the Indian's breath, but he didn't seem to be too drunk. He looked like he'd been worked over pretty bad. He had a scratch on the nose and a bruise on the right temple. It had been less than an hour, but Paul had already heard that a half-naked Indian had been tossed into the Legion Hall.

"Was that you that just gotten thrown in the Legion Hall?"

"Yeah, that was me."

"Who beat you up?"

"Four white boys, but I don't know who they were."

Paul told Yellow Thunder's niece the same thing he'd told her aunts when they'd come around making inquiries. He put their kin in a cell, and that was the last time he'd seen him.

Raymond Yellow Thunder needed medical attention that night, but that probably never occurred to Officer Paul. He was just a drunken Indian, after all. The officer who released him from jail Sunday morning saw the cuts and bruises before the Indian walked unsteadily out of the police station. As for driving Raymond to the emergency room, that probably never occurred to the cop. Paul knew several people were looking for Yellow Thunder. And he knew that intoxicated Indians often slept in the back of old cars behind Borman's Chevrolet. But walking the four blocks separating the police station from the dealership to see if the missing man was there may not have occurred to him. As for telling Arlene Lamont or

Harold Rucker to check there, that too, may not have occurred to him. Paul knew that Yellow Thunder was shoved half-naked into the Legion Hall. He knew that four white men had beaten him up. No one from the Legion Hall had pressed charges, so investigating that crime may not have occurred to him. Arlene Lamont had been in the police station and talked to Chief Case, too. Everyone in town seemed to know that Les Hare was responsible for pushing her missing uncle half-naked into the Legion Saturday night. Everyone but his family. As for telling Arlene, standing on the other side of the counter at that moment, that her uncle had been beaten up by four white men before vanishing, that simply may not have occurred to him, either.

Raymond's two oldest sisters, Annie Eagle Fox and Amelia Comes Last, had done just about all they could do. They stood in Morsett's Laundromat folding clothes, wondering what their next move should be. They had checked the hospitals, checked the jails, even in Pine Ridge and Rushville where he rarely ventured. The police said they hadn't seen him since Sunday.

Where was their brother Raymond?

At that moment, Raymond Yellow Thunder was across the street, about fifty yards away, behind some overgrown bushes in the back of a dilapidated truck. Just a few yards from the back door of Borman's Chevrolet garage, where his brother-in-law, Albert Crazy Bear, was fixing cars. Four blocks from where Toby Bayliss pounded away at dents at Messenger and Milburn Ford.

Raymond was slowly dying.

In the morning, children from the east side of town walked by the car lot in the chilly air on their way to the elementary school, and then returned in midafternoon. The truck sat between four other junkers; all were visible from the street. Other pedestrians passed by, but none ventured into the lot.

A gray hood of a sweatshirt covered Raymond's head, which rested just out of sight, in the crook between the driver's seat and the door. His right hand rested across his chest, his left arm underneath a thin blanket. Thermal underwear helped keep him warm. One shoe was off, lying on the floorboard, so he wrapped a dark blue suit coat around his foot to cover it. At some point, he'd sought out extra clothes, because he hadn't been wearing a gray-hooded sweatshirt when last seen. He'd gone somewhere to wash the blood off his face. Where he'd done this, no one would ever know.

The winter sun in the southeast came out for a few hours a day, sent its rays through the windshield, warming up the cab, until it sunk behind the towering grain elevators. The temperature dropped quickly at night and a few snowflakes landed on the windshield, but they didn't amount to much. Raymond started coughing, his lungs pushing up mucus.

Since Saturday night, the veins on the outer layer of Raymond's brain had been dripping microscopic amounts of blood. By the time he'd left the jail Sunday morning, the black splotch on his outer membrane was small, no bigger than a quarter. When George Ghost Dog came by later that day, it had spread, but it wasn't large enough to stop him from having a conversation. Hour by hour, the blood dribbled into the outer membrane, the leak spreading until it grew to the size of a pack of cards; big enough to stop his brain from functioning normally.

He slipped into a coma.

His brain was no longer able to command his muscles to cough up the phlegm, which dribbled down into his lungs, collecting in the bronchial tubes. Pneumonia invaded his body.

On Friday, five days after he first saw Raymond, George Ghost Dog was cutting through the used-car lot again when he saw his cousin lying in the exact same spot with his head resting against the door. He appeared to be asleep. He thought he might surprise him as he'd done Sunday, but the boy decided to let him rest instead. He kept walking.

It was Sunday afternoon and Michael Smith was playing a game of pickup basketball at the high school gymnasium when Officer Paul called him over to the side of the court. Smith took off his black-framed glasses and wiped the sweat off his brow.

Some kids had found the body of a dead Indian in an old truck behind Borman's Chevrolet, Paul told Smith. Probably a case of exposure, he reckoned. Smith went into the locker room to shower and change. Even on a Sunday afternoon, he would never go out in public looking like a slob. He was a fastidious dresser and didn't even like to take off his suit coat while sitting alone in the office.

Smith was the epitome of a small-town lawyer. He did it all. Wills, lawsuits, divorces—whatever helped pay the bills. Along with his private practice, he served as the county attorney. He'd spent his entire career in Gordon, moving there right out of law school in 1963. He had an offer to move to Washington DC to work at the Justice Department, but a desk job didn't interest him very much. Back then, western Nebraska was a land of opportunity for a young, ambitious lawyer. He wanted to try criminal cases and civil suits, and the West offered plenty of both. When he arrived at the age of twenty-six, the next youngest lawyer in the district was his forty-four-year-old partner.

Smith had lived a transient life as a kid. His father was a semiprofessional baseball player, who'd also worked for the phone company while moving his family from town to town. He'd spent most of his formative years on the east side of the state, but he'd always liked western Nebraska. His wife, Jeanne, was from O'Neill, down Highway 20 a few hundred miles, so they moved to Gordon with their three kids in 1963 and put down roots.

He showered, put on some clean clothes, and combed his hair back. His hairline was receding early; he was only thirty-five. But he was in shape. It was too bad about having to leave the game, but as the county attorney he also pulled double duty as the coroner. Not that he knew anything about medicine. The county didn't have the money to perform an autopsy on every corpse—it just wasn't practical. So whenever a body turned up, it was his duty to go to the scene and check out the situation. Usually it was an elderly man or woman at a remote farmhouse found dead in their bed. He always marked "coronary heart attack" as the cause of death. It was as good a guess as any. Years later, he would discover that someone had compiled mortality statistics in Nebraska using his data as a basis for their report. He was embarrassed to discover that Sheridan County had the highest heart attack rate per capita in Nebraska.

As Smith pulled up alongside the used-car lot, he saw Deputy Sheriff Dell Lennox—dressed in his brown uniform topped off with a cowboy hat and a camera dangling from his neck—peering inside a blue Chevrolet panel truck parked in the dirt lot. Officer Paul stood nearby. It was growing dark. Smith would have to hurry things up.

Smith squeezed between a pickup filled with scrap iron and the panel truck and peered in at the crumpled old man. His arm and a gray hood partially covered the face, and the waning winter sun threw shadows into the cab. His first thought was "exposure." The nights had been bitterly cold lately. He probably just crawled in there to sleep and froze to death. After Lennox finished snapping all the necessary pictures, they took the body out and laid it on the ground. The corpse was limp, no rigor mortis. Paul peeled back the hood.

"Raymond Yellow Thunder."

Paul told Smith what had happened eight nights ago. A puffy right cheek, a shiny bruise above his right forehead, and scratches on his nose told the rest of the story.

Arlene Lamont had also talked to Smith on Monday and demanded an investigation into the Legion Hall incident. But no investigation had taken place. Smith wouldn't be able to write "heart attack" or "exposure" this time. He'd have to call in the pathologist from Scottsbluff.

Smith had little confidence in the ability of Gordon's small-town cops or the sheriff's department, so he called the state patrol in Scottsbluff and asked them to send Investigator Max Ibach. He was about the same age as Smith and a good detective whom he'd called in many times on big cases. And this case was shaping up to be a big one. The coroner from Scottsbluff, the elderly Dr. W. O. Brown, drove to Rushville and performed the autopsy Monday morning. Yellow Thunder had died of a subdural hematoma, a brain hemorrhage, probably caused by a blow to the right side of the head. He'd died "mechanically," the doctor reported. Blood had slowly leaked into the membranes covering the brain until the pressure shut it down.

Ibach arrived in town at 3:00 p.m. Monday, February 21, and Smith immediately handed him a list of four suspects. This was hardly a murder mystery. Sheridan County law enforcement already knew who'd shoved Yellow Thunder into the Legion Hall. They just hadn't felt the need to do anything about it until the body showed up.

Toby Bayliss wasn't hard to find. The Ford dealership where he worked was directly behind the police station. By 5:45 p.m., Ibach had Bayliss sitting down to give a statement. What the bony mechanic gave him was part fact, part fiction. He wanted Ibach to believe that he was an unwilling accomplice to the crimes. He said Les Hare made him stop the car when he first spotted the Indian walking down Second Street. Les then jumped out of the Ford and punched Yellow Thunder. Les, Pat, and Butch insisted on loading the Indian into the trunk. Not him. He didn't want to give them his car keys, but they insisted. Actually, he never even got out of the car. Of course, he protested vehemently about what they were doing. The others were laughing and joking about how funny it was, but not Toby. Or so he claimed. He never mentioned going to Seger's Cafe afterwards. He said he went straight home after dropping everyone off at Dean Hare's house, south of town. Officer Paul and Chief Case had collected plenty of statements from diners at Seger's who'd overheard Les Hare bragging about the incident. According to the eyewitnesses, Toby Bayliss seemed to think tossing the victim into the Legion Hall was quite hilarious.

Bayliss did mention a possible eyewitness to parts of the incident—a nineteen-year-old meatpacking plant worker, Max Anderson.

After taking the statement, Ibach, the sheriff, and the police chief drove out with Bayliss to his home a few miles west of town. While Bayliss's two young boys watched, they removed a carpet from the car trunk, which appeared to have several spots of blood.

Earlier that day, Arlene Lamont was teaching a Head Start class. One of her volunteers delivered the news. Her uncle had been found dead inside a truck. He was the man who'd been pushed into the Legion Hall on Saturday night. Apparently a couple of the Hares had done it. Arlene had never put Uncle Raymond's disappearance together with the Legion Hall incident.

She was shocked, then angry.

She knew who Les Hare was. She'd heard ugly rumors about him for years.

At that moment, the town she'd grown up in and loved—where she'd felt no prejudice or hate—disappeared forever. Soon, the anger would turn to grief.

Before they had a chance to view their brother Raymond's body, word had reached his sisters Annie and Amelia that he'd been the victim of some kind of cruel humiliation at the Legion Hall. When they went to the mortuary in Rushville and demanded to see his body, the mortician wouldn't let them in. Perhaps he was still preparing the body after the thorough autopsy. Whatever the cause of the delay, it only added to their suspicion. What did their brother endure before he died?

The Oglalas knew that there were two kinds of justice in Gordon: one for the whites and one for the Indians. One popular story going around town had a bunch of teenagers who'd decided to bust in the door of an Indian family's home on the southeast side, run in, and terrorize the family. After they complained, the sheriff brought the culprits back and made them pay for a new door. And that was it.

What if a bunch of Indian boys had busted into a white person's house? They'd be in the reformatory for ten years. What about Vincent Broken Rope? Shot down by Gordon's chief of police back in '54? What about that Red Hawk girl? Pushed out of the back of a car the same year by those Gordon boys when one of them tried to sexually assault her! The one who pushed her got a slap on the wrist.

Every week the *Gordon Journal* ran the police report: a long list of Indians tossed in jail and fined anywhere from fifteen to fifty dollars for intoxication. No one ever saw a white man's name there. It was as if no white people ever walked drunk down the street. If the drunk Indian couldn't pay the fine, they put him to work. Cheap labor for the town. It wasn't so long ago that they'd be put on bread and water rations.

And no one had forgotten Wounded Knee.

Even the white man knew about it now. *Bury My Heart at Wounded Knee* was a number-one best-seller just the year before. One hundred ninety Lakotas slaughtered. Nothing happened to the commanding officer. Some of the soldiers were given medals! To the Lakotas, it was a massacre and an eighty-year wound that had never healed.

All this, Annie and Amelia knew. For the Oglalas have long memories about such things. What kind of justice would their brother receive?

Max Ibach sat Toby Bayliss down for a second time on Tuesday evening, February 22. The investigator showed him a series of photos of local Indians. He picked out Yellow Thunder as the one Les assaulted. He went through his statement again. Bayliss admitted that he'd made a mistake or two the first time they'd spoken. He did get out of the car when Les first beat up Yellow Thunder. He claimed he stood by and watched as Les punched him two or three times. And he was at Seger's Cafe with them after they tossed the old man into the Legion Hall half undressed. He said there was a fifth person in the car that night, Jeannette Thompson.

Michael Smith signed out warrants for the arrest of Bernard Jerome Lutter, Leslie Dean Hare, and Melvin Pat Hare the morning of February 23, 1972.

No one knew where or when the rumors started. But once they began, they swept over the reservation faster than a prairie fire.

Did you hear what happened in Gordon?

Some white boys killed an Indian.

They threw him half-naked into the Legion Hall.

The people inside made him dance "Indian style."

The boys led him there and everyone gathered around and they said, "Dance, you goddamn Indian!" Everyone was laughing and jeering. Making Indian whoops.

I heard he was castrated. They tortured him. Burned him with cigarettes.

How did he die?

His skull was crushed.

They took a tire iron and smashed his skull.

They're gonna let the guys off. Their dad is a filthy rich rancher. He'll buy their way out of it. They'll get off with a slap on the wrist. They're out on bail already.

There ain't no justice in the border towns.

Birgil Kills Straight was sitting in his office at Pine Ridge listening to a morning radio talk show broadcast out of Chadron. Some old ladies were prattling on about their wonderful community. Just a bunch of people with nothing better to do than call into their local station, he thought. He wasn't in the mood for this. They were really living in a fantasy world.

He didn't think Nebraska was that wonderful. He'd heard through the grapevine that his mother's first cousin had been brutally murdered in Gordon. Kills Straight was the director of the Talent Search Program. He was charged with finding promising high school students and setting them on a path to attend college. He was familiar with white justice in the border towns. Sometimes kids he worked with wandered down to White-clay and got caught on the wrong side of the law. The police were arresting them and sending them hundreds of miles away to juvenile detention facilities in the eastern part of the state without informing their parents or the tribal authorities. More than once he had to go in and file a habeas corpus writ to figure out where these kids were.

Kills Straight didn't know Yellow Thunder, but he knew his sisters. Amelia Comes Last and his mother were very close. Annie Eagle Fox had been the cook at his school in Kyle when he was growing up. Her husband, Bob, drove the school bus.

He couldn't take the mindless prattle anymore. He picked up the phone and called the station.

"Yeah, I've been listening to your show about how friendly the people of western Nebraska are. I just thought I'd let you know about my Uncle Raymond Yellow Thunder. He was drunk and these young men in Gordon were messing around with him and they took him around to the American Legion club where they were having a dance. And they pushed him in there, took his pants off, and people in there made fun of him—made him dance and somebody pushed him out eventually. They threw his pants out behind him into the cold. That was the last time they seen him alive. The next morning they found him dead in the back of a vehicle parked at a used-car lot."

The announcer hadn't heard anything about this. He was interested in hearing more. Kills Straight hung up the phone.

If there was someone on the reservation who hadn't heard the false rumor about Yellow Thunder being forced to dance "Indian style" to the delight of the jeering crowd, they had now. The story had gone out over the airwaves.

Kills Straight listened as more comments came in. Apparently the radio station's phone was ringing off the hook. The people calling in were interested. A couple of rednecks made some stupid comments, but most people wanted to know more. The show ended, and the host called him back right away. He wanted more details, but Kills Straight didn't know any. A few minutes later, the phone rang again. It was his cousin Severt Young Bear. He'd just heard him on the radio. His aunts Amelia and Annie had come to him and asked if he could do anything. They were afraid these men would get off without any punishment. They'd gone to the tribal chairman, Gerald One Feather. He wouldn't do a thing. One Feather was in the waning days of his two-year term. He probably wasn't going to stick his neck out over this.

Maybe Kills Straight could help.

Kills Straight started calling around. He phoned the sheriff's office, identified himself as one of Yellow Thunder's relatives, but they wouldn't tell him anything. He called the mortuary, but they wouldn't tell him anything, either. He called the NAACP, but they didn't seem interested. He called the office of Congressman James Abourezk and filled in one of his staffers on the crime. There was a Department of Justice community representative, Roman Gabriel. He called him, too.

There was one more person he could call.

There was a guy he'd worked with back when he was running the information management system at Pine Ridge four years ago. The fellow headed the same program at the Rosebud Reservation, and they'd worked together a few times. Kills Straight had heard that he was in Cleveland running the Indian center and was heavily involved in some new activist group. He couldn't remember the name of the organization, but he picked up the phone and dialed the center anyway. He wasn't in Cleveland, they said. He was in Omaha at a conference. They gave him his hotel room number, so Kills Straight made one last call.

The organization was the American Indian Movement, and the name of his acquaintance was Russell Means.

Russell Means woke up from a deep sleep to the sound of someone rapping on his door. He looked at his clock. It was almost 4:00 a.m. He flipped on the light and got his bearings, shaking off the disorientation one always feels when waking up in a motel room in the middle of the night. He was in Omaha. At the conference. He shuffled to the door and opened it up a crack. A big bear of an Indian wearing wire-rimmed glasses and a white cowboy hat stood outside. It took Means a moment, but he recognized him. Severt Young Bear. He was from Porcupine, up at Pine Ridge, his father's home reservation.

"Sorry to wake you," Young Bear said. "But we need your help."

Young Bear was tired himself. Only seven hours before, he was settling in to watch TV, relaxing after a hard day's work repairing wells for the tribal government, when a car pulled up to his house. It was two of his aunties, Annie Eagle Fox and Amelia Comes Last, there to talk to him about their murdered brother again. Along with repairing wells, Young

Bear was a district chairman in the tribal government representing Porcupine. And he represented his district well, for he was a full-blood traditionalist who wore his hair long and sang and drummed Lakota songs. Porcupine was one of the last bastions on the reservation for those who wanted to preserve the old way of life.

It was the second time his elders had come to him for help, but this time they had a plan. They'd read in the newspaper that a group of Indians was meeting in Omaha, and they knew that Young Bear had contacts in AIM. They were convinced that the Hares were going to get off free.

"We don't have any place to turn. So we came over—maybe you could help us," Annie Eagle Fox pleaded.

They begged him to go to Omaha and talk to this new organization. He was flat broke, though. None of them had any money. He jumped in his rickety car and drove to the trading post in Porcupine to ask the storeowner for a donation. When the gas tank was full, he set out on his midnight ride to Omaha.

Six hours later, Young Bear sat down in the hotel room and told Means the facts as he understood them.

Means had heard about Yellow Thunder when Birgil Kills Straight called a few days before. He knew a thing or two about Sheridan County's border towns. He'd spent an idle summer drinking and hanging out at the Jumping Eagle Inn at Whiteclay, one of the border town's rough-and-tumble bars. There was no justice in Sheridan County for Indians. Everyone knew it.

Means sent Young Bear to fetch Dennis Banks from his room. They would have to discuss this. The American Indian Movement had few followers on the reservation, and the leadership had been looking for ways to change that. AIM was made up of big-city intellectuals with roots in sixties activism; they had little cachet in the countryside.

Means was from Pine Ridge, but he'd been gone a long time. Now, maybe it was time to return.

Russell Means was the son of an Oglala father and Yankton mother, who was raised on and off the Pine Ridge Reservation. His parents met at Pine Ridge where his mother worked as a secretary to the superintendent and his father as a car mechanic. They both hated reservation life, and when

World War II broke out and workers were in demand, they moved to the Bay Area in California where his father found a job as a welder in the shipyards. His parents didn't speak Lakota. They were products of the Indian boarding schools, where the teachers' goal was to destroy the Indian culture and make the children adopt white ways. His father was an alcoholic and his mother could be physically abusive, but they both worked hard and neither wanted to return to the reservation. Young Russell never learned to speak Lakota and knew little about his own culture.

Russell spent his childhood in a racially mixed neighborhood in Vallejo, California, returning to South Dakota in the summers to visit his Oglala or Yankton relatives. When he was in high school in the 1950s, his mother bought a house in San Leandro, just south of Oakland. As a teenager, Russell began drinking booze and smoking dope. School held little interest for him, and he began cutting classes. He graduated from beer and marijuana to pills and, finally, heroin. Then he began dealing drugs to fellow students. After barely managing to graduate from high school, he enrolled for a semester at a city college until the local cops told him that they were on to his drug dealing. He skipped town, moved to Los Angeles, and found a mailroom job.

The United States, and its agent the Bureau of Indian Affairs, had never ceased its misguided social engineering policies. The scheme it invented in the 1950s and 1960s was to encourage Native Americans to leave their impoverished reservations and move to big cities where there were plenty of jobs. In Los Angeles, he met Indians in the relocation program from all over the country, although most of them had only exchanged rural squalor for urban squalor.

Means spent most of his early adulthood drifting with little purpose other than to make a living and drink. He worked at a series of dead-end jobs and attended several institutions of higher learning in several cities without gaining a degree. He'd been an assembly-line worker in a paint factory, a janitor, data processor, accountant, pool hustler, printer, dance instructor, bookkeeper, Indian fancy dancer for tourists, rodeo bareback bronco rider, and an administrator for the antipoverty program at the Rosebud Reservation east of Pine Ridge. He lived in San Francisco; Los Angeles; Rapid City; Mission, South Dakota; Albuquerque; Ottumwa, Iowa; and Phoenix. He'd married twice and had two families with Native American women: Twila, a Minneconjou Lakota he'd met in Los Angeles, and Betty, a Hopi he'd met in San Francisco.

After he got fired from his job at the Rosebud Reservation in 1968 for drinking, he applied for relocation, and the BIA sent Russell, Betty, and their two children to Cleveland—the least popular city in the program.

Means took his first steps toward activism in April 1969 when he and a few other reservation transplants decided to start an organization, the Cleveland American Indian Center, to serve the scattered families on the city's west side. There he helped Native Americans from all over the country: Choctaws from Mississippi, Crows from the Plains, and Ojibwas from the Minnesota woods. Until then, he'd carried the traditional biases of his ancestors—the Ojibwas and Crows were the Lakotas' old enemies—but he shed those old prejudices and began to adopt a pan-Indian attitude. Soon, Jess Sixkiller, an Oklahoma Cherokee who was trying to bind loosely affiliated Indian centers across the country into the National Urban Indian Organization, contacted him. Sixkiller flew Means out to a conference in San Francisco to help him rally support for the organization.

In the hotel ballroom where the conference was taking place, Means spotted two guys wearing their hair in long ponytails. They were draped in Indian jewelry and strode around the ballroom in moccasins. Means, dressed in semibusiness attire, thought they looked ridiculous. They were wearing "costumes," as far as he was concerned. He asked a man standing next to him who they were.

"They're from the American Indian Movement in Minneapolis," he replied.

Means didn't know it yet, but the two men's names were Dennis Banks and Clyde Bellecourt. And they were there to take over the organization.

Bellecourt and Banks were former convicts—a fact that their opponents through the years would never fail to bring up. Like Means, the pair had a perfect blend of good looks, street smarts, sharp intelligence, and righteous anger. Banks's eyes seemed to hold wisdom beyond his years. Etched on his angular face was a permanent scowl. He was an Ojibwa from the Leech Lake Reservation in northern Minnesota, but he'd been forced to spend eleven years of his childhood in boarding schools in North and South Dakota without ever seeing his family. After a stint in Japan in the air force, he spent his early adulthood drinking until he reconnected with his Indian spiritualism while doing an eighteen-month stretch in a Minnesota prison on burglary charges. While in his jail cell, he spent hours reading about the antiwar movement and all the social unrest and activism going on outside the prison walls.

As soon as he was released in 1968, he was ready to jump into the action. He called a meeting in a church basement, inviting anyone who was angry about the way Indians were treated in the Minneapolis Fourth Avenue Indian ghetto. One man who came to the church basement that night was a big, angry Ojibwa named Clyde Bellecourt.

Bellecourt was as wide as a linebacker, with a puffy oval face and two braids dangling past his shoulders. He was a former juvenile delinquent, spending his teen years in Minneapolis after the tribe kicked him off his native White Earth Reservation. While serving time in prison, Clyde passed the high school equivalency exam, earned a license to run steam plants, and had taken a Dale Carnegie course in public speaking. He was working for a power company maintaining dams in 1968 when he went to the church basement to hear what Banks had to say. He wanted to protest police brutality at the bars on Franklin Avenue. "Maybe starting tomorrow," Banks proposed.

"Why not now?" Bellecourt growled. "Let's go down there right now!"

And that's exactly what they did. That night, AIM was born.

At the 1969 San Francisco conference, Means knew nothing about the two fierce-looking Ojibwas. He just thought they looked like fools wearing their Indian regalia.

The pair delivered blistering attacks against Jess Sixkiller.

"You have two choices. Either radically change your organization or we'll destroy it!" Banks shouted.

Means stood up to defend the organization and made an impassioned speech telling everyone how much Sixkiller had helped Native Americans in Cleveland. Later, Banks and Bellecourt demanded that the NUIO move its headquarters to Minneapolis. When the leaders refused their demands, the pair stormed out.

A few weeks later, Banks called Means and invited him to join a protest at the National Council of Churches convention in Detroit. He wondered why they were inviting him since he'd spoken in defense of Sixkiller, but he agreed to go anyway.

Means watched in amazement as Bellecourt and Banks, denied the chance to speak at the convention, simply made the church leaders listen.

Bellecourt charged up to the podium, grabbed the microphone, and began a long harangue about the way the churches were collecting money in the name of impoverished Indians, then giving none of the funds to the people who needed it. Someone shut the microphone off, but he kept shouting in his loud, rumbling voice.

By the end of the conference, Bellecourt and Banks had extracted several important concessions from the church leaders.

"So how do I join AIM?" Means asked Banks.

"You just did," he replied.

When Means returned to Cleveland, he decided he was through working inside the white man's system. He quit his job as an accountant, opened an AIM chapter in Cleveland, and became the full-time director of the Cleveland American Indian Center. Means began agitating for Indian causes in earnest, first suing the Cleveland Indians baseball team for its offensive caricature, Chief Wahoo, then convincing the school board to review its outdated history books that portrayed Indians as savages.

All along, Means was honing his skills as an orator. Armed with little more than a college speech class, he learned how to speak extemporaneously and to hold an audience's attention. He also had a talent for organizing headline-grabbing protests. He organized occupations at Mount Rushmore and at a replica of the Mayflower at Plymouth Rock. After his marriage to Betty ended, he gave his life completely to the cause. In an election, he beat out Clyde's brother, Vernon, as the movement's first national leader. The political battle began a schism between Means and Vernon Bellecourt that would continue for thirty-two years.

But AIM was still in its ascendancy.

In 1972, as Means sat in the Omaha hotel room with Banks and talked about the tragic story of Raymond Yellow Thunder, there was no question in his mind about what they should do. Once again, urban Indians from around the nation had gathered to form some kind of unified organization. And once again, AIM was trying to assert itself as the one and only voice for Native Americans. But unlike at the San Francisco conference three years earlier, it was more than just Banks and Clyde Bellecourt with a silent Means on the sideline. AIM had showed up in full force, and Russell was now its most vocal and charismatic leader.

In conferences and workshops, AIM had taken an aggressive stance, acting belligerently and shouting down opposing viewpoints. Many delegates wanted to work within the system, while AIM wanted a more radical, aggressive approach. In Means's mind, his opponents at the conference were all red-on-the-outside, white-on-the-inside "apples" and "hang-around-the-fort Indians." He wanted reservation Indians to join the newly emerging movement and accused the others of ignoring their country cousins' needs.

Means and Banks promised Young Bear that help was on the way.

The next day, Means grabbed the microphone and spat out a string of criticisms at his opponents, each sentence a verbal hand grenade. Those who wanted to work within the system were fools. Bolder action was needed. He told them how savage white men in Gordon, Nebraska—a few hours' drive from where they were wasting time talking—had murdered a defenseless Lakota man. Raymond Yellow Thunder was humiliated, mutilated, and tortured. Meanwhile, his killers were walking the streets. Enough talk!

"This organization ought to go to Gordon where the action is!" Means shouted, punctuating every word with his index finger. "It should lead us to that racist town!"

The people of Gordon had no idea that a roiling river of anger was about to wash over their town.

Chief Red Cloud, circa 1880.
(Courtesy of Library of Congress.)

The Oglalas' Long
Journey to Pine Ridge

Dollie Pretty Cloud peered at the young white woman and the Lakota boy with suspicion. Why had they come to her cabin? She stood in her doorway, eyeing the stranger, as the boy explained why they'd come.

It was 1926, and Helen Blish was a graduate student at the University of Nebraska visiting Pine Ridge to study Lakota art. She'd heard that Pretty Cloud owned a book of drawings, traditional paintings portraying the old way of life. She asked if she could see it. The old woman softened a bit, for she was proud of what her brother had accomplished. She nodded, allowing the woman and the young man to step inside. She let them sit down on rickety chairs while she fetched the ledger from an old trunk. Her cabin was simple—a dirt floor, a potbelly stove, and a bed. The book once belonged to her brother, Amos Bad Heart Bull, she explained as she set it down on a wooden table. He died in 1913 at age forty-four. She removed a framed sketch of him off the wall and handed it to Blish, who studied it for a moment before turning her attention to the book.

She carefully turned to the first leaves. What she saw took her breath away. Pages and pages of drawings, hundreds of them etched in vivid colors, each sheet telling a story of a people, the Oglala Lakotas. Some of the sketches showed life before whites came to the prairie, when the warriors fought the Crows, when they performed the Sun Dance in the summer, when life was simpler. Others pictured famous battles, when the great Oglala chiefs defeated the bluecoats. There were sweeping images of skirmishes containing hundreds of figures, along with pictures of individual men locked in mortal combat. Slipped between the confrontations were scenes of everyday life: ceremonies, games, and dances.

The old woman began to talk of her long-departed brother as Blish carefully studied each page. Amos was the nephew of He Dog, an elder still living on the reservation. Amos had taught himself to draw. He bought the accounting book while he was serving as an army scout at Fort Robinson.

He was too young to remember the battles, but his father and uncles were there. They remembered everything. His father, Old Bad Heart Bull, was the band's storyteller and historian. Amos faithfully drew the stories of his elders, ignoring the ledger's rigid green lines, slipping in extra sheets when the book grew full.

When did he begin working on the book? Blish asked.

Right after the massacre at Wounded Knee, she said.

What was the significance of that, Blish had to wonder as she came across a scene from the tragic battle. Why did he feel the need to start drawing then?

Blish knew she was looking at something priceless, a pictographic history of a people during their most tumultuous years, all the stories passed down to the artist by eyewitnesses. The details on the clothing were stunning. The way the horses ran. So lifelike! And there were notes scribbled in Lakota on the sides to explain the scenes. Twenty years of Bad Heart Bull's life had gone into the book. She now knew how the egyptologists felt when they unearthed the Rosetta Stone.

The old woman would not sell the book. Not for any price. Blish and her interpreter left Pretty Cloud's cabin empty-handed, but she would return after contacting her colleagues at the university. She would come back with an offer that everyone could be happy with. She arranged for Pretty Cloud to receive a yearly stipend while they studied the book. After a few weeks of negotiations, the old woman acquiesced. Pretty Cloud understood that her brother had accomplished something important, that the white teachers wanted to study the book to understand her people's history better. But the cabin must have felt just a bit emptier, just a bit lonelier after they'd taken away all she had left of Amos.

Red Cloud, a tall, lanky Oglala warrior just twenty years old, sat among his friends in a circle around a campfire on a creek in the shadow of the Black Hills. Women and children gathered around to hear the young warriors' story. Underneath the vast prairie nighttime sky, one by one, each of the young men told the audience about their journey into the mountains. Everyone spoke except Red Cloud, who wasn't much of a storyteller.

While hunting in the mountains, they'd encountered an unlucky Ute returning alone from a hunt, his horse loaded down with deer meat, singing a happy song as he rode down a mountain trail through a pine forest. He shouldn't have sung so loudly. The Oglalas hid behind rocks and trees just as the hapless Ute emerged from the woods. One of Red Cloud's companions shot him through the heart. As the Ute lay bleeding and his horse stood idly grazing as if nothing had happened, they cut away his scalp, stripped him of his guns and possessions, and led the horse away.

Earlier that day, the Oglala party had come across a small, hastily abandoned Ute camp. The small band had left in a hurry; pots were still boiling over the campfires. The warriors pillaged the racks of drying meat and dined on the abandoned food.

The Utes once roamed over the western edges of the prairie, but they'd been pushed into the mountains like the Crows and the Shoshones. They'd all come up against the Lakotas and lost, retreating to the safety of the Rockies, only coming out to make furtive buffalo hunts.

Young Red Cloud and the other warriors left the mountains and returned to their camp in a happy mood. They had counted coup against the Utes and returned with food to share with everyone in their *tiospaye*, or small band. The Bad Faces, to which Red Cloud and his warrior friends belonged, was one of many *tiospaye* in the Sacred Hoop. For the Lakotas, the world was a circle. Everything in nature told them so: the moon, the sun, the earth, and the whirlwinds. Their tipis were round, and inside each tipi was a family. Kinship was unbreakable, a Sacred Hoop unto itself. A group of ten or so families would form a larger circle. And these bands formed the larger tribes. The Bad Faces, like the Koyas camping nearby, were part of the Oglala tribe. Theirs was a strong hoop—the hoop of a people who had ruled the prairie for decades.

Red Cloud was the son of a warrior, also named Red Cloud, who'd died before his birth. Red Cloud the elder was not a chief and his family had little, but young Red Cloud had distinguished himself as a warrior, returning from a fight against the Pawnees with his first scalp at age sixteen. A young man rose in Lakota society by counting coup—performing brave deeds in battle—and returning with the horses and scalps of the tribe's enemies.

The young warriors' triumphant return was tempered by tensions between the Bad Face and Koya bands. The Koyas were camped just to the north, and their chief and holy man, Bull Bear, was in a foul mood. Of all the Oglala bands, the Koyas were the strongest, and Bull Bear the mightiest of all the chiefs. One of the Bad Face boys had stolen a Koya woman to take as his bride, which usually wasn't a problem as long as everyone was agreeable to the arrangement. But Bull Bear didn't care for the young man, and the woman was his relative. All this was complicated by a barrel of whiskey brought to the Koya camp from Fort Laramie earlier that day.

A French beaver-pelt trader was probably the first to introduce whiskey to the tribe they called the Sioux back when they lived in the woods to the east. What could be more normal than sealing a business transaction by passing around a cup? North American tribes didn't have alcohol in their diet for thousands of years. Soon they would call it the "white man's wicked water." Just as with whites, there were Indians who loved it too much. Just as with whites, there were Indians who lived only to drink, to hang around the fort or the trading post hoping, sometimes begging, for a cup. Just as with whites, the whiskey made them lose control of their emotions, made them quarrel, do foolish things—sometimes kill. It wasn't long before the "drunken, lazy Indian" stereotype fixed itself in the minds of white settlers. There were plenty of "drunken, lazy white men" on the frontier, of course. But no matter. By 1834, Congress outlawed the sale of intoxicants to all Indians.

That same year, fur traders opened a trading post on the North Platte River at Fort Laramie. For a few buffalo robes, the white men would give them sugar, coffee, glass beads, black kettles to cook their food, iron ax heads to chop wood, and metal arrowheads so they wouldn't have to spend hours chipping away at stones. The laxly enforced law banning alcohol sales to Indians didn't dissuade the traders from distributing fourth-rate, watered-down whiskey. Some Lakotas drifted to the forts and trading posts, where they sank into the depths of alcoholism. They were derisively called "Laramie Loafers" or "hang-around-the-fort Indians." They curried favor with the white men, and sometimes acted as go-betweens.

Red Cloud knew whenever whiskey found its way into the camps, trouble soon followed. As his friends sat around the campfire regaling the women and children with tales of the mountain excursion, they continued to gnaw on the deer meat. They had already distributed some of their spoils to the widows and the elderly. Greed in Lakota society was taboo. For those who could not hunt or provide for themselves, food and shelter were given to them. To give to the needy in one's tribe was honorable, and to share your good fortune expected. For everyone—widows, orphans, the crippled—were all part of the same family. Several times a year, usually during a funeral or during the Sun Dance, families would sponsor a "giveaway" where many of their possessions were distributed to other families.

The warriors heard a commotion from the direction of the Koya village. There were slurred words, the sounds of drunken quarrelling. And then the crack of a rifle. The young men stood up.

"Are you going to lie there and be killed?" Red Cloud heard an uncle yell out from the dark. "Where are all the young men?"

They grabbed their rifles. Were they under attack from the Crows?

"Where is Red Cloud?" his uncle said, appearing from the dark. "Red Cloud, are you going to disgrace your father's name?"

Bull Bear was the problem, Red Cloud realized, not the Crows.

The Bad Face warriors ran outside the village in the direction of the gunfire. In the light of the moon, they saw lying shot on the ground the father of the boy who had stolen the woman. Bull Bear and a handful of his warriors hovered over the fallen man. Red Cloud could smell the whiskey from where he stood. The Bad Faces opened fire on the Koyas. A bullet ripped into Chief Bull Bear's leg, bringing him down to his knees. Red Cloud charged up to him. "You're the cause of all this!" he said, raising his rifle and shooting the Koya chief between the eyes.

In 1841, the year Red Cloud killed Bull Bear, whites were both a nuisance and a convenience. There weren't yet enough of them around to threaten their way of life. But that would soon change. For almost one hundred years, Lakotas had ruled the prairie. Amos Bad Heart Bull's drawings showed life the way it used to be.

Before the Lakotas stepped out onto the prairie, no single tribe ruled the Plains where millions of buffalo covered the grasslands like the shadows of dark clouds. Two generations before Bad Heart Bull's father and uncles were born, the tribes were forest dwellers and left the woods only to hunt in the summer. And then two Lakota tribes, the Oglalas and the Sicangus, known to the French as the Brulés, or Burnt Thighs, left the forest for their summer hunt and never came back. The five other Lakota tribes soon followed. Their Santee Sioux cousins stayed behind in the woodlands of Minnesota, a choice they would one day regret. The Yanktonais settled on the eastern edge of the prairie, while the Lakotas, also known as the Teton Sioux, pushed out to the western fringe.

When the Lakota tribes stepped out onto the prairie, they discovered horses, which had made their way to the Plains from the south and north. They discovered the gun, brought to them by fur traders from the northeast. They discovered that these were two excellent tools for making war on their neighbors.

When the Lakotas stepped out onto the prairie, about 1750 or so, the vast emptiness was full of buffalo. Where they once brought down the beasts through stealth, they now did so with the speed of a horse. Whereas once they moved from camp to camp, carrying their tipis and belongings on their backs, or on dog-pulled travois, the horses allowed them to follow the herds with ease. They learned how to shoot. They learned how to ride. They learned how to do both at the same time.

When the Lakotas stepped out onto the prairie with their horses and guns, it was bad news for the other Plains tribes like the Crows and the earth-lodge-dwelling Pawnees who were among their favorite targets. They booted rival tribes out of the Black Hills. Native Americans had etched carvings into their sandstone cliffs for as long as five thousand years, and an untold number of tribes had hunted there. Now it was the Lakotas' turn to occupy the sacred hills

By the time Lewis and Clark passed through in 1804, the Sacred Hoop was powerful and strong. The Lakotas had divided into seven tribes, a sacred number for the Sioux. The northern Lakotas—the Hunkpapas, Blackfoots, and Sans Arcs—made war on the Mandans, Arikaras, and Hidatsas in what is modern-day North Dakota. The Minneconjou and Two Kettle tribes roamed the middle plains. And the strongest of them all, the Brulés and Oglalas, ruled the south.

The settlers brought the Lakotas something besides horses and guns. Disease, like the horse, came indirectly. But when it came, its impact was profound. When smallpox spread among the village-dwelling tribes along the Missouri River, the nomadic Lakotas broke into smaller bands, headed for the hills in self-imposed quarantine, and let the microbes weaken their enemies further. When the Oglalas or Brulés came galloping over the hills to attack the villages, the Omahas, the Poncas, the Otoes— all decimated by disease—never had a chance. The Lakotas forged alliances with the Cheyennes and the Arapahos. They could also call on their

Yanktonai cousins when needed. Within a few short years, they ruled the middle of the continent—from the Yellowstone River in the north to the Platte River in the south, from the Rockies in the west to the Missouri in the east. The settlers always claimed that the Indians didn't understand ownership of land. Of course, Plains tribes didn't have deeds; they didn't know what an acre was, and no individuals owned plots. But territory was something they understood very well. The Lakotas set out to acquire as much prime buffalo hunting land as possible. They did it swiftly. They did it effectively. And they did it without mercy.

The Lakotas tangled most often with the Crows. Inside the Bad Heart Bull ledger are pages and pages of the legendary fights with the tribe rendered from stories passed down from his father and uncles. Stories of young warriors like Red Cloud charging into camps, counting coups, slaying their enemies, and fleeing with their captured horses. There were defeats as well. Occasionally, the Crows counted coup against the Oglalas, but they eventually found themselves pushed into the mountains like many other vanquished tribes. Soon, no tribe in the middle of the continent was mightier than the Lakotas, and none were more powerful than the Oglalas after Bull Bear's death.

Life was good for a while. Buffalo were plentiful, and there were still enemies around to count coup against: Pawnees to the south and Crows to the west. The tribes hunted buffalo in the summer and fall, using every part of the beasts to some useful end. The women gathered chokecherries, wild onions, and fruits to supplement their diet. The bands gathered in the summer to meet with other tribes, sometimes with their Santee and Yanktonai cousins, to hold councils and perform the Sun Dance, their most sacred ceremony.

Pages five and six of the Bad Heart Bull ledger show the women gathered around in a circle as the men, stripped from the waist up, with whistles made of eagle bones in their mouths, strain against the sacred pole, to which they were tethered through piercings in their chests, staring at the sun until the flesh rips through and they collapse.

Susan Rouleau looked up at her French-Canadian father as he spoke to the schoolmaster in broken English. She was seven years old, too young to understand the foreign language, but old enough to understand what was happening. She and her two younger brothers were being left at a school in the town of Highland in Kansas Territory, within sight of the Missouri River. Abandoned. She may not have known the word in English, but she could feel it.

Her Oglala mother, White Buffalo, had died shortly after giving birth to her infant brother Jesse in 1859. Now, her father, Hubert Rouleau, didn't want the half-breed children anymore. Her younger brother, John, stood by her side as the two men conversed.

Many French-speaking Canadians like Rouleau followed the Lakota tribes. The beaver-pelt boom brought them down from Canada, and Hubert and his brother Charles settled on a spot along the Missouri to trap. Hubert, in his fifties and barely five feet tall, was still a tough mountain man despite retiring from the life of a trapper years ago. He'd lost all his toes to frostbite, but soldiered on and became a trader at Fort Laramie. Opportunities brought the trappers farther west, and many, like Rouleau, settled at the fort along the banks of the Platte River. The fort was the trading hub of the west, where two new kinds of Indians began to emerge. One was made up of the offspring of traders who'd taken Indian wives. Sometimes, these "squawmen" abandoned their families. But some stuck around and taught their boys the ins and outs of business. Soon, there were Lakotas who bore their names: Bordeaux, Pourier, Roubidoux, Janis. These children occupied both worlds and weren't accepted by either race. But they were often called upon to settle disputes and serve as bridges between Lakotas and whites.

The other new Indians were the "Laramie Loafers." Most Lakotas came to the fort only once or twice a year when it became the distribution point for goods allotted to them by treaty. But some Lakotas didn't want to go back to the wilds, and they stuck around the fort all year. Some of these so-called loafers also served as cultural bridges; others simply fell into the depths of alcoholism and couldn't leave a ready supply of watered-down whiskey.

In the white world, the half-breeds were just Indians. The number of white institutions that would take mixed-blood orphans were few, so Hubert traveled the length of the Kansas Territory to a place near where his brother and he began trapping twenty years before. The Highland University Preparatory School was south of the town of Rulo, phonetically named after his brother, Charles Rouleau, and run by a sympathetic Presbyterian minister who would educate and look after the children.

After Hubert concluded his business with the minister, he left his children in the school's care, returning west, never to see them again. The two boys would be raised as whites. But Susan would one day return to her Oglala roots.

The French traders came in a trickle until the 1860s. But the following years Susan Rouleau spent in the school would see a flood of whites washing over the prairie to claim it for themselves, just as the Lakotas had taken it from their rivals over a century before.

Red Cloud had been waiting on the ridge above the white man's fort along the Big Horn River for several days. His harried bluecoat enemies remained inside the stockade, too afraid to stick their noses outside. The chief knew from painful experience that he could never take the fort in a frontal assault. The log walls were nearly impregnable, and inside the soldiers bore new repeating rifles and howitzers. The men inside were scared out of their minds and hungry enough to eat their horses, but even in their reduced state they maintained the advantage of superior weapons. But there were other ways to beat the U.S. Army, and Red Cloud was patient.

For several days, runners came to his camp with entreaties from the generals at Fort Laramie. Would Red Cloud come in to make peace and sign the treaty? The answer was still "no." Not until they abandoned the forts and the road running through the Powder River Country, the Lakotas' hunting grounds acknowledged by treaty.

It had been two decades since Red Cloud shot Bull Bear. His black hair reached down to his waist. His sleepy eyes betrayed hard cynicism from years of dealing with the lies of whites. He was now in his forties, still tall and lanky with wiry muscles. Old enough to be wise, but young enough to cut an imposing figure. Because he wasn't a hereditary chief, he had had to battle to become the most powerful Lakota leader, distinguishing himself in skirmishes with the Crows as a young man, then proving himself to be a brilliant tactician against the army when he was older. He was now the Lakotas' most famous war chief, or infamous, according to his opponents.

For two years, he'd fought the bluecoat generals. The seven Lakota tribes had banded together, and with their Arapaho and Cheyenne allies they'd staved off the Powder River invasion that began when gold was discovered in the Montana mountains to the north. In 1866, the Great Father Andrew Johnson in Washington had sent a treaty commission to Fort Laramie, and Red Cloud had gone there to see what the whiskered men had to offer. But Red Cloud discovered during the negotiations that the generals had already dispatched soldiers to build forts on the Bozeman Trail. Red Cloud quietly walked out of the negotiations, took his band into the hills, and began a bloody guerrilla war.

Now Red Cloud and his warriors watched Fort C. F. Smith from above. At last, the log doors swung open. Were they sending out cutters to gather wood for their fires? No. There were horses and wagons. They continued to stream out. The soldiers were abandoning the fort.

It was a gratifying moment for Red Cloud. Little had gone well for the Lakotas, especially when it came to dealing with whites. When he was young, the only caucasians the Oglalas knew were traders. But more Europeans boarded ships, crossed the Atlantic, and crowded the eastern cities. Some stayed in the slums. Others were farmers and wanted their own land to till. As each year passed, the fertile land in the East was swallowed up acre by acre, and the children of the original settlers had to move farther west to stake their own claims. The politicians, hoping to reduce unemployment in the cities, passed laws making it easy for would-be sodbusters to try their hand at farming.

When gold was discovered in California, Conestoga wagons began cutting a trail along the southern edge of the Sand Hills near the Platte River. The white men's animals overgrazed the land, and their wagon trains chased away the game. The migrants cut down all the trees they could find along the river, ruining the campgrounds where the bands had spent the winters. In 1851, Lakotas, Crows, Southern Cheyennes, and Arapahos signed a treaty allowing safe passage for pioneers traveling along the Platte River in exchange for tobacco, coffee, and other goods. But every summer, more and more encroachers came. They built forts and trading posts, and strung telegraph wires along the way.

The same decade, more than one hundred thousand settlers arrived in Minnesota. They grabbed what land they could, forced the Ojibwas and the Santee Sioux onto tiny reservations, then proceeded to starve them by breaking every treaty they ever made. Promised annuities never arrived, disreputable traders cheated them out of land, game disappeared, and starvation set in. In 1862, as the Civil War raged in the South, the Santees entered a war they couldn't win. The army and settlers defeated the Woodland Sioux, sending them off to unlivable land in the Dakota Territory, grabbing every acre they'd left behind.

Minnesota was now made safe for the white settlers.

The politicians in Washington never thought they'd need that Indian land out west. The country seemed so vast. There was plenty of room for everyone. But European ships kept coming, unloading the huddled masses yearning to breathe free. Even so, the territory north of the Platte River was considered worthless. The "Great American Desert," as one early explorer called it. The forty-niners, Mormons, and other migrants, seeing the desolate Sand Hills to the north, never had any reason to believe otherwise. They just kept moving.

The Rocky Mountains yielded enough gold to spark a new rush there. White men began to push Arapahos and Southern Cheyennes out of their traditional territory in Colorado. In late 1864, seven hundred Colorado militia men led by Colonel John Chivington attacked a peaceful Cheyenne camp on Sand Creek. Most warriors were off hunting, so it was easy for his men to slaughter the one hundred elders, women, and children left behind.

Colorado was now made safe for the white settlers.

Oglalas and Brulés were having a difficult time finding buffalo. The white leaders in Washington knew that to kill the buffalo was to kill the Indian. And there was a ready market for their hides in the East. The buffalo hunters proceeded to wipe out the Plains Indians' food source.

After the end of the Civil War, the white invasion began in earnest. The Union Pacific Railroad cut across Nebraska along the path the forty-niners traversed. The Lakotas retreated to the Powder River Country, the land between the Black Hills and the Rocky Mountains where there was still plenty of game, and the Yellowstone, Tongue, and Powder rivers ensured there would always be water.

But then the new gold rush began in Montana. Army generals came after the Lakotas, and their Cheyenne and Arapaho allies, with orders to kill every Indian male over the age of twelve. Red Cloud and the other chiefs fought them with bows and arrows and antiquated trading guns. Red Cloud made overtures to his old enemies, the Crows. He told them that together they could defeat the white man. But the Crows and the Pawnees, who had never experienced a moment of mercy when the Lakotas ruled the prairie, signed up as army scouts instead.

Despite the entry of the Lakotas' traditional enemies into the fight, snow, poorly trained troops, arrogant generals unfamiliar with the territory, and the tenacity of the Lakotas led to the treaty negotiations in 1866. The nation found it had little stomach for war after four years of bloodshed between the North and South. But the federal government's duplicity at the negotiations forced Red Cloud to continue fighting. The chief had spent the first summer making allies. He gathered around him three thousand warriors, and several chiefs who would one day become legends.

The Brulé chief, Spotted Tail, preferred peace and went to hunt buffalo in the south. Spotted Tail had served time in Leavenworth prison for attacking a mail train in 1851, and the experience had left a strong impression on him. The whites could never be defeated, he believed. But many of his warriors broke away to fight. Chief Dull Knife of the Northern Cheyennes and his warriors joined Red Cloud, as did the Arapahos and their leader Black Bear. Among the Lakotas were Sitting Bull and Gall of the Hunkpapa tribe, and a young warrior who would soon make a name for himself, a quiet but determined young Oglala named Crazy Horse.

Red Cloud used a network of hang-around-the-fort Indians and mixed-blood traders to obtain modern guns. He still couldn't defeat the bluecoats in head-on battles, or penetrate their forts, but he could wage what would one day be called asymmetric warfare. His warriors demoralized the isolated soldiers by attacking wagon trains and cutting off their supplies. No one traveling the "bloody" Bozeman Trail was safe.

A Civil War hero, Captain William Fetterman fancied himself a real Indian fighter. He didn't have much respect for the "red men," let alone his superior officers who, in his opinion, weren't doing an adequate job in cleaning them out of the Powder River Country.

"With eighty good men, I could slice through the whole Sioux Nation," he bragged.

On a cold day in December 1866, he took about that many horsemen out of Fort Phil Kearny to pursue a small band of Indians harassing the fort's woodchoppers. His superior officer warned him not to venture too far, but Fetterman wouldn't listen. The eight braves galloped away, taunting them, drawing them farther into the hills.

Waiting there were thousands of Lakota, Arapaho, and Cheyenne warriors, who wiped out the hapless soldiers. Red Cloud was the mastermind of the plan. And one of the decoys was the warrior Crazy Horse.

The Fetterman Massacre brought the United States to the negoti- ating table. Several chiefs traveled to Fort Laramie to accept gifts and see what the U.S. government had to say. "Where is Red Cloud?" the white men asked. They knew there wouldn't be any peace until the Oglala chief made his mark on the treaty. For months, the white generals at Fort Laramie did everything they could to bring in Red Cloud. They sent him gifts. They practically begged. Red Cloud, through a trusted emissary, gave them the same answer every time. "I'll come in when every last sol- dier has abandoned the forts."

Finally, the white chiefs granted his demand.

As Red Cloud watched the column disappear down the trail heading south, he knew that he'd finally won. He and his warriors left the ridge, the young men whooping as they rode into the empty fort. Red Cloud watched from atop his horse as others searched for anything useful to loot. Soon the wood buildings began to crackle and spark. Smoke reached his nose.

Red Cloud had won a war, not just a battle, and forced the U.S. gov- ernment to bow to his demands—a feat that few Native Americans had accomplished. He returned to Fort Laramie to sign the Treaty of 1868.

The United States ceded the Lakotas the entire western half of present-day South Dakota from the Missouri River to the Wyoming border. This land would be forever known as the Great Sioux Reserva- tion. Included in this vast reservation was the Black Hills, the Paha Sapa, their sacred land. No white settlers or soldiers could step onto this great chunk of prairie without the Lakotas' permission. The U.S. government also ceded them hunting rights to the Powder River Country, all the land in Wyoming north of the North Platte River and east of the summits of the Big Horn Mountains. The Sand Hills, south of the Dakota Territory border in Nebraska, remained a part of their unceded territory "so long as the buffalo may range thereon in such numbers as to justify the chase." The hardliners in the military didn't want to relinquish the upper half of the Nebraska Panhandle, but the skilled diplomat Spotted Tail insisted that it be preserved as their hunting grounds.

They were an odd-looking bunch of tourists, the sixteen Lakota men and four women with their long hair, brown skin, and dour expressions. They didn't look like they were having any fun at all on their trip to the nation's capital. Their handlers took them to all the impressive places. But they didn't seem to be impressed. And Red Cloud, looking at the giant stone houses of the white men through his sleepy eyes, appeared positively bored. They stopped at the Navy Yard to watch the sailors fire a giant fifteen-inch cannon. It made a thunderous noise as it launched a shell down the Potomac River, but Red Cloud scoffed at it. It was too big to haul around the mountains and plains, and what warrior would be foolish enough to ride into its range of fire?

For decades the U.S. government had employed a successful formula to subdue troublesome chiefs. Invite them to Washington, let them see the multitudes of whites in the cities, display their superior technology and military might, then sit them down with the president to make them feel important. They would realize how futile it was to make war.

Two years after the signing of the Treaty of 1868, there was still trouble on the Plains. From the beginning, both sides disagreed on what the piece of paper meant. The United States had promised rations. And rations had to be distributed in one place. So the federal government established the Red Cloud Agency. For the first couple of years, Red Cloud's people still clung to the old life by hunting the Powder River Country in the summer with the bands of so-called wild Lakotas such as those of the Hunkpapa chief, Sitting Bull, who'd never signed a treaty with the whites and never would.

For two years, the two sides had squabbled. Red Cloud wanted the agency to be located at Fort Laramie on the Platte River. The U.S. government wanted the Indians to go to a site on the Missouri. Red Cloud claimed the agents were cheating them of promised goods. Meanwhile, the treaty clearly stated that the Lakotas and their allies were to put down their guns and become peaceful, sodbusting farmers. The adults were to deliver their children to schools where they would be taught English. Meanwhile, white settlers agitated to be allowed into the Wyoming mountains to seek gold, but the army knew that would just stir up trouble.

In 1870, Red Cloud accepted an invitation to visit President Ulysses S. Grant in Washington to straighten out these matters. He was to bring only twelve men. He insisted on twenty, and three of his own interpreters, or he wouldn't go.

When Red Cloud arrived in Washington, the press and political leaders were under the impression that he spoke for all Plains Indians. If only they could pacify him, then peace would come to the prairie.

Spotted Tail, Red Cloud's rival and leader of the Brulé band, had made peace, but neither chief had the power to force the "wild" Indians to abandon their way of life. The free Lakotas were happy to come to the agencies in the winter to collect their annuities, but as soon as the snow melted, they dashed off to the Powder River Country—the land they'd fought so hard to keep—to hunt buffalo.

Spotted Tail and his Brulé delegation dined in the White House with Red Cloud and President Grant. The two Lakota chiefs had been bitter rivals for the past two years, but they'd put aside their differences to show a united front. Their entourages met the next day with the secretary of the interior and the commissioner of Indian affairs. They tried to convince Red Cloud to adhere to the Treaty of 1868—to abandon the buffalo hunt for the plow. If they thought they'd cowed the chief with their displays of military and technological might, they were wrong. Red Cloud stood up and spoke.

> I have offered my prayers to the Great Spirit so I could come here safe. Look at me. I was a warrior on this land where the sun rises, now I come from where the sun sets. Whose voice was first sounded on this land—the red people with bows and arrows. The Great Father says he is good and kind to us. I can't see it. I am good to his white people. From the word sent me I have come all the way to this house. My face is red, yours is white. The Great Spirit taught you to read and write, but not me. I have not learned. I came here to tell my Great Father what I do not like in my country. You are close to my Great Father and are a great many chiefs. The men the president sends there have no sense of heart. What has been done in my country, I do not want to ask for it. White people going through my country. Father, have you or any of your friends here got children? Do you want to raise them? Look at me. I come here with all these young men. All are married, have children, and want to raise them.
>
> The white children have surrounded me and have left me nothing but an island. When we first had this land we were strong, now we are melting like snow on the hillside while you are growing like spring grass.

Red Cloud asked them to send him honest agents and not to build any roads through the Black Hills or Big Horn Mountains.

He made similar speeches to the president that night and to an audience in New York before he returned west. He finished his trip by saying he would refuse to acknowledge the Treaty of 1868 because the men who'd interpreted it to him were liars.

Red Cloud remained a skilled and tough negotiator.

Just as the slaves had their abolitionists agitating in the North prior to the Civil War, the Indians of the West had their "friends" in the East. These well-meaning Indian sympathizers, many of them Quakers, had a simple solution. Turn the Indians into whites as soon as possible. The adults would be converted from hunters to farmers, the children sent to schools to learn to read and write, and all would be converted to Christianity.

"Farmers?" the Oglalas thought. "Who do they think we are? A bunch of Poncas?"

The "friends" allocated to each reservation a Christian denomination. And for Red Cloud's people, their designated missionaries were the Episcopalians.

The first Red Cloud Agency was near the familiar Fort Laramie. The "friends" insisted that the army shouldn't administer the Indians' affairs, so control of the agencies was handed to civilians. Good Christian men, of course, so there was a new chief of sorts: the Indian agent. Agents were political appointees. Sometimes they were corrupt. Sometimes they were simply incompetent. Often, they were both. Red Cloud immediately began feuding with his appointed agents. He accused them of cheating. They accused him of being a stubborn traditionalist only out for himself, and of inflating tribal rolls to take more than the tribe's share of goods. The chief would remain a cocklebur in the butt of the agents for decades to come.

In 1871, the federal government forced Red Cloud to move his people thirty miles downriver from Fort Laramie. But there was no firewood there, and white settlers nearby complained of raids. Again, Red Cloud's tribe was forced to move, this time to an unsettled area in northwestern Nebraska along the White River.

The army established Camp Robinson up the road to keep an eye on the Oglalas, while the Brulés had an identical setup at Camp Sheridan and the Spotted Tail Agency forty miles east. Due to sketchy surveys of the remote area, the army believed the agencies were within the boundary of the Great Sioux Reservation in the Dakota Territory. In fact, they were several miles south in Nebraska.

Free bands of Lakotas, Arapahos, and Cheyennes arrived annually to line up for their treaty-allocated goods. They began to look upon the agency Indians with scorn as they took their rations and returned to their hunting grounds. Soon, there was a rift between those who believed that it was futile to fight the white man and those who wanted to cling to the old way of life. There were "wild" Indians and "agency" Indians. The wild Lakotas still wanted to make war against the Crows, to hunt buffalo in the Powder River Country, to camp in the Black Hills in the winter. However, Red Cloud and Spotted Tail, designated by the federal government as the spokesmen for their peoples, believed it was useless to make war against the whites.

The Indians had "friends" back East, but in the West enemies surrounded them. White settlers had stepped out onto the prairie themselves and were taking over what would soon be eastern South Dakota. They pushed up against the Missouri River looking across the vast empty plains hungrily, like kids with their faces pressed up against a confectionery window. They asked why the Sioux, numbering no more than twenty-five thousand, had the entire half of the territory for themselves. Why are they given free food? When the locusts eat our crops, we starve. Why are they given free farming supplies when we have to borrow from the bank to buy ours? The Treaty of 1868 wasn't a sufficient answer for them. America, after all, was meant for whites. It was their Manifest Destiny. The settlers' hunger for land could never be sated. They screamed and hollered at the politicians in Washington.

We want more land!

And more alluring than unbroken sod, they relished gold.

The United States broke the Treaty of 1868 by sending Colonel Custer into the Sioux's sacred Black Hills in the summer of 1874. John Gordon and his party of twenty-six followed. The army instigated the gold rush and then had the impossible task of keeping gold-crazed miners off the reservation. While John Gordon's wagon train burned in the Niobrara River ravine, thousands of others were hightailing it for the hills. The army escorted some of the lawbreakers out, depositing them with civil authorities who quickly turned them loose. Most went right back to prospecting.

War was in the air.

President Grant again called Red Cloud, Spotted Tail, and other chiefs to Washington.

Wouldn't you like to sell us the Black Hills?

The answer was either "no" or a ridiculously high price meant to show the U.S. government just how much the Paha Sapa meant to them. The Treaty of 1868 stipulated that any ceding of territory had to be approved by three-fourths of the adult males. Red Cloud and Spotted Tail returned to the agencies without a deal.

Captain Anson Mills watched with some trepidation as more and more Indians gathered near the lone cottonwood tree on the edge of the vast Nebraska prairie. One hundred fifty of his men, mounted on steeds they'd ridden from Camp Sheridan, also watched nervously as thousands of warriors, representing almost every Lakota, Arapaho, and Cheyenne tribe, trotted in on their swift horses, their faces painted for war, every one of them carrying weapons: bows and arrows, war clubs, and guns. Chief Spotted Tail had ordered his loyal Brulé warriors to take positions near the soldiers, which gave Mills some comfort.

Mills had to wonder, though, whether the cavalry and the "friend-lies" could truly protect the commissioners. The old men wearing suits and gray beards, sitting in the shade of a canvas awning, had to notice the force gathering outside. The negotiations had sputtered for days, but now it looked like something was about to happen. But what? There were already five warriors for every one of Mills's men.

It was September, four months after Mills had ordered the burning of John Gordon's wagon train, an act that prompted the Sioux City news-papers to call him the vilest of names and had done nothing to deter the would-be miners.

Iowa Senator William Allison and the other commissioners came to see if the Lakotas would sell the Black Hills. The negotiations were supposed to take place inside the walls of Fort Robinson, but the chiefs insisted on neutral ground. How they'd chosen this lonesome, unprotected spot near the cottonwood tree, Mills would never know. It was hot. Flies swarmed around, joyously buzzing on top of the manure the cavalry and Lakota horses had plopped on the ground. The thousands of warriors sur-rounding Mills and his men wore their stoic expressions or scowls, but there was tension in the air, buzzing as thick as the flies.

Red Cloud and Spotted Tail took their places across from the com-missioners. Dozens of lesser chiefs like American Horse sat in a line to the left. Absent was the Hunkpapa medicine man Sitting Bull. When asked if he would come to the council, he replied that he would never sell any land to the white man. He pinched some dust between his fingers. "Not even as much as this!"

As the leaders parleyed, warriors lined up on horseback in front of the open tents. Many were angry young men, convinced that Spotted Tail and Red Cloud, now derisively called "government chiefs," were going to give away their sacred land.

Senator Allison sat on one side of the tent facing the throng. Next to him sat a missionary, a trader, and some military officers—every part of white society with a vested interest in the Lakotas. With his mixed-blood interpreters beside him, the senator began a long rambling speech. Mills noticed Young-Man-Afraid-of-His-Horses, a hereditary chief of the Oglalas, standing on one side watching the proceedings.

Suddenly some shots cracked outside the tent.

Little Big Man, a cousin of Crazy Horse, galloped between the chiefs and the rows of seated commissioners. He was painted for war, bare chested, his rifle barrel smoking, two six-shooters strapped around his waist. Two other mounted warriors rode at his side.

"I will kill the first chief who speaks for selling the Paha Sapa!"

His rifle split the sky again.

"And I'll do the same to any white man who tries to take them!" he added.

Young-Man-Afraid-of-His-Horses put himself between the warriors and the frightened commissioners while his loyal men began a song of peace.

The message from Sitting Bull and Crazy Horse had been delivered. Sell the Black Hills and break the Sacred Hoop forever.

Spotted Tail and Red Cloud whispered to each other for a moment, then rose to their feet. Spotted Tail signaled to Mills that it was time to leave. The commissioners stood up in a hurry. Mills's riders, and two companies from Fort Robinson, surrounded the negotiators while warriors loyal to Red Cloud and Spotted Tail provided a second, thin layer shielding them from the jeering Lakotas, Cheyennes, and Arapahos, who were singing war songs as they passed. It was eight long miles back to Fort Robinson. Mills was relieved to see its gates.

A few days later, Allison asked if the Indians would simply sell the rights to mine the Black Hills. After they took all the gold, then the whites would leave. The army simply couldn't keep all the people out of the Black Hills, he said. He offered them four hundred thousand dollars per year to lease the land, or they would buy it outright for six million dollars paid in fifteen installments.

By that time only Spotted Tail had bothered to stick around. He delivered the message: the Paha Sapa weren't for sale. The commission returned to Washington, where the country's leaders had already decided to take the hills away anyway. President Grant gave a secret order to Generals Phil Sheridan and George Crook. Make no further resistance to the miners. If only John Gordon had waited a few more months . . .

Many Indians left the agencies, scalping and killing miners and settlers as they made their way back to the Powder River Country.

The war for the Black Hills had begun.

Crazy Horse prayed to the Great Mystery to show him a way to defeat the bluecoats, and his prayers were answered. In Amos Bad Heart Bull's ledger are pages and pages of the two legendary fights, the Battle of the Little Big Horn—known to the Lakotas as the Battle of Greasy Grass—and the Battle of the Rosebud. The artist had been just a toddler at the time, barely old enough to remember bits and pieces. He drew the mounted warriors with their coup sticks and rifles, their war bonnets flowing in the breeze, their swift horses charging the enemy. In the Battle of the Rosebud, he drew a Cheyenne chief riding his horse too close to General George "Three Star" Crook's flank. The warrior was shot down, but his sister rode out on her horse to save him. He drew Red Cloud's son Jack shooting his way out of a horde of Crow mercenaries to make a miraculous escape.

During a Sun Dance, Sitting Bull had seen a vision of bluecoats falling into an Indian camp. Colonel Custer, the man who'd led one thousand men into the Paha Sapa two years before, fell into the Indians' camp just as Sitting Bull had seen in his vision, not from the sky, but on their horses. The colonel and his men were slaughtered in the Battle of the Little Big Horn. It was the U.S. army's greatest defeat in the War for the Great Plains.

Red Cloud and Spotted Tail remained at the agencies in Nebraska as the wild Indians derisively called them "treaty chiefs." When news of the bloody rout reached the East only days after the joyous July 4 centennial celebration, the nation called for revenge. Red Cloud and Spotted Tail's peaceful bands were put under virtual arrest. Their weapons were confiscated and their horse herds taken away and given to Crow scouts. A new commission arrived and demanded that they sign away the Black Hills for good. The battle at Little Big Horn gave the U.S. government an excuse to break the Treaty of 1868, including the requirement of attaining the signatures of three-fourths of the adult males for any exchange of land. The chiefs refused to sign at first, even though they were surrounded by troops. The commissioners threatened to take away their rations, a tactic they would come to use again and again over the years to bend the stubborn Lakotas to their ways. Faced with starvation, a few chiefs signed the new agreement, Red Cloud and Spotted Tail included.

The federal government also demanded that the two bands leave northwestern Nebraska and move to spots on the Missouri in central South Dakota. The army wanted a river port to ship their supplies. Nebraska's state legislature and the settlers, discovering the true location of the border, wanted the "savages" removed.

Nebraskans were incensed that the Treaty of 1868 allowed for hunting rights in the Sand Hills. White hunters had all but exterminated the buffalo, and no one believed the so-called wasteland was habitable, but the legislature passed a resolution demanding the Lakota tribes' removal. The Pawnees had already been booted out to the Indian Territory by 1875. The Poncas' treaty was torn up, and they were forced to abandon their cornfields and march to a miserable speck of land five hundred miles away in Indian Territory. Only the Omaha tribe managed to hang onto its small reservation north of the thriving city that bore its name. Red Cloud and Spotted Tail didn't want to move. White settlers had ruined the land along the Missouri. They were afraid of what the whiskey traders would do to their people, now idle and with nothing to do but drink all day.

As for the Indians in the Powder River Country, the life of freedom they had known was coming to an end. After Custer's Last Stand, the bluecoats attacked with vengeance in their hearts. The cavalry cut through their villages, destroying every living and nonliving thing. The holdouts had no time to hunt for food, and their ammunition ran low. Hounded by the army, Sitting Bull and his band fled to Canada. Crazy Horse had to surrender or watch his small band starve.

On page 156 of the Bad Heart Bull ledger, the artist wrote, "In the season of 1877, Crazy Horse was killed. A Lakota seized him. His name was Little Big Man."

Crazy Horse believed he was being escorted to Fort Robinson to make a trip to Washington. He arrived inside the walls to find his cousin, Little Big Man, on the army payroll and part of the detail guarding him. Little Big Man: the warrior who'd bravely threatened Red Cloud, Spotted Tail, and the treaty commissioners with death if they sold the Black Hills.

Little Big Man knew Crazy Horse's road would not lead to Washington. For now, the chief was going to a small jail cell. The older chiefs at the agency had grown jealous of Crazy Horse's influence. The generals and the reservation chiefs both decided that it was time for him to go, and he was taken into custody.

When Crazy Horse realized the soldiers were taking him to jail to put him in leg irons, he struggled. Little Big Man grabbed him from behind, and a soldier stuck him in the gut with a bayonet. The great Oglala warrior chief died that night.

Red Cloud, Spotted Tail, and the other chiefs took a train to Washington to discuss the plan to leave their agencies for the Missouri River site. President Rutherford Hayes promised them that they'd have to stay there only one winter. It was easier and cheaper to deliver their rations by boat, he explained. The federal government would not deliver the food and clothing the Lakotas now depended upon for survival to the Nebraska agencies. Red Cloud returned to Nebraska hoping that the president would be true to his word. Faced with starvation that winter, Red Cloud and nearly five thousand Oglalas left northwestern Nebraska under the escort of two companies of soldiers.

Nebraska was now safe for the whites.

When spring came, another commission tried to convince Red Cloud to stay, but he refused, and the officials left with him and two dozen other chiefs to select a new spot.

They settled on an area along White Clay Creek. The Badlands were to the north; Nebraska's border marked the southern edge. Spotted Tail's Brulés chose a spot just to the east. It was within sight of the sacred Paha Sapa. Even though the hills were lost to them forever, they could still see their outlines in the distance. After eight locations, Red Cloud's agency would move no more.

They once roamed freely in an area that spanned three states and parts of two others. After that, they had most of South Dakota. Now, the Lakotas were surrounded by a sea of land-hungry white settlers, merchants eager to make a buck, and railroad tracks threatening to pierce through what remained of their territory. The buffalo were gone. The tribes they'd pushed off the Plains a century before had been forced onto their own reservations. The Crows, Shoshones, and Pawnees who'd helped the cavalry defeat their Lakota enemies suffered the same fate.

When Red Cloud arrived at his people's final destination in the autumn of 1878, the federal government dropped the name "Red Cloud Agency" and changed it to "Pine Ridge Agency" after the razorback line of rocky, tree-covered hills that bisected the land. It was a small effort to deflate Red Cloud's ego and standing among his people. His next war would be one of wills with the new agent, Dr. Valentine McGillycuddy.

Spotted Tail's land was now called the Rosebud Agency. Both chiefs had concluded correctly that waging war with the U.S. government was futile. If the Lakotas were to survive, they had to put down their guns. But the leaders would now have to fight for the souls of their own peoples. The generals were gone, but the missionaries, schoolteachers, and Indian agents took their places to wage a culture war.

The U.S. government's sole plan was to convert the Indians into farmers. But they soon discovered that the soil at the new agency was nearly worthless. Idleness and despair set in. Merchants set up shops at nearby "whiskey ranches" to fill a void in the men's souls.

From the East, a new railroad line would creep across their former hunting grounds thirty miles south. Ahead of the iron rail, settlers would fill in the land. Until then, the Sand Hills were thought to be barren and worthless. But a few ranchers were about to find out otherwise.

Amos Bad Heart Bull's drawings of the old days came to an end. There were no more fights with Crows. No more great victories over the bluecoats. The stories his uncles and father told him were complete. Now, he began to draw life on the reservation—scenes he'd observed with his own eyes. There was one more battle to record. It would be the most tragic of all.

The White Folks' Journey
to Sheridan County

The wagon wheels cut through the sandy soil as the horses' tails switched back and forth. Mari Sandoz, just fourteen years old that spring of 1910, looked up at her father, an unkempt man with a scraggly beard clumped together by tobacco juice. In a time when bathing was a once-a-week occurrence, Old Jules Sandoz was known to go much longer than that. He drove the team hard into the depths of the Sand Hills, which were colored pale green in the wake of the spring rains. Mari's ten-year-old brother James sat beside her. Both children wondered what lay ahead. Their father, a French-speaking Swiss immigrant, was a stubborn and mean-spirited man with a penchant for beating his wife and children. They didn't dare question his motives.

For more than two decades, Old Jules had farmed a claim south of Hay Springs in the western section of Sheridan County known as the Mirage Flats. He'd also run a side business locating claims for would-be settlers in the Sand Hills. Many had come and gone, for it was a tough land to make a living on. Old Jules didn't like most people. And most people didn't like Old Jules. So he located some unclaimed land for himself in the heart of the county's largest ranch. Mari gazed at the towering grass-covered dunes enveloping them. She'd seen them from a distance from her home on the flats, but she'd never ventured there. It was said a man could get lost in those hills forever. Some went in and never found their way out. The Lakotas called them a place of mystery. They would chase game there, but preferred less desolate spots to pitch their tipis. To Mari, they were both frightening and alluring.

Old Jules whipped the team over the last ridge, revealing a mile-long valley with a small shimmering lake at the opposite end. Cattails ringed its edge and domed muskrat dens stuck out like miniature islands in a vast ocean. Next to the small lake stood a windowless wooden shack her father had built the previous summer. As soon as he pulled up, he ordered the

Oglalas and Sheridan County residents pose together in Gordon, June 1919. (Courtesy of Sheridan County Historical Society.)

Nebr.
ler

children to unload the supplies. He wouldn't bother lending them a hand as he watered the horses. His offspring knew better than to complain. That would only earn them a swift beating. Old Jules had a gimpy leg, but that wasn't why he wouldn't work. Children and wives were put on earth to do his bidding, he believed.

Mari stepped onto a dirt floor as she lugged a sack of dried beans inside. Cobwebs were the shack's only decorations, and cracks between the boards its only light. When they were done unloading, their father climbed on the wagon, turned around, and headed back to the flats, leaving Mari and James behind to protect his claim.

While hated by most of his neighbors, Old Jules was also an amateur horticulturist, a community builder, and a staunch opponent of the cattle barons, who were attempting to monopolize every inch of land. He was also a friend of the Oglala Lakotas in a county where few had any use for the "red man." Yet, his story would have been lost to history if not for the fourteen-year-old girl he'd dumped off in the middle of nowhere that spring. For Mari Sandoz would go on to write the biography of her father's life, *Old Jules*, a book that would also trace the history of Sheridan County and introduce the Sand Hills and its settlers to the world. She would also write volumes about the Oglalas, a people she grew to love because of her father's friendship with the bands that camped near their Mirage Flats home.

As her father disappeared over the hills, she looked out as far as she could see. There wasn't a single tree; nothing but grass. Some might have seen emptiness. Some might have been afraid. But with her tyrannical father gone, Mari felt the lightness of freedom. When she gazed out at the Sand Hills, she saw only immense beauty.

Thirty-one years before the day Old Jules dumped off his children in the Sand Hills, Jim Dahlman and Bennett Irwin packed their horses to lead a trip into the unknown. They were a couple of young, rough-looking Texas cowboys recently transplanted to the vast, empty land of northwestern Nebraska. Many like them had made the journey north on cattle drives, navigating a line of mooing, bawling longhorns through Texas, Indian Territory, and Kansas, more than one thousand miles until they arrived near the Nebraska border and the Indian reservations. Many of these men stayed in the north and hired on at ranches or located a patch of land to plow. As for Dahlman and Irwin, they traveled north in the relative comfort of a train.

Dahlman was blessed with a bit more smarts than the average cowpoke, but he kept his intellect to himself. He was a fugitive from justice, and the other cowboys knew him by an alias, Jim Murray. Dahlman had shot his brother-in-law in Texas. The snake had abandoned and dishonored his sister, so putting a hole in the low-down dog didn't bother him one bit. Believing he'd killed him, Jim slipped away to the untamed north where no one asked too many questions.

He found work as a hand at the Newman Ranch, which was located thirty-five miles east of Camp Sheridan. The Newman brothers had a good little business going. After Red Cloud's Oglalas settled at the Pine Ridge Agency in 1878, the federal government needed beef to feed them, and lots of it, delivered at two-week intervals. The agency was hundreds of miles away from the nearest railroad line, so anyone who could deliver beef "on the hoof" to this remote land could nab himself a lucrative government contract. The Newmans staked a claim that year farther west on the Niobrara River than any settler had ventured, thus beginning the long, intertwined economic relationship between the white settlers of what would one day be Sheridan County and the Oglalas to the north.

Just south of the ranch lie the Sand Hills, a good-for-nothing wasteland, everyone said. Nebraskans had complained bitterly about the Treaty of 1868, and agitated for the Lakotas' removal from the territory, but after the federal government expelled the Indians in 1877, no one jumped in their wagons and whipped their horses in a mad dash to settle there. A grasshopper plague in the eastern half of the state had stemmed the tide. If it was so tough making a living on the fertile soil there, it would be impossible to do so out west, the would-be settlers reasoned. Nothing could grow there. There was little rainfall, and the soil was sandy. While the lands to the north, south, east, and west quickly filled up with homesteaders, the Sand Hills remained untouched.

This was the land Irwin, Dahlman, and their party ventured into during the spring of 1879. A terrible blizzard had struck a few weeks earlier. The ranch hands had done their best to keep the cattle from drifting away in the storm, but the whiteout conditions, with snow driving like stinging bees into their faces, forced them to take cover. Thousands of head drifted south, vanishing into the confusing dunes. The Newmans charged Dahlman and Irwin with leading the salvage party, but they held little hope of finding many longhorns as they packed their horses and loaded up the chuck wagon. Two days into the trip, a mid-April blizzard convinced them the mission was a bad idea. The men had no choice but to hunker down, with nothing but the wagon to shield them.

Two days later, as the April snow melted away to reveal pale, green patches of grass, Irwin and Dahlman rode ahead of the party to scout the land. They crested a hill and looked down into a meadow where a small herd of fat, happy cows were lazily grazing. They were plump enough to send to market that very day! They returned with the others, rounded the cattle up, and pressed on to discover more herds. They didn't all have the Newman brand. Some were escapees from the trail drives of years gone by. Some of these mavericks—three or four years old at least—had never laid eyes on humans before and bore no brands at all. Grass grew in the hills in abundance. Nutritional grass, it seemed, and contrary to popular belief there was apparently enough water around to slake the beasts' thirst. By the end of the five-week ordeal, the party rounded up one thousand more cattle than the Newmans had lost. It was like finding twenty-dollar gold pieces lying on the ground. Dahlman and Irwin realized that everything assumed about the Sand Hills was wrong. You don't keep cattle out of the Sand Hills in the winter. By God, you send them there!

Old McDonald had a ranch. And on this ranch, he sold whiskey. In fact, the man known as McDonald did not raise cattle, corn, or wheat. He had only John Barleycorn to offer, something Oglalas were willing to spend what little money they had to buy. Not long after the Newman brothers arrived, a different type of entrepreneur set up their businesses south of the Pine Ridge Agency. Selling liquor to Indians had been illegal since 1834, but since then, bootleggers had been making tidy profits breaking the law. The so-called whiskey ranches in Nebraska were simply the latest in a long-established tradition of selling liquor to Lakotas. McDonald and his competitors first sold booze outside Camp Sheridan to thirsty soldiers. After the army abandoned the site in 1881, the bootleggers found new customers at the agency.

The first Pine Ridge agent was Dr. Valentine McGillycuddy, a strong-willed twenty-nine-year-old Episcopalian who believed, like many others in his day, that the Indians were to be treated like children. They needed to be molded into a white image, and the sooner the better. The adults were a lost cause, he believed. But the children were clean slates. He had two major annoyances. One was Chief Red Cloud. The two men despised each other and waged a war of wills over what was best for the Oglalas. His second problem was the bootleggers. He couldn't stop the Sioux from drifting below the state line to imbibe illegal liquor. And he couldn't stop liquor from being smuggled in, despite the best efforts of his well-trained Indian police force of fifty men.

When the Oglalas settled at Pine Ridge in 1878, everyone believed the Nebraska state line lay twelve miles to the south of the agency head-quarters. In fact, it was only two miles, and as soon as the bootleggers realized this, a twenty-four-hour whiskey ranch popped up within sight of McGillycuddy's office. On still, summer nights, when he left his bed-room window open to let in a breeze, he could hear the men carrying on over the border. The sound was maddening. Almost as infuriating as the thought of Oglalas not following his orders.

The Oglala men had about every reason under the sun to drink, and drink hard. Their way of life was gone. Where they were once self-sufficient, providing for their women and children by hunting the Plains, now they had nothing to do but sit and wait for their beef rations. Where they once were able to prove themselves in battles against their mortal enemies, now they had no way to earn their names. The U.S. government treated them like children. And their own children were sent to Christian schools, where the boys' long ponytails were sheared off. The whites wanted them to farm. But they were warriors and hunters. For those who tried to plant crops, the soil was of no use. Drought and grasshoppers were swallowing up homesteads all over Nebraska and the Dakota Territory. European immigrants whose families had been farming for generations had given up. How were Oglalas to succeed?

Boredom. Grief. Hopelessness.

Time to have a drink.

Red Cloud and McGillycuddy, though avowed enemies, could agree on one thing. The whiskey ranches were a threat. Going back to when Red Cloud killed the drunken Chief Bull Bear, he'd hated what the wicked water had done to his people. McGillycuddy ordered his Indian police to patrol the border and lock up or expel the smugglers, who were mostly men married to Oglala women and mixed bloods, but his crackdown wasn't enough to stem the flow. Bootleggers such as McDonald were out of his jurisdiction despite being only two miles down the road. And there were no lawmen in this unsettled section of Nebraska. The Oglalas needed a buffer zone, McGillycuddy believed.

After much complaining to the Indian commissioner in Washington, McGillycuddy finally received his wish. In 1882, President Chester A. Arthur signed an executive order granting a ten-mile-long, five-mile-deep strip of land in Nebraska to the Pine Ridge Reservation for the protection of the Oglala Sioux. It was a rare instance of the U.S. government giving land back to the Indians.

The strip would be forever known as the "Extension."

In the spring of 1884, Jim Dahlman and a half-dozen hired hands east of the Newman Ranch sat on a stockade and watched with some amusement as an old gent with a long black beard attempted to ford the Niobrara while leading a team of oxen. There wasn't much to do in the middle of the prairie, and they saw few visitors, so a wagon train full of settlers making their way west was quite a spectacle. As soon as the gentleman's oxen stepped into the river, the beasts made up their minds to head downstream. Try as he might, the man could not force the team to pull the wagon across the shallow river instead of down it. The cowboys jumped in the river to lend the tenderfoot a hand, and together they managed to set the oxen on the right course.

By the time the settlers reached the Newman Ranch a day later, the cowboys there had caught wind of the chaotic crossing, so they waited to see if the old man would provide them with the same entertainment. To their surprise, the easterner jumped in front of the oxen, grabbed them by the reins, and led them waist deep through the murky water.

The cowboys cheered his success and went out to greet him. He introduced himself as the Reverend John A. Scamahorn. He and his wife, along with about one hundred followers, had left Sullivan, Indiana, to start a town from scratch in the middle of the empty prairie. The Fremont, Elkhorn & Missouri Valley Railroad was crawling west, and smart settlers knew they needed to jump ahead of it to claim the choicest land. The Methodist minister may have been a tenderfoot out west, but he was no fool. During the Civil War, he'd escaped a Confederate prisoner-of-war camp, not once, but twice. Since the war, he'd been living in southern

Indiana, but the moist weather there didn't suit him, so he came looking for a drier climate. He'd come to the right place.

It was his second trip to the area. The previous summer, the reverend and some church elders had traveled as far as the new train line extended to Valentine, Nebraska, then rode west to scout a location for the planned settlement. They found a viable spot along Antelope Creek on the hard ground above the Sand Hills, so they returned to Indiana and recruited more settlers from the flock. The following summer, they rented several train cars, loaded their livestock and meager possessions, and rode as far as the line could take them. They trudged one hundred miles, narrowly avoiding two prairie fires, before arriving at the isolated ranch.

After another day's journey beyond the ranch, the Hoosiers pitched their tents along the banks of the creek. They were a long way from timber, and their canvas homes would have to do for quite some time. They weren't wealthy people. Scamahorn arrived with a team of oxen, a cow, a pig, two horses, and sixty dollars in his pocket. Before leaving Valentine, he'd been appointed postmaster. As soon as he pitched his tent, he opened up the "post office," which consisted of some stamps in a cigar box. The first Sunday after they arrived, the reverend delivered his first sermon underneath a wide tent.

The settlers had to decide on a name for their new settlement. "Scamahorn" might have been a logical choice, but the reverend was probably too modest to accept that (and it wasn't exactly the most mellifluous name). However, the fate of the Gordon party, which had met its end a decade ago twenty-five miles southeast of town, was still well known. The settlers believed that John Gordon had been done a great injustice, so the transplanted Hoosiers named the settlement after the "resolute sooner."

It didn't take alcohol long to make its appearance among the churchgoers. A reformed outlaw, Doc Middleton, pitched a tent, stuck a long board atop two barrels, and became the town's first saloonkeeper. Middleton was as close to a celebrity as one could find in the remote northwest, having made his reputation as a horse thief in his younger days—one with a Robin Hood–type reputation. He stole Indian horses from Chief Spotted Tail's tribe and occasionally gave away some of his spoils to less fortunate settlers. So he stole from the poor and gave to the slightly less poor. He was legendary for his ability to escape the law, but they caught him eventually and he served nearly four years in the state penitentiary. New towns on new railroad lines went through predictable cycles. As soon as the railroad workers set up camp, the men who made a profit from them set up nearby. Whiskey, prostitution, and rowdiness followed. The good Christians just had to put up with it for a while.

Scamahorn's prediction on where the railroad would build its depot was off by a mile or two; so by the middle of 1885, after officially incorporating itself, the town pulled up its stakes and moved a mile west. The train carried with it lumber, and construction began in earnest. Middleton moved out of the tent and into a more permanent structure on Second and Main. Dry goods stores and banks surrounded his saloon. The railroad built a depot next to the tracks, and a dusty road running north of it bisected the wooden structures. Gordon's population swelled to five hundred, and it began to resemble a real town.

The sodbusters arrived on the tails of the Methodists to stake their claims on the hardtop land between Gordon and Rushville where the Sand Hills stopped and the earth flattened out enough to plant a field of corn, wheat, or potatoes. Czechs, Swedes, Germans, a mishmash of European cultures and tongues, filled in the land. Some were second-generation Americans, the sons and daughters of Iowans or Nebraskans who grew up on homesteads back east and now wanted their own 160 acres. Every one of them was hungry for land. Some came by train, others by covered wagon. Most had seen advertisements or newspaper articles extolling the virtues of the new territory. The railway wanted to bring in as many settlers as possible to make its line viable, and spreading the promise of free land in "gardens of Eden" always worked. The land up north went quickly, and the settlers began to look south to the flats west of the Sand Hills.

The Scamahorn party was only the first in a flood of settlers in newly established Sheridan County, named in tribute of the army camp that used to lie in its northwestern corner. Three towns would spring up to the west in anticipation of the railroad: Clinton, which would never amount to much; Rushville, the future county seat that would thrive as a shipping point for goods and travelers heading to Pine Ridge; and Hay Springs, the last whistle stop before the county line. A contentious political battle for the location of the county seat resulted in Rushville grabbing the honor. Allegations of ballot box stuffing did not change the results.

A few weeks after Scamahorn's Methodists settled Gordon in the spring of 1884, Jules Sandoz stood outside his dugout on the Mirage Flats watching a campfire across the Niobrara River send smoke among the pine and cottonwood trees. He'd dug the hole that had become his home less than a week before in the side of a small hill, reinforcing it with wood found on the banks of the river. Since then, would-be settlers had come and gone, preferring to grab their piece of land closer to the railroad line. He wondered if the fire belonged to some prospective neighbors, so he waded across the shallow river, which was barely a foot deep in this part of the country.

He was surprised to find a small band of Indians camping along the banks. They greeted each other with "Hous," and Jules sat down to smoke the pipe. The band's chief was named White Eye. Somehow, through broken English, they managed to communicate.

Sandoz was twenty-five years old and spoke English with a thick French accent. Although he dressed like a dirty bum, he came from elite stock in Switzerland. Unlike many of the landless third or fourth sons who'd left the old country for America, he was the eldest from a good family with four years of medical school under his belt. But he had a short temper and quarreled with his father over money and a woman. To prove a point, he left his homeland in the Alps forever. He settled for a couple years in northeastern Nebraska near where the Niobrara emptied into the Missouri. He married a woman, slapped her around a bit, then left there in a huff as well, hitching a team of horses to a wagon, heading west along the Niobrara until he found a new patch of land along the river.

Jules and the Oglalas talked about hunting game and of old days when the buffalo roamed the land, before the whites came. The band had camped on the same spot for generations, and despite Agent McGillycuddy's restrictions against his charges traveling outside the reservation, they returned there every summer.

White Eye took Jules on a hunting trip into the Sand Hills, until then a place of mystery to the young immigrant. The chief gave him a few pointers on how to navigate the confusing hills, the Land of Gone Before, as they called them. He taught Sandoz their methods for tracking and killing game. Jules was a crack shot, so White Eye dubbed him "Straight Eye."

As the years passed, more settlers arrived on the flats, some at his urging through letters to relatives or articles submitted to Swiss-American publications back east. Although he was still a young man, he was the eldest of the Swiss settlers, so his neighbors began to call him Old Jules. Over the years he would feud with his neighbors, go through three more wives, all of whom he beat, and periodically clash with the ranchers, who were doing their best to run the farmers out of the territory. In short, he was as ornery as a badger.

But he liked the Oglalas. And the Oglalas liked him.

Sandoz was the exception rather than the rule among settlers. The bloody battles with the tribes were a recent memory, and most of the pioneers knew only what they'd read in newspapers. In the press, the Indians were "savages." Custer was a hero rather than an incompetent general. Crazy Horse and Sitting Bull were renegades, not freedom fighters. They'd heard countless stories of how the Sioux massacred pioneers, and some of these stories were true. The papers neglected to say why Indians were on the warpath in the first place. But Sandoz accepted the Oglalas and approached them with intellectual curiosity rather than fear.

As settlers came and went on Mirage Flats, the ranches expanded outward, and mean-eyed cowboys and so-called vigilantes did their best to intimidate the farmers, who were derisively called "grangers" or "nesters." If it wasn't fear of the cattle barons, it was a lack of rain. For the railroad propaganda was a lie. Sheridan County was no "Garden of Eden" for dryland farmers. It was a tough, unforgiving country.

But Old Jules stuck it out. An amateur horticulturist, he searched for crops that could survive drought conditions. He continued to write optimistic letters to prospective settlers and sent for some of his younger brothers, who claimed land nearby. He charged a finder's fee to help the hopeful emigrants stake unclaimed or abandoned plots.

His final marriage to a Swiss-German woman, Mary, would last, but only because she was destitute and couldn't escape his clutches. Their first born was Mari. With a father who saw his wife and children as little more than servants, Mari's few happy childhood memories were the yearly visits from the Oglalas who continued to pitch their tipis near the Sandoz residence. They sat around the campfire and spoke of the old days. Listening in was Mari, who soaked up their stories like rain in the Sand Hills soil. One of the Oglalas sitting near the campfire was He Dog, a cousin and loyal friend of Crazy Horse. It was He Dog who first told Mari of the mystic and warrior who was killed at Fort Robinson. And there were many other stories as well.

In the summer of 1888, Bartlett Richards walked with Bennett Irwin at Irwin's ranch deep in the Sand Hills. Richards, a baby-faced twenty-eight-year-old rancher with a New England accent and a patrician bearing, liked what he saw. Nestled in a valley, surrounded by hills browned by the summer sun, Irwin's ranch sat near Bean Soup Lake, named for the meager dish Dahlman, Irwin, and the other cowboys shared in the final days of their fateful excursion. The Wyoming rancher was on a buying trip and he had a motivated seller. Irwin was the last of the original ranchers remaining, one of the few who remembered what the land was like before the home-steaders and the Scamahorn party arrived. The Newman brothers were long gone. They felt crowded on their ranch along the Niobrara River after settlers began claiming the hardtop land to the north. Competitors were also horning in on their lucrative Sioux cattle contracts, and a devastating prairie fire had swept through the grassland, leaving their cattle with nothing to eat. They pulled up stakes and drove their herd to Montana. Jim Dahlman gave up ranching to find his fortune in the newly founded town of Chadron forty miles west. There, he began a career in politics. By that time, Dahlman had received word from Texas that he'd only wounded his brother-in-law instead of killing him, so he'd dropped the "Jim Murray" alias. When he became mayor of Omaha years later, his political opponents would dig up the scandal and use it against him. But he simply said "the scoundrel deserved it," and that was good enough for the electorate. "Cowboy Jim," as the Omaha residents called him, would go on to serve five terms.

That left Irwin behind on his ranch deep in the hills, and he was ready to move on. Word of the ranch's availability had reached Richards's ears, so he made the arduous trip from Wyoming. Unlike the rough, uneducated cowboys who'd made their way up the cow trails from Texas, Richards had come to the West from Andover, Massachusetts. He was the youngest of six from a middle-class family who'd fallen on hard times since the untimely death of their father. Fueled by stories of the untamed West and the pros-pect for adventure, he convinced his mother to let him make a temporary trip to Wyoming even though he was only seventeen years old. He never returned.

He began as a cowboy, learning the cattle business from the bottom up, and soon made connections with wealthy investors who'd come from the East to make their fortunes grow. He acquired capital through his connec-tions at the Wyoming Stock Growers Association and bought one thousand head of cattle. By the age of twenty, he'd become a bona fide rancher.

Irwin told Richards about the rolling hills that provided shelter to cattle during winter storms. He told him about the long, nutritious grass that fattened the cows for market. He picked up a fistful of the sandy soil.

You can't farm this land, Irwin insisted. No granger will want it.

On the last point, Irwin was only half right; some would attempt to till the soil. But Richards had heard what he wanted. In Wyoming, troubles were festering between the ranchers and homesteaders who wanted to farm. Oh, to be free of the farmers. They were such a nuisance, Richards thought.

As for the hills themselves, Richards didn't need Irwin to tell him about their benefits. It had been a tough winter on the High Plains. Zephyr's biting winds had swept down from the mountains with its driving snow. The cattle had nowhere to take cover on Wyoming's featureless range. Hundreds of thousands of head had perished. As Richards gazed up at the hills, he was convinced that he was standing on the finest ranchland in the United States of America.

Richards and his well-financed business partners bought out Irwin, along with two other adjacent properties, and named it the Spade Ranch, with a brand in the shape of the playing card suit. He set about turning Irwin's small outfit into an efficient factory-like operation. He strung barbed wire in rectangular sections, separating the pastures for more efficient grazing. He sunk wells, using windmills to pump out water for thirsty cattle. The parched-looking Sand Hills had plenty of water underneath the surface because the sandy soil soaked the rain up like a sponge. He had his men build firebreaks—long earthen barriers designed to halt devastating prairie fires. He hired scores of men—cowboys, cooks, and foremen—to oversee the operation. He disassembled the Newman brothers' old cabin along the Niobrara, moved it to the Spade, and converted it into a cookhouse. Train tracks to the north and south of his burgeoning operation allowed him to ship cattle to the Chicago slaughterhouses. He built a house and stockade in the town of Ellsworth, twenty miles to the south of the Spade on the Chicago Burlington & Quincy Railroad line. His corporation's profits soared when he secured government contracts to sell beef to the Pine Ridge Reservation.

And he created much of this "empire of grass" on land in the public domain. When the grangers came to settle on land that was rightfully theirs to claim, they found barbed wire and ornery cowboys blocking their way.

Jack Coon put on his Sunday best, packed a lunch, hitched up his wagon, and headed north from his sod house near Wolf Creek, a few miles south of the Pine Ridge border. Although he was wearing his finest accoutrements, he wasn't heading to church. Coon was born in Wisconsin and raised in Iowa, but by the time he reached manhood, there wasn't a patch of available land left to homestead in the Hawkeye State. So he left for Sheridan County with his parents and brothers in tow in 1884 and staked out his own spread just a few miles south of Pine Ridge. He wasn't there long when word reached him of a spectacle up north among the Indians, so he decided to see it for himself. There wasn't a lot of what they called "entertainment" in those days on the prairie, just a lot of hard work trying to eke out a living on land where raindrops rarely had an inclination to fall. Everyone had to witness an "on-the-hoof" beef issue at least once. It was said to be better than any "Wild West show" and more thrilling than any rodeo.

In the short time that Coon had lived on the Nebraska side of the border, much had changed. It had taken months, not years, for the unsettled land to fill up. Suddenly, there were two distinct communities and cultures living side by side. Sheridan County was never uniformly white. Nor was the Pine Ridge Reservation uniformly Indian. A few black and Chinese families settled in Gordon and Pine Ridge to take menial jobs, as they had in nearly every town in that era. Cherry County, just to the east, had several black homesteads, including the town of Brownlee, settled entirely by former slaves and their children.

On the reservation, the full-blood Oglalas struggled to make a living farming off the land. But whites with more agricultural acumen saw opportunity there, especially on the eastern edges where the land was flatter and there was enough topsoil to plant wheat.

Susan Rouleau, abandoned by her French-Canadian father in Kansas when she was seven years old, was now a young married woman. As an Oglala, she had the right to take an allotment on the reservation. She met a white boy, William Sears, at a school in Highland, Kansas; and after marrying, the young couple made their way to Pine Ridge in search of opportunity. More and more white men like Sears settled on the reservation to set up trading posts, ranches, or farms. As long as they were married to an Oglala, it was perfectly legal. And there would soon be ways to get around that rule.

Since traveling was so difficult then, the Oglalas and white settlers had little interaction. Sheridan County newcomers knew little of their neighbors to the north other than the sensational, violent stories they had read in dime-store novels and newspapers. Now, there was reason to make the arduous trip north. After several hours traveling under the warm sun, Coon guided the wagon toward a corral surrounded by a throng of natives. Surrounding him were a dozen other settlers, standing on their carriages and buckboards, shading their eyes, ready for the excitement about to unfold. Coon pulled his wagon up alongside one of his neighbors. He exchanged pleasantries. It got awfully isolated and lonesome out on the homestead in the 1880s, and any human contact was a godsend. Most of the other spectators Coon didn't recognize. They'd come from all over, sometimes traveling for several days to watch the issue.

Inside a wooden pen, bawling cattle shuffled about, nervous because they'd been raised on the rangeland and weren't used to the crowded conditions. Outside the pen, Oglala men, their hair in ponytails, some wearing cowboy hats, others dressed in traditional garb, were mounted on their best horses forming two long lines in a gauntlet—Winchesters and bows and arrows at the ready. The women and children stood behind the men next to their wagons.

And then it began.

A crier at the stockade chute called a family's name.

"Red Owls!" An assistant prodded the first steer, and it bolted out of the chute between the line of men. The frightened animal dashed for the open range, but it wouldn't go far.

The Red Owl men rode after the beast, whooping and hollering as they shot bullets and arrows into its side. The terrorized steer looked left and right for an opening, then charged into an Oglala family who was standing too close. The women and children parted as the steer sought escape. Three more arrows pierced its shoulder.

Before it went down, the crier called another family's name.

"Hollow Horns!"

Another victim dashed out of the chute to meet its doom.

"Fool Heads!"

A third steer came out. And then another, and another. The sound of rifles, snapping like popcorn in a skillet, filled the prairie. Soon, dozens of steers with arrows stuck in their sides lurched about, attacking their tormentors until they collapsed.

Coon had never seen such chaos and mayhem. It wasn't so long ago when these same men roamed the Powder River Country hunting buffalo on their swift horses. They were still good shots, and despite the pandemonium, their bullets and arrows rarely went astray.

The women and children descended on the carcasses and butchered them where they fell. One steer wasn't quite dead yet, and it made a final lunge at a family who'd arrived too quickly. An Oglala woman delivered a swift ax blow to its head, putting it down for good. She cut out the tongue first, which was considered a delicacy. They flayed the hide on the ground and began systematically to cut up the meat as the horses from other families galloped by, hunting down their own steers.

The cattle were not buffalo migrating on the Plains. The Oglala men were no longer warriors. The beef issues would be their last taste of what a real buffalo hunt was like.

When it ended, Coon and his neighbors had a picnic behind the corral as the Oglalas on the other side started boiling kettles for their own feast. The whites loaded up their wagons and made the long journey home. For the settlers, the on-the-hoof beef issues were their first cultural contact with their neighbors to the north. For Coon, it was a spectacle he would never forget and would one day tell his grandchildren about. The beef issues were held every two weeks, and he would make the trip several more times.

The road traveled both ways. Once a year, the Oglalas hitched up their teams and made the trip south for the Fourth of July celebrations in the nascent towns of Rushville and Gordon. They wore their finest feathered and beaded ceremonial dress to dance for the white folks. Oglala men, sitting in a circle around giant round drums, sang as the dancers—with their beads vibrantly lit under the July sun—moved to the rhythm around a sacred pole. The spectators would politely applaud. The Oglalas' reward was more beef provided by the town businessmen. The dancers and singers returned to their camps next to the fairgrounds to cook their free beef in black cooking pots over fires, and to smoke the pipe with their friends.

Agent McGillycuddy eventually phased out the on-the-hoof beef issues, calling them too dangerous and inhumane. With so many arrows and bullets flying around, accidents were bound to happen. Mundane slaughterhouses took their place. But Oglalas dancing at the county fair was a tradition that would last until the 1950s.

These two examples of early cross-cultural exchange in the late 1880s, however, did little to stem the hysteria that was about to sweep over the prairie. In 1890, settlers like Coon made the trip north again to see a new spectacle. It was called the Ghost Dance. The mutual distrust, misunderstanding, and fear it provoked would lead to disaster.

Sheridan County settlers pose in front of Fort Nendle during the Ghost Dance scare, circa 1890. (Courtesy of Sheridan County Historical Society.)

A New World

Charley Allen rode his horse alongside his three companions on a crisp late December evening in 1890 on his way to Wounded Knee Creek. It was unusually warm for midwinter, and there wasn't a flake of snow on the ground. But he knew from his days as a freighter that winter on the prairie could go from halcyon to hell in a matter of hours.

Allen had an angular face, bushy black eyebrows, and a matching mustache that all but covered his mouth. He was a newspaperman from Chadron, Nebraska, temporarily employed as a stringer for the *New York Herald*. For that job, he felt quite qualified. As far as he was concerned, he was one of the few journalists who bothered to tell the truth about the troubles in Sioux country that year.

The Nebraska and South Dakota settlers had thrown the Plains into a panic over the so-called Ghost Dance craze, so the army had invaded the reservations to prevent the Sioux from going on the warpath. Unlike the "war correspondents" who arrived by the dozens over the past few weeks, Allen knew a thing or two about the Indians. He was married to a Lakota of mixed blood, which made him a "squawman" in the eyes of his peers. That epithet always made him bristle. He spoke some basic Lakota, and unlike these Johnny-come-lately correspondents—two of whom were riding next him—he'd lived in the area since the founding of the Pine Ridge Agency twelve years earlier.

Although it was nearly ten o'clock, these were strange times and the road east of the agency was full of fellow travelers—mostly mounted cavalrymen and scouts. Some rode as if they were in no hurry at all; others galloped madly.

Allen wasn't supposed to be there. He had a newspaper to run in Chadron, and the young apprentice he'd left to fill in for him was anxious to leave. He was all set to send a wire to the *New York Herald* giving his notice when a reporter for the *St. Paul Pioneer Press* told him that Big

Foot and his band of wayward Minneconjous had agreed to surrender to the Seventh Cavalry the following morning. The reporter implored Allen to come. This was Custer's infamous Seventh after all, there to accept the surrender of a chief who'd fought at Little Big Horn. What an opportunity for a gripping story! Allen reluctantly agreed, for news correspondents, while rivals, generally enjoyed each other's company.

The Minnesotan had suddenly received a telegram calling him back to St. Paul and had to depart that night. Unbeknownst to Allen, Charles Cressey, the lanky reporter from the *Omaha Bee*, and the beefy *Nebraska State Journal*'s William Kelley had attached themselves to the excursion. Neither man had much regard for the truth, and both were disgraces to the profession as far as Allen was concerned, but he kept his mouth shut and off they went in the middle of the night to Wounded Knee.

The three joined up with a hotelier from Gordon, Nebraska, Mr. Swiggart, an acquaintance of Allen's whose first name escaped him. Cressey, who didn't care for horseback riding, gave his steed to Allen and placed himself in back of Swiggart's small wagon. The hotelier was a curiosity seeker who'd made his way to the reservation just to see what was what. There were a few sightseers like him around, but most Nebraskans were afraid the Indians were going to pour over the border at any moment and had fled to the safety of the towns.

Kelley, who rode alongside him, was a baby-faced, clean-shaven young man who didn't have the qualifications to report on a grammar school picnic, let alone a complicated fiasco such as this. He was working in Lincoln at the business office of the *State Journal* when an editor decided he was qualified to be a reporter. Now, he was riding alongside Allen with a six-shooter strapped around his waist, attempting to look the part of a Deadwood tough in a dime novel.

As for Allen, he carried no weapons. Why would he? This Ghost Dance craze was a bunch of hoopla. Few of these phony correspondents knew anything about what had led to the so-called unrest.

Red Cloud faced one of the Lakotas' old nemeses, General George Crook, on a field at Pine Ridge in the summer of 1889. Behind the chief were resolute leaders like Young-Man-Afraid-of-His-Horse. And behind them were about four hundred Oglala men who were dressed and painted for war. This wasn't a battle, but it was a war of wills. Now sixty-eight years old with failing eyesight, Red Cloud had ordered the warriors to arrive with their weapons as an act of intimidation—just as the federal government had done when it sent Crook to the Great Sioux Reservation as their chief negotiator in yet another land grab. "Three Star," as the Indians had named the general when he fought them from 1876 to 1877, looked rather perturbed as he sat under the shade of the canvas negotiating tent.

Red Cloud squinted at Three Star and told the general that he might as well go home. The Oglalas had already decided that they weren't signing away any lands. But Crook wouldn't leave. He may have felt annoyed by the show of force, but he wasn't afraid. He was there on a mission to break up the Great Sioux Reservation into small islands and open up South Dakota for railroads and settlement.

The white settlers wanted more patches to till, and the U.S. government was attempting to take it for them. The pioneers were champing at the bit in central South Dakota, waiting across the Missouri for the situation to change. The influential railroad companies also needed a clear passage to the West. Standing in their way was the "Great Sioux Nation," which cut a strip down the center of the territory. South Dakota was also making preparations to become a state, and what good was a state if a reservation split it in half?

The white men had overrun the Black Hills in 1875. The Lakotas fought valiantly for the land, only to watch it taken away without compensation. By the late 1880s, mining companies were extracting untold millions in gold and silver from the Sioux's sacred land. Now commissioners arrived at the agencies with a new treaty that they promised would bring progress and happiness to the Sioux.

Congress in 1887 had passed the Dawes General Allotment Act, which provided individual allotments of reservation lands to Indians. If they wanted to make a farmer out of an Indian, they had to give him a patch of land, they reasoned.

To bust up the reservation legally under the terms of the Treaty of 1868, they had to convince three-fourths of the adult males to agree to it, which was a major problem since the Lakotas had no reason to trust the U.S. government after so many broken treaties. With the lure of individual allotments and the promise of millions of dollars to be generated by the $1.25 per acre fee the homesteaders would pay into an interest-bearing account, Congress dispatched Crook to explain a complicated twelve-page document to the Lakotas. His mission: to present a pile of horse manure to the Sioux and make them believe it was chokecherry pie.

The commissioners traveled to the Rosebud Agency first. The skilled negotiator Chief Spotted Tail was long dead, shot down by a rival named Crow Dog. The leaderless tribe was suspicious at first, but Three Star and the other commissioners started pulling chiefs aside to sway them over. They used mixed bloods and traders married to Indian women to coax them, along with alcohol, bribery, threats, and whatever trick they could pull to make the men sign. Without the strong leadership of Spotted Tail, and under the impression that the nonsigners would lose out on the perceived benefits, the once mighty Brulés caved in.

By the time Crook arrived at Pine Ridge one hundred miles to the west, Red Cloud knew better than to sign the treaty. An eastern group of liberals who sympathized with Indian causes, the Indian Rights Association, had written the chief warning him not to sign the papers. They'd spread leaflets throughout the reservation telling the Oglalas not to trust old Three Star.

Red Cloud's traditionalists broke up a second meeting by rushing in on horses, scattering the participants. Not only did they not want to sign the papers, they didn't even want to discuss it. A scowling Red Cloud told the commissioners they hadn't fulfilled their past promises.

"My friends, when a man owes ten cents or fifty cents up here at these stores, these storekeepers want that paid before he gets anymore. And I looked around to see if I could see any boxes of money that you brought here to buy more land, and I could not see any."

The commissioners distributed copies of an indecipherable twelve-page treaty that would cause native speakers of English to run for *Webster's Dictionary*. What did "severalty" mean? the Oglalas asked. It meant that each adult male would own a patch of land, 160 acres—*after* it was held in trust for twenty-five years. What is an acre? Why would a man want to own land? The concept was foreign to the Lakotas' thinking. Territory belonged to the tribe. No individuals owned land. Once a man had a deed, no one could ever take the land away from him, the commissioners explained.

Does this mean our rations will be cut?

Absolutely not!

A few days later, Red Cloud and the four hundred mounted warriors asked the commission to leave the reservation. Crook wouldn't be bluffed so easily. The general finally told them the truth: Congress wouldn't make a better offer, and if they didn't sign, they were just going to take the land anyway. The talks continued.

The Oglalas, however, had a secret weapon: Chief American Horse. The chief was considered a progressive, and therefore a possible ally to the commissioners. He was also the Oglalas' best orator. He arrived with his entourage at the negotiating tent and launched into a harangue about how the white settlers' cattle had encroached on the Pine Ridge borders. He went on to muse on everything from the unfair prices at the traders' stores to the inferior quality of their government-issued rations. The mixed-blood translator strained to keep up. The chief went on and on. He never shut up. The commissioners sat, sweat running down their backs in the June heat, with smiles frozen on their faces, trying not to offend their potential progressive ally.

And then the verbose chief came back the next day and started all over again. It was a filibuster unseen outside of the U.S. Senate. American Horse delivered a three-day gripe, bringing up every point of contention on every treaty the Lakotas ever signed.

Finally, one of the commissioners could take no more.

"Is it the intention of the chief to kill us with words?"

As his comment was translated into Lakota, the assembled Oglala audience erupted in guffaws. American Horse didn't crack a smile. After the laughter died down, he continued, the words flowing from his mouth like water down the Niobrara.

But after the third day of speechifying ended, Crook took American Horse aside for a private meeting. The general used an old ploy. If the chief didn't sign, the Oglalas would lose all their lands. American Horse changed his rhetoric, voiced his support for the treaty, ended his filibuster, and touched pen to paper. He would live to regret it.

As the negotiations wore on in the dry summer heat, the Chadron town leaders appointed Charley Allen to invite Red Cloud and his people to attend their Fourth of July celebration. The newspaperman had known the chief for years and was happy to do it since he could kill two birds with one stone and file another story about the land commission.

Like many pioneer men, Allen had had his pick of professions when he first came to the territory. He was a nineteen-year-old Kansan with one semester of college under his belt when he joined a cattle drive heading north. He settled down near Fort Laramie, the distribution point for the Lakotas' treaty goods. He fell in love and married the mixed-blood daughter of a trader, Emma Hawkins, and began freighting goods from the fort to points all over Sioux country. A freighter's life was well paying, but tough. The roads were a constant challenge. Renegade Indians and bandits of every ilk could lurk behind any boulder. Horses came up lame. And the weather was seldom ideal. Wheels became mired in mud, and in the winter deadly blizzards struck without warning.

When business began to slack off in 1879, Allen moved his family to the Pine Ridge Agency when the paint was still drying on Agent McGillycuddy's new house. There was plenty of construction work there, and Emma had family among the Oglalas. He built schools and hauled freight until he moved to Valentine, Nebraska, to take up blacksmithing when the town was the terminus of the new railroad. As it stretched farther west, a friend who owned a printing press wanted to move his operation to the newly established town of Chadron, about thirty-five miles southwest of the Pine Ridge Agency. He asked Allen to be his partner on the condition that Allen would write the editorials and stories for the *Chadron Democrat*. His friend just wanted to run the printing press. Allen had no journalism experience, but he quickly got the hang of it as the pair worked in a floorless shack.

Allen found the chief in his house across White Clay Creek, sitting cross-legged on the floor, in deep discussion with his followers. The federal government built the structure, grandiose for an Indian, to appease the old chief. For seven years, Red Cloud had feuded with Agent Valentine McGillycuddy. The younger, and equally obstinate, former army surgeon unilaterally declared Red Cloud "deposed as chief" a half-dozen times, and did everything possible to undermine his authority. McGillycuddy called Red Cloud a drunkard. Red Cloud accused McGillycuddy of corruption. Both their claims were false, but throughout the rancorous power struggle Red Cloud managed to hold on to the house.

Despite his weak eyes, Red Cloud recognized Allen and greeted him as a friend. The chief was in an agreeable mood, despite the underhanded politicking going on over the General Allotment Act, and he promised to go to Chadron, where the Oglalas would dance and sing for the townspeople.

Red Cloud arrived in Chadron the morning of July 2 along with a thousand of his followers dressed in their finest regalia. The sight of so many Indians descending into the town from the north threw some of the fainthearted women and children into a tizzy. They thought the Sioux Nation was launching an uprising.

The next day, on a platform across from the courthouse, Red Cloud and an interpreter took the stage alongside the town dignitaries and listened to their speeches and patriotic songs. And then it was the chief's turn to speak. After a short preamble thanking the citizens for their hospitality, he felt the need to say a few words about the land commission.

"The Great Father has sent commissioners here to try to fool me like a child and take my land from me. They told me that if I did not give up the land it would be just like a big fish in the pond with little fish—the big ones would eat the little ones all up. They said that the white people would take all the good land from me, and that I would have nothing but bad lands where I would starve to death. They said if I had a high stone wall around me, the white people would get over it, and that if I did not sign the paper there would be no more Indians—they would be wiped out. But I am no child, so I did not sign the paper. The Great Father has bothered me so much about my land that I am getting tired of it. I have told him that I would never give up my land, and I want you to understand me . . ."

Red Cloud certainly wasn't one of the legendary Oglala orators, Allen thought, but he printed the speech in its entirety in his newspaper. The celebration went well. There was little inebriation, no tension, and the townspeople loved the dances and singing. A hat was passed, and everyone chipped in to buy some cattle so they could treat their Indian neighbors to a feast.

After Red Cloud returned to the reservation, he found Crook waiting with a new deal. He offered the chief and Young-Man-Afraid-of-His-Horses two hundred dollars each in bribes. The two leaders were longtime rivals, but on this point they were united. They still refused to offer their support. The general departed Pine Ridge with only a few hundred signatures.

General Crook and the commission pressed on to the Cheyenne River and Standing Rock agencies still fifteen hundred signatures shy of the three-fourths needed. Cheyenne River was controlled by Chief Hump, a fervent traditionalist. And Standing Rock was Sitting Bull's domain. The stubborn chief had never signed anything, and came back from exile in Canada only after the government there booted him and his followers out.

Crook bribed, cajoled, threatened, divided the opposition, and ultimately conquered. Soon, the commission had the approval of the three-fourths of the male population needed. The Great Sioux Reservation had shrunk into manageable, square islands. Settlers poured over the Missouri boundary to claim the prime land. The price for proving up: $1.25 per acre. The fees went into the Lakotas' account for the first three years after the law was enacted; then the price for marginal land dropped to only seventy-five cents, and later fifty cents. Nine million acres were to be ceded to the settlers. And any "surplus" land on the reservation could be settled as well. The federal government also deducted accounting and surveying expenses. In exchange, individual allotments would be given to male heads of households, with their ownership being held in trust for twenty-five years. So the plots were theirs to do with as they pleased (after two and a half decades). But the Lakotas had a big pile of money in an account in Washington (to be spent however the bureaucrats there saw fit with no input from the account holders). The secretary of the interior proudly proclaimed that the bill was "a long step toward the disintegration of their tribal life."

A few months after the U.S. government practically gave the nine million acres away, Congress, in a budget-cutting mood and with a little social engineering in mind, decided to slash the Lakotas' food rations in half. The Indians had to learn to be self-sufficient, the politicians rationalized. And the best way to accomplish this goal was to make them grow their own food. Learn to farm or starve. The politicians really just wanted to save a few dollars, though.

After just being cajoled into signing another treaty, the Lakotas were convinced that they'd been duped once again. Crook had promised them that signing the treaty wouldn't affect their rations. Although there was no relation between the land deal and the ration cuts, they were convinced otherwise. The traditionalists who spoke out against the treaty focused their anger on those who had signed, like Chief American Horse, rather than the true source of their predicament, the U.S. government. Bitter feelings erupted between the traditionalists and progressives. Meanwhile, their children began dying of diseases caused by malnourishment.

As Allen rode along the trail with his three companions on the unusually warm December night, he remembered the Independence Day celebration and the land commission dispute. Allen, for one, supported the General Allotment Act's goals. The Lakotas had to separate themselves from the old way of life once and for all, and the best way to do that was for them to become landowners, just like the settlers. However, there wasn't one word of input from the Lakotas, Allen thought. The Washington bureaucrats printed up the document and sent it west to be signed whether the Indians liked it or not. Allen believed what Crook had told the chiefs, that if they didn't sign, somehow, some way, the Lakotas would still lose their land.

For many town residents who hailed from the East, the Fourth of July celebration eighteen months earlier was their first contact with Indians. The ceremonial dress and dancing enthralled them. Now the same people in Chadron, as well as Hay Springs, Rushville, and Gordon, were cowering in their homes, afraid the "savages" were going to go on the warpath and scalp every last one of them. Nothing could be further from the truth. But the truth was a rare commodity these days.

What a difference a year and half could make, Allen thought.

The troubles began with a dream.

Over the Rocky Mountains, past the Great Salt Lake, and through the forests of northern Nevada, nine hundred miles from Pine Ridge, Wovoka lay near death in his round brush-covered hut in an arid valley nestled between high, craggy mountains. The Northern Paiute Indian was wracked with fever, his broad forehead burning; his mind, waging a battle within, slipped away, allowing his spirit to break free from his sick body. Outside his hut, the moon began to swallow the sun.

His spirit journeyed to a better place, where green forests surrounded lush valleys, where deer and other game ran in great herds. There were people there, too. Laughing and smiling, playing games, eating roasted meat and fish. The people were those who had gone before, his dead mother, and generations of his ancestors. They were all there and living happily with no sickness. He saw Jesus, hands bleeding, spear holes in his sides, living among the people. This was paradise on earth. Wovoka knew this was not the past or present, but the future.

And then the Great Mystery spoke: "Your people must be good and love one another. They must end their quarreling and live in peace with the whites. They must work hard. They must not lie. They must not steal. They must abandon the ways of war. I will teach you a dance, and this dance you must do every ninety days, for five days, and then purify yourselves by bathing in a river. And if the people do so, all that you see before you will come to pass; the world will be reborn and you will be reunited with your ancestors. There will be no more sickness or death and you will live in this beautiful place."

The fever broke, and Wovoka returned to the material world. He rose from his pallet, wrapped a blanket around his body, and weakly stumbled outside where an eclipse had thrown the world into darkness. Slowly the sun began to reemerge, turning the dusk back into day.

Wovoka looked to the heavens. He had a message of hope to deliver.

The Lakota pilgrims entered the valley more than a year later in the spring of 1890. Wovoka, the Wood Cutter, was from a distant tribe, a people the Lakotas had never encountered in a distant land where they'd never ventured. Word of his prophecy had spread east. It was said he could control the weather. During a drought, he predicted rain, and the rains came. Letters began arriving for Wovoka, the man named Jack Wilson. This was the name given to the messiah by the white, Christian family who'd adopted him as a boy. He wrote the correspondents back, passing on his message of peace and hope. He sent them magical red paint to wear while they performed the special dance. Emissaries from the Shoshones, Crows, Arapahos, and Cheyennes had ventured to the barren sage-covered valley to see the new holy man themselves. They returned as disciples to teach the special dance that would return the world to the way it was before.

Short Bull and Kicking Bear had passed the hat on the Lakota reservations to pay for the nine-hundred-mile pilgrimage. The Lakotas were eager to hear a message of hope, for there was little of that on the reservations after the federal government had slashed their rations. The plan to make farmers out of the Lakotas had failed. The men's role as providers and protectors had been wiped away. Game on the small territory in which they'd been confined had been hunted into oblivion. Their attempts to grow crops or raise gardens in the poor soil resulted in withered patches. Sacred customs such as the Sun Dance had been driven underground. When disease came, they could no longer flee to remote camps and isolate themselves. Death had spread through their settlements the previous winter, taking the lives of young and old. Rancor had further torn the Sacred Hoop apart when the traditionalists blamed progressives like American Horse for signing the treaty and falling into Three Star Crook's trap.

Kicking Bear was among those who held the treaty signers in contempt. He was a veteran of the Little Big Horn battle who'd ridden beside his cousin Crazy Horse. The tall, thickly built former warrior, now middle aged, had lost little of his disdain for the white man's ways. His brother-in-law Short Bull was a stocky Brulé medicine man who had an affinity for the white man's suits and coats, although he was Indian to the core.

The pair made their way to the land of the "Fish Eaters" and found Wovoka, the tall, broad-shouldered messiah, who gave them the same message: live in peace, do the dance, and the world will be reborn. The Lakota emissaries returned to their reservations in the spring of 1890 as fervent disciples. The pair spread their own interpretation of Wovoka's words. All but forgotten was the command to live in peace with the white man. If the messiah's vision included white men in paradise, Kicking Bear conveniently forgot about it. He told his followers their tormentors would once and for all be wiped off the face of the earth, and this could be done by dancing rather than fighting. Kicking Bear invented Ghost shirts and Ghost dresses, white muslin with blue designs painted into the fabric. As long as the dancers wore the magical garments, bullets could not harm them, he promised.

That summer, their converts began to dance. Settlers like Jack Coon, bereft of entertainment since the end of the on-the-hoof beef issues, once again hitched their wagons and made the trip north to watch this new spectacle. The Oglalas didn't mind the observers. It was a religious ritual that would bring them heaven. Didn't the white man preach that it was good to go to heaven? The Nebraskans watched the dancers emerge from the sweat lodges in the harsh afternoon sun, the men and women gathered around a stripped tree trunk forty feet high with a white flag tied on top. A holy man began with a prayer:

"Great Wakan Tanka. We are ready to begin the dance as you have commanded us. Our hearts are now good. We would do all that you ask. In return for our efforts we beg that you give us back our old hunting grounds, and our game. Oh, transport such of the dancers as we are really in earnest to the Spirit Land far away and let them see their dead relatives. Show them what good things you have prepared for us and return the visitors safely to Earth again. Hear us, we implore."

The great circle of dancers, dressed in their white, magical shirts; stars, crescents, and birds painted on their faces, began by lifting their hands to the messiah in the west and singing without drums:

> The Father says so
> The Father says so
> The Father says so
> The Father says so
> You shall see your Grandfather
> You shall see your Grandfather
> The father says so
> The father says so
> You shall see your kindred
> You shall see your kindred
> The father says so
> The father says so

As they sang, first loud, then soft, they intertwined their fingers, shuffling slowly to the left in short rhythmic steps. They wore no beads or anything made of metal, for the white man made these.

Their voices rose. Up and down, each verse loud, then soft, repeating the song for hours and hours until they were in a trance. After awakening, they collapsed outside the circle. Some would cut pieces of flesh from their skin. This went on for days.

The Nebraskans put their own interpretation on what they saw.

The dance is intended to wipe white men off the face of the earth! They're wearing special shirts meant to stop bullets. This must mean they're getting ready for a fight! Why, this is a war dance! Hell, after the federal government cut their rations in half and grabbed their land, who can blame them? By God, the Sioux are fixing to go on the warpath!

The Nebraskans hightailed it back to their farms, ranches, and towns. Hysteria began to spread among their communities. The unknown bred fear, and the fear grew out in concentric circles. On the farms and ranches to the south of Gordon, where rumors and ignorance about the

Oglalas flourished, word of an uprising reached the settlers' ears. Some tossed all their belongings in their wagons and drove hard for Sheridan County's towns. Those who didn't want to leave dug forts into the sides of hills.

On Mirage Flats, Old Jules laughed at the settlers. He knew the Indians and he didn't fear them one bit. When his neighbors began building a fort and stockpiling weapons, he scoffed. The Flats were eighteen miles south of Hay Springs, which was twenty-five miles south of the reservation. Still, the panicky homesteaders locked their doors, kept their rifles loaded, and waited for the Sioux Nation to invade.

Allen first heard about the Ghost Dance in May and had written an article for the *Chadron Democrat* describing its followers' messianic beliefs. Since the medicine men were foretelling of the Second Coming of Christ that August, he predicted that the hoopla would die out soon thereafter.

But it didn't die out. The frightened Nebraskans, reinforced by the frightened South Dakotans on the other side of the border, began howling for protection. Joining them was the newly appointed agent at Pine Ridge, D. F. Royer. He was a Republican political appointee who wouldn't have known the difference between an Oglala and an Eskimo. He was a weak man, and the Indians only respected strength. He thought it was his duty to stop the dancing, but he couldn't.

His terror mounted until he fled the reservation with his family in the middle of the night. As he whipped his team into Rushville the next day, he proclaimed that the Indians were coming! A few townsmen believed him and ran north with their Winchesters to have a look-see. No Indians.

Royer went straight to the telegraph office and sent a wire to the commissioner of Indian affairs: "Indians are dancing in the snow and wild and crazy."

He asked for troops, and the troops came. The sight of bluecoats on their reservation panicked the dancers. Kicking Bear, Short Bull, and their followers headed for the safety of the Badlands, while merchants in the Nebraska border towns began licking their lips in anticipation of the fat profits they'd make from a good old-fashioned Indian uprising. Indian trouble meant soldiers, and soldiers had to be fed, had to drink whiskey, and had to have female companionship. The bluecoats were followed by the brown suits. Newspapers dispatched a gaggle of reporters: would-be war correspondents anxious to make a name for themselves, space writers who were paid by the inch, and staffers from all over the East, especially the Omaha dailies.

One day a telegram arrived from an editor of the *New York Herald* at the *Chadron Democrat* offering decent money to Allen if he would cover the unrest; so he joined the throng at Pine Ridge. The assignment turned out to be both stultifying and boring. General Nelson Miles, the commanding officer in charge of the operation, declined to take an aggressive stance. The disciples were allowed to carry on with their ever more desperate dancing in the safety of the Badlands. The would-be war correspondents were disappointed to say the least. However, since many of them were paid by the amount of newspaper column inches filled, they began inventing incidents and wiring editors wild rumors, passing them off as facts. The way they described events, an all-out war was going to break out at any moment.

Two of the worst culprits were riding alongside Allen the night they left for Wounded Knee. He'd called Cressey and Kelley "liars of the first water" in an editorial only three weeks before.

> From the very beginning of the present trouble they have shown a marked proclivity to enlarge upon every trivial incident and distort the truth far beyond the bounds of reason, besides having at times manufactured stories of blood and rapine in order to pander to the depraved tastes of the lovers of the marvelous and create sales for the papers they represent.

Cressey was a freelance space writer and was paid by the amount of senseless drivel he could produce. His copy was the source of much amusement with the other reporters. But Kelley's inaccuracies did the most damage. His Lincoln newspaper was affiliated with the United Press, so his sensational dispatches were transmitted throughout the world.

By the time December came around, the border towns were once again boomtowns. Rushville, the closest to the train depot, was the largest beneficiary. Boozing soldiers filled the saloons, merchants made a killing filling orders for the hungry troops, and ladies of ill repute arrived to negotiate for their virtues. The army was paying top dollar to any man with a wagon and team who could haul goods to the agency. As soon as a train pulled into the station with supplies, the freelance freighters— mostly refugees who'd fled the countryside in terror—lined up at the boxcars hoping for a load to supplement their meager income.

How long would the "war" last? Forever, the profiteers on the border towns hoped. When some Rushville businessmen overheard the reporter Thomas Tibbles sending dispatches to Omaha reporting that there was in fact no war, no uprising, and no breakouts, they let him know that he was no longer welcome in town. Tibbles had to reach into his coat to fake them into believing he had a concealed gun, just to make the men back off.

Meanwhile, the Nebraska National Guard supplied volunteer militia with five hundred rifles and twelve thousand rounds of ammunition. Having five thousand federal troops on the reservations to the north and five hundred guns wasn't enough. The border town citizens pleaded with the governor to send in the Guard.

Old Jules Sandoz never bought into the paranoia. Three of his Indian friends had come looking for him on his place on the Flats while he was in jail. (He'd been charged with attempting assault on one of his neighbors during another one of his never-ending feuds.) His wife refused to open the door and sent the Oglalas away. After his release, Sandoz went looking for the three men at a camp north of the Rushville tracks, but the spot where the Indians usually stayed had been abandoned. He wondered what his friends had wanted. On his way home, he met General Miles in the street. Knowing Old Jules's reputation as a friend of the Indian and a superb tracker, the general offered him a job as a civilian scout. Perhaps he could convince the Oglalas to turn themselves in. Old Jules spat a stream of tobacco at the general's feet.

"You mean hunt Indians? I have lost no Indians. You lose any, you hunt for them!"

Fort Nendle was a potato and root cellar converted for war. Just two miles south of the Nebraska border on Wolf Creek, neighbors of the settler Jack Coon dug slits between the sod and wooden planks and prepared to fight off attacks with their rifles and six-shooters. Such makeshift forts dotted the border from Valentine to Chadron. Coon, who'd once traveled north to watch the on-the-hoof beef rations, found a new way to occupy his time. He accepted the army's offer to become a scout during the troubles. The settlers remaining behind spent their days outside, but when night fell, the women and children went underground while the men slept outside, taking their turns as sentries. They spent restless nights with frayed nerves caused by rumors, speculation, and dreams of savage Indians descending from the border to take scalps. One night a sentry sounded the alarm.

"The Indians are coming!"

The outlines of horses approached them under the light of a waning moon. They heard voices and whoops. The men took their positions and cocked the hammers on their guns as the women and children cowered in the corner. Just as they were about to fire, the outline of one of their neighbors emerged. He was driving a herd of horses from pasture.

In Gordon one night, the volunteers posted on the north side of town heard the clomping of horse hooves galloping from the northeast. A sentry rang a warning bell and the citizens hurriedly dressed and dashed to the safety of the school, where volunteers had erected a defensive wall earlier that fall. The thunderous pounding convinced them the Sioux were finally making a massive assault!

It turned out to be a stampeding herd of horses.

In Hay Springs, rumors ran rampant that renegade Sioux were hiding in the timberland on the pine ridge within sight of the town and were poised to attack. When someone's gun accidentally went off in a pasture south of town one night, the volunteer sentries deduced that the sneaky Indians were launching an attack from the opposite direction! The men ordered the women and children to stay inside their houses as the militia, with their National Guard-issued rifles in hand, dashed into the streets.

Of course, the Lakotas weren't attacking from the south or north. The thought of attacking anybody never crossed their minds. Most of the Pine Ridge Agency population didn't believe in the Ghost Dance religion. Chief Red Cloud, nominally a Catholic convert, had endorsed the new religion, but declined to take part and remained in his house on the agency. But some of the disbelievers, seeing the army invade their land, fled with the Ghost Dancers into the Stronghold, a well-protected valley in the Badlands where the army was keeping a close eye on their every move. They couldn't have broken out and attacked anyone if they had wanted to. And they didn't want to. If they followed the messiah's instructions, as interpreted by Kicking Bear and Short Bull, the whites would be wiped off the face of the earth without them ever having to fire a bullet.

Rough Feather looked down at the flat area next to Wounded Knee Creek as the soldiers escorted him and the long line of bedraggled Minneconjou Lakotas to their camp for the night. He was twenty-five years old, tired and hungry. But there were hundreds of women and children with him who had suffered the same biting winds and gnawing in their stomachs during their journey from the Cheyenne River Agency.

His band had spent the summer and fall singing, praying, and waiting for the new world to arrive. A new world where the buffalo roamed and there were no white men. But the white men had not vanished. In fact, they wouldn't leave them alone.

Chief Big Foot, sick and coughing up blood, was in a wagon rolling down into the campground. The bluecoats' doctor had attended to the band's chief, but Rough Feather, like many Lakotas, didn't have much faith in the white man's medicine. Chief Big Foot was known to all as a peacemaker. But to General "Bear Coat" Miles, he was simply a troublemaker.

Unbeknownst to Rough Feather and the other Minneconjous, the army had decided to arrest the chief and send his people off to a South Dakota fort. Like the Nebraska settlers to the south, the South Dakotans had come to believe that the Indians were going to go on the warpath. Like the Oglalas, the Minneconjous had an agent who sent warnings to Washington pleading for troops. And what would soon be called "yellow journalism" was adding kerosene to a campfire.

Big Foot, who had once traveled to Washington and met with the Great White Father, did not want war. He just wanted to perform the dance as he understood it so the world could be reborn and made into a better place. Still, when the soldiers asked the chief to bring his people to the fort, he agreed. They needed to go there to collect their treaty annuities anyway. Big Foot had also received an invitation from several chiefs at Pine Ridge to broker peace between the dancers and the army. For his services, they promised him one hundred horses.

Rough Feather remembered seeing the two wounded Hunkpapa Lakotas arriving in camp, one limping as they made their way to Big Foot's tipi. The pair had traveled one hundred miles from the nearby Standing

Rock Agency to bear the terrible news. Sitting Bull was dead—Lakota police working for the white soldiers had killed him. The medicine man had decided to go to the Badlands and join those resisting General Miles. The Hunkpapa chief had nothing to do with the spread of the Ghost Dance, but as a longtime enemy of the U.S. government, he supported the dancers' goals. The army suspected him of being a fomenter of the craze and saw the unrest as a good opportunity to eliminate him once and for all. Forty-three Indian police, most of them with personal or intertribal grudges against Sitting Bull, were sent to arrest him, while two cavalry companies stood at the ready three miles away. When the police arrived at his cabin, he agreed to go peacefully. Outside, more than a hundred of his followers angrily watched. As the police were escorting him out of his cabin, he abruptly declared that he wouldn't go. The crowd erupted, the shooting started, and a bullet killed Sitting Bull instantly.

After hearing the bedraggled men's story, the band believed the army intended to slaughter or imprison them. Despite the chief's misgivings, the other headmen recommended fleeing at once for the Badlands. They set off into the bone-chilling wind with little food in the middle of the night, much to the surprise of the nearby army officers.

During the long trek, the chief came down with the flu, which developed into pneumonia. He began coughing up blood. General Miles, infuriated that Big Foot had broken his promise to go to the fort, dispatched hundreds of troops to stop him. After traveling several days, a cavalry detachment intercepted the Minneconjous on Pine Ridge land. By that time, the tribal members were too weary and ill to travel farther.

After Rough Feather and his kin reached the flat area where the soldiers commanded them to pitch their tipis, he helped his family set up camp as the boys tended to the horses. The soldiers erected their tents in straight, regimental fashion facing the Indian camp. After days of harsh winter weather, a balmy breeze began to blow from the south. The bluecoats distributed bacon and hardtack to quell their wards' growling stomachs. Rough Feather saw soldiers put Chief Big Foot in an army tent where they installed a small stove to keep him warm. It was good they showed him such kindness, Rough Feather thought.

A second group of soldiers and thirty Oglala scouts arrived on their horses just before nightfall. They set up small cannons, the ones that spat out shells without reloading, on the nearby ridges. Word soon began to spread through the scouts that the Minneconjous were to give up their weapons the next morning. Rough Feather couldn't believe such talk. To ask a man to give up his rifle. He'd paid for it himself! Then another disquieting rumor began to spread. These were the horse soldiers of Long Hair Custer. Not the same ones, of course, for most of them were wiped out on the Greasy Grass fourteen summers ago, and these soldiers were too young, even younger than Rough Feather.

The Lakotas had long memories. But did the bluecoats? Rough Feather and the other young men began to eye them nervously.

Allen and his three companions' nighttime ride finally ended as they guided their horses into a wide ravine where dim moonlight outlined scores of tipis. It wasn't such a bad spot to camp, he thought. It sat next to Wounded Knee Creek, so there was water, and it lay in a bowl-shaped valley in case foul winter weather struck. Beyond the Indian camp, a few lanterns glowed in the cavalry tents. After finding shelter in an abandoned cabin, the three reporters sought out the officers to see if there was any news. Allen was happy to see the Seventh's commanding officer, Colonel James Forsyth, and one of his troop captains, George Wallace, inside the tent. They warmly greeted the reporters, whom they'd come to know over the past few months. Everyone seemed to be in good spirits as they celebrated the band's capture with cigars and whiskey. Chief Big Foot was ill and had surrendered peacefully, they said. There were rumors that Kicking Bear and Short Bull's followers, still holed up in the Badlands, were going to surrender at the agency the next day. Allen wondered if they'd made the right move. Maybe the bigger story would be in Pine Ridge. Much to the chagrin of his two inventive colleagues, it was beginning to look as if their much-hoped-for war wasn't going to materialize.

After a short night's rest, the three reporters left the abandoned cabin at the break of day to see if there was any news to gather. Allen didn't waste any time separating himself from the others. What fine weather for late December, he thought. He breakfasted on bacon, hardtack, and strong coffee, then took a stroll around the camp. He couldn't have been the only groggy one, with all the whiskey flowing through the camp the night before. He'd stayed up late listening to Forsyth's fascinating anecdotes of traveling through Europe after the War Between the States with the late General Phil Sheridan.

Allen was in a good mood, although he had to admit the Indians didn't seem to be. He meandered over to the open space between the Lakotas' tipis and the army's tents where Forsyth was informing morose men dressed in ghost shirts that they had to give up their weapons. They went quietly back to their tents to retrieve them.

Allen recognized an old friend, the mixed-blood scout Baptiste Garnier, "Little Bat" to all, and walked over to say good morning. Meanwhile, the warriors returned with their weapons and tossed them in a pile. The colonel was not pleased. He berated the men for not following his orders. The few guns they'd brought back were old, beat-up models. Forsyth knew they had better weapons and ordered his soldiers to search for them.

Allen tagged along as Little Bat and another scout carried out a tent-by-tent inspection. Not everyone in the Indian camp was so sullen. He noticed eight or nine boys, dressed in the gray uniforms of their day schools, playing bucking horse and leapfrog on a patch of grass. He smiled as he remembered playing the same game as a boy. He recalled helping build the Wounded Knee district schoolhouse, just a few miles down the road, when he first came to the reservation a dozen years before.

When the warriors returned, he saw a medicine man, his shirt and face painted red and blue, arguing with his followers. He strained to hear what the wiry man was saying. Allen knew enough Lakota to grab the gist. The medicine man was imploring them not to be afraid of the soldiers. Their shirts would protect them. Forget Big Foot. Forget the general, he said, and picked up a handful of dirt, tossing it into the air.

"We can scatter the enemy like this dust!" he told them.

Allen walked away, noticing for the first time that a line of sightseers, including Mr. Swiggart, had parked their wagons on a butte overlooking the camp to watch the proceedings. He took out his pipe, filled it with tobacco, and lit a match on his boot heel. As he puffed and looked around he saw several troops above him manning four Hotchkiss guns on the opposite side. "Gun" wasn't an appropriate word. "Miniature cannon" was a more accurate description for the 3.2-inch-caliber weapon. He followed a couple more soldiers around as they inspected the remaining tipis. They found plenty of guns and were confiscating anything sharp as well: knives, hatchets, awls. Forsyth had been right. They were holding out.

Allen walked back to the center of the camp, drawing puffs on his pipe. He couldn't see much over the throng, but he could make out the medicine man, still jumping about in an agitated state. Little Bat stood a few feet away, listening in while holding his rifle. Allen took the pipe out of his mouth and started tapping it against his leg to empty the dead embers.

The medicine man screamed something, and Little Bat froze for a moment, turned to Allen, wild-eyed, scared.

"Look out Charley!"

Crack. The first bullet snapped.

Silence for a moment. Then the camp erupted in gunfire.

Allen turned to run as bullets whizzed past his ears. The swifter Little Bat lit out ahead as they ran west toward the buttes. The half-breed scout was so fast, Allen soon lost him and found himself running alongside three cavalrymen on the road beneath the Hotchkiss guns, now spitting their shells into the Indian camp. One of the soldiers stopped to shoot at two Lakota women trying to hitch their horse to a wagon. He sprinted away from these men so he wouldn't become a target, stumbling underneath the buttes until he doubled over, his lungs wheezing. Bullets began smacking into the ground around him, kicking up dirt into his eyes. Behind him, he saw a dozen braves with their backs to him shooting at the soldiers. Anyone returning fire could easily cut him down with a stray bullet. Allen crawled up, heading for a notch at the top of the ravine. He turned to see the camps enveloped in smoke; the Hotchkiss shells were shredding the canvas tipis like newsprint. God help anyone inside. He realized he still had his pipe in his hand. He stuffed it in his coat pocket, praying he would live to smoke it again. He inched up the hill, never daring to raise his head until he reached a line of troops.

"I thought you was an Indian!" one of the soldiers told him. "I had you in my sights!"

Allen sat down on a wooden box. His hands were trembling as if they had a mind of their own. He borrowed a plug of tobacco from a soldier and began to chew as the others continued to empty their rifles into the camp below.

Rough Feather collapsed as the first volley crashed like thunder into the men around him. He'd been standing with a blanket over his head, gathered with the others next to Big Foot's tent, when the shooting began. He was unconscious for a moment, maybe two, three seconds, but to him it was an eternity that had turned the whole world into darkness. He opened his eyes to the sound of cracking guns. All he could see above was smoke blotting out the once clear, blue sky. He saw a warrior pull himself up and run into the haze. He instinctively followed.

Shapes of men with guns surrounded him. Bluecoats or Minneconjou warriors, he couldn't tell. His ears rang, but through the din he could hear women and children screaming. The fleeing warrior in front of him collided with a bluecoat, and the pair tumbled to the ground, their hands reaching for each other's throats. Rough Feather leapt over them and ran a few feet until a cavalryman appeared out of the smoke and slammed the butt of his rifle into his ribs. He fell, the breath knocked out of him, but the soldier didn't stay to deliver a deathblow. As he writhed in agony, he heard the cannons above pounding faster than a drum. He had to get up and take cover! He staggered through the smoke until he reached the side of a hill. There was nowhere to go but up. Up where the soldiers were firing their guns.

"Come over here," he heard a man call out. He knew him, a warrior his own age, Ghost Bear. "Come on! Quickly!" he shouted from a coulee that cut down into the creek below. Rough Feather followed his voice and slipped down into the small gorge where women and children were cowering in terror.

Around them, the Hotchkiss cannons spoke, sending a jolting message out over the prairie. The cacophony broke out from the bowl-like valley, traveling at the speed of sound. The shells' popping reached the settlers at the makeshift Fort Nendle, less than six miles away. The settlers held their rifles tight, futilely peering north attempting to discern what was happening. The balmy breeze carried the thunderous noise to the ears of Susan Sears-Rouleau and her five-year-old girl, Lulu. The abandoned daughter of the French-Canadian trader was a traditional healer now, and she instinctively ran inside the house for her medicine bag. By the time the sounds of the Hotchkiss shells reached the soldiers and the Oglalas at Pine Ridge, the popping was muted but no less menacing. The winds carried an unmistakable message: tragedy had struck Wounded Knee. The guns would echo for more than a hundred years.

Hours later, Allen walked among the carnage. How had he managed to escape? Bodies lay everywhere among the tattered tents and tipis. Soldiers. Braves. Women. Children. Blood oozed out onto the ground. Most of the dead lay only feet away from where Little Bat and he had been standing. Soldiers crept among the shredded canvas with their rifles at the ready, looking for any holdouts. Allen spotted Chief Big Foot lying on the ground, his face tilted into the glaring sun. Then the old man began to move. He'd been playing possum. He slowly began to lift his head.

Snap. Snap.

Two shots from a rifle put the old chief down for good. His middle-aged daughter dashed out from a tent where she'd been hiding, distraught and wailing.

Two more cracks and she fell face first into the ground next to her father.

Allen reeled away, sickened by these two needless deaths. He watched as soldiers chased another survivor into a tattered tent, then filled it with bullet holes.

An order finally went out for the men to cease fire.

He watched as Colonel Forsyth strolled around the carnage, surveying the scene. Allen looked down to see the boys, the ones playing leapfrog on the grass while their elders bickered a few yards away over the surrender of the guns. They were all dead. Cut down on the spot he'd last seen them with no chance to flee. Their gray uniforms blackened with blood.

Rough Feather and the others heard a voice call out to them in Lakota. "Come out! We won't shoot you anymore!"

Slowly they emerged from their hiding place. The man who called out was a half-breed interpreter. His nose was nearly sliced off from a knife wound. It dangled by a thin piece of skin.

"You better go up and help load the wagons with the wounded," the man said. Rough Feather followed him up to the ridge. Below him, women, men, boys, girls, horses, dogs were strewn between the shredded canvas tents.

There were seven wounded in the wagon; the only one he recognized was Big Foot's wife. What had happened to his kin? The soldiers ordered them to depart for Pine Ridge. He was forced to leave behind on the bloody brown grass hundreds of dead, and a few that were still barely living.

Old Jules was in Rushville when rumors of the tragedy swept into town at the same time as a snowstorm. He spat on the dirt street in disgust. He packed his horse and rode into the biting winter storm to see for himself.

After traveling into the fierce winds all day, he whipped his tired horse up a hill and looked down on the pathetic scene. The soldiers had taken their dead and wounded, then left the remains of Big Foot and his people in a lonely patch of earth now blanketed in snow. Their faces were contorted, their ghost shirts frozen stiff with blood.

Years later, he would tell his daughter Mari about that horrible tragedy. A tragedy he called a "blot on the American flag."

Shortly after the disaster at Wounded Knee, a twenty-one-year-old army scout, Amos Bad Heart Bull, walked into a dry goods store in Crawford, Nebraska, the town closest to Fort Robinson. His uncle Short Bull—no relation to the Ghost Dance leader—had been a scout for seven years and had helped his nephew secure a job with the cavalry. Amos searched the wares until he found what he was looking for. He picked up a wide accounting ledger and thumbed through it. There were faint lines for writing numbers, but he wasn't interested in checks and balances. The wide paper would suit his purposes just fine. He paid the storekeeper a portion of his small salary and took the ledger back to the barracks. Now that it was all over, and the old ways would never return, it was time for him to record the story of the Oglala Lakotas. The stories Short Bull and his other uncles had told him—of fights with the Crows, and Sun Dances and the Battle of Greasy Grass—and the story of the massacre at Wounded Knee that had just reached his ears. He had no formal art training. But he had talent. And a strong desire to record history that should not be forgotten.

He began to draw.

Indian Scare

They crammed into their cars, rented a Greyhound bus, and headed north to the Omaha and Winnebago reservations. They stopped and made speeches. Savage white men in Gordon, Nebraska, killed an Indian man. His skull was crushed. He was humiliated, tortured. They gathered more followers, and the caravan grew. They drove to the Santee reservation next, picked up more protesters, and then entered Lakota territory at Rosebud.

The FBI and state patrol Teletypes tapped furiously away in a staccato rhythm.

URGENT.
SEVERAL HUNDRED INDIANS PLAN TO GO TO
GORDON, NEBRASKA NIGHT OF MARCH SIX
TO BURN BUILDINGS IN REPRISAL FOR DEATH
OF RAYMOND YELLOW THUNDER.

All day long the machine spat out messages.

The URGENT Teletypes backed off the "burn buildings" claim, but the radicals were heading to Gordon nevertheless. AIM was planning a rally in Billy Mills Hall at Pine Ridge, South Dakota, at 7:30 p.m. A march on Gordon would take place the following day. The leaders were threatening to "wipe the town off the map." Some reports stated they were coming with weapons. Citizens of Whiteclay and Gordon were said to be arming themselves.

Meanwhile, County Attorney Michael Smith sat in front of a reporter at his Main Street office pounding his desk, on the cusp of shouting. False rumors were being reported in the press as fact, he told the Associated Press journalist. The program director of the Nebraska Indian Commission, Ken Bordeaux, had written him an indignant letter:

Throwing his stripped and naked body into the American Legion Club while a dance was in progress is something unrealistic and certainly must be related to the dark ages of history.

We are quite aware that retribution will transpire in the form of due process of the law, but what is happening in western Nebraska to our Indian citizens? Will [these] kinds of atrocities and outrages against our Indian people persist? Must other citizens stand by and let this happen or are they, too, still fighting the Indian wars of the last century?

Now, the state's Indian commissioner was telling reporters that Yellow Thunder died of a crushed skull. He was calling for a grand jury investigation. Meanwhile, Smith had been fielding calls from the Justice Department, the FBI, and numerous reporters.

Smith's voice raised a notch as the reporter scribbled in his notebook.

"The commissioner hasn't even been in touch with me. He doesn't know what the autopsy said. Only I and the pathologist know that, and Raymond Yellow Thunder did not die of a crushed skull!

"I really wish the Indian commissioner had bothered to call me. I really wish he'd done that!"

The reporter went through the allegations one by one.

All the suspects were in police custody and charged within a week of the body's discovery, Smith insisted. The judge had set bail for all of the accused. Yellow Thunder was in the American Legion Hall less than thirty seconds. He was not forced to dance "Indian style" to the delight of a jeering crowd.

"There really isn't much of a story," Smith told the reporter.

Assignment editors from newspapers and radio and television stations all over the country didn't agree. Journalists were about to descend on Gordon like hungry grasshoppers.

State patrol investigator Max Ibach and Smith drove over the Pine Ridge, making their way to the reservation on Route 87 in a last-ditch effort

Protesters march up the Gordon City Auditorium steps, March 8, 1972.
(Reprinted with permission of the *Omaha World-Herald*.)

to diffuse the situation. It was nearly dusk, and the scattered lights of Whiteclay and the town of Pine Ridge to the north blinked at them as the car descended the razorback hills.

It had already been a busy day. Earlier, Ibach, Smith, and police chief Bob Case had met at Smith's Main Street office to discuss a plan of action. The FBI and the state patrol's Omaha bureau told town officials to expect several busloads of AIM "leftwing radicals" and "militants." Now, they had to figure out what to do about it. Smith, as the county's top law enforcement official, was in charge of responding to the situation rather than the affable, but out of his depth, Chief Case. Ibach said there wasn't enough time to gather a sizable force of state troopers. Smith decided law enforcement would take a nonconfrontational stance. The twenty patrolmen Ibach expected from the western Nebraska division were to keep a low profile and stay out of sight, he insisted. To further complicate matters, Smith wouldn't be in Gordon the next day. He was scheduled to argue a case four hundred miles away in Lincoln at the Nebraska Supreme Court.

Not everybody was on board with the "nonconfrontation" plan. Mayor Bruce Moore informed them that several hotheads at the volunteer fire department were planning to greet the Indians with guns and fire hoses. It wasn't so long ago when their counterparts in Selma, Alabama, had gone down in infamy by turning their high-pressure nozzles on civil rights protesters. The volunteers apparently thought it would be a good thing for Gordon to be seen on NBC getting tough with the "commies." So Moore, Smith, and Ibach walked to the station to deal with the firemen. They told them to let law enforcement handle the situation. Plus, they might be needed for other duties besides shooting Indians. For example, putting out fires.

Now, Ibach and Smith had their own fire to put out. They had to convince these so-called radicals to stay out of Gordon. Three meetings were on their schedule that night. First would be a private negotiation with AIM leaders and tribal government officials. That would be followed by a public rally at Billy Mills Hall. Smith would assure the angry AIM members that he had the situation under control and that the Hares would receive a vigorous prosecution. Then maybe they would call off their march. Gordon's Oglala community was also meeting at the Neighborhood Center to diffuse tensions and make plans for the march. Smith hoped everyone would listen to reason. He was taking care of the Yellow Thunder case. The rumors weren't true. There was no need to march or protest.

As they drove through Whiteclay in the fading light, Smith noticed Ibach's .45 underneath his suit. He told the investigator to leave his gun behind.

"I've got to have something when I go in there."

"You leave that damn thing in the trunk!"

Ibach reluctantly agreed.

They walked into a meeting room at the tribal office's administrative building and sat down at a table in front of several Bureau of Indian Affairs officials, including the tall superintendent Stanley Lyman, a few Legal Aid representatives, and about fifty scowling AIM members and sympathizers. The small, private meeting would be neither private nor small. The shouting began the moment they sat down. Russell Means and Dennis Banks ripped into the BIA officials and Smith, calling them "racists" and "pigs," peppering them with questions without giving them time to answer.

"Why didn't you file murder charges?"

Smith could barely open his mouth before the next question was fired at him, followed by jeers from the assembled AIM supporters. The "radicals" were hopping mad. Smith wouldn't be talking anyone out of marching into Gordon.

The one-sided grilling lasted several minutes until Banks handed them a list of demands. First, they wanted the manslaughter charges to be refiled as first-degree murder, and false imprisonment charges refiled as kidnapping. They wanted Yellow Thunder's body exhumed and a second autopsy carried out at Sheridan County's expense. Next, they demanded a grand jury investigation into law enforcement officials at Sheridan County. Plus, they wanted the resignations of Smith, the head of the Nebraska State Patrol responsible for the Gordon area, and police chief Bob Case.

Means told them they weren't welcome at the Billy Mills Hall rally that night. Then Banks stood up.

"If you're not willing to meet our demands, I suggest you get out of Pine Ridge."

Ibach and Smith were taken aback by the hostile atmosphere. They left believing that there very well could be violence the following day.

Later that evening, Lulu Trueblood accompanied her daughter Gladys Shald to the chilly Neighborhood Center and sat down on one of the cold, hard folding chairs. She was eighty-eight years old and possibly the only one there who had memories of the last "Indian scare." They were dim memories, the memories of a six-year-old girl. Her mother was Susan Sears (Rouleau), the half-Oglala, half-French girl abandoned by her father in Kansas who moved with her white husband to Pine Ridge. Susan had given birth to seventeen children afterward, and Lulu was one of the thirteen who survived infancy.

Lulu recalled little of the hysteria that gripped the border towns in 1890, but the aftermath remained with her. She remembered hearing the bursting Hotchkiss shells at Wounded Knee, and later that day, accompanying her mother to the Church of the Holy Cross near Pine Ridge where the army had sent the wounded victims.

Susan was a healer, and she carried a black doctor's bag with her everywhere. The bag's contents, like herself, were a mix of both cultures: Western medicines and traditional roots and herbs used by the Oglalas. Lulu watched as her mother went from one wounded person to another, doing whatever she could. She saw injured children, some younger than herself, lying on makeshift beds, which were nothing but straw bunched up on the floor and covered by old blankets. She would never forget the image of the warriors, tapping the beat of their death songs on the floor with their bloody hands.

Lulu later married Benjamin Trueblood, a child of one of the original Scamahorn party settlers, and they settled on a farm near Lake Wakpamni. Like her daughter Gladys sitting next to her, Lulu had inhabited both worlds and had friends in both communities. Two of Lulu's sons, Tom and Buddy, had married Oglala women, so she had grandchildren all over the reservation. Her daughter Gladys was born in Gordon, but spent two years attending an Indian day school. One of Gordon's Oglala elders had called Gladys and asked the family to attend the meeting. Lulu, her sister Maxine, granddaughter Susan Phillips, and daughter Gladys were the only white faces there until Smith and Ibach strolled in and took their seats at a folding table.

The four women sat quietly as the local Oglalas, silent for so many years, finally had a forum to speak. Anger over Yellow Thunder's death had been festering for weeks, and perceived racism and mistreatment by the local whites festering for decades. Gordon's silent minority would be silent no more.

Smith sat and listened as they went through a litany of complaints:

Why were the Hares walking free?

Why were Indians locked up for days for having a few beers while drunken white folks were allowed to drive home?

Why aren't there any Indians working as clerks at stores? You take our money, don't you?

What about that cop shooting Vincent Broken Rope back in the 1950s?

What about those white boys shoving Jessie Red Hawk out the back of their car? Did they ever serve any time?

There were two kinds of justice in Sheridan County: one for the whites and one for the Indians.

An intoxicated man stood up and took off his shirt, displaying several scars he said the Gordon police had inflicted on him.

"Look at what they did to me!"

An elder escorted him out of the building.

Despite all the complaints, the meeting was at least more civil than what Smith and Ibach encountered at Pine Ridge. Smith agreed that the city would provide a makeshift stage and a public address system to be set up in front of the Neighborhood Center the next day.

No one ever asked Gladys Shald or Lulu Trueblood to speak, so they offered no opinions. They sat in a silent show of support. And when they left, they could only wonder what the latest Indian scare would bring.

To the northwest at Billy Mills Hall, a raucous rally with seven hundred angry Oglalas was under way. For the first time, residents of Pine Ridge were getting a taste of their fiery native son, Russell Means. If they didn't know who he was before, they did now.

Severt Young Bear and his troop of traditional singers from Porcupine huddled around the drum and began the rally with a song. Next came prayers in Lakota. A speech infused with righteous anger from Banks followed. Then Means took the crowd to the next level. The Oglalas had never heard an Indian like Means before. He was one part American Horse, one part Malcolm X, and one part his Iowa Technical College speech professor who'd given him a "C" seven years earlier for moving around too much and not making eye contact with the audience.

Means took the microphone and started in a slow, evenly paced voice.

As Yellow Thunder's sisters sat in front, Means told the audience crammed on the bleachers how a quiet, innocent man had been brutalized. He paused at the right moments to let the image of Raymond, alone, naked on the dance floor while the white citizens of Gordon laughed, set in. How they thought it would be a hoot to make him dance like the "injuns" in the movies.

He brought them through the history of the reservation as he paced in front of the crowd. He reminded them about the hundreds of women and children slaughtered at Wounded Knee by ruthless white soldiers fifteen miles west of where they sat. How everything had been taken away from them. The Black Hills. Their way of life. Their culture. Their language. And most all, their pride.

He waved his index finger and said they were going to march into Gordon and show the white man that they weren't going to take it anymore! The crowd erupted in agreement as the drummers pounded their approval.

Calls to bring arms came down from the bleachers. Let's take our guns. We'll show them! That touched off a rancorous debate on whether to bring weapons, some advocating a more militant approach, others nonviolence.

Means asked Leonard Crow Dog to pray over the matter. Crow Dog was a Brulé Lakota from Rosebud and a direct descendant of the Crow Dog who'd murdered Chief Spotted Tail in 1881. He was a traditional to the core, wore his hair long, and bragged that he'd never attended a white man's school. He was looked upon by some as AIM's official medicine man. He told other members that his forefather killed Spotted Tail for signing away the Black Hills. That may have given him street credibility with AIM, but the circumstances of Spotted Tail's death were reported quite differently in reputable history books. While Spotted Tail was an early proponent of peace with the United States, like Red Cloud, he also stubbornly opposed the foolish Indian bureau policies that were forcing the Lakotas to become "imitation white men." At the negotiations for the

Black Hills in 1875, he told the treaty delegation that their lands weren't for sale at any price.

Crow Dog was a former chief of the Rosebud Indian police who wanted to take Spotted Tail's place. He shot the old chief in an ambush, was convicted of murder, and sentenced to hang. But the U.S. Supreme Court intervened, ruling that the Dakota Territory courts had no jurisdiction when Indians killed Indians on a reservation. The incident split the Brulé reservation into factions and took away the tribe's strongest leader, which allowed the Crook commission to run roughshod over them in 1889.

Until that night, AIM didn't have a history of violence. They hadn't even broken a window, let alone invaded a town with rifles and dynamite as some were advocating. Means said they didn't know who or what was going to be waiting for them in Gordon the next day. Rumors were fueling fear on both sides. They'd heard the governor might call up the Nebraska National Guard. There could be redneck vigilantes waiting to take matters into their own hands, or state troopers willing to crack heads. It could turn into a bloodbath.

But later that night, Crow Dog performed a ceremony. The spirits told him they should go armed with their spiritual strength only.

In Gordon, word came down from the reservation to expect trouble. With hundreds crammed into the Billy Mills Hall stands, it was easy for BIA Superintendent Lyman to send in informants to gather intelligence. A Justice Department Community Relations official was also feeding info to Ibach, reporting that tensions were running high. Lyman told Ibach that AIM leaders were openly advocating a riot. Means had threatened once again to "wipe Gordon off the map." Ibach posted around-the-clock lookouts north of Rushville and Gordon to forewarn of any invasion. He asked liquor stores and bars to close. The governor hadn't called up the Nebraska National Guard. There wasn't enough time, let alone the political will. In fact, Ibach was having a difficult time scraping up a force of two dozen state troopers he could only hope would be in place by the following morning. That would hardly be enough men to stop hundreds of angry, rioting Indians. Fears of an armed invasion by militant Indians swept through the border towns just as they had in 1890. Folks locked their doors and made themselves scarce.

On a chilly Tuesday morning in Porcupine, a bastion of traditional Lakota culture ten miles north of Wounded Knee, Crow Dog sprinkled Means, Banks, and the Bellecourt brothers with gopher dust, the same medicine Crazy Horse used to make himself impervious to bullets. Everyone boarded the rented bus or piled into cars and headed south.

The night before, Means had come up with a plan. He remembered a term paper he'd written in junior high about flags on ships being flown upside down when they were in distress. The Indian was in distress, so he asked everyone to bring as many American flags as possible.

With the bus leading the way, eighty cars following, and upside-down American flags flapping outside their windows, they drove over Pine Ridge, past the Wounded Knee Massacre site, where eighty-two years before the army had tossed hundreds of victims in a trench a few days after the horrific fight.

After the massacre, the fickle and imaginative press had turned on the army and blamed it for the disaster. General Miles tried to have Colonel Forsyth court-martialed for improperly positioning his troops during the attempt to disarm the Minneconjous. Many of the twenty-five soldiers who died that day had been struck by friendly fire, caught in a cross fire of their commanding officer's making. But Forsyth was cleared of all charges. Many soldiers, in fact, received medals. The Lakotas petitioned the U.S. government for compensation, but never received a dime.

The massacre faded from the public's consciousness. Perhaps because most of the victims were Minneconjous, it was easy for the schoolteachers and white reservation administrators to systematically make the Oglalas forget about what happened there. They renamed the Wounded Knee district "Brennan," after the agent who lorded over the reservation at the turn of the century. Charley Allen wrote a memoir of his life on the prairie, including seven chapters on the Ghost Dance hysteria and Wounded Knee Massacre. By the time he died in 1942 at the age of ninety-one, he'd failed to find a publisher. It would be another fifty-five years before it saw print.

The collective amnesia changed in 1970 when a white librarian, Dee Brown, published *Bury My Heart at Wounded Knee: An Indian History of the American West*. The number-one best-seller sold millions of copies and would be called one of the most influential nonfiction books of the twentieth century. The Wounded Knee Massacre was the final chapter in a relentlessly depressing but powerful book. Historians debated over who fired the first shot. Was it a battle or a massacre? Did the soldiers deserve medals or court-martials? For those driving past the site, it was a ruthless massacre. They had to wonder what the white man had in store for them that day.

The caravan turned east toward Rosebud, then south at the Lake Wakpamni district. At eleven o'clock, the bus parked on the shoulder of Highway 27 under a sign:

WELCOME TO THE LITTLE CITY WITH THE BIG SMILE

Despite Crow Dog's proclamation and the leadership's order to march into Gordon unarmed, many of the rank-and-file members had handguns tucked away.

Just in case.

The white folks of Gordon, with the exception of the Shalds, were afraid to stick their heads outside.

Susan Rouleau's descendant Pat Shald stood with his apron on outside the Jack and Jill on the north end of town as marchers filed by, many carrying upside-down American flags. Always the contrarian, Pat wasn't afraid. In fact, he was ticked off he had to stay and watch the store. He wanted to follow the march to see what was going to happen.

Out front, Means, Banks, Crow Dog, and the Bellecourt brothers led the column. Raymond's sisters and cousins followed a few steps behind. Severt Young Bear brought his nine-year-old son, Severt, Jr. They walked down Main Street, between the rows of nicely painted houses. The doors were closed, and the drapes drawn tight. The Associated Press had reported that the Indians were marching in with firearms.

Pat's sister Susan Phillips stood at her front door on Main Street as the marchers walked by. She looked up and down the block and glimpsed only one neighbor brave enough to show his face. The town residents, especially the elderly, were terrified. She was afraid, too. Not for her own safety, but for what might happen later. As Gladys Shald's daughter, she was sympathetic to the Oglalas' plight and had many Native American friends in town. She taught at the Head Start program with Arlene Lamont and knew most of the families. She'd heard the rumors that the marchers were coming with weapons. She was a fervent pacifist and abhorred violence of any kind.

The protesters left the tree-lined residential section and entered the downtown area. Means made for the post office. Everyone cheered as he pulled down the American flag, then draped it around his shoulders. They walked past the nearly finished theater, past Messenger and Milburn Ford where Toby Bayliss had been fired the previous week for his involvement in the crime, past the Coast to Coast store, Saults and Son Drug, and the old Sheridan Hotel where Ibach watched from the top floor through binoculars. Past the *Gordon Journal* office, Saub's clothing store, and Borman Chevrolet. Gordon looked like a ghost town.

There were no cops or guardsmen there to bust heads. The marchers didn't know about the woefully inadequate force of twenty troopers, plus assorted local sheriffs and town cops, positioned at the state's maintenance yard a few blocks away. Ibach, watching from his makeshift command post, was ready to radio the squad cars if needed, but everything seemed peaceful.

Means, Banks, and Crow Dog led the marchers over the railroad tracks, between the towering grain elevators, down to Highway 20, then turned around. A few protesters broke off, dashed over to the American Legion Hall a block away, and snatched the command flag. Considering the rumors about how Yellow Thunder was treated there, the Legion got off lightly. Except for the flag thefts, there was no vandalism or violence of any kind. They had heeded Crow Dog's words.

The column marched back up Main Street, arriving at the Neighborhood Center, where Means mounted the platform and took the microphone.

Gordon's Oglala community started to arrive one by one to hear these so-called radical Indians, dressed in native jewelry and beads, chokers around their necks, their long hair in braids and headbands around their foreheads. Fifteen-year-old George Ghost Dog, the last person to speak to Yellow Thunder, was among them. A couple AIM members encouraged the boy to climb up on stage to tell the audience what he knew, how Yellow Thunder told him that four white men had beat him up, but he was terrified of speaking in front of all those people.

Means, still wrapped in the American flag, delivered yet another powerful speech, this time for the CBS and NBC affiliate camera crews.

"We came here today to put Gordon on the map. But if our demands aren't met, and met soon, we'll come back and take Gordon off the map!"

The crowd cheered.

They didn't stay outside long. This was AIM, and AIM occupied. It was a cold day, the temperature hadn't reached the thirties, so Means announced that they were taking over the city auditorium. They would occupy it until the governor and the city of Gordon met their demands.

They walked the three blocks en masse and found City Manager Art Britton and Chief Case there to greet them. The horde filled the entire street. The auditorium was much more than a combination basketball court and stage. The multipurpose building, constructed in the Depression era, housed the mayor and city manager's offices, as well as the police station and city jail at a separate entrance on the south side. The mob was a human flood the two men were helpless to stop, and they had orders to be nonconfrontational. They unlocked the doors to the gymnasium as Means snatched Case's hat off his head. He had no choice but to allow it. Smith had instructed him to keep his cool. That normally wasn't a problem for the mild-mannered police chief, but this day would test his resolve.

Means demanded that the city council and mayor come to hear their grievances. The city manager, Britton, really ran the town. The mayor was an elected official who had few duties. Bruce Moore obeyed the summons, though, leaving his job as manager of the Farmer's Co-Op.

In the center of the gym, organizers set up tables and a public address system as protesters filled the seats above. Banks had come up with the idea to hold an all-Indian "red-feather" rather than "blue-ribbon" grand jury to take testimony about the Nebraska border towns.

Moore, an even-tempered lifelong resident of Gordon, wearing thick black glasses and a plaid shirt, stood and listened patiently with the other officials to hours of testimony. As the only white men of authority there, they became the punching bags. The mayor, Britton, and the three council members sat on their folding chairs as Means berated them, asking pointed questions but interrupting them before they could respond. The audience, packed all the way up the arena-style seats, looked down on them, some jeering like a Greek chorus. Soon, Means was shouting in Moore's face, calling him and his town "racist." The mayor tried to get a word in edgewise, but there was no talking to this angry man.

Police Officer John Paul's name repeatedly came up. Allegations, never proven, emerged that the lumbering, baby-faced town cop was a thug and had sexually abused Indian girls in the back of his police car. A doctor at the town's hospital and a salesman at Borman Chevrolet were also high on their list of racists. The locals accused the doctor of refusing treatment to Indians. Moore believed the stories were exaggerations and trumped-up charges (except for that Chevy salesman, whom he believed truly was a redneck), but he had to sit for hours on a folding chair and take it. He had no way of knowing that the notoriously inaccurate Gordon rumor mill was reporting to his wife, Sheila, that town officials had been taken hostage.

Clyde and Vernon Bellecourt demanded that Moore adjourn with them to his upstairs office. The mayor was asked to phone Governor J. J. Exon to demand a grand jury investigation into Yellow Thunder's death. Moore made the call as the Bellecourts listened in. Moore reported that the governor was sending his representatives to Gordon and that they should arrive shortly.

Robert Two Crow had listened to the speeches at the Neighborhood Center and followed the marchers to the city auditorium. He was quite upset. He wasn't angry about all the social injustices they were talking about at the "red-feather" grand jury. He was angry because all the bars and liquor stores were closed.

Two Crow had been living on the streets for a couple of years. He was one of the dozen or so regulars the Gordon police rounded up for intoxication and tossed in jail. He remembered Raymond Yellow Thunder. He was a quiet, elderly man he ran into at the bars every once in a while.

Two Crow was twenty-three years old and a chronic alcoholic. He'd done two tours of duty with the army, one in West Germany and one in Vietnam as an infantryman. The Lakotas, despite the abuse inflicted upon them by the U.S. government, had a long, proud history of serving in the military dating back to World War I, which some whites found ironic considering everything the government had taken from them. Scores of Oglala eighteen-year-olds like Two Crow volunteered for Vietnam. Others were drafted. Through the Great War, World War II, and Korea, the Lakotas had fought. When the passenger trains still ran through Rushville and Gordon, the Pine Ridge American Legion post arranged receptions at the stations. Veterans dressed in their uniforms, bearing drums and American and tribal flags, greeted the returning soldiers with traditional Lakota honoring songs, just as the warriors returning from battle received in the nineteenth century.

By the time Two Crow's last stint ended, the passenger trains were a thing of the past and so were the receptions. Two Crow alit from a Greyhound bus, emotionally scarred from combat, with no one there to greet him. He left the army with no skills, no education, and no direction, so he wandered down to the border towns and started drinking and smoking dope. He hitchhiked from town to town, drinking in Whiteclay, Chadron, Alliance, sometimes as far away as Denver. He'd been locked up plenty of times in Gordon. And like Yellow Thunder, he'd slept in the back of Borman's lot, too. He agreed with some of those testifying that the Gordon police could get rough sometimes, but that was usually when you gave them a hard time. The garrulous drunks were the ones who received rough treatment. He'd seen John Paul knock a drunk around in a jail cell once, but the dude had been fighting back and mouthing off.

In the summer, they'd let you work off your fine picking up trash, mowing grass, or raking up leaves; then you could be released early. It was a source of cheap labor for the city. If you were arrested in the winter, that was tough luck. You just had to sit around jail and sober up. Funny, how no white men ever had to rake leaves for the municipality. It was as if no white person ever walked down the sidewalk with too much beer in him.

Two Crow thought he'd go to one of the AIM meetings when they set up a chapter, just to see what they were all about.

The press had to love Means. He gave good quote. He stepped outside to do an interview with the network television crews and assembled reporters, still wrapped in the post office's American flag, Case's police chief hat worn crookedly to the side.

"I am like a rubber band, stretched as far as it can stretch, and when I snap the first man I get a hold of in Gordon who has European heritage, they won't be able to exhume his body. There won't be anything left of him!"

Did he mind being called a militant?

"No. It's about time somebody in the Indian population got a little militant. We've been the 'good niggers' for too long."

Do you have any weapons?

"The only weapon we have is the peace pipe!"

Are you willing to take up violence?

"Indians don't have to 'take up violence.' The violence is already there. It was put there by the white man, and violence is the only thing he understands."

Governor Exon's representatives, Clive Short, director of buildings and grounds, and the Indian Commission director, Robert Mackey, arrived in the middle of the day from Lincoln. Mackey told the audience that he'd asked Washington officials to empanel a grand jury to investigate Yellow Thunder's death. He'd also asked that the charges be changed to first-degree murder. The crowd applauded, welcoming his comments.

But Short wasn't well received. Exon had sent the Lincoln bureaucrat to be his "eyes and ears" because he'd lived in nearby Chadron. His other qualifications for being there were lost on the AIM leaders. Means called him a "bellboy," and the red-feather grand jury sentenced Exon "to hell" for sending him. Means then demanded that John Paul arrive that evening to face the abuse allegations, and if he didn't, he would "hunt him down and castrate him if necessary."

Into the storm walked Ed Hollstein.

The lanky and elderly attorney considered himself a "friend of the Indian." He was also the court-appointed attorney for Jeannette Thompson. As someone who'd represented dozens of Oglalas over the years, he felt he could explain the American justice system to them. He was an old-fashioned country lawyer who'd practiced law in the district before many in the crowd were born.

He took the microphone and began by telling the crowd he was an attorney for one of the defendants. This news was met by catcalls. It was true that he had defended many Indians over the years. But as a former county attorney, he'd sent plenty of them to the hoosegow as well. In private practice, he was the Whiteclay liquor storeowners' favorite mouthpiece.

"As one of the defendants' attorney, I will call for a neutral autopsy . . ."

"Goddamn slum lord!" someone yelled.

(Hollstein also owned several pieces of property on Gordon's southeast side.)

"Get off the stage!"

He tried to speak.

Who were these people? Didn't they realize he was a "friend of the Indian"?

Three Oglala women rushed up and grabbed the microphone. They took him by the arm and escorted him by force out of the auditorium as the crowd applauded his exit.

Later, he billed the district court one hour for "defending the American judicial system."

Banks walked up to Moore and asked if the city could provide them with supper that night. The Ojibwa wasn't screaming and shouting like Means. He seemed to be a levelheaded guy. Moore agreed to supply some food.

"You know, what we're trying to accomplish here is when you see an Indian walking down the street, you see him as a human being, not just an Indian," Banks said.

Moore thought that was reasonable. Maybe it was time Gordon looked at the way it treated the Oglalas, he concluded.

Meanwhile, Arlene Lamont was furious. Still angry over the cruel death of her uncle, she was ready to join AIM and take up the cause. A *New York Times* reporter cornered her for an interview, and she quickly turned on the town she once loved.

"The harassment just has got to stop. Yellow Thunder wasn't the first of us to be mistreated, but he'd better be the last. We're tired of being cursed on the streets, tired of being beaten in the alleys. And we're tired of doing the white man's dirty work."

The reporter later wrote that she was one of Gordon's most militant Indians. He neglected to mention that she was also Raymond's niece and deeply hurt by his death. To add to her stress, her husband Ray was becoming increasingly belligerent about her involvement with AIM. They'd argued several times, and he told her not to go to any demonstrations. He didn't seem to want her to have any life outside the home. He didn't support her in her teaching aspirations at Head Start or her night classes, and this was just one more thing he didn't condone.

Still, a creeping ambivalence came over her.

She saw Means verbally abusing Bob Case and Bruce Moore. She hated the way the larger Means was humiliating the police chief by wearing his hat. She heard Moore and Case called "red-necked racists" and "white savages." She'd known these men her whole life and knew that simply wasn't true. As for John Paul, he was another matter.

The testimony from local Indians continued throughout the day. Occasionally a reporter wandered over to Main Street to grab a quote from a white resident or store owner. The white locals blamed the occupation on "outside agitators." Of course, that was true. AIM had organized it all. But if any of the white residents had worked up the courage to go to the auditorium and listen to those testifying at the ad hoc grand jury, they would have learned about a different side of Gordon. But the only white people at the occupation were Moore and the councilmen, members of the media, a few clergymen, two undercover state troopers posing as reporters, and the Shalds.

Three generations of the Rouleau-Trueblood-Shald clan arrived to listen to the testimony. Gladys Shald, her daughter Susan Phillips, and Debbie Harris, Gladys's adult granddaughter, walked up the auditorium steps. Susan, who had watched the marchers come into town earlier that day, was still a little apprehensive. Her mother assured her that she would be all right, but Susan wasn't entirely sure. When they went through a line in the basement, Debbie asked an AIM member what she had to do to join the organization.

"The first thing you can do is slit that wrist and drain that white blood," he said.

Susan's brother Pat, however, was ecstatic when he received a call from a city councilman, who put in an order for that night's supper. At last, he had an excuse to leave the Jack and Jill to see what was going on. He loaded up bags of potatoes, bread, lettuce, and lunchmeat in the back of the supermarket's El Camino, "Shald's Jack and Jill" emblazoned on the side, and drove down to the auditorium, parking in front where an NBC television crew filmed him arriving. He climbed up the steps where he encountered a frazzled and still hatless Chief Case.

"What the hell are you doing here?" Case said.

"I got an order for food. Where am I supposed to take it?"

"Downstairs, I guess."

Pat went down to the kitchen where he saw one of his reservation cousins, Gary.

"Hey Gary. Got food. Need help!"

His cousin rounded up some strong arms, and they went outside to help unload the car. The camera crew ended up showing a snippet of the delivery and the El Camino on the Nightly News.

The next day, the store received several calls from angry residents accusing the Shalds of donating food to the radical Indians. Pat, always happy to be in the town gadfly, found it all amusing.

Reva Evans, editor and publisher of the *Gordon Journal*, sat down to type her weekly column. She was fuming mad, sick and tired of these outside reporters besmirching the town she loved, and she was about to let them have it. Her weapon would be her Royal manual typewriter.

The petite and bespectacled publisher was a true daughter of the Sand Hills—proud and patriotic. Her loyalties were to the town of Gordon, God, and country, in about that order. Evans was in her third decade publishing the *Journal*, and she'd never seen anything like this.

She'd studied journalism briefly at the University of Nebraska in Lincoln before returning in the late 1940s to the Sand Hills where her father was a rancher and former sheriff of Cherry County. That was enough experience for the new owners of the *Gordon Journal* to hire her as an associate editor. Their tenure at the paper was brief, though, and when they announced plans to leave after only a few months, she borrowed the money to buy the paper herself. It was unusual in 1949 for a young mother to own and run a business, let alone a newspaper. The chamber of commerce types, all men of course, said she wouldn't last.

She'd been the family breadwinner ever since then. Her husband, John, had never fully recovered from a car accident early in their marriage, and he lived in the family basement, occasionally emerging to set type at the paper until he passed away in 1965. She'd raised two children, but the *Journal* was her true calling.

For twenty-three years she'd settled into the routine duties of a small-town weekly newspaper. She'd never once missed a city council meeting, never missed the annual 4-H banquet, never failed to run the stories important to the people in her patch of Sheridan County: marriages, engagements, homecoming kings and queens, high school sports, car accidents, obituaries, and the occasional break-in.

She didn't attend the meeting at the Neighborhood Center the night before the march and wouldn't set foot in the auditorium for two days. For nothing negative about Gordon ever appeared in her newspaper. Occasionally, a big-city reporter would blow through town and do a write-up about the old "tent city" before it was removed, or a piece about the poverty of Gordon's Indians. The articles, their existence hinted at but their writers and publications never revealed, were followed up with a stinging attack in her weekly "Reva-lations" column. These outsiders could never understand Gordon, she believed.

She'd watched the marchers pass by the office the day before, flying the flag upside down, some wearing it like a cape. It was a disgrace. Her pressman, Errol Brakeman, a staunch Republican like herself, had brought his rifle and kept it handy in his pickup out back in case there was trouble.

For Evans, anyone who spoke out against America, like those Vietnam War protesters in Washington, was simply wrongheaded. Now she had hippies on her own doorstep. These outside agitators were coming in and scaring the local Indians half to death. Spreading pernicious lies. Slandering her town. But the worst part of the whole fiasco was her colleagues in the media.

They were repeating outrageous rumors in their stories, sending them over the airwaves, comparing Gordon to the Deep South. Why, that just wasn't true. And this idea that Yellow Thunder was forced to dance Indian style as the American Legion crowd cheered. That was the worst lie of all. It slandered the entire town, made them sound like a bunch of sadistic, cruel monsters with no human feelings whatsoever. One of her employees was at the dance that night, as were nearly two hundred others, including some Indian couples from the nicer parts of town. The so-called reporters weren't interviewing anyone there. And then there was the reporter from the *Des Moines Register*. She'd let him use the office phone as a professional courtesy, and she heard him use the words "forced to dance Indian style" while calling in a story. This after she'd granted him an interview explaining that it wasn't true!

"Gordon's always been good to the Indians. They live in every part of town. We have a housing authority that's trying to get rid of those shanties on the south side of town where some of the Indians live.

"Just look at the school activities. Why, for the last two years the 'King of Sport' award has gone to an Indian.

"Our Indians, the ones who live and work here, are good people and they get along with the whites. It's these outside Indians who are wearing those flags that have everyone upset, and they're scaring the local Indians so bad they don't know what to think."

She wondered if anything she'd said had gotten through to the Iowan. She called his editor in Des Moines and let him have it. Evans was a stickler for accuracy and spelling. The reporter was quoting Ted Ghost Dog as Ted Dog. She told the editor to make the change.

And then there was the lead paragraph of the *Washington Post* story. A story that had been reprinted all across the country, including the *Los Angeles Times*: "On Feb. 12, an Oglala Sioux Indian, Raymond Yellow

Thunder, 51, involuntarily entertained a crowd at the Gordon, Neb., American Legion hall by dancing without trousers or undershorts."

Where did this reporter get his information? He cited no one. He filed the story from Washington. He'd never left his desk there.

Other news sources, the Associated Press, the *Rapid City Journal*, the *Omaha World-Herald*, had repeated the lie to various degrees, slipping in the fact that Yellow Thunder had been stripped and shoved onto the dance floor in the same paragraph, making it sound as if the terrible act had happened right there in front of the crowd. Yes, the door he was shoved in led directly onto the dance floor, but he wasn't in there more than a few seconds.

Her weekly page 2 column, "Reva-lations," was normally reserved for musings on small-town life or wry commentary on national affairs. The comfort of holiday traditions was a favorite topic, patriotism, the seasons, or some community betterment project she was promoting. But not this week. She slipped a sheet of yellow paper into her manual Royal typewriter and rolled it around the drum. She used no other color but yellow and had always stuck with her reliable manual despite the purported advantages of electric. She began to type.

REVA-LATIONS
Truth in Reporting—now out-moded

I am ashamed of my profession.

I am deeply, abjectly ashamed of being identified with a profession which I had thought, until now, was dedicated to digging for the truth and presenting facts to the public.

That concept, I find, is idealistic, old-fashioned and out-moded.

The cardinal rule of modern journalism is sensationalism, not accuracy.

Why waste time interviewing eyewitnesses to an event, why present a factual account when highly-colored rumors with shock-value impact are buzzing around and guaranteed to sell more newspapers, attract more listeners or viewers?

People of the Gordon community had a good and painful look last week at "big city" reporters of every media in action. They saw and heard the truth distorted beyond all belief.

The Legion club affair—the cause celebre for our recent ordeal—is a classic example.

One hundred twenty-seven people signed the register the evening in question and NOT ONE of them was interviewed by the visiting press.

Had this been done it would have established that not more than 30 seconds elapsed from the time the front door of the Legion club burst open and the victim of the cruel act was propelled inside until, immediately shielded from general view by a man who had been seated close by, he was assisted from the hall. This is a fact.

The published story is entirely different. The rumor that began to circulate a week after the affair, was never verified—but it was broadcast to the world. Not because reporters weren't aware their stories were riddled with lies. They knew—they deliberately proceeded.

One downy-faced neophyte from the *Des Moines Register* sat at a *Journal* telephone filing his story. When he started on the same "forced to dance" hearsay, an eyewitness who was in this office said, "I was there—that wasn't what happened at all." He looked up and said "that's tough" and went right on with his gossipy account.

How about Carl Akers' KBTV, Denver story?

When the AIM group came here from Omaha and other points to hold a rally and demonstration, a KBTV reporter was dispatched to Gordon. After the group had marched from the neighborhood center to the community building, the KBTV man dashed to a nearby home and asked to use the telephone to call in his story.

Imagine the utter amazement of those within earshot to hear him describe the Indians as decked out in warpaint and feathers, brandishing tomahawks and bows and arrows! He had apparently seen too many sleazy tv westerns and his imagination did the rest. Carl Akers on the 5:30 p.m. news broadcast that silly story . . . of course he was the victim of inept reporting. The only dress seen; other than ordinary attire, consisted of hippie-type garments which are pretty standard everywhere even in remote areas like Gordon, and the American flags which had been ripped from homeowners' standards along Main street and draped shawl-like around the shoulders.

It seems reporters should investigate rumors—and establish facts. This includes Paul Harvey, 'champion' of truth. Only one did, from the

New York Times, which figures. The *New York Times* has a reputation of being a responsible newspaper. The majority with representatives here were less than responsible and from henceforth all of their stories can be doubted.

I, one of the least in the field it is true, am ashamed of my profession. It is a sad day for this country when rumor, hearsay, gossip and lies take the place of verified facts in the public press.

Of the hundreds of page 2 columns Evans had written over the decades, it was perhaps her best work. However, the local Indians were not "scared half to death" as she believed. Many of them were at the auditorium listening to the speeches or testifying at the "red-feather" grand jury. If she'd gone there, she would have known that. Despite her stinging column, the "forced to dance Indian style" rumor would live on for decades.

For the Oglalas, the chance to speak at the ad hoc grand jury was cathartic. Finally, they had a forum to voice their complaints. The local leaders and Evans dismissed their stories as "exaggerations" and told the press in patronizing tones that they "treated their Indians good." Evans told an outside reporter, "These things they're saying about discrimination just aren't true. Indians are treated just like everyone else in this town."

She was living in a fantasy world.

Perhaps some of the stories were exaggerations. But many of them weren't. Either way, both sides missed an opportunity. The white citizens of Gordon could have come down to the auditorium to learn how their neighbors lived. And AIM could have welcomed them. Instead, Means's bombastic quotes went over the airwaves. Who the hell wanted to go to the auditorium and be castrated?

Evans believed Gordon was a perfect town beyond reproach, where whites and Indians lived together side by side in perfect harmony. Means believed the town was inhabited by uncaring white devils, who looked at Indians as subhuman. The truth probably lay somewhere in between.

After returning from Lincoln, Michael Smith had another potential conflagration to put out. The Legionnaires and fire department were threatening to go to the city auditorium and "clean the radicals out." The next day, Gordon's card-carrying conservatives were up in arms about the desecration of the flag. Of all the things AIM did during the occupation, the disrespect shown to the Stars and Stripes would remain burned into their memories for decades. Once again, he had to walk over to the station to cool off the hotheads.

Now, it was time to negotiate an end to the occupation.

Both sides wanted a second autopsy to put the matter to rest. AIM was accusing pathologist W. O. Brown of being a "racist" bent on covering up atrocities. Smith had seen the autopsy report and was convinced the coroner would be vindicated.

Disinterment for an Oglala family is a difficult religious decision, but Annie Eagle Fox, Amelia Comes Last, and their brother Russell finally agreed. AIM's demand that Sheridan County pay for the procedure wasn't going to happen, so the Native American Rights Fund volunteered to pay for a top-notch coroner from Denver, Dr. George O'Gura, to perform the second autopsy. John Echohawk, a Pawnee attorney from the organization's main office in Boulder, Colorado, was arriving to ensure that everything was done correctly. AIM paid for Dr. Jesse Samuels to fly in from New Haven, Connecticut, to assist. A Rapid City pathologist, Dr. Wayne Geib, would observe, along with approximately seventy others, including Russell Yellow Thunder.

As the occupation dragged on into its second day, both sides were looking for a way to bring it to an end. Smith agreed to meet with the AIM leaders at his Main Street office at 11:00 a.m. Wednesday. With him was Governor Exon's emissary Clive Short, Bob Case, and Bruce Moore.

Means, Clyde Bellecourt, and Banks entered the room shouting accusations as several of their supporters watched from outside. Once Smith convinced the AIM followers to clear the room, and the Nebraska state emissaries left, the four remaining men quieted down and began to talk. Smith was determined not to negotiate away anything that mattered.

Bellecourt was mostly quiet. Banks just sat there looking fierce. Means took the lead and again demanded that the second-degree manslaughter and false imprisonment charges be dropped and changed to murder and kidnapping. On that point, Smith would not budge. He knew murder, with the burden to prove an intentional act to kill, would never stand up in court. He'd consulted with the state's attorney general and he'd agreed. What the Hares, Bayliss, and Lutter did was horrendous, but he believed it couldn't be legally defined as anything but manslaughter and false imprisonment. Smith knew, and the AIM triumvirate knew, they needed an agreement that would allow AIM to declare victory and clear out of town.

Means, glaring at Smith from across the desk, saw the attorney as a closed-minded white man of privilege who wouldn't listen to reason. Smith betrayed no fear. And no other emotions, either. He wouldn't acknowledge that he'd done anything wrong and insisted that the investigation had been completed.

Skilled negotiators represented both sides. And both sides would receive just about everything they wanted. AIM leaders wanted a signed piece of paper that would show their followers that they'd made the white man bow, and Smith didn't want to give away anything of substance.

They agreed to the second autopsy, which was already in the works. Smith never opposed the idea and knew it would show no signs of torture or a crushed skull, but the body was buried in South Dakota, so he had no jurisdiction in the matter. He agreed to be present at the second autopsy and a press conference announcing the results.

Smith also agreed to suspend John Paul and carry out an investigation into his conduct. The locals at the ad hoc grand jury had repeatedly accused the cop of being rough with drunken Indians and sexually assaulting local Indian girls. Means insisted Paul should be suspended without pay (which never happened).

They agreed to set up a human relations council made up of local clergy and Oglala leaders. They were also to release two Oglalas recently arrested for intoxication being held in the Rushville jail. Gordon's officials were to join AIM in calling for grand jury, Justice Department, and congressional investigations into Yellow Thunder's death. And the town was to assist local Indians in running for elected office by leaving them information at the Neighborhood Center.

Smith was pleased because, in reality, he'd promised them very little. AIM leaders were pleased because they could proclaim victory.

Banks, Means, and Bellecourt returned to the city auditorium with a notarized paper in hand, declaring that they'd forced the white man to capitulate to their demands. Singing and dancing followed. The peace pipe was passed around between AIM and the reservation traditionalists, but they didn't invite Gordon town leaders to join in.

It was a paper victory. The autopsy was already being arranged. The two inmates in Rushville were released. Incarceration for intoxication usually lasted a day or two, and they had served their time. The town of Gordon and AIM's joint call for investigations wouldn't amount to anything. No one at the Justice Department or Congress was interested. And leaving information at the Neighborhood Center on how to run for local elections was easy enough.

AIM considered the suspension of John Paul a major victory. Its leaders would exaggerate its importance. History books reported that "AIM forced the police chief to be fired." In fact, John Paul was not the police chief, was never fired or suspended, and no investigation was ever carried out. Less than two months later, he was hired as a deputy sheriff for the county, which involved a raise in both pay and stature. The Hares would cry "conspiracy," claiming Paul was part of a cover-up.

Only the human relations council would survive.

Means declared "complete and total victory" at the auditorium that afternoon. Severt Young Bear was asked to sing a victory song. He wasn't sure what to sing, but he remembered a wordless song he'd once heard at a powwow. As he and the Porcupine Singers beat his forefathers' drum, the powerful melody came from his lips. The song would become the AIM anthem.

Yellow Thunder's second autopsy the following day at a Rapid City mortuary confirmed the results of the first. He died of a subdural hematoma. There was no torture, mutilation, or cigarette burns. Both pathologists agreed that the bruise on the right side of the forehead didn't amount to much. They didn't believe the mark corresponded with the hemorrhage.

As Smith observed the procedure, he was already thinking about how he would prosecute the case. The bruise would pose a problem. He knew he had a difficult trial ahead of him. He'd already convinced Lutter to testify against the others in a plea deal, but he didn't know if that would be enough. Proving even second-degree manslaughter wouldn't be easy. And this was shaping up to be the most important and high-profile case of his career. Smith was, by nature, a competitive man. That was one reason he came to western Nebraska, to do battle in court. He could have taken that desk job as a Justice Department paper pusher in Washington DC, rarely having the chance, if ever, to see the inside of a courtroom. The upright citizens of Gordon wanted to see the Hares go away; there was no doubt about it. But that didn't matter much to Smith. He wanted to win.

Echohawk and Smith faced the reporters at the Rapid City press conference to announce the autopsy's results. Means, Banks, and Clyde

Bellecourt, instrumental in spreading the false rumors to the press, were conspicuously absent.

Finally, most of the sensational rumors could be put to rest. All except the "forced to dance Indian style" one. The newspapers would continue to print that as fact, some not even bothering to stick the word "allegedly" in the sentence. For the next three decades, prominent authors and historians would regurgitate the newspaper articles and the rumor would live on. (As would the belief that Yellow Thunder was castrated and tortured. Not everyone read the *Rapid City Journal*.)

A reporter asked Echohawk if he knew how such rumors began.

"The question is then, why did these rumors start? . . . They relate to the mistrust of the Indian people to white communities. . . . There is tension due to numerous incidents, of which Yellow Thunder's death was only one. . . . No one needs to ask why there is tension when Indians are humiliated in this fashion."

By that weekend, the commander of the Nebraska American Legion arrived in Gordon to conduct his own self-serving investigation into the allegations. He cleared the Legion of all wrongdoing. Bernard Sandage would state to them, and at the upcoming trials, that Yellow Thunder had simply refused their offer of help, and once he did that, they didn't feel the need to call the police or an ambulance.

An American Legion press release later said that Sandage offered to call the police, but Yellow Thunder refused. It also said that the Gordon police arrived within ten minutes. Max Anderson's testimony would later cast doubt on that assertion. If someone had called the police, it wasn't Sandage.

The Legion's internal investigation failed to address why the post did not press charges against the Hares. A vigorous investigation into the incident may have led the police, or Yellow Thunder's family, to the old truck before he died. The truth was less sensational, but equally as tragic for Yellow Thunder. He could have been helped, but no one bothered.

Soon, another sensational rumor began circulating around the reservation. This time it involved a fourteen-year-old boy who was allegedly choked by the white proprietors at the Wounded Knee Trading Post. A group of AIM activists heading to Yellow Thunder's reburial ceremony in Porcupine broke off from the funeral procession to stop there. They invaded the trading post and private museum, looted and stole artifacts, and assaulted one of the storeowners.

AIM could no longer claim they'd "never so much as broken a window." The skirmish at the trading post would be the opening shot in a six-year war, with AIM and the "traditionalists" on one side and the federal government and "progressives" on the other. A year later, AIM would occupy Wounded Knee for seventy-one days. A small-scale dirty war would claim dozens of lives, tear the community apart, and make AIM a household word.

Gordon did change after the march, but change didn't happen overnight. There would be growing pains. But first, Michael Smith would have to find a way to convict Bayliss and the Hare brothers. It would not be a simple task.

Two Paths

Charley Allen sat in the Pine Ridge Post Office waiting for Sam Deon to come in the door with that day's installment of the life of Chief Red Cloud. It was three years after the Wounded Knee Massacre, and Allen had left journalism to take up a new career as Pine Ridge's postmaster. His fervent support for the Democrats had paid off with the appointment, thanks to the election of President Grover Cleveland and the political patronage system. He supplemented his income by opening a general store in the same building.

Although he was one of only three correspondents at the massacre, he'd received little notoriety as an "eyewitness to history." The know-nothing *Nebraska State Journal* clerk turned "reporter," William Kelley, who'd accompanied him that day, did grab a moment in the sun. He was celebrated as an "Indian fighter" after picking up a rifle and shooting his way out of the melee, putting down three braves before making good his escape, according to several soldiers. (The other imaginative reporter, Charles Cressey, made an identical claim, but no one could corroborate his story.) Wounded Knee created quite a sensation at the time, but three years later the massacre had faded from the thoughts of the general public.

Allen was keeping his writing habit alive by working on a side project. Chief Red Cloud, now so nearsighted he had to rely on one of his grandchildren to walk him to the post office, was unwittingly handing over his life story to Allen by way of the French-Canadian trader Sam Deon. The stubborn old chief had been offered a handsome sum to sell his life story to a publishing house, but he'd turned it down. So Allen and Deon conspired to do it for him.

Red Cloud came through the door that day with his hand on the shoulder of his grandson and greeted Allen as an old friend. After retrieving his mail, the chief stepped outside to sit for a spell next to Deon. The two men had been close since their days at Fort Laramie. Like Allen,

Deon had married an Oglala woman, although the Canadian spoke the language much more fluently. For six months, Deon and Red Cloud had sat outside the post office and reminisced.

"Tell me about the trouble you had with Chief Bull Bear," Deon would say, and Red Cloud, squinting through his poor eyes, seemed to peer back in time while recalling his glory days as a young warrior. After sitting a spell, the chief would grow weary of talking, take the arm of his grandson, and leave for the day. Deon would step inside where Allen sat ready to record the secondhand words.

That day, Allen had instructed Deon to move into the juicier stories. For the past few months, he'd recorded stories of the chief's fights with the Crows, Shoshones, and Utes. Deon tried to prod him into a conversation about the war for the Bozeman Trail.

"I don't want to talk of such things. We're friends with the whites now," he said. "I'm tired of talking."

And that was the end of the book. Red Cloud was happy to share his stories of fighting the Crows, but he would go no further.

Allen's plan to make a buck off Red Cloud's story came to nothing. Publishers weren't interested in Red Cloud's life prior to his victory over the U.S. Army on the Bozeman Trail. It would be one hundred years before the manuscript saw the light of day. Meanwhile, Amos Bad Heart Bull, sitting in a cabin on the reservation, continued to spend his free time drawing pictures in his accounting ledger of the way things used to be, with no dreams of book deals with New York publishers, only a desire to record stories that would otherwise be forgotten.

Red Cloud lived for another sixteen years. He didn't live fast and die young like Crazy Horse. He was the old soldier who faded away, passing in 1909 at age eighty-eight. He was a strong-willed voice for his people, forced to shepherd them through traumatic upheaval. His power as a leader faded quickly after the Wounded Knee Massacre, and no strong Oglala leader would emerge to replace him. In the year of his death, economic, cultural, and political forces were beginning to sap any hope the tribe had of creating a viable society. By the time AIM arrived at the reservation to protest Yellow Thunder's death six decades later, the once-mighty Oglalas were the poorest people in America.

Sam Hinn *(left)* and unidentified bartender pose at the Barrelhouse Tavern, Rushville, Nebraska, date unknown. (Courtesy of Sheridan County Historical Society.)

Bartlett Richards and his business partner William Comstock sat in an Omaha courtroom with their high-priced attorneys to await their verdict. It was November 13, 1905, and much had changed since the day the New Englander arrived in Sheridan County to purchase Bennett Irwin's remote spread nestled in the Sand Hills. The Spade was by then the largest ranch in Nebraska. Its territory reached from Ellsworth on the Chicago, Burlington & Quincy Railroad rail line in the south to the Chicago Northwestern line to the north. A contract supplying beef to the Pine Ridge Agency had also helped Comstock and Richards secure a lease for ten thousand acres on the reservation. But not all the land in Richards's sphere belonged to him. Much of it was in the public domain. The Spade Ranch cowboys had fenced off the unclaimed public land, and that was against the law. To ensure that no one homesteaded near vital streams and watering holes, the company recruited "friendly filers," also known as "Civil War widows." The term was a catchall moniker for anyone who could file a claim stating his or her intention to live on the property for five years. Once they "proved up," they would then sell out to Comstock and Richards's Nebraska Land and Feeding Company. The Spade also surrounded prime spots with its deeded property, stringing up barbed wire to make access to the public domain land all but impossible for would-be settlers.

A wave of Populist sentiment was sweeping over the prairie, especially among the small farmers like Old Jules Sandoz. The cattle barons were as reviled as the rail barons and the oil barons. It just wasn't a good time to be a baron.

The respectable churchgoing citizens of Gordon had their own opinions of Richards. His brother DeForest, a Chadron banker and future governor of Wyoming, had a pretty young daughter named Inez. In 1897, Bartlett took a trip with DeForest's family to Germany, where uncles marrying nieces wasn't against the law. Bartlett and Inez returned from their European trip as man and wife. Back in Gordon, the tongues began wagging.

Settlers arrived in the Sand Hills, broke the sod, and quickly went bust. The 160 acres allowed under the old Homestead Act wasn't a viable amount of land in western Nebraska, and a handful of powerful ranchers were the only ones profiting from the Lakotas' old hunting grounds. In 1904, Nebraska representative Moses Kinkaid, sticking up for the tens of thousands of farmers who made up most of the western Nebraska electorate, pushed the Kinkaid Act through Congress. Settlers in Sand Hills counties could now claim 640 acres of nonirrigable land. If they could stick it out five years and prove they made $1.25 worth of improvements per acre, the land was theirs. The law was supposed to give the "little guy" a fighting chance.

Many cattlemen refused to give up this prime rangeland easily. They tried to push the sodbusters out by waging a dirty war. Old Jules was among the grangers who pushed back. Since arriving in the county, the stubborn Swiss immigrant had been collecting fees by locating claims for settlers. As soon as the Kinkaid Act passed, he aggressively sought out plots in the public domain under the control of the Spade and Spring Lake ranches and the notorious Krause Brothers. In response to the influx of grangers, the cattlemen signed on hired guns as "ranch hands." More than a few Kinkaiders were found bullet-ridden in their fields. Witnesses to these crimes on the isolated prairie were few. John Krause shot a farmer in a fencing dispute and stood trial in Rushville. The jury believed his claim of self-defense and pronounced him "not guilty."

One day, the hired gunmen came for Old Jules's brother Emile, who'd settled a homestead on the edge of the Sand Hills. These assassins weren't too concerned about witnesses. They shot Emile down as his wife and children watched. His death was a message for Old Jules, who began toting his Winchester at his side, his reputation as a crack shot serving as a deterrent. He received some measure of revenge when he traveled to Omaha to testify in the fencing trials against the cattle barons, trials like the one where Richards and Comstock awaited their verdict in November 1905.

When Theodore Roosevelt became president in 1901, the cattle barons rejoiced. One of their own had made it to the top. Teddy knew a thing or two about the business. Before relaunching his political career, he'd been part-owner of a ranch in North Dakota. Representatives of the powerful stockman's associations had been to Washington to lobby the new president. They wanted laws on the books that would allow them to lease public lands—for no such mechanism existed.

Richards and the other cattlemen rationalized that it was okay to break the law because Sand Hills soil was unsuitable for farming. They reasoned that they were doing the small, poor farmers a favor by keeping them off the public lands. The topsoil was too thin. Once the sodbusters plowed fields in the small strips of land between the dunes, it was ruined. Farming caused blowouts, the sandy bare patches that exposed the earth like gaping wounds. Under certain conditions, the blowouts could spread like cancer.

For the grangers who wanted to try their hand at small-scale ranching, 640 acres didn't amount to much. If only there were a way to legally lease the land, then the cattle barons could legitimize their monopoly.

But Roosevelt proved to be less than sympathetic to the wealthy cattlemen's sad plight. The city slums were bursting with the unemployed, and policies to move immigrants to the countryside were in vogue. The president wanted a high-profile conviction, and Richards and Comstock were among the most egregious lawbreakers. There were accusations and suspicions that the Spade Ranch had resorted to violence after several nearby Kinkaiders died under mysterious circumstances. But for the most part, Richards's reputation as an eastern gentleman had remained intact. The business partners were nevertheless brought to court in 1905 on charges of illegally fencing more than two hundred thousand acres of U.S. government land.

Richards and Comstock's attorney advised the pair to plead guilty because they would never receive a fair trial in eastern Nebraska. Jurors there had shown little sympathy for western fat cats. He told the judge before sentencing that the company was in the process of tearing down the barbed wire. If there were any remaining fences, they must belong to the Spade's neighbors, he insisted. His clients were doing their best to comply with the law.

The judge fined Richards and Comstock three hundred dollars apiece and sentenced them to six hours in the custody of a U.S. marshal. The newspapermen on hand didn't report whether Richards rubbed his wrist from the slap he'd received.

Comstock and Richards—in the presence of their lawyer and the clerk of the district court—served their lighter-than-air sentence at the posh Omaha Club. The federal marshal who'd been tasked with overseeing the ranchers' six-hour sentence remanded them into their attorney's custody and excused himself from duty. Everyone was in a good mood. Cigars and spirits followed the steaks.

But the Populist press discovered how the wealthy ranchers had spent their six hours of punishment. The headline writers had a field day. In Washington, Roosevelt slammed a newspaper down on his desk in the Oval Office and called for the heads of the clerk, judge, and marshal. And he wasn't done with Bartlett Richards.

As the sun crept up over the horizon and the roosters crowed to greet its appearance, Andrew Yellow Thunder sent his children out to do their chores on their small patch of land next to American Horse Creek near the village of Kyle. His son, Raymond, tended to the horses and cattle, while his older sisters fetched water from the stream, named after their mother Jennie's father, the warrior turned "progressive" chief who caved into General "Three Star" Crook's demands in 1888.

The same morning seventy-five miles to the south, James Hare sent his son Dean out to tend the horses on his homestead in the heart of the Sand Hills. After their chores were finished, Raymond and Dean made their way on foot to small schoolhouses.

They spoke different languages, came from different cultures and races, but at the end of the day, life was just as tough for Dean as it was for Raymond. When the two communities arrived in the area two decades earlier, the standards of living of the white farmers in the Sheridan County countryside and the Oglalas on Pine Ridge weren't so different. The Oglalas lived in tipis and log cabins. The cabins were warm in the winter and the tipis cool in the summer.

The settlers lived in dugouts, or soddies, because lumber was scarce and expensive. The sod houses were warm in the winter and cool in the summer. Most of the Oglalas couldn't speak English, but neither could many of the Germans, Czechs, Scandinavians, and other immigrants who settled Sheridan County.

The Oglala children went to small schools with white teachers, many of whom had a hard time understanding their students' culture. Education south of the border was also basic. Schoolteachers could be as young as sixteen and needed only to pass a written test to secure a low-paying job in a one-room schoolhouse where they had to juggle multiple grades.

Both communities endured the same tiresome weather: blazing hot in the summer, freezing cold in the winter. When a blizzard swept out of the Rockies, the deep snow killed livestock on both sides of the state line. If drought withered the corn, or a swarm of voracious grasshoppers devoured the wheat, that was just too bad. Government subsidies and crop insurance were decades away.

The Oglala full bloods tended to live near their *tiospaye*, their extended families, and when times were tough, they could lean on their band to help them through rough patches. For many pioneers, all they could see near their homes were miles and miles of empty grassland.

When they needed money, they had to go to a bank for a loan, which usually involved a mortgage. If the crops failed, and they couldn't pay off their notes, they lost their homesteads.

There was one major difference between the two communities, and that was freedom. In Sheridan County, the unforgiving land weeded out the hapless, the spineless, and the brainless. Those remaining—the ones who'd survived the blizzards, the crop failures, the market collapses— would eventually do much better than the Oglalas. The settlers who went bust could at least pack up their wagons and move to better pastures. However, the Oglalas were not free people. They didn't have that option. They had no power, little control over their destiny, and few in Washington to defend their rights.

Within decades, Sheridan County would thrive while the Pine Ridge Reservation would sink into despair. Sadly, it didn't have to be that way.

When Raymond Yellow Thunder, his two brothers, and four sisters first attended the nearby day school, they spoke almost no English. They sat in their chairs bewildered by the foreign language the white adults jabbered at them. But in the 1920s and 1930s, teachers at the one-room schoolhouse did little in the way of reading, writing, and arithmetic. Vocational education and busywork took up most of the day. But there was one lesson they wouldn't forget. Students caught speaking Lakota would suffer a paddling. Indian culture was bad, Christian ways were good. Their father Andrew cut his hair short and insisted that his three sons do the same. American Horse's progressive values had been handed down.

Raymond's education ended after eighth grade. The brighter students, like his older sister Amelia, were chosen to attend boarding school in far-off locales. It was a poor reward for academic achievement. The institutions were designed to eradicate the Indian and turn the students into imitation whites. The "educators" carried out this plan through corporal punishment. The child molesters of yesteryear also found helpless victims at the boarding schools, where they were free to do unspeakable acts to children belonging to parents with no power. Graduates returned to their homes speaking English well, but they paid a dear psychological price.

The Yellow Thunders' economic survival depended on a variety of sources. They received some money through leases on their land. This money went into Andrew's individual Indian account. Any time he wanted to spend the money that belonged to him, he had to go to a subagent in his district known as the "boss farmer." The boss farmers were intended to be extension agents charged with helping the Oglalas grow crops, but their role evolved into carrying out administrative duties and promulgating BIA policies in the districts. When Andrew wanted to access money from leases, or for wages earned working at the agency, he had to go to the boss farmer and beg for it. The subagent had the right to turn down a request if he didn't feel the family needed the money. Even if the subagent decided to relinquish some funds, Andrew didn't receive cash. He would receive a voucher to be redeemed at the nearby white-owned trading post. The chit could only be used to buy the items listed by the boss farmer. Naturally, the trading post prices were high. And naturally, the boss farmers and the storeowners could make secret deals resulting in kickbacks.

The Yellow Thunder children tended a garden to add to their diet. Raymond and his brothers hunted rabbits, squirrels, and other small game to put meat on the table. The family had about sixty to seventy horses, a modest herd in those days, but another source of income. The girls picked chokecherries along the creek in the fall and pounded them into dried beef pemmican, just as their ancestors did with buffalo meat. Once or twice a year, the boss farmer would distribute rations. By this time, the commodities were more of a symbolic contribution of what the United States owed the Oglalas than a means to stave off starvation. The amount of bacon, flour, and coffee distributed wasn't enough to live on for an entire year. Yet these meager goods would be proof to some border town whites that the Indians were lazy and lived on taxpayer handouts.

The agents and the boss farmers tried to stamp out Lakota culture, but they had little success. Nearly every community had a public hall, where the community gathered to do the Rabbit and Omaha social dances. Agents banned such gatherings, but the subagents didn't have the ability to shut down every dance. When they did close a hall, the dancers would simply move to someone's home. It was the same for the Sun Dance. Agent McGillycuddy had outlawed their sacred ritual in the early 1880s, but it lived on in remote canyons out of the boss farmers' sights.

Nothing aggravated the Christian overlords more than the "give-away," though. The Oglalas' custom for sharing manifested itself several times a year, mostly during Independence Day. Ironically, the Fourth of July emerged as one of the year's biggest festivals. The Oglalas loved celebrating the independence of the country that had subjugated them. Amos Bad Heart Bull drew the parades, with riders flying American flags as they paraded through the villages. But the Oglalas had their own twist. The day's festivities included a reenactment of the Battle of the Greasy Grass, Little Big Horn, their greatest victory over the white man.

The giveaway was a time-honored tradition that taught the youngsters the Oglala ethic of sharing. The leaders, especially the traditional chiefs, would give gifts to the less fortunate. Kids received coins. Others received star quilts that had taken weeks to sew; horses, cattle, virtually anything of worth was handed out, and it was considered bad etiquette to present anything to your own family. The practice infuriated the missionaries, teachers, and agents who were trying to mold the Indians into white folks. How would they ever build up personal wealth if they gave everything away? (Apparently these devout Christians weren't familiar with the Sermon on the Mount.)

The Yellow Thunders instilled a strong work ethic in their children. Their daily chores, tending gardens and the horses, helped the family survive. Even when times were tough, the Lakota custom of sharing remained strong. The others in the American Horse *tiospaye* would help one another in times of need.

On Saturdays, they would hitch up a wagon and ride the seven miles to Kyle to shop at the trading post. Andrew didn't have to trade there. If he had cash outside the control of the boss farmer, he could find cheaper prices at Pine Ridge. And Whiteclay and Gordon had prices even lower than the agency. But those destinations were a good day's ride from Kyle, and a trip to the border towns was a once- or twice-a-year occurrence. Outside of their teachers, the white traders, ranchers, or boss farmers, the Yellow Thunders had little contact with the white folks of Sheridan County.

Cancer claimed Jennie in the early 1940s. A few years later, Andrew hitched up his team to make an unexpected weekday trip to Kyle. It had been a stormy June day, and when he didn't return, the family went out to search for him. They found him and the two horses dead beside the wagon, struck by lightning. With their parents' passing, the family land passed out of their control. The Yellow Thunder children scattered throughout the area, looking for ways to make a living.

By the time Dean Hare was born in 1923, the Spade had broken up into a patchwork quilt of smaller ranches owned by former ranch hands.

The once powerful cattle baron died in 1911 in prison. President Roosevelt had gone after the Spade Ranch owners again, and the federal government filed a thirty-five-count land fraud indictment. The felony charges were significantly more serious than illegal fencing. All the old tricks Richards had used to monopolize the public lands came to light in a trial beginning in 1906. A jury convicted Richards and Comstock, but appeals kept them out of prison until 1910. One year later, Richards died in a Hastings, Nebraska, prison from complications following surgery to remove gallstones.

Two years before Richards's death, Old Jules, perhaps sensing the rancher's predicament, staked a claim five miles north of the Spade's headquarters where he would dump off his daughter Mari and son James the following year. He would eventually move to the house in the long valley and spend the remainder of his life there.

The Spade's "empire of grass" began to disintegrate, and the ranchers blamed the government. After Richards's death, the South-hills community grew more insular. The perceived persecution of one of their own would fuel their independent, almost libertarian brand of conservatism for decades.

The Kinkaiders' day also came to an end. Ultimately, a force more powerful than the federal government, stubborn grangers like Old Jules, or the wealthy cattle barons decided who would control the Sand Hills. And that was the land itself. For the ranchers were right. The soil was good for little besides raising cattle. Old Jules planted orchards on his small spread north of the Spade to prove something other than grass could grow there, and the trees bore fruit, but the idea never caught on. The Kinkaiders sold out to the ranchers and moved away.

The small ranchers who took over the lands from the failed Kinkaiders felt little connection to the outside world. The road to Gordon was rough. They did much of their trading in Alliance to the west. Few of their hired hands were Oglalas, and the Sandhillers knew little of Indian culture. Aside from watching the Oglalas dance at the county fair, person-to-person contact with the Indians was rare. The stone arrowheads, scrapers, awls, and flint knives littering the blowouts were the only reminder of those who once hunted the land.

Dean Hare's world was this insular community. Like Raymond Yellow Thunder, he attended a one-room schoolhouse. The community made its own entertainment by throwing dances in barns where the band was whoever showed up with whatever instrument they could play. Folks were so desperate for something to do, when the cantankerous, smelly

Old Jules sponsored a barn dance to make a few dollars, he had a good turnout.

Dean's home had no electricity and no running water. Midnight trips to the outhouse in the winter would harden any man. Even before the Depression hit, the Hares never had much money. Dean's father, James, was a World War I veteran who came back from Europe after being gassed in the trenches. His neighbors knew him as a tough man. One had to be to make a living in an unforgiving land with four children to raise. The Sand Hills farmers and ranchers were in some ways protected better from the economic storm. There were gardens to provide vegetables and chicken, hogs and cattle to provide meat. Wild game, deer, ducks, and geese supplemented their diet. Dried cow manure heated their stoves and cooked their food. Hunting coyotes was part sport, part necessity. The canines had roamed the hills long before humans arrived, but the animal the Lakotas called "the trickster" was considered a pest. The county paid a bounty for their ears, so along with the thrill of the hunt, the Hares earned a little extra money as well.

A journey to Alliance or Gordon was an all-day affair that came only a few times per year. Roads cutting through the Sand Hills were little more than well-worn paths. Automobiles, still a rarity, could reduce the time of the trip as long as the tires didn't bog down in the sand.

When Dean Hare was eight years old, and the country in the throes of the Great Depression, his mother Wilma fell ill with a high fever. His father hitched a team to a wagon, for the family was too poor to own a car, put his wife in the back, and set out for Rushville. She died of appendicitis a few days later.

James Hare declined neighbors' offers to take the four young children off his hands. He did the work of two adults, the ranching, the cooking, and cleaning—too proud to accept charity. But it was too much, and James remarried a woman not of Dean's liking.

As with Raymond Yellow Thunder, Dean's education stopped at the eighth grade. His father promised him the deed to a 160-acre plot upon his death if he quit school and came to work on the homestead. And as with Raymond, the loss of his parent broke up the family. Life in his father's house became intolerable. James, who could be a mean and violent man, was no help to a suffering boy. When he was sixteen and old enough to strike out on his own, he left his father's home with nothing but the clothes on his back. He didn't go far. He ended up on the doorstep of Pat Hooper, a friend of the family and neighbor who owned a horse ranch a few miles away. Pat took him in. And Hooper's daughter, Norma Lhee, and son Sandy accepted him as part of the family.

As Sam Hinn guided his horse-drawn wagon over the sandy hill toward the homestead on the bright July afternoon, he could make out specks running toward him from the direction of the house. The dry wind carried shouts of joy over the grass to his ears. The children could spot a peddler's wagon quicker than a hawk could spot a field mouse. He gave his team a little flick of the whip to hurry them up. The horses' reward would be a cool drink of water. The sun was high and bright enough to wash the colors out of the hills. Horseflies had harassed him for miles. There hadn't been rain in weeks.

All over the Sand Hills, makeshift dwellings constructed of lumber or sod had sprung up like black toadstools on the tan-colored grasslands. Most of the residents were Kinkaiders, trying to eke out a meager living from the marginal land. They were poor, but they still needed supplies. Gordon, Rushville, and Hay Springs were a day's ride. The Sears Roebuck catalog required planning. Small country stores, like the one owned by Old Jules, had few items, but could also be a long trek. So itinerant peddlers like Hinn provided a much-needed service.

The children, huffing and puffing, their hair clumped with sweat, reached the wagon as they screamed out Sam's name. The kids knew, and Sam knew, that their parents were known to buy some sweets, and undoubtedly these barefoot rascals, their faces dirty from playing in the fine dust all day, were hoping their folks had a few extra pennies for a stick of licorice. A towheaded boy hopped up on the passenger side as the others tagged along. Hinn smiled, laughed, and teased them in broken English.

Not every child on his route was so happy to see him. Some looked at Hinn with hard eyes. They knew their parents were too poor to indulge in a treat. They tossed rocks at his wagon, called him "Dago" because of his dark complexion. But Sam wasn't Italian. He was from Ain Arab, Syria.

Hinn had stepped off the boat at Ellis Island shortly before the turn of the century at the age of fifteen. He had little but a smattering of English and the address of relatives in Ottumwa, Iowa. At the advice of his cousins, he made his way west, doing various jobs in Nebraska and Wyoming until he wound up in Rushville where he invested his savings in a peddler's wagon. He crammed it with every necessity and sundry a pioneer could need: bolts of cloth, medicines, tonics, spices, flour, yeast, perfume, harmonicas, ink, combs, mirrors, pots, needles and thread, hammers and nails, silk handkerchiefs for the ladies, and tobacco, pipes, and paper for the men. Every nook and cranny of the wagon was stuffed with every anticipated need.

As he pulled up to the soddy, the lady of the house stepped outside to greet him. Hinn said "hello" with a big grin. He was always friendly, even to those who never bought. Some day they might. And there were other Syrians plying the same back roads. It wouldn't do to be unfriendly or to cheat one of the impoverished settlers.

The Czech immigrant invited him inside, always a good sign, for him and the children, who were hanging on his arms. There were few distractions in the summertime and Hinn's arrival would be the most exciting part of their day. The lady of the house, who spoke broken English as he did, needed some cloth. He brought in a few bolts and she bought a half-dollar's worth, which was enough for him to hand out some complimentary licorice sticks to the children.

After watering the horses and finishing his business, he set out for the next rustic hovel, which stood only a few miles away. The children tagged along as far as they could walk. It was several hours until sunset. He usually spent the night wherever he arrived when the sun went down, paying for his room and board in cash or goods. He had several stops before then, for it was a long summer day. The more stops, the more potential profit.

Sam Hinn plied the Sand Hills in his wagon until the roads became better and the automobile age arrived. Trips to Gordon or Rushville were by then a once-a-week occurrence rather than a few times a year. By the mid-1920s, the age of the Kinkaider was finished. The abandoned soddies and dugouts collapsed, eroding over the decades back into the soil like melting hail on a warm spring day. Gravity and wind took the wooden hovels, reducing them to piles of rotting boards.

Hinn saw the change coming and invested his savings in a pool hall in Rushville. He would start other business ventures as well, and loyal customers who knew him from his days as a peddler traded with him when they came to town. To succeed in the white man's world he knew he had to assimilate. He converted from Eastern Orthodox to Catholicism, for Rushville was a Catholic town. He married a Syrian woman named Helen, and they would have seven children, but he didn't allow Arabic to be spoken in his house. It was English only. When World War II broke out, his four oldest boys all served proudly. And his fifth went to Korea.

Merchants in Gordon and Rushville like Hinn began to thrive as the automobile changed the way the farmers and ranchers did business. Every Saturday was like Christmas to the shopkeepers. The Oglalas, escaping the economic control of the boss farmers, made their way to Whiteclay, Rushville, and Gordon as well to purchase what they needed at better prices and, in some cases, to secure whiskey from bootleggers. Even after the end of Prohibition, selling alcohol to Indians remained illegal.

Ferd Shald, a hulking German-American from Stuart, Nebraska, came to the area as an itinerant butcher, traveling from homestead to homestead like Sam Hinn, selling his skills until he settled in Gordon in 1927 where he found a full-time job in the butchery of a general store. The already large Shald grew larger hauling slabs of meat in the locker. In 1930, he bought his employer's store on Main Street and married Susan Sears's granddaughter Gladys Trueblood, who gave birth to nine children.

The soil on the flattop land stretching from Gordon to Rushville was fertile ground for potatoes. When the harvest came, the farmers needed cheap labor, and lots of it. Entire families descended from the reservation to work as seasonal laborers. The day schools cancelled classes, and the reservation became eerily empty. The Oglalas pitched their canvas tents on farms, and at the edge of Gordon, working from sunup to sundown. There was money to be made, money the boss farmer could not control. Some of the Oglalas who came for the potato harvest or the Sheridan County Fair stayed behind and searched for year-round menial labor. A tent community sprang up on the southeast side of town over the railroad tracks, near the sale barn where the ranchers came to buy, sell, and trade livestock.

The border town merchants' accounts grew fat from several sources. They had the country folk arriving by buggies or Model T's on Saturdays, the townspeople all week, and the Indian trade when they had some cash to spend.

In 1937, Hinn bought the Barrelhouse Saloon in Rushville and renamed it the Stockman's Bar. As a distributor of liquor, Hinn sold truckloads of booze that made its way to the reservation. He and his sons adopted a "just don't tell us what you're doing with it" attitude when the bootleggers came down to stock up for trips to Whiteclay and the reservation.

Raymond Yellow Thunder was born into a long line of horsemen. The Oglalas had once used their equine knowledge and skills to conquer the upper plains. Tribes with large herds in the pre-reservation era had both wealth and prestige. And Andrew Yellow Thunder, the descendant of Oglala men who depended on the horse to hunt and wage war, passed his knowledge on to his sons. The Yellow Thunders kept a small herd of horses and a few cattle on their land next to American Horse Creek. In the early part of the century, that wasn't uncommon, even for the full bloods. The "friends of the Indians" who'd wanted to turn the Lakotas into farmers when the reservation was settled simply had the wrong strategy. Most of the reservation land was marginal for tilling the soil, but the Pine Ridge prairie was a rancher's paradise. The Lakotas were natural cowboys, so the tribe's cattle and horse herds began to grow, with the mixed bloods and intermarried white men leading the way.

The Oglalas had gardens, small herds (although they couldn't slaughter their own cattle unless they had permission from a boss farmer), small game to hunt, and seasonal harvesting work in Nebraska. Full bloods could join the Indian police force or work on roads. Mixed bloods took jobs teaching in schools or as clerks at white-owned trading posts. Apart from the token treaty rations, there was no welfare or food stamps on the reservation.

By the time Raymond was born in 1921, the brief period of self-sufficiency on the reservation was nearly over. When World War I broke out, beef and leather prices skyrocketed. Watching all that Indian land "go to waste" supporting Indians was too much for the South Dakota and Nebraska ranching outfits to bear. They made a deal with a corrupt agent to "lease" the ranchland on the Pine Ridge Agency. The Oglalas could only watch as the white ranchers ran herds onto their pastures, mixing their cattle with that of the Oglalas, trampling their gardens, tearing down fences, fouling up their clear streams with cow dung. The agent decided the Oglalas, who had no economic or political power, should be responsible for collecting the grazing fees. Naturally, the ranchers forgot to put their checks in the mail. By the end of the Great War, a white man-made disaster had ruined the thriving Oglala livestock industry.

They had no cattle, and soon they would have no pastures. The General Allotment Act, which General "Three Stars" Crook rammed down the Lakotas' throats in 1888, had slowly begun to take away all they had left: their land. The Oglalas never wanted the act, but they suffered its insidious consequences. At first, many tribal members refused to accept their allocations. But the federal government began divvying up the land anyway in 1904. When the head of the household who held the title to his 160-acre allotment passed away, it was divided among his children. Soon, the allotment was too small to be of any use. Agent John Brennan, who owned cattle himself and had a cozy relationship with the South Dakota Stockgrowers Association, devised a leasing plan. The nearby ranchers had been illegally running their cattle on reservation land for years, but now they had a legal way to exploit the grassland. The lease money was divided up and put into accounts controlled by the boss farmer. The owners of the land had no say on who could lease their property and how much they should be paid per acre.

The mixed bloods were also given land, sometimes against their will. Some of these tribal members went off to fight in the trenches of Belgium in World War I and returned to find their allotted land repossessed for nonpayment of taxes and sold to a white farmer or rancher. The mixed bloods became a landless class and began gravitating toward Pine Ridge where the whites were more apt to give them jobs.

The General Allotment Act also allowed for "surplus land" to be sold to homesteaders. The valuable, farmable flattop land in the reservation's southeast quarter was hence declared "surplus." Whites grabbed enough of this prime land to organize Bennett County and cede themselves from the reservation. One-fourth of the reservation was gone, and only a few patches of trust land remained there. The U.S. government wasn't finished grabbing land from the Oglala. Later in the century, it would requisition land for a military firing range and take the Badlands for a national park.

But first, another white man would arrive in Lakota country promising a new order. Once again the adult males would be asked to vote for something they did not want. The result would be a growing schism between the full bloods and mixed bloods that would tear the reservation apart.

Old Jules Sandoz's life was coming to an end in 1928. His eldest daughter, Mari, had traveled from her small apartment in Lincoln to be at his bedside in Alliance. The tough immigrant whose violent temper once struck fear into his family was now a frail man lying in a dingy hospital ward. Mari was by then a struggling writer. She'd married an older neighbor while still young to escape her father's house, but she dreamed of a life of letters in bigger cities, so after five years she divorced her husband and moved to Lincoln to reinvent herself, never mentioning the marriage to any of her new friends.

Her father had never supported any of her efforts to make a life of her own. When she was sixteen, she had to sneak away to Rushville to take a teaching qualification test. When she was twelve and had a story published in an Omaha newspaper's children's page, he beat her and threw her in the cellar.

She arrived east with a headful of stories heard from men stopping at her father's first homestead along the Niobrara: cowboys, Indians, freighters, hunters, and homesteaders. There was little to do on the prairie in those days other than listen to their tales. Living in a spartan Lincoln apartment, she began to put these recollections on paper. When one of her stories set in the Sand Hills won a contest in a national magazine, Old Jules sent her a slap in the face by way of the U.S. mail.

"You know I've always considered writers and artists the maggots of society," he wrote.

As Mari looked down at her sick father, she had to wonder at the hold he had over her. Old Jules. Straight Eye. American. Immigrant. Iconoclast. Wife beater. Child beater. Friend of the Indians. Enemy of the cattle barons. Amateur horticulturist. A community builder, but hated by his neighbors. Lazy, smelly, gimpy, unshaven, tobacco juice–spitting Old Jules.

Despite his meanness, he was still her "papa."

Old Jules looked up at this daughter from his deathbed and said, "Why don't you write something about my life?"

It was the first time he'd ever encouraged her to write anything. What was behind this change? A dying man's bid for immortality? If that were the case, he would receive his wish.

After Old Jules passed away, Mari returned to Lincoln to record her father's life story. Through the lean Depression years, she wrote and revised; sent out manuscripts, only to have them rejected; revised and sent them out again.

In 1935, *Old Jules* beat out 582 other manuscripts and won the prestigious *Atlantic Press* nonfiction contest, which came with a $5,000 prize, a nice sum in the middle of the Depression for a struggling writer. *Old Jules* was historically accurate, but told in a literary style. It was chosen for the Book-of-the-Month Club, and soon the Swiss immigrant became the epitome of the tough homesteader, since Mari pulled no punches while portraying her father. The reading public learned about the little-known patch of America known as the Sand Hills, and along with it the history of Sheridan County, the rivalry between the farmers and the ranchers, and a bit about the Lakotas, including the tragedy at Wounded Knee.

Mari's career took off. Her fascination and love of Native American culture led her to write a biography of Crazy Horse. *Cheyenne Autumn* told the story of Chief Dull Knife and his people's escape from Indian Territory. *These Were the Sioux*, a cultural history of the Lakotas, followed. She wrote histories of the cattlemen, the fur trappers, and the buffalo hunters. She scandalized the upright citizens of Gordon when she published a novel, *Slogum House*, which depicted a tyrannical woman who ran a house of ill repute in a fictional county called Dumur. The county seat of the same name was easily recognizable as Gordon. The Southhillers were always scandalizing the Gordonites, it seemed. First Bartlett Richards married his niece, and then came *Slogum House*.

In March 1934, at Rapid City, South Dakota, a slight, bespectacled man stood before hundreds of tribal representatives from throughout the upper plains and told them a new day was dawning between the U.S. government and the American Indians.

Sitting quietly in their chairs were chiefs and elders from Lakota bands representing every reservation. Sitting with them were Cheyennes, Shoshones, and members of other tribes from nearby states. Boss farmers, agents, BIA bureaucrats, mixed bloods, and white priests and ministers from all the churches with flocks on the reservations had also come to hear what this rather ordinary-looking man had to say.

He told them the General Allotment Act was an abject failure. It was time to put the land that had melted away into white hands back into community ownership. It was also time to let the Indians govern themselves. Each tribe, if it agreed, would have a president and a council elected by the people. No more edicts from Washington. "Sovereignty" was the word. Furthermore, Indians would be allowed to live as they saw fit. They would be permitted to practice their own religion and speak their own language. The Lakotas could even practice the sacred Sun Dance without fear of arrest.

A murmur went through the crowd. Who was this man? Was he serious? Bring back the Sun Dance? Practice their own religion! The Catholic and Episcopal brothers fidgeted uncomfortably in their cassocks.

Even more astounding than the speaker's revolutionary ideas was the fact that he was the new Indian commissioner.

John Collier had been a critic of the Bureau of Indian Affairs and its principal gadfly since he fell in love with Indian culture in the 1920s. When the Democrats came into power with their "New Deal," President Franklin Delano Roosevelt appointed Collier to see if the critic could straighten out the disaster known as the reservation system.

Before Collier arrived in Rapid City for the two-day conference, he'd already been warned by the Rosebud agent that his self-government plan might not work with the Lakotas. What worked for the Navajos in the Southwest or the Seminoles in Florida might not be the best fit for the Sioux in South Dakota. By that time, the schism between mixed and full bloods had grown deeper than ever. Direct elections might tip the balance of power in favor of the more numerous, landless mixed bloods, he was warned.

But Collier delivered his proposals anyway. He was there to listen to their ideas and was open to suggestions, he insisted. And he received plenty of them from all sides. The Catholic Lakotas were afraid of losing federal government funding for their schools. The white and mixed-blood landholders were afraid the "communists" would take over their property. The full bloods were afraid the mixed bloods would seize political power. In short, everyone was afraid of the unknown. Besides, Pine Ridge had just written a new constitution and formed the Oglala Tribal Council based on the consensus style of government they'd practiced for hundreds of years. The reservation was a mess, but at least it was a mess they understood.

Collier was an idealist, though. His vision was to wipe out poverty on the reservations. He returned to Washington with his one-size-fits-all approach to lifting the Indian out of squalor. As the bill that would soon be known as the Indian Reorganization Act wound its way through Congress, senators and representatives with vested interests in the status quo made amendments and struck lines. No matter what version Congress passed, the new law would have to be put to a referendum. So the BIA launched a public information campaign by sending representatives to reservations like Pine Ridge to do chalkboard discussions explaining the benefits of the new plan. The plan envisioned by Collier, anyway.

The landless mixed bloods who'd put down roots in Pine Ridge village favored the law, which made the full bloods suspicious. It was an old schism with a new label. It was "hostiles" and "friendlies" during the Indian Wars, "progressives" and "nonprogressives" in the early years of the reservation, and now became "Old Dealers" and "New Dealers."

During the preceding forty years, the mixed-blood population had grown exponentially. While many mixed bloods did not own land, their economic clout on the reservation had grown as the white bureaucrats who ran the reservation favored them for better-paying jobs. There were full bloods who favored the New Deal, and mixed bloods who opposed it, but the schism was now largely seen as a matter of blood quantum.

In late 1935, a referendum on a new constitution passed by a two-hundred-vote margin. The New Dealers had won. A watered-down version of Collier's utopian vision became law. The Sun Dance returned to Pine Ridge. But there was a restriction: no piercings.

In addition, the new tribal council and tribal president could pass new laws, but not without the "review" of the reservation's agent (now called a superintendent). Any law that would in any way affect a white resident would be subject to the BIA commissioner's approval as well. Self-government was, in fact, a sham.

And the full bloods were ultimately right. The mixed bloods seized power, and Frank Wilson, a Bennett County resident who grew up in Lawrence, Kansas (possibly as little as one-eighth Lakota), became the first tribal president. Wilson attempted to pass a series of laws designed to wipe out traditional culture. Graft, corruption, and nepotism took hold immediately. Collier's sham "sovereignty" was sticking the proverbial square peg into the round hole. The "us and them" feelings between the "progressives" and "nonprogressives" grew deeper. Collier's dream to wipe out poverty on the reservation was a beautiful one, but it was every bit the abject failure that the General Allotment Act was.

Norma Hooper, her brother Sandy, and Dean Hare explored the Sand Hills together, completing chores, riding horses through the grasslands, doing all the things kids did to occupy their time in the middle of nowhere during the Depression.

The Hoopers were a family of horse tamers, and had been for generations. Pat Hooper started out as a hand at the Spade, then bought his own property nearby when Richards's empire began to crumble. Theirs was a literate family that believed in education. Books by Nebraska's most famed writer, Willa Cather, as well as others by Pearl Buck and Jack London, lined their shelves. Norma attended a one-room schoolhouse where Mari Sandoz's youngest sister Caroline was her seventh-grade teacher. Norma enjoyed a happy childhood. Her father made enough money raising horses to live comfortably, or as comfortably as one could live on the desolate prairie in the first half of the century.

Dean arrived on the ranch with a streak of bitterness in his heart, but Norma saw the good in him. She knew his young life had been rough. As they grew older, their friendship grew into something more. In 1942, when they were both eighteen, they eloped to Mullen, Nebraska, in nearby Hooker County.

It was a stormy union. Raising livestock was all Dean knew. He'd failed his army physical, and didn't go to war, so he spent their first years of marriage working at a series of low-paying cowboy jobs, dragging Norma from ranch to ranch, earning little while living in hired-hands' quarters. Dean was easily angered, frustrated that life had dealt him bad cards, and that anger turned violent. Norma, a strong-willed young woman and Dean's intellectual superior, would retreat to her parents' home when the arguments grew intolerable, but she always returned to Dean.

Their firstborn, Leslie Dean Hare, arrived two years after they were married. Norma took Les with her and moved to Gordon to look for work, leaving Dean in the South Hills. When she returned to him, things weren't much better. Two years after Les was born, when the marriage was nearly at its end, their second son, Melvin Pat Hare, arrived.

During a particularly violent fight in October 1946, Dean shook Norma, twisted her arm, and smacked her so hard she nearly passed out. A month later, her doctor advised her to leave his house and return to her parents' ranch. Dean showed up at the Hooper residence angry as a badger, and the pair quarreled until dawn. That was their last night together.

A judge found Dean guilty of all of Norma's allegations and granted her a divorce on the grounds of extreme cruelty. Although she expressed fear for the safety of her children, he allowed Dean normal visitation rights, declining to spell out exactly what that meant.

Norma married Bob Strasburger, the son of another former ranch hand who'd bought a piece of the Spade. When Pat was six, the family moved to Kansas City, Missouri, so Norma could study for a teaching certificate at Calvary College.

Les went back and forth between his mother's home and his father's leased property on the banks of the Niobrara River. Norma did everything she could to raise Les as a gentleman—dressing him in nice clothes, teaching him Sunday-school manners—to ensure that the Hare mean streak wasn't passed down to a third generation. But every time Les returned to Dean, his dad tried to take the "sissy" out of him, attempting to undo Norma's influence. As a boy, Les worshiped his father. Life with Dean meant hunting, fishing, and chasing coyotes in the Sand Hills. Was there any doubt which life a boy would choose?

Pat rarely went along. In fact, he barely knew the man whose last name he bore. Perhaps it was because Pat was delivered toward the end of the marriage that Dean never believed his secondborn was his son or wanted much do with him. When stepfather Bob Strasburger would not claim him either, that left Les as the only male who accepted Pat. And so Pat learned to follow Les everywhere. Even into a dark used-car lot hunting for human prey.

Highway 20. March 1954. Somewhere just east of Chadron, Nebraska. Sometime in the middle of the night. Robert "Curly" Walton was riding shotgun as his buddy Mickey Shelley drove out of town toward Gordon in their four-door sedan. The roads were better. The cars were faster. Gas was cheap, and young men from Gordon in their early twenties had money to spend. Cruising the border towns was the new thing. Gordon to Rushville to Hay Springs to Chadron, and back again, stopping at each one to take a spin up the main drag, keeping an eye out for the cops, looking for cars full of girls doing the same. Curly and Mickey began the

evening drinking at an American Legion dance in Rushville, then grew tired of the scene and lit out for Chadron.

As they approached the edge of town, the pair spotted an Indian guy about their age with his thumb out. Standing next to him was a dark-skinned girl, a bit younger, with her arms crossed. She was cute, so they pulled over to give them a ride.

Twenty-eight-year-old Ward Red Hawk had been out drinking as well, starting the night off in Whiteclay with three pals and his sixteen-year-old sister, Jessie, tagging along. One of his running partners had wheels, so they piled in and drove the back roads to an Indian camp in Chadron where they continued to party in canvas tents. Jessie didn't drink and begged her intoxicated brother to take her back to Pine Ridge, so they walked to the highway where Ward stuck out his thumb.

After driving a mile or so, Curly looked back at Ward. "Hey, I wanna get in the back seat with your sister," he announced.

"She's just a kid," Ward told them as the car rolled to a stop. Jessie and Ward jumped out and fled into a pasture as Curly shouted a string of obscenities at them.

Ward and his sister spent a half hour walking blindly through the soggy fields as the car's headlights, like a pair of cat's eyes, hunted for them up and down the highway and gravel county roads. The car at last sped off toward Rushville. They came out of hiding and started back toward Chadron, walking in a ditch for a while until Ward decided the white boys had given up on them. A trucker ignored his frantic waving and rushed by, but they were both relieved when the next car slowed down. As it pulled over, they realized it belonged to their tormentors.

"You better get in the car or I'll bash your head in!" Mickey told Ward as Curly grabbed Jessie by the arm and pushed her in the back seat.

Mickey hung a U-turn and headed east again as Jessie tried to push Curly's hands off her dress. Ward could only stare straight ahead, scared, shamed, humiliated, as the two struggled in the back. Jessie scratched Curly's face, making him angrier.

Ward heard the back door open. Air rushed in with a roar.

Jessie's body hit the blacktop, flopping for a few yards until the bumper of an oncoming car slammed into her. She died instantly.

Walton and Shelley hired attorney Charles Fisher to defend them. The portly attorney had been practicing in western Nebraska since the Depression and knew the territory. At the trial in Chadron, Curly Walton claimed he had no idea how Jessie Red Hawk flew out of the car. Shelley and Ward Red Hawk testified that they'd been looking straight ahead. Did Walton push her out of anger, or did she jump to escape a sexual assault? The judge gave the jury, comprising eight white housewives and four white men, a choice: they could find them innocent or convict them of manslaughter, assault and battery, or leaving the scene of an accident. The jury chose "assault and battery" for Curly Walton. The judge, expressing his unhappiness with the jurors' decision, had no choice but to sentence Walton to a mere six months in jail. Shelley received six months for leaving the scene of an accident.

Gordon Journal editor and publisher Reva Evans had a problem. This was usually the case when her beloved town's reputation was being besmirched. She dutifully reported the two Gordon men's arrest for the death of Jessie Red Hawk, but later couldn't find the time to file a story about their trial or conviction. Ten days after their arrest, she had a bigger story in her own backyard.

Like most border town episodes, it began with a night of drinking.

Vincent Broken Rope, his wife, and a few buddies were driving around Gordon knocking back bottles of fortified wine. They pulled over in a parking lot on the southeast side, near "Indian town" where the temporary village of canvas tents had become a year-round Oglala settlement. A frightened white woman phoned in a noise complaint, bringing police chief Clarence "Sailor" Lane over to the "wrong side of the tracks." Broken Rope was a World War II infantryman who'd fought in Normandy, North Africa, Sicily, and the Rhineland, receiving a good conduct medal, a Purple Heart, and a Bronze Star for serving his country. Lane was a hard-nosed former boxer. The police chief and his deputy Merle Spindler had reputations for being rough with Indians.

Lane flashed his lights, signaling Broken Rope to pull over. He ordered him out of the car and told him to go sit by the cruiser, which he did without complaint. When Lane told Broken Rope's wife to step out, she refused. Lane grabbed her by the arm, and Broken Rope ran over to stop him. Lane whipped out a blackjack and took a swing at the vet's head. The police chief later testified that he felt something graze against his abdomen as the Indian swung wildly before turning to run away. Lane pulled out his gun and shot three times. The third bullet ripped through Broken Rope's side and brought him down face first onto the gravel road. His wife jumped out of the car and came at Lane with a screwdriver. He briefly considered shooting her, but thought better of it and wrenched the tool out of her hand.

Lane radioed Spindler for backup, and when his deputy arrived the police chief produced a knife he claimed came from Broken Rope's hand. Lane had a bruise and a scratch on his abdomen, but the wound, wherever it had come from, hadn't drawn blood.

The two cops loaded the bleeding Broken Rope into a cruiser and drove him to the police station to book him before taking him to the hospital. The veteran foot soldier, who'd made it through three bloody campaigns against the fascists, didn't survive his encounter with Chief Lane. He spent five weeks in the hospital before dying from the gunshot wound.

Reva Evans's initial story on Broken Rope's death included a detailed account of his drinking that night, but not a word about his distinguished service record. For such a resolute patriot as Evans, this was a glaring omission. She felt no need to mention Chief Lane by name or the fact he'd shot Broken Rope in the back. (As if there were a single citizen in the town who didn't know the identity of the police chief. Still, she wouldn't want to embarrass him.) To call the *Gordon Journal*'s reporting on the matter "biased" would have been charitable. Meanwhile, Evans's rival, Rushville's *Sheridan County Star*, included all these facts in front-page stories.

Gordon held a coroner's inquest, appointing five white merchants, including Ferd Shald, to determine if the town should take disciplinary action against Lane. Several white residents who'd witnessed the confrontation from their nearby homes testified that they'd never heard Lane say "halt." A couple of bystanders who'd arrived just after Broken Rope fell said they hadn't seen a knife. Despite the excessive use of force, the white men absolved Chief Lane of all wrongdoing. Only then did Evans print his name.

The Oglala Tribal Council passed a resolution condemning the finding and threatened to boycott Gordon's businesses if Lane wasn't dismissed. The BIA "studied" the circumstances surrounding the deaths of Broken Rope and Red Hawk, but the inept, corrupt agency had no power outside the reservation.

It was 1954. The civil rights movement rising in the South hadn't touched northwestern Nebraska. Blatantly biased reporting, whitewashed coroner's inquests, cops shooting unarmed Indians in the back, and signs on public bathrooms declaring "No Dogs or Indians Allowed" were the norm in Sheridan County. The notion of Indians marching down the street to demand justice was still eighteen years away.

Beneath the soil in a small graveyard on the Pine Ridge Reservation, Amos Bad Heart Bull's book of drawings lies next to his sister, Dollie Pretty Cloud.

The graduate student, Helen Blish, who'd brought the ledger to light, made good on her promise to return the book. She studied it for thirteen years, paying Pretty Cloud a rental fee while she analyzed its hundreds of meticulously drawn pictographs, each a window into a world that had vanished. Blish had completed a master's thesis based on the book, and there were hopes that the complete ledger and its drawings could be published, but there were no funds around for such an undertaking in the middle of the Depression. Blish unexpectedly died in 1941; then Pretty Cloud followed her in 1947. It was the Oglala elder's wish that the book go with her, and so her beloved brother's ledger was interred six feet under the prairie.

The University of Nebraska Press finally had the funds to take on the project in the 1950s and asked Pretty Cloud's family if they could retrieve the ledger from its resting place. The answer from Pretty Cloud's family was "no." Disinterment was taboo for the Lakotas. The book was precious to Pretty Cloud, and her family would respect her wishes.

In 1966, Mari Sandoz passed away of cancer in New York City, as far as one could be from the Sand Hills. Never again would an author write so lovingly of the two neighboring communities. In the 1930s, one of Blish's professors had the foresight to photograph the Bad Heart Bull ledger. They were black and white photos, but they were better than nothing. One of Sandoz's final published works was an introduction to Blish and Bad Heart Bull's *A Pictographic History of the Oglala Sioux*. Now long out of print, it sits mostly forgotten in stacks of university libraries, wedged between other 970s in the Dewey decimal system, waiting to be discovered again.

Native American activists march through downtown Alliance, Nebraska, May 25, 1972. (Courtesy of Knight Museum, Alliance, Nebraska.)

Thunder in the Courthouse

ow that the family crisis was over, twelve-year-old Dennis Yellow Thunder returned to school. As he walked up to the schoolhouse doors, the other students were talking noisily, smiling and laughing, but his heart was full of grief and hate. His uncle Raymond would no longer bring him paint, drawing pads, and colored pencils. He remembered how Uncle Raymond and his father had pooled their money to buy him a pony, bridle, and saddle when he was seven years old. It was Raymond who taught him how to ride.

Now his uncle's grave was covered in flowers and sage; hundreds of people had gathered to bury him again after the second autopsy, most of them strangers. Russell and Amelia Yellow Thunder tried to shield Dennis from the pain. His parents didn't allow him to attend either funeral or to march with AIM into Gordon. Russell was a quiet, peaceful man like his older brother. And like his older brother, he drank hard and worked hard. He was deeply hurt and shocked over the circumstances of his brother's death. He would attend the upcoming trial, but after that he would rarely speak of the tragedy.

Dennis had never seen color before. His childhood friends were both Oglalas and the sons of white farmers who lived nearby. Two of his best pals had been Harold and Wayne Sipp, white kids his own age who lived nearby. They'd grown up together, exploring the prairie, fishing in the lake, sitting next to each other on the school bus. Only half of the students in his school were Oglalas.

Now, Dennis saw color. He saw it clearly. His parents' efforts to protect him failed. He'd been told how his uncle had been brutalized, humiliated, tortured by white men who despised Indians. A hatred festered inside Dennis, spreading over his soul.

He stepped inside the school and made his way to the restroom, where he walked up to the first white boy he saw and unleashed a punch, hitting him squarely on the nose. He once considered the kid a buddy, but that didn't matter. The other boys gathered around, screaming, not knowing or caring what the fight was about. Dennis's victim fought back until the white principal barged in and broke them up. He grabbed the pair by the arms and escorted them to the locker room where he handed them boxing gloves.

"All right, you boys want to fight, then go to it," he said, without bothering to ask what had started the scrap. The other kid put up a good fight. Dennis was fueled by rage, though, and kept pounding him until he'd had enough.

If the principal thought that he'd settled the matter, he was terribly wrong. Dennis came back to school the next day and started another fight with another white kid. The anger would eat away at Dennis for years until it nearly consumed him. He fought. Took drugs. Got expelled from school. He was headed for an early violent death or life in prison until a medicine man saw what his parents and teachers did not and rescued him.

The Hares, deep in the Sand Hills, felt under siege.

At the time of her sons' arrest, Norma Hooper was living on her parents' ranch near the Old Spade, helping her ailing mother after her father's death. Les and Pat had been forced to leave Colorado and move to the ranch while awaiting trial. Since February, lifelong friends had abandoned them. People they'd known all their lives refused to say "hello" when they saw them in Gordon. They changed their phone number. They peered out from behind the window blinds with suspicion at any car approaching.

Norma was convinced that her sons were innocent. She never believed that they would do such a thing. They were actually trying to help the Indian at first, they insisted. It was just a prank that had gone wrong. They did take his pants off and throw him into the Legion Hall, but they never harmed that old Indian, they told her with tears in their eyes. She believed them and mortgaged her cattle to raise the bail and retain the lawyers.

The cantankerous Dean Hare, however, refused to contribute a nickel. Norma blamed Dean for making Les "rough." As a young woman, she'd seen how James Hare had passed his meanness on to his son Dean.

It was like a hereditary disease, and she was certain she'd done everything to raise her sons as gentlemen, like the upright cattlemen she'd admired as a girl.

After Norma divorced Dean in 1944, he'd remarried twice and raised three more boys with a third wife. They were all teenagers and were faring better in school than Pat and Les ever did. The middle boy, Miles, was considered one of the most gifted athletes Gordon High School had ever produced. Dean had inherited some money, but he wasn't giving any of it up to pay for a lawyer. In fact, he wouldn't attend the upcoming trial.

Dean had become a bitter man. He could be charming and entertaining with his customers when trying to trade a horse, but everyone knew not to end up on his bad side. Pat Vinton, a neighbor he blamed for injuring one of his cattle in a fencing dispute, found this out when Dean and Les encountered him on a dirt road near their properties. Dean jumped out of his pickup and sicced one of his greyhounds on him. As Les watched Vinton struggle with the dog on the ground, his father planted a cowboy boot in Vinton's crotch. At the hospital later that day, doctors had to remove one of his irreparably damaged testicles. Everyone in town knew the story.

Norma retained Chadron lawyers Charles Fisher and son Charles Frank Fisher to defend her boys. The senior Fisher was in his sixties and had been practicing law in the Panhandle for decades. In 1954, during the Jessie Red Hawk trial, Fisher had managed to get Curly Walton and Mickey Shelley off with light, six-month sentences. Fisher also had a reckless driving charge against Les dismissed in Gordon.

But this was no driving infraction.

And it was no longer 1954.

Michael Smith sat in his Main Street office and sorted through his mail. A white envelope from a far-off city where he knew no one and a return address with the name of a stranger tipped him off that he'd received another piece of "fan mail." He quickly ascertained that it was from another misinformed yahoo who'd read about Yellow Thunder in the newspaper and concluded that he wasn't doing a very good job. He tossed it in a cardboard box with the hundreds of other missives. Some of the letters were insulting, some were threatening. A few were thoughtful. One fellow from St. Louis claiming to have clairvoyant powers said he knew the "true story" behind Yellow Thunder's death and he would be leaving for Gordon "that Thursday" and Smith should expect him to drop by the office. Of course, he never did.

Even with all the free advice from the concerned citizens of America, Smith still had a tough case ahead of him. The preliminary hearing had gone well. On March 24 at the Sheridan County courthouse, Judge Wendall Hills found enough evidence to bind the Hares over for arraignment in district court. Testifying was Officer John Paul, the pathologist W. O. Brown, American Legion Hall manager Bernard Sandage, and Bernard "Butch" Lutter.

Turning the itinerant carpenter against his buddies had been relatively easy once Max Ibach, the state patrol investigator, discovered that Lutter's uncle was a longtime sheriff in neighboring Cherry County. His uncle talked some sense into his nephew, and Lutter agreed to testify. In exchange, the manslaughter charge against him was dropped, leaving only false imprisonment. This was the best possible solution. Smith could never convince Pat to turn against his brother. Toby Bayliss and Les had been close since childhood. And then there was Jeanette Thompson. She was madly in love with Les, and wouldn't be a friendly witness. Plus, she hadn't physically taken part in the crimes and remained in the car during the beating in the used-car lot. For the meantime, the charge of false imprisonment against her would stay on the books.

Even with Lutter's cooperation, Smith felt he had a delicate and difficult case. Lutter had testified during the preliminary hearing that he'd seen Les jumping on Yellow Thunder from the other side of the truck, but he didn't directly witness it. He did see Bayliss lift up the victim's head and strike him twice in the mouth, but Smith didn't think those blows could cause a fatal head injury.

He didn't believe the subdural hematoma was the result of these assaults. Maybe Yellow Thunder's head had slammed against something in the trunk. The bruise above the right eyebrow was in the same spot as the hemorrhage, and he would try to tie them together. Somehow, he had to convince a jury to make the connection.

And he could expect no favors from the judge assigned to the case.

Robert Moran was a no-nonsense district court judge who took his job seriously. He was short in stature, but long on intellect and big on propriety. He was a proud Irishman, Catholic to the core, who had a keen intellect and a love of history and literature. He was known to make obscure references to Chaucer in court that would zoom right over the heads of the attorneys.

Members of the bar remembered him in the old days when he was a country lawyer like themselves. They used to golf and have a good time together. As soon as he went to the bench, those days came to an abrupt end. His strong belief in ethics meant no more social outings with attorneys trying cases before him. If they ran into him in the hallway, they were free to chitchat about the weather or the Cornhusker football team, but they knew better than to bring up a case.

Moran's first ruling was to consolidate the Hares' cases so the brothers would be tried together. Then he changed the venue to his hometown of Alliance, sixty miles southwest of Rushville in Box Butte County. The Fishers had filed the change-of-venue motion, arguing the Hares would never find a neutral jury in Gordon. And they were probably right. Few in Gordon wanted a "not guilty" verdict. Many had preconceived notions about Les, the wild child of the Sand Hills. Others were angry that Gordon had been disgraced in the national media. And there were those who were simply afraid of what the radical Indians would do if the Hares were declared innocent. Among them were the border town businessmen who'd come to depend on the Indian trade since Great Society welfare programs had given the impoverished Oglalas the freedom to spend their food stamps and checks wherever they pleased.

It would be up to the citizens of Alliance to proclaim the Hares guilty or not guilty. Like Gordon, Alliance had a small Lakota community and its own troubled history.

For a brief time, AIM had the respect of many on the reservation. Marching into one of the border towns and making the white folks capitulate to their demands—it was unprecedented. They chartered an AIM chapter in Gordon and organized another at Pine Ridge. This was what leadership wanted all along: respect on a reservation.

After leaving Gordon, they celebrated the victory by partying in Porcupine for several days. But their newfound respect began to erode when a small group of mourners on their way to Yellow Thunder's second funeral attacked the Wounded Knee Trading Post. The assailants heard a rumor that a white merchant had assaulted an Oglala boy. Some also found the private museum attached to the post offensive. The store sold tacky souvenirs to the ever-increasing numbers of tourists who arrived after reading Dee Brown's *Bury My Heart at Wounded Knee* best-seller. The storeowners made a buck selling postcards of the dead Chief Big Foot lying in the snow. Why should whites profit from the tragedy? During the Gordon ad hoc grand jury, some had criticized the owners' trading practices.

Members of the mob pulled the seventy-two-year-old Clive Gildersleeve out of the post, pushed him to the ground, and spat on him while others looted the museum. The Gildersleeves were well liked in Gordon, and the assault on them and their business became another reason for the whites in Sheridan County to fear and despise AIM. There were local Oglalas who respected the family as well. Dennis Banks apologized for the incident, but the "militant" label the FBI had hung on them was beginning to fit for some, most notably the newly elected tribal president, Dick Wilson.

AIM declared that fifteen to thirty thousand Indians from all over the United States would arrive at Pine Ridge the Monday after the march on Gordon. They proclaimed that any Democratic presidential candidate running in that year's primary wishing to garner the Indian vote should join them. Neither the candidates nor the thousands of Indians from across the nation ever arrived. Despite the no-shows, AIM repeated the grand jury format at Billy Mills Hall. It had been a rousing success in Gordon, allowing normally reticent people to vent their frustrations. They then took the show on the road, traveling to reservations all over South Dakota to take affidavits on racial prejudice, while leaving AIM chapters in every community they visited.

In May, a week before the Hare trial, AIM leaders and hundreds of rank-and-file members traveled to Banks's home reservation at Leech Lake, Minnesota, to hold their annual convention. They may have earned the respect of many on Pine Ridge, but not so among the Ojibwas there. AIM attempted to insert itself in a local dispute over the rights of whites to fish and hunt on the reservation. But local leaders preferred to handle the matter in the courts, and Banks received a chilly reception. Leaders began to spar over who would be the movement's official medicine man. The Bellecourts and Russell Means preferred Leonard Crow Dog, while Banks wanted Wallace Chips, an Oglala from Pine Ridge. The convention split into pro-Means and pro-Banks parties and ended in turmoil with the two well-armed sides trading angry words. The two camps left Leech Lake in separate caravans. But they were both going to the same place.

Alliance, Nebraska.

Mark Monroe unlocked the doors of Alliance's American Indian Center and watched the rough-looking AIM members file in. It was two days before the beginning of the May 21 trial, and the AIM vanguard, mostly from Vernon Bellecourt's Denver chapter, had arrived to organize the protest. Rolls and coffee spread out on folding tables awaited the long-haired, blue-jean-wearing crowd. Monroe didn't know much about AIM, and he didn't like what he saw.

A portly man with thick, black-framed glasses and closely cropped hair, Monroe stood out in this crowd. He spotted a few handguns and knives. Many in the group looked like they'd just been sprung from the joint. Despite the early hour, some appeared to be drunk.

And Monroe would know.

He was Oglala with a smattering of Cheyenne who'd spent most of his life in Alliance. He was born in 1930 on the eastern edge of Pine Ridge, but his father Bill left the reservation during the Depression with the family to look for work, and they never returned. When he was ten years old, his father moved his family to Alliance for the potato harvest, and except for a stint serving in the Korean War, the farming and trans-portation hub had been Monroe's home ever since.

Sitting just west of the Sand Hills amid beet and potato farms in the Nebraska Panhandle, Alliance's population of six thousand plus amounted to a good-sized town in such a sparsely populated land. In a lily-white area, its population was amazingly diverse. In the early part of the century, it was a stop for the Chicago Burlington & Quincy Railroad, which housed hundreds of black porters there. A sizable population of Mexican and Oglala families who arrived for the seasonal agricultural work in the beet fields decided to stay and make their homes there as well. Nearly four hundred Native Americans lived in the town. Shortly after Monroe moved to Alliance, World War II broke out and the Army Air Corps set up a training base a few miles to the east, bringing thousands of airmen and construction and support jobs. Diversity didn't mean tolerance, though.

The three minority groups lived on the "other side of the tracks" to the south. The blacks and Latinos, who looked at each other with disdain, in turn looked down on the Oglalas, who lived in a tent city.

Alliance's Indians hadn't fared much better than their reservation cousins. Poverty was high. Racism was rampant. Oglala kids were allowed in school, but they were shoved into the so-called Opportunity Room, the academic ghetto where children had the "opportunity" to sit in a chair and stare at the wall while the white kids learned their ABC's in the classroom next door.

When Monroe was a boy walking down the street with his mother, they saw a sign:

NO INDIANS OR DOGS ALLOWED—
WHITE TRADE SOLICITED ONLY

He turned to his mother and asked, "Am I a dog?"

After returning from the Korean War with two bullet wounds, Monroe struggled with alcoholism. He'd turned his life around after running for police magistrate in 1968. Like Gordon, Alliance did little for the local Indian alcoholics except put them in jail a few days, fine them fifteen bucks, then put them to work raking leaves to pay off their fines. It was cheap labor for the city, and there was no attempt to rehabilitate anyone. The police magistrate, a woman who'd held the office for twenty-five years, was the functionary who carried out this unprogressive policy. Monroe knew her job well. He'd been arrested for drunkenness more times than he could count.

Monroe became the first Indian to run for a public office in Alliance, and his candidacy made news across the state. There were plenty of bigots in town who didn't like the idea. He'd awake to find his house egged, and he received more than a few threatening phone calls. He ultimately lost the election in a close vote, but it was an empowering experience that helped him become the community's best-known Indian advocate. After the election, he convinced Alliance's leaders to do more for its Oglala population. He set up the American Indian Center in an abandoned army barrack, organized an Alcoholics Anonymous chapter and a Boy Scout troop. Monroe was an "establishment" Indian, everything AIM had been rebelling against. He believed in working within the system.

But he had one thing in common with the tough-looking AIM activists crowded into the Indian Center basement. He was equally furious about the way Yellow Thunder had been treated. And for that, he could put up with their gruff behavior. After a lifetime of suffering racist, redneck attitudes from some Alliance residents, Monroe wondered if his hometown could deliver the verdict that justice demanded.

The Box Butte County courthouse sat at the end of the town's main commercial block in the middle of a manicured lawn, shaded by towering trees as old as the community. Dennis Banks, Russell Means, Vernon Bellecourt, and one hundred of their followers marched into the turn-of-the-century building, each one of them convinced that a Nebraska jury would never convict white men for killing an Indian. They were there to make their presence known. For this they had brought an awesome weapon: a traditional Lakota drum made of buffalo hide, four feet in diameter, along with several drumsticks. They set it down in the center of the rotunda on top of the Nebraska state seal laid in tile on the first floor.

So far, Alliance hadn't caved in to AIM's demands as Gordon's leaders had two months before. The movement's leadership called ahead and told Alliance officials to expect anywhere from one thousand to fifteen hundred protesters. The Denver vanguard, led by Vernon Bellecourt, immediately set out to see how far they could push the town leaders. They demanded that the city give them emergency food and money. The city turned them down. So they asked for another place to pitch their tents. The town had arranged for a camping area in a park, which was not to AIM's liking. Alliance said "tough." They asked that the city organize a human relations council similar to the one they'd left in Gordon, and that liquor outlets be closed for the duration of the trial. The city was okay with those requests.

AIM was just getting started. The drummers sat in a circle and started a thunderous beat.

BOOM BOOM BOOM BOOM BOOM BOOM BOOM BOOM BOOM BOOM

The singers lifted their voices, not to the Great Mystery in heaven, but to the courtroom above. The building was all marble and wood. There was nothing to muffle the pounding as it traveled up the central staircase—like smoke up a chimney—for two flights until it arrived in the courtroom, shaking the windows, mingling with other drums from the green lawn out front. The thumping pounded in the chests of the sixty-five prospective jurors, each aware that they'd been summoned for one of the most sensational trials in recent Panhandle history. It pounded in the chests of Raymond's siblings, Annie Eagle Fox, Amelia Comes Last, and Russell Yellow Thunder, who sat patiently in their seats. It pounded in the chest of the Hares' mother, Norma Hooper, who'd been brought up through an entrance in back and seated inconspicuously in the press section. It pounded in the chest of *Gordon Journal* publisher Reva Evans, who clutched a pad and pen in the row behind Norma. It pounded in the chests of the law enforcement officers, who'd taken AIM at their word when they told them to prepare for fifteen hundred activists. It pounded in the chests of Pat and Les, dressed uncharacteristically in neatly pressed suits and neckties, sitting glumly at the defense table. It pounded in the chests of Mike Smith and the Fishers, who gathered their thoughts as they eyed the jury pool. It pounded in the chest of Judge Moran, who took his place at the bench and began the voir dire jury selection process without mentioning the thunderous beat rattling the windows.

Yellow Thunder's niece Arlene Lamont didn't hear the drums. She did not attend the trial. For her, Gordon would never be the same. She once believed she would spend the rest of her life in the town she grew up in. But her thirteen-year marriage to Ray Lamont was finished. Her image of Gordon had changed irrevocably. She left her husband and the kids, cleared her debts at the Main Street stores, and drove north, never to return.

AIM's first plan was to flood the courtroom with its supporters. Seating had begun at 9:00 a.m., but the one hundred spectators led by Banks and Means began climbing the stairs at 10:10. By that time, there were only four open seats left in the room with a capacity of 104. The jury pool alone took up more than half the spots. Those arriving on time had taken the rest.

A combination of city cops, state patrolmen, and sheriff's deputies stopped the protesters before they reached the third floor. Since there were only four seats left, they were free to send in a delegation of four, the sheriff said, but that was all until after the noon recess. Then the seats would be open on a first-come, first-served basis. An angry confrontation ensued. Banks was outraged. This was a racist attempt to keep Indians out of the courtroom, he proclaimed. Some of the female protesters at the foot of the staircase egged on the men. They told them to force their way in. Banks turned to his followers gathered below him on the steps, choosing not to take on the cops.

"This proves the court and the judge are racists, and they're just going to let those men go free!"

Banks left to lodge a complaint with a Justice Department Community Relations representative monitoring the trial, then called a press conference at the city auditorium. Since the reporters didn't want to sit through jury selection, most of them showed up. Banks, Vernon Bellecourt, and Means awaited, ready to give some quotable quotes, which was one of their strongest talents. Banks took the lead this time instead of Means, who was feeling glum from all the infighting. Bellecourt stood behind with his arms crossed as Banks launched into a tirade. He was glad that they'd been barred from the courtroom. They were going to have their own parallel trial the next day, an "all-Indian red-feather grand jury" to call attention to injustice in Alliance.

"Instead of sitting in the courtroom for nine hours a day and doing nothing, we can now expose Nebraska as the number-one racist state in the country!"

Means left out the bombastic, violent threats that had marred the Gordon takeover, but he complained about the city putting them in the Bower Field campsite. "They've got us down in the slums in what the honkies call 'Indian park.'"

Means just wasn't himself. Ever since the Leech Lake fight over the medicine man issue, he'd been feeling down. The infighting was discouraging. Banks's insistence on Chips as the movement's holy man was fraying their unity. Clyde Bellecourt wasn't there to back him up, only his brother Vernon, whom he'd previously tangled with over the movement's leadership. They were trying to work together and show the public a united front, but it was an illusion.

Vernon had only an eighth-grade education, and like Banks and his brother he was a convict. He was sent to prison at age nineteen for robbing a bar in St. Paul, Minnesota. Like Clyde, he'd spent his time in prison learning a skill. His was cutting hair. After serving three years, he emerged from prison, went to cosmetology school to refine his techniques, and became one of the most talented hairstylists in St. Paul. Soon he owned a chain of salons, got married, and had three kids. He had ambitions to become rich and even more successful, and he thought the path would be real estate. He moved to Denver and styled hair as he pursued his new career. One day Clyde called him and accused him of selling out. "I'm trying to win back the land," he told him. "And you're selling it!" Vern joined his brother in a life of activism and established an AIM chapter in Denver. Although he had a shrill voice, he was as articulate and intelligent as the others. He was still sore that Means, and not he, had been named the movement's de facto leader. The two would snipe at each other for decades.

The night before the trial, Banks and Means walked into a church basement they'd been using as a headquarters only to find some Oklahoma toughs pointing handguns at Vernon and threatening to kill him. He'd gotten into an argument with them over the medicine man issue, and they were about to blow his brains out all over the church.

Fortunately, Banks talked them out of it.

A dejected Means complained to the reporters about the unbalanced coverage they'd received during the Gordon protest. He claimed the journalists had given more ink to the results of the second autopsy than they had to the circumstances of Yellow Thunder's horrific death.

"This is probably the last press conference I will ever have," he declared.

Michael Smith was beginning to worry. The pool of sixty-five prospective jurors was nearing its end, and they still hadn't seated the required twelve, plus one alternate. The Fishers had brought in an Alliance-based lawyer to conduct the interviews. It was three against one. Smith didn't like to work with a co-counsel, so being outnumbered was his choice. The Fishers' hired gun asked one woman if the sound of the drumming and singing intimidated her. She said it did, and Judge Moran dismissed her. Every juror wanting to escape now knew those were the magic words. Suddenly they were all declaring the drums scared them. They were coming down to the last row of candidates.

John Haller, a thirty-eight-year-old auto mechanic, took the stand.

"Does the sound of the drums and singing bother you in any way?" the Fishers' consultant asked.

"No, sir."

He asked Haller if he'd heard about the case, and if so, where.

"Radio, TV, the *Omaha World-Herald*. Just about everywhere."

"Have you formed an opinion about the case?"

"Well, I reckon I have. Yes."

"Can that opinion be changed by solid evidence?"

"Yes, it could," he said, thinking he'd have to be an idiot not to be swayed by solid evidence.

He was accepted as a juror.

There were nine Native Americans in the jury pool, but they were all dismissed for cause. By lunchtime, the court was still three jurors short.

Smith spent the noon break in the empty jurors' room mentally preparing for his opening statement. He honestly didn't know what was going to happen. The state was required to disclose all its evidence, but the defense was not. He didn't know what the Fishers had. He'd gone against the elder Fisher many times and he was a worthy adversary. And would an all-white jury convict the Hares for killing an Indian? It was hard to tell with a jury. He had to prove proximate cause: that an illegal act—assault or false imprisonment—had led to Yellow Thunder's death. He had to link the bruise on his right forehead to the subdural hematoma. The problem was, he didn't personally believe that to be the case. He postulated that Yellow Thunder had either knocked his head on the edge of the trunk as he was being unwillingly shoved inside or that he slammed it against something hard as Bayliss was driving over the railroad tracks. That was still proximate cause, but he wouldn't bring up the railroad track theory in court. And he was beginning to second-guess himself for filing the false imprisonment charges. When given two options, a jury would sometimes choose the lesser of the charges. One of the worst-case scenarios was a "guilty" verdict on false imprisonment and "not guilty" for manslaughter.

A bailiff knocked on the door, pulling Smith out of the puddle of self-doubt he was wallowing in, and announced that Judge Moran wanted to see him in his chambers.

He found the judge, the court clerk Don Gilbert, and the Fishers waiting for him. The sound of pounding drums wafted up from outside.

"Don't ask me why we're here," Moran said as Smith took a seat. "I thought you'd better be here because I don't know what this is about either."

The fierce-looking Banks entered the judge's chamber with a young man who introduced himself as the Justice Department's Community Relations representative.

"My name is Dennis Banks. I'm an Ojibwa Indian and the father of nine children."

"I'm Judge Robert Moran. I'm an Irishman and the father of eight children. What are you doing here?"

The Community Relations representative said the Justice Department and the American Indian Movement wanted the trial postponed for one day and moved to the Alliance High School gymnasium to accommodate all the spectators.

Judge Moran sat and listened patiently to his reasoning while Gilbert took notes.

"Can I have the name of your supervisor and his phone number please?" Moran asked. The young man gave it to him as Moran dialed. The supervisor answered within a couple rings.

"I have this Community Relations representative here asking me to postpone my trial a day and that it be moved to a high school basketball court. I just wanted to let you know what he's proposed and that he's offered this as if he has the authority from you and your department," Moran said.

He handed the phone to the young man.

"He wants to talk with you."

The man put the phone to his ear. "Uh-huh. Uh-huh. Yes, sir," he said, then hung up and walked out of the room without saying another word, leaving Banks behind.

The Community Relations representative was not seen in Alliance again.

Jury selection resumed after lunch as the singers in the rotunda lifted their voices to the third floor and the drum vibrated throughout the building. Now that most of the jury pool had been cleared out, about twenty AIM members, including Means, easily found seats. He wore a tight T-shirt and an Indian-power medallion dangling from his neck. He kept his arms crossed as he glared at the judge.

"You will be happy to know that the commissioners plan to air-condition this courtroom this summer," Judge Moran said cheerfully as the proceedings commenced. The room was stuffy, and the body odor of one-hundred-plus spectators crammed together made the ordeal worse.

The jury pool was down to its final six candidates, and Smith wondered if they would have enough jurors to proceed, but they agreed on their twelfth and the one alternate juror with a couple to spare. Now they could get down to business. Judge Moran had set a few new rules. If anyone left the courtroom during the trial, they wouldn't be let back in until the next recess. He'd posted extra bailiffs and sheriffs at the doors to enforce his rules. Several undercover state patrolmen were also scattered among the spectators. Since closing the windows in the jackhammer heat would have been unbearable, the protesters chanting on the lawn outside were as clear as a hi-fi. Moran was normally a stickler for proper business attire, but he allowed the male jurors to take off their suit coats. Smith, always a sharp dresser, wouldn't have taken off his jacket if it had been 110 degrees. He would wear a different suit every day of the trial, and they were the latest in men's fashion. The portly elder Fisher, with a pink hearing aid wrapped around his ear, was as usual wearing white socks with a dark suit, a fashion no-no as far as Smith was concerned. He once asked his longtime adversary why. "I have a foot condition," was the reply. Whatever that meant.

Smith stood up and addressed the jury, telling them how the Hares and three others were driving around drunk, how they first saw Yellow Thunder and how Les jumped out to push him, then later found him, beat him, and threw him half-naked into the Legion Hall while a dance was in progress. He concluded by saying the state would "effectively link blows that Yellow Thunder received during the incident to his eventual death, which was caused by a brain hemorrhage."

Fisher told the jury that they could disprove the false imprisonment charge because Toby Bayliss's car had a special latch installed that would allow someone inside to escape. He said there was more than one car driving around that night, and someone else may have injured Yellow Thunder. Leslie and Pat Hare did not harm the victim. They had actually helped Yellow Thunder. The state would not be able to prove beyond a reasonable doubt that the Hare brothers caused the injury, he declared.

Sitting in the hallway waiting to be called, George Ghost Dog was fidgety and nervous. Speaking in public frightened the fifteen-year-old. His boss at the Neighborhood Center had given him a ride to Alliance, and as they walked through the AIM protesters outside, Vernon Bellecourt stopped him and shook his hand.

"Don't be afraid," the elder said. "Just tell them what happened and you'll be all right."

The bailiff called him in, and as he walked up to the witness box, he felt the eyes on the back of his neck. Smith asked him a series of questions, and he tried to tell everyone what his cousin Yellow Thunder said when he came across him in the car lot, but Fisher kept standing up and interrupting him.

"Do you remember what he said to you?" Smith asked.

"I asked him if he . . ."

Fisher leapt up. "Please. He can answer that yes or no."

"Do you remember what was said? Do you? Just yes or no, George."

"Yeah."

"Would you tell us what you said to him and what was said to you, please?"

Ghost Dog was about to answer when the old lawyer jumped up again.

"That is objected to as incompetent, irrelevant, and immaterial; hearsay; not binding on the defendants!"

"Overruled," Moran said. George didn't understand what was going on, but finally he was able to deliver what Smith wanted the jury to hear. The mark above Yellow Thunder's right eyebrow was there Sunday when Yellow Thunder said some white boys had beaten him up, and it was there the next Friday when he thought he was sleeping.

Prior to Ghost Dog's testimony, Legion Club patron Virginia Wheeler had testified how Yellow Thunder was pushed into the dance and how her husband went to cover him up. She noticed a bruise on his hip before they escorted him out, she said. Sandage was next and related his version of the story, admitting without embarrassment that once Yellow Thunder said he didn't want any help, he saw no reason to take any action.

Unfortunately for Smith, Wheeler and Sandage both said Yellow Thunder had covered his face in shame while inside the Legion and neither had noticed an injury above his right eyebrow. Officer John Paul, however, testified that he'd seen Yellow Thunder with a bruise above the right eyebrow before he admitted him as a sleeper, and then again when he found him dead eight days later.

Smith wanted the jury to connect the wound above the eyebrow with the subdural hematoma. But what if he couldn't establish that the wound was there at all?

By the end of the day, AIM had a press release out listing its grievances against the city of Alliance. They had been barred from the courtroom. They had been denied emergency food aid. A promised spot in the National Guard armory had been changed to the park. The local paper would print it in its entirety the following morning.

The press release ended on an ominous note.

> Let White America know that from this day forward once again we state that the native sovereign people will no longer tolerate abuse and mistreatment of our people. And we will take whatever action necessary to protect our people and our rights.
>
> From this day forward let this white racist sick community of Alliance, Nebraska, State of Nebraska and the United States of White America be aware that the American Indian Movement will take any and all steps to insure the protection of our people. The American Indian Movement will take any and all steps to insure justice for our people. WE ARE PREPARED TO DIE FOR THESE BELIEFS AND AS IN ANY WAR WE ARE PREPARED TO TAKE THE OFFENSE TO INSURE OUR PEOPLE MAXIMUM PROTECTION.

For the time being, only AIM knew what the final sentence in capital letters meant. For the next two days, downtown Alliance would be devoid of shoppers.

Despite the brouhaha over the lack of seats during the first day, the gallery was half empty the next morning. Several reporters went to the "red-feather grand jury" scheduled for 10:00 a.m. at the city auditorium, but no one was there. It had apparently been canceled.

Judge Moran had finally had enough of the drum in the rotunda. He ordered the police to move the drummers and singers out to the lawn with the other protesters. The distance between the open windows and the singing groups below was still only about thirty feet. While the drums wouldn't reverberate up the stairwell anymore, AIM could still make its presence felt.

Smith had a problem. The wound above the right eyebrow he wanted to connect to the subdural hematoma kept appearing and disappearing depending on who was testifying.

The first to take the stand on the second day was the prosecution's star witness, Bernard "Butch" Lutter. He didn't describe a savage or pro- longed beating. Bayliss had slapped Yellow Thunder a couple times on the face, and Les Hare had said "I really stomped him," after jumping up and down on the other side of the truck. But a boot heel coming down with the weight of a grown man's body would have left a lot more damage. The second autopsy Smith had observed in Rapid City showed a very small bump on the brow, and both independent pathologists had agreed that it didn't amount to much. A subdural hematoma was usu- ally the result of a blow to the opposite side of the head, a fact he hoped wouldn't come up.

The elderly pathologist W. O. Brown took the stand and did his best to explain how a subdural hematoma was like a ticking time bomb and would cause death only several days after an injury. But Fisher did a good job casting doubt on the approximate time of death. Brown said that the scabs and marks on the victim's face appeared to be only a few days old, implying that some other beating took place later in the week, long after the encounter with Bayliss and the Hares. Dr. Brown also admitted that subdural hematomas sometimes occurred naturally without any trauma. That didn't help Smith's case at all.

Dr. Brown also couldn't nail down the time of death. The problem was Ghost Dog. He'd said he thought Yellow Thunder was asleep on Friday the 18th. He didn't say he was alive or dead. Only that he was resting in the exact same position he'd seen him in on Sunday.

On Fisher's cross-examination, the pathologist almost sunk the case.

"Do you have any way of telling, Doctor, if one of those injuries to the head was from—caused by an instrument or . . ."

"The skin wound looked like it had probably been caused by some fairly broad-surfaced instrument. Anyway . . . it didn't have the appear- ance of a cutting wound or a wound produced by some sharp edge. And that is about as far as I would go."

"Could it have been caused then by running into the sharp edge of a door?"

"It could be."

"Falling down or striking something."

". . . our findings here would be compatible with any one of a great variety of blows or injuries."

After Brown gave a brief description of a subdural hematoma, Fisher went on.

"And so, it is apparent here that this particular subdural hematoma was of some duration, however. It had been, say, just the day before or two days before?"

"It was recent. I wouldn't rule that out."

"It could have been two or three days?"

"Yes. Uh huh. That's positive. Yes."

"It could have been ten days?"

"Well, I doubt if it were ten days because by ten days changes occur in the hematoma . . . such as the blood begins to break down and things like that. I don't think it was ten days old."

"And that hadn't occurred?"

"No. That hadn't occurred."

On redirect, Smith asked him if a blunt object such as a boot heel could cause such an injury. Dr. Brown said that was possible.

The doctor hadn't helped Smith's case at all. The problem was that no one knew when Yellow Thunder had died. It could have been hours after Ghost Dog had seen him. Or it could have been days. In all probability he'd died long before Ghost Dog saw him that Friday, but there was no way to prove that. The doctor went on to say that the scabs on the face from the scratches didn't look like they had been formed more than twelve hours to three days before death.

The nineteen-year-old meat cutter Max Anderson was next. He told the jury how Les had asked him to turn off his pickup truck's lights and how he witnessed Butch Lutter and Pat Hare shoving Yellow Thunder into the Legion Hall. He later jumped in the car with the others and saw them snatch the old man a second time and load him back into the trunk, then drive around with him for at least another half hour.

Fisher reminded Anderson that he had made three statements, two to the police, and that none of them matched. One was made to Max Ibach on February 22 and another to Bob Case on February 28, and now a different story under oath. He then showed him a picture of Yellow Thunder as he was found and asked if he looked the same.

"He didn't look like this."

Smith on redirect treated Anderson as a hostile witness. Neither of the statements he made mentioned the condition of Yellow Thunder's face. In the first, Anderson claimed never to have witnessed anything after Les asked him to turn off his lights. He said he drove right home.

Smith made a motion to impeach his own witness.

The lawyers conferred with the judge, and a short recess was called. When they came back, everything seemed to be straightened out. Smith dropped the motion.

"Now which of these three statements you've made is true?" Smith asked.

"The one I'm up on oath on. I didn't want to say any more because I was afraid of what might happen to me."

Anderson was dismissed. But he never backed down on claiming that Yellow Thunder did not have any bruises or marks on his face that night. It was another case of the appearing and reappearing bruise. But according to his own police statements, Anderson never left the car or put himself in a position to look at Yellow Thunder closely, Smith reminded the jury.

Smith rested his case. The jury left the room, and old man Fisher made a motion to dismiss both charges. The state had not proven false imprisonment or that any blow by either of the Hare brothers had led to Yellow Thunder's death.

Moran dismissed the motion and called a half-hour recess.

Once again, representatives of the Shald clan arrived to offer their support. Two of Lulu Trueblood's granddaughters, Doyle Bixby and Peggy Harris, came bearing sandwiches for the protesters outside the courthouse.

Doyle left Gordon after high school, marrying the son of Lawrence Bixby, who'd taken over what remained of the Spade Ranch after the demise of Bartlett Richards. Even though the Bixbys and Hoopers had been close neighbors, she was taking the side of the Indians. Like many of her siblings, she had embraced her mother Gladys's Oglala heritage. Earlier that day, she called the eldest Shald child, her sister Peggy, who was married to an Alliance bread distributor, and the two made their way to the courthouse. The protests brought the Indian out in Doyle—only if it was just a sixteenth. After her marriage, the liberal, Catholic townie had found herself living in the conservative, insular Sand Hills. She knew Les and his mother, Norma Hooper. Doyle was one of many who saw Les racing his cars along the dirt roads of the Spade Ranch during his wild teenage days. As Peggy and Doyle handed out the sandwiches, some of the recipients were rather surly and unappreciative. But she didn't mind. It was for a good cause.

Since the law didn't require the defense to reveal its evidence, Smith had no idea what the Fishers had up their sleeves. He was about to find out.

First came a Gordon High School student, Dan Hooper, who said he knew about a special latch inside the trunk of Bayliss's car that would allow anyone inside to free himself. Hooper was Les and Pat's first cousin.

So the Fishers were going to use that as a defense?

Then the Hares's sixteen-year-old half brother Miles took the stand and claimed that he'd encountered the party in question at the laundromat while Yellow Thunder was putting his pants back on. He testified that he hadn't seen any marks on the victim's face or any indication that he'd been beaten up.

The jury certainly wouldn't see him as a credible witness, Smith hoped. He didn't bother to cross-examine him or the Hooper boy.

Fisher then called Police Chief Bob Case and Sheriff George Pochon to establish the fact that Yellow Thunder was an alcoholic. It was a ploy to tap into the drunken Indian stereotype. Case said Yellow Thunder had been in jail for voluntary sleepovers or intoxication arrests 217 times since 1951. Smith took the opportunity to cross-examine both lawmen and asked them if they'd seen any special latch inside Bayliss's trunk. Neither had.

Fisher then called the dispatcher and magistrate Kay Lou Peterson, who from her vantage point about fifteen feet away had not seen any bump or cut above Yellow Thunder's right eyebrow, although he did have scrapes on his right cheek and nose. She insisted that she had a good look at him under a fluorescent light. This directly contradicted John Paul, who had arrived at the station shortly afterward. On cross-examination, Peterson said Yellow Thunder had told her that "four white boys beat him up."

Bayliss was the last witness of the day. He testified that he'd installed a special latch inside his trunk because one of his two small boys had once locked himself inside during a camping trip. The lock existed, then didn't exist. The wound above the eyebrow existed, then didn't exist. Who was the jury going to believe?

Fisher asked for an early adjournment since the next witness was going to be a long one. Did that mean one of the Hares was going to take the stand? Smith hoped so. He believed putting a defendant on the stand was almost always a mistake.

Alliance began to gird itself for what might be the final day of the trial. AIM supporters were seen as left-wing militants who'd already trashed a trading post. Its leaders made violent threats. They hadn't arrived in the numbers they'd anticipated—only a few hundred at the most—but several were armed.

And then there was the threat made in the press release. They were willing to die for their beliefs? What did that mean? The state patrol was urging Judge Moran and his family to leave their home so troopers could protect them in a safer location. But he refused, so they posted around-the-clock guards there.

The next day, in front of a packed courtroom, Pat Hare took the stand. The tall, good-looking brother put his hand on the Bible. He took an oath to tell the whole truth and nothing but the truth. He solemnly swore. With a loud, confident voice and an open, smiling face, Pat told his side of the story as the drums outside kept a steady beat.

Pat, his brother Les and his girlfriend Jeannette, Butch Lutter, and Toby Bayliss were driving around Gordon drinking beer when they happened to drive by an old man. Les said he wanted to stop and talk to him, so he jumped out of the car, exchanged a few words with him, and then he gently turned the man around.

He got back in the front seat and said: "By God, that guy is as drunk as we are!"

They all had a good chuckle.

Pat didn't even realize he was an Indian. And he didn't know what was said between the two. They cruised around town for a while longer, bought another case of beer at the Wagon Wheel liquor store by the railroad tracks. They started driving around again when they happened to see the Indian gentleman walking into the used-car lot.

"Why, it's too cold out tonight," Les said. "That Indian gentleman will pass out and freeze to death if we don't help him."

The four men spread out into the parking lot out of concern for the old man. Les managed to locate him in the front seat of an old truck. He opened the door, but the man had passed out. He fell into his arms and Les gently pulled him out of the truck as Pat grabbed his feet. Together they lowered him to the ground. About that time Toby flew around the other side of the truck and drunkenly ran into Les and they both fell to the ground. Les got mud on his hands.

Just about then Butch arrived, so he couldn't have seen what had happened.

"Well, let's depants him. Maybe that'll wake him up," Les suggested. So Pat and his brother took off his pants and shoes. The refreshing air seemed to wake the man out of his stupor.

"Do you want to go for a ride?"

"Yeah, it's cold here," the Indian gentleman replied.

They helped him walk to the car. They were all a bit unsteady from the alcohol, but they made it back without falling down.

"Hey, I've got my car cleaned up too well, and he smells so bad I don't think I want him to ride in there," Toby said.

He went to the back of the Ford and opened up the trunk.

"You can ride in here," Pat said, and the Indian gentleman climbed in the trunk by himself.

"Now, there's a lever here. You can lift it and it'll open up the trunk."

"Okay." The old man felt around to make sure he knew how to operate the device.

Someone started to close the trunk.

"Be careful! Be careful!" Pat said. "Don't get his fingers caught in the latch. Watch out for his fingers!"

Jeannette and Les both suggested taking the man to jail where it was warm.

"How are we going to take him to jail and explain that he ain't got any pants on?" Toby said.

"Besides, we're so drunk ourselves the police will give us a ticket," Pat added.

Butch remembered that there was a dance in progress at the American Legion Hall.

"It would be a funny joke if we pushed him in there," Butch said. "Then they'll call the police and take him to jail."

"No, sir!" Les said. "I ain't going down to that Legion Hall! I ain't gonna have nothin' to do with it!"

Both Les and Jeannette were dead set against the idea.

"By God, I'll push him in!" Pat said, so Toby drove down the street to the Legion.

There they saw Max Anderson sitting in his pickup. Les asked him to turn off his lights. Pat and Butch went back to the trunk, opened it up, and found the man asleep. Pat gently nudged him awake.

"We're here."

"Okay," he said as they helped him out.

The pair walked the man to the east door. Butch opened it and Pat pushed him on the back of his shoulders. Not very hard, though. Gently, in fact. Then Butch closed the door.

They ran off to meet the car, then drove around awhile before heading back to the Legion Hall about ten minutes later. Anderson joined them in the back of the car and started drinking beer. He said they brought the Indian gentleman right back out. And that was all there was to it. So the six of them started driving around again, heading north, when they saw the old man walking without his pants back toward the used-car lot.

"Let's give him his clothes back and give him a beer," Les said.

The Indian walked over as Butch opened the trunk for him to voluntarily climb back in. Butch shut the trunk and they started driving around again. About this time, Pat was feeling sick. He asked to be taken back to Dean Hare's place.

And that was about all he knew. At no time did anyone strike or kick the Indian gentleman. There were no marks on his forehead or face.

The story would have been laughable if Yellow Thunder's death weren't so tragic.

Michael Smith stood up, walked over to the cocky and confident Pat Hare. With sarcasm oozing from his voice and etched across his face, Smith commended Pat Hare for his altruistic deeds. He then proceeded to rip into his story like a coyote with a prairie dog in its jaws.

"You were trying to act like a Good Samaritan. Is that right?"

"Yes, sir."

All the cockiness and self-confidence drained from Pat's face.

"And do you commonly make a habit of helping sleepers?"

"No."

"So your original intent was to help him . . ."

"The original intent was to find the man and wake him up so he could find a better place to sleep."

"And your second humanitarian act was taking off his pants?"

As a "breather, refresher," he replied, his voice not so loud.

Was the trunk he was placed in heated?

"No, not by a heater . . ."

He asked if someone nearly passed out could understand how to operate a trunk latch.

"He had said something about the cold, so I thought he could understand about the latch," Pat replied weakly.

"And your third Good Samaritan gesture was to push him inside the Legion club so he could get to the police?"

"Yes," now barely audible above the drumming outside.

"Another added benefit was that it would be a good joke."

The jurors had to strain to hear his answer.

"I thought it might be a bit humorous."

A defeated Pat stepped out of the witness stand and sat down next to his brother.

Smith called state patrol investigator Max Ibach as a rebuttal witness to testify that he hadn't seen any latch in the trunk. He asked Ibach about the trunk mat he removed on February 22. He said it had three reddish brown spots of foreign substance on it, and the FBI report was entered into evidence, but it wasn't remarked upon again. Smith was pulling out every piece of ammunition. In fact, the FBI report stated that the red spots weren't blood, but the Fishers passed up a chance to expose the ploy.

After the noon recess, the two attorneys made their closing remarks.

"The testimony given to you by the defendant Melvin P. Hare is incredible. In fact, the word was created for this kind of testimony," Smith said. He then recounted Pat's story in its entirety, highlighting each absurd point. He added that Officer John Paul's testimony about the wound above the right eyebrow alone would be enough to convict them.

In his closing statement, Fisher reminded the jury that the testimony did not prove that the hemorrhage was caused by external blows.

"They may be guilty of something, but it's certainly not manslaughter."

As the jury went into deliberations, Means put the finishing touches on his plan.

AIM would infiltrate as many warriors as possible into the gallery. If the verdict was not guilty, each AIM member had a person to attack. Means chose the judge for himself. Others were to go after the jury, the attorneys, and the Hares. They were going to fight until they were hauled off to jail. Means told a couple members of the press to expect something big when the verdicts were read.

Meanwhile, Les, Pat, their mother Norma, and some other staunch friends waited out the deliberations in a small, hot room. Outside, beating drums intermingled with chants of "the Hares must die." There was nowhere to go and nothing to do but listen. A deputy sheriff had strongly advised them to not stick their heads out of the window. They hadn't heard a word from their attorneys since the end of the trial.

Finally, the elder Fisher opened the door.

"Boys, they're railroading you and there's not a damn thing I can do about it," he said, then closed the door without another word.

After six hours, the jury had a verdict. AIM runners dashed to the city auditorium to spread the news. Means, Banks, and Vernon Bellecourt interpreted the relatively short deliberations as bad news. Means was certain the all-white racist, redneck jury, as he called them, would come back with "not guilty" and he would have to lead a fight.

The drummers on the lawn began pounding and singing a war song as the gallery filled. This was the biggest show in town. Annie Eagle Fox, Amelia Comes Last, and Arlene Lamont's older sister, Inez Johnson, sat in the front row. Smith's wife Jeanne rarely came to his trials, but she wanted to see this one and took a seat next to Raymond's family. To her side, Ibach scanned the assembled crowd with his lawman's eye.

Norma Hooper sat in her usual spot among the reporters as Reva Evans in a back row flipped open her notebook. She would write about the nice, conventional attire worn by Mr. Yellow Thunder's family. (As opposed to the hippie element sitting nearby.)

Pat and Les came in, still dressed in their suits, and took their places, their hands in their laps. Les felt a gnawing pessimism in his gut.

There were, in fact, few optimists in the courtroom. Smith didn't have any idea which way the verdict was going to go. He knew that Fisher was right. He hadn't proven beyond a reasonable doubt that the beating resulted in the hemorrhage. He didn't believe it himself. But did the jury?

Means and the assembled AIM warriors—primed to do battle with the bailiffs and whomever they could put their hands on—were equally pessimistic, convinced the whites would never convict one of their own for killing an Indian.

The state patrol had an inkling that Means was planning something big. Several undercover officers were spread throughout the gallery, ready to put down any courthouse riot. Ibach turned to Jeanne Smith and told her if the verdict was "not guilty" she was to follow him over the railing and make for the side door. She hadn't realized until that moment that she might be in danger.

Judge Moran entered the room. The first thing he did was compliment the spectators for their orderly conduct during the past three days. He said no matter what the verdict was, no one would be allowed to leave the courtroom until all of the jury members were escorted home. There would be no demonstrations or outbursts.

The jury shuffled in and took their seats as five uniformed law enforcement officers stood along the wall as a show of force. A couple of Nebraska Game and Parks officers had even been brought in as reinforcements.

The drumming and singing outside abruptly stopped.

The judge asked foreman Robert Neely if they had reached a verdict.

Means, who'd found an aisle seat, plotted his route to the judge, while several patrolmen sitting nearby plotted their routes to Means.

The foreman stood up and proclaimed Melvin Patrick Hare "guilty" on the charge of false imprisonment. "Guilty" on the charge of manslaughter. For Leslie Dean Hare. The same. "Guilty."

Fisher made a motion to poll the jurors. Each one confirmed his or her decision as Pat and Les listened without betraying any emotion.

The drummers below began pounding a victory song as the jurors began filing out.

Annie Eagle Fox stood up, walked over to Smith, and simply said, "Thank you." A reporter came over to ask if she had anything else to say.

"My heart aches so I cannot talk," she replied, then began weeping.

A patrolman escorted juror John Haller to his car.

The drummers and singers were still celebrating on the other side of the courthouse and beginning to make their way to the city auditorium for a celebration. The noise didn't bother the mechanic at all. It never had.

One day, an attorney representing the Hares for their appeal of the case would call him and ask if there was an atmosphere of intimidation. He said "no." He wasn't afraid of any Indians. He and the other jurors felt perfectly safe. He was more afraid of the Hares than AIM. A year or two after the trial, he would spot Pat Hare walking through his repair shop door. He didn't know what he wanted, so he casually picked up a tire iron just in case. It turned out he just needed his pickup fixed. If Pat recognized him as one of the twelve who'd put him away, he didn't say anything.

In deliberations, Haller immediately voted guilty, as did about eight other jurors. Pat Hare had done more to sink their case than anyone as far as Haller was concerned. His story was a lie from the beginning to the end, the mechanic believed. He also didn't like the way Fisher was trying to tap into their alleged prejudices by playing up the fact that the Indian man smelled. He tried to portray Yellow Thunder as nothing but a drunk.

There was one fellow on the jury who'd bought into all that. He was one of the last holdouts.

"Well, if he wants to be a drunk and live in a truck, that's his goddamn right!" Haller said.

The whole latch argument was the stupidest goddamn thing he'd ever heard. How was a man nearly passed out supposed to operate a latch in a cold, dark trunk? And what was he supposed to do? Jump out of the car when they were driving forty miles an hour?

As they came to Haller's car, the patrolman asked him if he wanted an escort home. He took a pass. He was anxious to return home and tell his kids about his big day. They thought it was quite exciting that their dad was on the jury for such a big case. The cop checked the back of his seat just to make sure no one was hiding there; then Haller drove home.

The trial would be one of the most memorable events of his life.

The Hares were heading home at that moment as well. They were still free on bond pending a probation report and a possible motion for a new trial or an appeal. The state patrol escorted the brothers and their supporters all the way back to Sheridan County, thirty-five miles east, near their mother's home by the Old Spade Ranch. In their minds, it was an unfair trial. AIM had intimidated the jurors into pronouncing them guilty. They firmly believed that the pathologist had proven that they couldn't have caused the injury that killed Yellow Thunder. The jurors must have been afraid of a large-scale riot. They were bitter against the town of Gordon and the judicial system. They just couldn't understand why people had turned against them. They spent the night looking out their windows in case AIM came seeking revenge, but the Indians were too busy celebrating at the city auditorium. The dancing and singing lasted into the night.

Reporters came by seeking comments.

"Perhaps there is a ray of hope in the justice system of white America," Vernon Bellecourt said. Still, there was a strong institutionalized racism in northwestern Nebraska, he added.

"People are born into this type of racism. They don't recognize it until it is pointed out to them."

He told two reporters working for the conspicuously absent Reva Evans that AIM intended to send a small task force to Bayliss's trial scheduled for July. As for Gordon, AIM "has sensitized the community, but more has to be done."

In fact, AIM's senior leadership, torn apart by infighting and their self-destructive militant strategies, would largely forget about Gordon. But they weren't done making news. AIM's biggest, boldest newspaper headlines were still to come. One of the organization's lieutenants would take on Sheridan County's border towns. His name was Bob Yellow Bird Steele. The Gordon police, Michael Smith, Mark Monroe, and he were about to go to war.

Bob Yellow Bird gives the Gordon City Council a piece of his mind, March 11, 1976. (Courtesy of *Sheridan County Journal Star*.)

Billy Jack Goes to Gordon

Robert and Richard Yellow Bird Steele were playing by a pond near Bridgeport, Nebraska, when they spotted the outlines of a rowboat sticking up above the muck. The eleven-year-old Robert wondered if he could make it float, and soon he had his younger brother, Richard, wading with him knee-deep into the mud.

The two boys were 150 miles from their home on the reservation. It was early fall 1956, beet-picking season when their parents, Charles and Sarah, packed up their brood of ten children and pitched their tent on a farm in the heart of the Panhandle to earn some money. Charles had to do whatever he could to feed all the hungry mouths.

The Yellow Birds were part of the Red Shirt band and lived at Red Shirt Table on the northwestern section of the Pine Ridge Reservation in the heart of the Badlands. Three generations ago, a white man had married into the *tiospaye*. No one remembered much about him, but the "Steele" had remained—at least on their birth certificates. Many family members informally dropped the name.

As a seasonal worker, Charles kept his family on the move. Occasionally, he landed a job working as a foreman on a ranch and they'd stay in one spot for a year, but schooling for the kids was inconsistent. In the winter, the children attended the Pine Ridge boarding school. Bob and Richard, only a year apart, were bright kids who never gave their folks any trouble.

For the next few evenings, Bob and Richard scraped the mud out of the boat until it was nearly ready to go back on the water again. But they never had the chance to test it.

They didn't hear the cop behind them until he slammed the cruiser's door.

"Where'd you get that boat?"

"We pulled it out of the water there," Bob said.

"Don't lie to me. You stole it," he said.

"No we didn't. We took it out and cleaned it up." The cop wasn't interested in their explanation. He grabbed Bob by the arm and loaded him into the back of the car.

Richard watched as the policeman drove off with his older brother.

He wouldn't see him again for several years.

On August 25, 1972, in Alliance, Nebraska, Judge Moran looked down from his bench at Les and Pat Hare and asked if they had anything to say for themselves.

"I never did it," Les said.

"Well, I am not guilty of the charge," Pat added.

Their attorney, Charles Fisher the elder, asked for probation.

"This is a matter that came about by reason of the drinking of all the parties concerned, including the man who was supposedly killed by these boys . . . it was a practical joke, and it certainly backfired," Fisher said.

Moran wasn't having any of it.

"The one thing you did say, Mr. Fisher, which is certainly appropriate of this case . . . was that alcohol played its usual significant role in a crime of this type. And without depreciating in any way the seriousness of what you two gentlemen did, the said part of it is the root problem; that it is the excessive consumption of alcohol—that was not touched upon by the people who sought something sensational in these events.

"You were not so intoxicated that you did not know what you were doing. It is not understandable under any circumstances, and it becomes more difficult to understand what motivated this when we review your age. . . . It seems to me that it indicates a feeling that the [deceased], being a member of an ethnic minority, somehow or other was an inferior being, who in your own judgment . . . could be properly subjected to the humiliation that you intended to subject him to."

Moran could have given them both ten years. But since there was no weapon involved, and neither had any felony convictions, he gave Les six years, describing him as the "ringleader." Pat received two years. Moran fined them both five hundred dollars for the false imprisonment convictions. There would be two appeals before either of them saw the inside of a prison cell.

Three days later, Vernon Bellecourt and about sixty other Denver-based AIM members arrived at the courthouse to protest the light sentences. They lowered the Nebraska and U.S. flags from the pole and hoisted the AIM flag in its place. Bellecourt issued several demands to Governor Exon, including the removal of Judge Moran from office, the release of all Indian prisoners in Nebraska, the reversal of the light sentences, and an investigation into the double standard of justice in Nebraska.

"The national officers of the American Indian Movement have taken a position that they will not be held responsible for the acts of individuals who desire to institute their own actions against the State of Nebraska and the Hare brothers," said an AIM statement. The governor had forty-eight hours to meet their demands. The statement also recommended revoking the Hares' bond and that they be taken into police custody for their own protection.

It was all bluster. Before the forty-eight hours were up, the AIM members returned to Denver.

If they could have known how long Les and Pat would actually serve, they might have come right back. After the Hares exhausted their appeals, they entered the penitentiary in Lincoln in the fall of 1973. Les served two of the six years, and Pat ten months of the two-year sentence.

When Bayliss faced Judge Moran in November, the trial took place in the Sheridan County courthouse in Rushville rather than Alliance. The only sounds outside were cars and trucks passing by on Highway 20. There was no AIM protest, no Yellow Thunder family in attendance, no press horde. Only Reva Evans reported the proceedings.

Bayliss's court-appointed attorney, L. E. Mitchell, did his best to poke holes in Smith's case. He pointed out that no one knew Yellow Thunder's exact whereabouts for eight days. He revealed discrepancies between the clothes in which Yellow Thunder was found and what he'd been wearing the night of the assault. Meanwhile, testimony revealed that the sheriff's department had lost Yellow Thunder's clothes while building a new storage shed.

When the hulking John Paul took the stand, it was Smith, not Mitchell, who exposed the indifferent attitude of the Gordon Police Department.

"Did you have occasion to see [Yellow Thunder] at any time between the visit at the police station and the time that you found him dead?" Smith asked.

"No, I didn't."

"Did the police receive any missing person's complaint or anything about him at that time?"

"I am sure we did; we had different people inquiring about him."

"You did?"

"Yes."

"Were you, or any of the people in the department, successful in finding him during this period?"

"No, they weren't."

"Had you been called to the—or have you ever found people in this parking lot or used-car lot sleeping or occupying any of these used cars before this case?"

"Oh yes. We have. Yes."

Paul testified that he'd asked some street people if they'd seen Yellow Thunder. They hadn't. He said he also asked Yellow Thunder's employer, Harold Rucker, which made no sense since Rucker was among those inquiring about Raymond. That was the extent of John Paul's investigation. Police Chief Bob Case testified that he was investigating the Legion club incident that week. If that were true, it wasn't a vigorous investigation to say the least.

Neither Smith nor Mitchell asked why the Gordon police didn't tell Yellow Thunder's family that their loved one had been the victim of a crime. Neither lawyer directly asked why no officials had bothered to walk or drive the four blocks to the used-car lot where it was common for drinkers to sleep. Or why they didn't, at the very least, recommend that Arlene Lamont or her aunts look there. Neither of the attorneys wondered aloud how Max Ibach was handed a list of four suspects the moment he showed up in Gordon. For that would suggest that the police department knew the perpetrators' identities, but that they had no intention of filing charges against four white men for beating up and throwing a naked Indian in the trunk of a car. Mitchell inquired how the sheriff's department managed to lose the clothes Yellow Thunder was found in, but he didn't ask how and why John Paul had managed to secure a better job and a raise a month after he became the focus of allegations of abuse.

None of this was brought up in court. After all, the incompetence of the Gordon Police Department and the county's dual standard of justice were not on trial here.

It was Robert "Toby" Bayliss.

And Robert "Toby" Bayliss was found guilty.

He received four years. Moran said his actions were less than those of Les Hare's and more than Pat's. Like the Hares, he served far less time than the sentence.

Nevertheless, his role in Yellow Thunder's death would largely be forgotten. He would rarely be mentioned in newspaper articles or history books. It would always be "the Hare brothers."

From Reva Evans's Royal typewriter came this odd admission: "In contrast with the outside demonstrations at Alliance in May, the scene at Rushville was marked with an almost total lack of spectators. An officer was quoted as attributing this lack of outside interest to two factors: The newspaper reports that the 'agitators' were in Washington and the cooperation of the news media in omitting pre-trial publicity on this hearing."

AIM was indeed in Washington DC. In fact, its members had taken up residence there. AIM and other Indian groups organized the Trail of Broken Treaties. From Los Angeles, Seattle, and San Francisco they caravanned east while gathering followers and staging small demonstrations along the way, timing their arrival in Washington on November 1, the week before the 1972 Nixon-McGovern election.

They expected to arrive with several other Indian organizations in a show of unity. They expected to be fed and put up in church basements. They expected to meet with dignitaries, politicians, and other power brokers. But those expectations were not met. They found themselves sleeping in a rat-infested ghetto church. Plus, all the politicians were out of town on the campaign trail. The more conservative Indian groups were wary of AIM and their radical tactics. Local police were equally wary and were expecting some kind of occupation. They were right. They thought it might be the Washington Monument. They didn't predict that it would be the Bureau of Indian Affairs.

Tired of living in the scummy church basement, more than one thousand Native Americans marched downtown and occupied the bureau's headquarters. For several days, they expected to be forcibly evicted. They set up barriers and made Molotov cocktails. On the afternoon of

November 6, as the Bayliss trial began, negotiations for a peaceful end to the occupation collapsed. The fear of an imminent attack set off a wave of vandalism and looting inside the building. The day after Bayliss was convicted, AIM and the other participants agreed to end the sit-in for sixty-six thousand dollars in travel money.

Means, Banks, and the Bellecourts returned to the prairie and began to gather their forces. To police agencies, many border town whites, and conservative Indians, they were militants and thugs. To many young, angry Indians, they were heroes.

When they went to Custer, South Dakota, in February 1972 for the trial of Darld Schmitz, a white man accused of stabbing Wesley Bad Heart Bull, Means got the courthouse riot he'd anticipated in Alliance nine months before. AIM had been looking for another case similar to Yellow Thunder's, and they thought they had it with Bad Heart Bull. However, Bad Heart Bull was not a gentle soul like Raymond. He was a street tough who'd engaged in a knife fight with Schmitz, who was another violent drunk.

The trial was to be held in Custer, a town in the sacred Black Hills named after the hated general who'd slaughtered Lakota women and children, violated the Treaty of 1868 by invading the hills, and met his timely end in the Battle of Little Big Horn. AIM, always conscious of such symbolic battlegrounds, arrived in full force for the trial. Like Alliance, there weren't enough seats in the courtroom gallery. As snow began to fall, police and protesters began a shoving match on the courthouse steps, which quickly escalated into a full-scale riot. Means and dozens of others were taken away in handcuffs.

The Oglalas left the cold late fall air and filed into Gordon's theater, settling into their seats with bags of popcorn, boxes of Milk Duds, and paper cups topped with soda. They were there to see their celluloid hero, Billy Jack, a karate-kicking, part-Indian Vietnam War veteran who wore blue jeans and a black hat. Writer, director, and lead actor Tom Laughlin had already starred in two Billy Jack movies. In the second movie, *Billy Jack,* he defended a Southwest Indian tribe and the New Freedom School, an unstructured educational institution for wayward hippies led by the fervent pacifist Jean, Billy Jack's platonic girlfriend, and portrayed by Laughlin's wife, Delores Taylor. Their foes were a gang of redneck bullies led by the evil scion of a white fat cat.

Laughlin was not a "half-breed" like his character, but the script included plenty of invented Indian mysticism. And despite Jean's admonishments, Billy Jack did kick the asses of small-town rednecks who persecuted the peaceful, powerless Native Americans and freedom-loving hippies. Indian scholars ridiculed the film's inaccurate tribal ceremonies. The movie critics ridiculed the movie's "peace through violence" message. Billy Jack wanted to live in peace. He wanted to walk a spiritual path. But when he saw the bullies beating up hippies and Indian kids, well, he just went "berserk!" Despite the critics, moviegoers, both Indian and white, loved *Billy Jack*. The film was one of the most popular independent films to date.

In the final scene, the police hauled Billy Jack off in handcuffs for crushing the windpipe of the Indian-killing son of the fat cat, and three years later the Gordon audience was about to find out what happened next in *The Trial of Billy Jack*.

A lot had happened since the first Billy Jack movie opened in 1971. Watergate sowed distrust in the electorate and fueled liberal Americans' suspicions of big government. Laughlin was an anti-establishment left-winger, and for the third installment of the series he threw in every liberal cause célèbre from the past ten years he could reasonably fit in a script, including thinly veiled re-creations of the My Lai massacre in Vietnam and the Kent State shootings in Ohio. Near the end of the movie, after the popcorn, Milk Duds, and soda had run out, those watching began to squirm. On the screen, a carload of cowboy hat–wearing, redneck thugs snatch Billy Jack's Indian friend, Blue Elk, beat him up, strip him of his pants, and take him to a dance. They carry the bloody, unconscious Indian into an American Legion–like club where the Stars and Stripes and red, white, and blue streamers festoon the back of a stage. A country band plays a waltz for the all-white dancers. The thugs dump Blue Elk onto the dance floor as the whites gather around. One couple is shocked enough to leave, but the others stay.

"Ladies and gentlemen, we got a special attraction here tonight," the rednecks' leader says. "Our good friend Blue Elk is going to do an authentic Indian war dance for ya, ain't ya boy."

A middle-aged man in thick, black glasses tells his wife it's time to leave. "Why? It's time they got theirs!" she declares.

One of the rednecks pushes the drummer aside and starts a tom-tom beat, while the leader lights a cigarillo, burning Blue Elk on the bottom of his foot. The burn jolts him awake as the whites look on sadistically.

Jean rushes in to throw herself between Blue Elk and the bullies.

"How could you possibly enjoy this?" she says to the assembled crowd. "What are you? A BUNCH OF ANIMALS!"

Fortunately for Blue Elk, Billy Jack and his Korean hapkido-master pal arrive to kick some honky butt. If only Billy Jack had been around February 12, 1972, at the American Legion Hall in Gordon. He could have at least called an ambulance.

Oglalas flocked to the border towns to see *The Trial of Billy Jack*. In Chadron, it was held over for a second week. (Even *The Sting* didn't get held over a second week.) If they missed it on the big screen, the movie was shown on network television several times over the next five years.

The "forced to dance Indian style" rumor of 1972, reinforced by sloppy, inaccurate reporting, had reached the eyes of Tom Laughlin and made it into his script.

More than thirty years later, many Oglalas still maintain Raymond Yellow Thunder was forced to dance to the delight of the Gordon American Legion crowd. Curiously, they will also throw in the fact that he was burned by cigarettes on the bottom of his feet, a rumor disproved by the second autopsy.

In March 1972, Bob Yellow Bird, his wife, Joann, and his brother-in-law, Bill Cross, were among the throng standing outside Gordon's Neighborhood Center to listen to what the American Indian Movement's Russell Means had to say about Yellow Thunder's death. AIM was exactly what the three were looking for. Bill had been active in Indian rights causes and had traveled to some meetings outside Nebraska, so he had a passing familiarity with AIM. When he heard the organization was coming to Gordon, he grabbed Bob and Joann and the three drove from Chadron, where they'd been living, to help pave the way, taking testimony from local Oglalas on the mistreatment they'd received there. Bill would serve on the "all-Indian red-feather grand jury."

Bob Yellow Bird had been a rebel with a cause. And now his cause had a name: the American Indian Movement.

It's hard to say what path the young Oglala boy would have taken if it weren't for the fateful day when the policeman wrongly arrested him for stealing the boat. Unjustly snatched from his family and thrown into a reform school in Kearney, Nebraska, four hundred miles from his home, Yellow Bird grew up to be a bitter and angry young man. The reform school "re-formed" the kid who'd never been in any trouble into a juvenile delinquent. He did two stints in juvenile detention, spending the better part of his adolescence imprisoned. When he ran afoul of the law again at age seventeen, a judge told him he had a choice: join the military or go back to Kearney.

He chose the navy.

If he thought that he could avoid Vietnam by serving on battleships, he was wrong. The navy recognized his keen intelligence and made him a radio specialist, sending him to help man landing craft utility boats, which plied the twisting rivers near the Demilitarized Zone to deliver supplies to camps upstream. Yellow Bird saw plenty of fighting as the boats zipped in and out of hot zones while taking enemy fire. His little brother, Richard, joined the navy and ended up in Vietnam as well. The only respite they had was the occasional rendezvous in Saigon to share war stories over some beers.

After Vietnam, Yellow Bird returned to western Nebraska. By then, his parents had passed away, and his brothers and sisters had drifted apart. Unlike the fortunate sons of the wealthy whites, young Lakota men went to Vietnam in droves. Of those lucky enough to return, many had fallen into a world of alcoholism or drugs. No jobs awaited them. Counseling for their post-traumatic stress syndrome, if they could receive it, didn't seem to help. But Bob channeled his anger into something other than a life of crime. He became an activist. He investigated and protested suspicious jailhouse suicides of Oglalas in Alliance. He told a jury once that he first became aware of racism in this period of his life when a less qualified white man in a Panhandle town was hired over him for a job. But that awareness undoubtedly came earlier when the cop robbed him of his childhood.

Bob had grown into a tall young man, with striking good looks and the long black ponytail sported by most male Indian activists. He possessed both ambition and a fierce intelligence, to complement his physical charisma. He wanted to be the new Russell Means, and he had the talent to rise as far as he did. But like Means, Yellow Bird had a drinking problem. It was a habit that would bring him nothing but trouble in the years to come.

In the late sixties, Yellow Bird skipped around from low-paying job to low-paying job in the Nebraska Panhandle, hopping from bar to bar on the weekends until one night at a Chadron tavern he spotted an Oglala woman, Joann Cross, a cute, short drink of water, who'd been trying to make a living in the white man's world herself. They soon became inseparable.

Joann came from a large, well-respected Oglala family from the reservation town of Kyle. Her brother Bill, like her, was small in stature and also possessed a sharp intelligence. He would become Bob's right-hand man in their fight against injustice.

When Bill was nine years old, his father Frank brought his boys and some nephews down to Gordon to the Sheridan County Fair to watch the rodeo. When they departed for Kyle that night, Frank became disoriented and tried to cut through an alleyway. The wheels sunk in a mud puddle, and the boys jumped out to push. Suddenly, two cop cars came in with their lights flashing. Frank, naive in the ways of border town law enforcement, thought they'd come to help. A neighbor had called to report some drunken Indians behind his house, and the cops chose to believe him, despite the fact that the car was full of kids and one adult teetotaler. The police told him to get the hell out of Gordon or he'd be put under arrest. Fortunately, the boys freed the car from the puddle. The cruiser tailed them all the way to the edge of town.

By the 1970s, Bill and Joann's father had moved to Gordon and become a spiritual leader. Like many in his generation, he'd blended his Christian beliefs with traditional Oglala spiritualism. Many thought the Ghost Dance religion had died out after the Wounded Knee Massacre, but bits and pieces remained in his church, where Frank led a congregation on the southeast side of Gordon in a rundown house. While there were no ghost shirts, and the ceremonies took place indoors out of view of the white folks, there was plenty of trancelike singing.

Joann and Bob got married and started a family. She'd brought a boy, Wesley, to the relationship, whom Bob adopted. Wesley's brothers and sisters began arriving at a rapid pace. After Joann, Bob, and Bill traveled to Gordon to hear the AIM leaders speak, they pledged their support to the movement.

While leading his nomadic life, Bob took pre-law and political science classes at Chadron State University. Bob and Bill bought a second-hand mimeograph machine, and soon they were cranking out copies of a newsletter, the *Crazy Horse Advocate*.

The Yellow Birds settled for a while in Crawford, Nebraska, the closest town to Fort Robinson. Unlike Camp Sheridan, which had been dismantled and plowed under eighty years before, Fort Robinson had survived into the twentieth century and become a popular tourist destination for history buffs. The historical and symbolic significance of the site where Crazy Horse in 1877 was killed was not lost on Yellow Bird, who plotted his own small-scale AIM occupation. The federal government rendered it surplus property and announced it would hand the fort over to Nebraska. Bob believed that under the Treaty of 1868 surplus federal land should be returned to the Lakota Nation. Less than a week after the BIA occupation ended, Yellow Bird and about fifty other Indians staged a takeover of the fort's museum. He patterned the demonstration on AIM tactics. Occupy. Make demands. Give explosive and highly quotable quotes to the press, then leave. State troopers moved in, awaiting orders from Governor Exon to end the occupation, but those orders never came. The takeover lasted about fourteen hours and ended without violence.

Prior to ending the occupation, Yellow Bird agreed to plead guilty to two misdemeanor charges. A few days later, he found himself before Judge Moran. It would be their first of many encounters. Moran deviated from the plan, though. He asked Yellow Bird to acknowledge in court that Fort Robinson sat on state property. He refused, and Moran sent him to county jail.

Yellow Bird, like the karate-kicking Vietnam vet Billy Jack, would one day return to Gordon to clean out the "rednecks." A small-scale war of wills between him and the Gordon police would end in tragedy. But first, he would return to the reservation to take part in AIM's most sensational occupation.

Calico was a wide spot on the road that didn't amount to much. Just a dozen or so buildings and a log cabin–style community center on the west side of the reservation. But dozens of AIM activists and Oglalas had crammed into the dilapidated center on a cold February afternoon to decide how to fight the police state that had taken over Pine Ridge.

It was 1973, one year and a week from the day Yellow Thunder was found dead in Gordon. Dennis Banks, Russell Means, Clyde Bellecourt, and Leonard Crow Dog listened along with dozens of AIM members from tribes all over the nation who'd come to the prairie to support their cause. One by one, locals like Severt Young Bear voiced their frustration with the government of Dick Wilson, the president of the tribal council, whom they accused of corruption. To AIM, Wilson represented the status quo. He was a puppet of the Indian Reorganization Act tribal government and part of the wealthier mixed-blood class who wanted to suppress the traditional Lakota ways. They accused him of continuing the longtime practice of handing out lucrative jobs to his cronies and cousins. He, in turn, banned AIM from the reservation. A local front for AIM, the Oglala Civil Rights Organization, led by a small, wiry Oglala, Pedro Bissonette, had sprung up in its place.

As it had in 1890, the federal government invaded the reservation to quell the "troubles." Wilson, with the backing of BIA superintendent Stanley Lyman, called in federal marshals and the FBI. Instead of the bluecoats, it was the marshals dressed from head to toe in blue jumpsuits. FBI agents in dark suits and uniformed BIA police joined the fight. And then there were the GOONs, Guardians of the Oglala Nation, as they liked to call themselves, vigilantes on Wilson's payroll who wanted to stamp out AIM.

Wilson definitely had it out for the native son Means. The two had been exchanging foul words since AIM members looted the Gildersleeves' trading post on their way to Yellow Thunder's second funeral. The reservation soon became polarized between the traditionals and the mixed bloods, the old schism that dated back to the days of Fort Laramie. Shots were being fired into residents' homes at night. Thugs were roughing up their opponents. The victims were both AIM supporters and AIM foes. Many Oglalas chose one side or the other, but the majority simply kept their heads low and tried to avoid trouble.

Yellow Thunder's cousins, Birgil Kills Straight and Severt Young Bear, had joined AIM after the Gordon protest and were later elected to the tribal council. They promptly launched impeachment proceedings against Wilson on corruption charges. Three days earlier, Wilson had squirmed out of the trial by waiving a twenty-one-day waiting period, giving Kills Straight no time to gather evidence. They lost the vote.

Now what? The traditionals inside the community center were fed up.

It was Sunday evening and growing dark. One by one, hereditary leaders, medicine men, and elderly women stood up and asked the warriors to take action. The BIA offices and tribal headquarters were the most obvious targets for a takeover. So obvious that they were covered in sandbags and surrounded by armored personnel carriers (APCs), federal marshals, tribal cops, and scores of FBI agents.

But there was a better spot.

Although they were totally unprepared for what they were about to do, the AIM members piled into dozens of cars. They drove through the dark countryside speeding toward the heavily fortified BIA offices in Pine Ridge five miles to the south. Lookouts spotted the caravan as soon as it reached the town fringes. The police scanners crackled; panicky officers sent a warning over the airwaves. The radicals are coming! The radicals are coming! But the radicals passed the BIA offices and tribal government buildings, honking their horns, flashing their headlights, and flipping the scowling feds the bird.

The caravan sped east on Highway 18 with one FBI car tailing them to radio back reports. When they reached Highway 27, they turned north—on their way to Wounded Knee.

The following day in Chadron, Bob Yellow Bird heard about the occupation and made his way north. He had to make his way past APCs, marshals, helicopters, FBI agents, network television crews, BIA police, Wilson's GOON squad, white vigilantes, and assorted curiosity seekers. They were all forming a ring outside Wounded Knee, and it was closing fast.

As Bob made his way into the bowl-shaped valley, the topography looked much the same as it did when the reporter Charley Allen and his companions rode their horses over the ridge in December 1890. The only major change was a country road bisecting the site. Instead of rows of army tents and tipis, more than eighty rust-bucket cars were parked near the trading post near the creek. Where a Hotchkiss gun on a small bluff to the northwest once spat death on Big Foot's band, a small white church stood next to a cemetery where a mass grave held more than one hundred massacre victims. Bob greeted armed AIM warriors standing guard next to the church.

As he walked into the general store and museum to the south of the church, he found it already looted. Shelves were now empty, glass cases shattered, relics gathered in the museum had been "repossessed."

The Indians inside were hard at work concocting Molotov cocktails with empty Coke bottles and gasoline.

Nearby guards stood watch over the Gildersleeves and an elderly Catholic priest. Clive Gildersleeve and his part-Ojibwa wife, Agnes, had run the trading post since 1930, but they'd recently sold the business to Jan and Jim Czywczynski. The new owners—who were away when the takeover began—tried to capitalize on the notoriety Dee Brown's book had brought to Wounded Knee by opening the museum. To AIM, their so-called museum and gift shop were travesties, nothing more than whites profiting off the massacre of the Lakotas. The Gildersleeves, and an elderly couple who'd been visiting when AIM invaded, were released a few days later. In the final days of the occupation, the businesses were completely destroyed, burned to the ground, and the two families would never return. Their departure would mark the end of white-owned mom-and-pop stores on the reservation.

For the first time since 1890, the words "Wounded Knee" appeared on front pages across the nation. Means wasted no time using the pay phone inside the trading post to call major media outlets. And TV crews wasted no time arriving there. Means and Banks soon became household names. They were now the most famous Indians in America—heroes to some, dangerous subversives to others.

Yellow Bird discovered that the occupiers hadn't brought nearly enough ammunition, guns, and food, but they'd brought plenty of people, including women, children, and teenagers. He joined other Vietnam veterans, who dug bunkers and patrolled the perimeter just as the military had taught them in the war. Yellow Bird found seventeen-year-old Tom Poor Bear pitching in.

AIM had once again demonstrated a genius for making headlines by occupying Wounded Knee, but as far as a strategic position to hold, it was a disaster in the making. The vets knew they couldn't allow the feds, who were manning APCs less than a half-mile away, to take the high ground surrounding the concave valley. And they had only an odd assortment of hunting rifles, shotguns, and handguns to hold them back. Some of the weapons were so obsolete they had no usable ammunition. Within a few days, the occupiers constructed nine bunkers and a system of connecting trenches and foxholes, each manned around the clock. The bunkers were made of old logs, cinderblocks, and pillowcases filled with dirt.

The vets knew a thing or two about military tactics, and Means knew a thing or two about propaganda. As spokesman for the occupation, he'd already sent AIM's demands out to the world: sovereignty for the Indian peoples, the abolishment of the Indian Reorganization Act tribal government, and the enforcement of the Treaty of 1868, including the return of the sacred Black Hills to the Lakotas.

In Gordon, strangers with out-of-state license plates began passing through town. The border town businesses were again having a heyday. FBI agents in a helicopter once swooped down to Rushville, landing in an empty parking lot, just to buy a few bags of groceries. Pat Shald's older brother Mike had recently left the grocery business, selling the Jack and Jill north of Gordon to invest in the Hacienda Motel on Highway 20. It would prove to be a fortunate business move. Mike ran the restaurant and lounge, which would host scores of marshals and G-men for years to come.

As it was in 1890 and during the Yellow Thunder march, fear gripped the communities. AIM members and sympathizers from tribes across the country were making their way to the new battle site, many of them passing through Gordon, Rushville, and Whiteclay. Who were these hippies and out-of-towners? Residents began locking their doors and sleeping with guns next to their beds. Gordon was abuzz when the communist Angela Davis arrived at Gordon's Neighborhood Center on her way to show solidarity with her Indian brothers and sisters. A six-foot-tall black woman walking down the streets of Gordon? And a commie, at that! These were indeed strange times.

Yellow Bird's brother-in-law, Bill Cross, lent a hand at spiritual leader Frank Fools Crow's place in Kyle, helping guide those wanting to join the occupation into Wounded Knee. If they weren't there on the day of the takeover, they were brought in through the same gullies where Big Foot's people fled to escape the Seventh Cavalry's bullets.

Cross snuck reporters in, along with white radicals and AIM members from all over the country. Crow Dog's property on the Rosebud Reservation and Severt Young Bear's residence in Porcupine also became staging points. Left-wing sympathizers organized airlifts to drop in supplies. Vernon Bellecourt, who hadn't been at Calico the night of the takeover, drummed up support on university campuses throughout the nation. Wounded Knee rallies broke out all over the country.

One day, as a wet snow fell on the brown hills outside of Kyle, Bill watched as a middle-aged Indian man and his young wife walked up to Fools Crow's place. They'd arrived penniless, but they felt a calling to go to Wounded Knee, to be a part of the spiritual awakening. Bill was shocked to see that the woman didn't have any shoes. They said an eagle had led them there. It wasn't the first time Bill had witnessed Indians arriving at Fools Crow's who said they'd been guided there. It was a thirty-mile trip from Kyle to Wounded Knee and taking the well-guarded main roads was impossible, but Bill felt compelled to help them complete their pilgrimage. They walked the entire way, the woman stoically pressing on in the cold without any shoes. Her only respite came when her husband carried her on his back over the damp ground.

One night, Bob was keeping watch in a bunker with two other warriors when a sniper's bullet came flying through a cinder block, missing him by inches. He grabbed his rifle, cursing the unseen assailant as he shot wildly into the darkness.

Firefights were common. Both sides accused the other of starting the exchanges. Others believed white vigilantes or BIA cops were provoking them. The first death came on April 17 when a U.S. government bullet killed a white man posing as an Apache, Frank Clear Water. Many dubious characters such as Clear Water had made it into the village. FBI informants, spies, and right-wing radicals acting on their own had an easy time talking their way in.

On the night of April 26, gunfire burst over the prairie, red tracers darting over the now burned grass. Both sides fired thousands of rounds at each other. The FBI shot teargas into the perimeter, flushing an Oglala army veteran, Buddy Lamont, into the open where he caught a sharpshooter's bullet in the chest. His death marked the beginning of the end.

Means and Clyde Bellecourt left Wounded Knee for Washington to negotiate an end to the occupation, leaving Banks behind. Food began to grow scarce as the feds became better at stopping couriers bearing backpacks full of provisions. Negotiations for a settlement proceeded in fits. More were leaving through the gullies at night than coming in.

The occupation ended after seventy-one days with another paper victory. As the end neared, Banks melted away into the night. Bob Yellow Bird made it out unmolested, returning to Joann and his kids in Chadron without detection. Meanwhile, FBI agents began arresting everyone they could put their hands on.

The occupation's end didn't stop the tensions and dirty war on Pine Ridge. In fact, life there worsened.

Bob Yellow Bird and his thirty followers gathered near his home in Gordon's southeast corner to stage their first protest. It was two years after Yellow Thunder's death and one year after the Wounded Knee occupation. The only concrete result of the march on Gordon, the Human Relations Council, would be meeting shortly in the high school gymnasium.

Yellow Bird had to be disappointed with the small turnout. Joann and Bill were there. The others were from the younger generation. It was the elders, those he believed were so accustomed to the racism around them that they didn't notice it anymore, who were absent.

The protesters hoisted their signs and started up Main Street.

Yellow Bird believed Gordon needed his help. He'd recently moved his family into a white frame house on Ash Street near the edge of Indian town, close enough to Highway 20 to hear the semitrucks roar past. As far as Bob was concerned, the council was a failure. Gordon had made no progress in the way it treated Indians. The AIM chapter left behind had withered away. He was there to change the status quo, and that day's march would be his first opportunity to do something.

Joann had given birth to a child nearly every year since 1969, and the one-bedroom house that would eventually house seven kids was already a noisy, chaotic place. Despite the "Indian town" moniker, several white families lived nearby. The sweat lodge in the front yard and the tipi and occasional bonfire in the back irked some of his elderly neighbors. The house soon became AIM's unofficial headquarters in western Nebraska, and cops stopped by on a regular basis.

After the small group of protesters arrived at the gymnasium, Bob delivered a long list of grievances to the council. The streets in the southeast side of town were unpaved and poorly maintained. Doctors at the hospital were not providing equal treatment to Oglala patients. Indians could find only low-paid, menial labor. Drunks arrested in Gordon and brought to the new county jail in Rushville were not given transportation back home. Yes, there was now an Indian on the Gordon police force, but he wasn't to their liking.

"We want a full-blood Indian on the police force," he told the council.

He criticized the school curriculum and demanded an Indian be hired as a teacher or counselor. (He did not specify the blood quantum.)

Russell Means's brother Ted drove down from the reservation and joined the meeting, telling the council that "the national leaders of AIM are very concerned about the situation in Gordon. It has been two years since we were here and the council has failed drastically. AIM stands ready to focus national attention on Gordon if needed."

Yellow Bird gave the council thirty days to meet his demands for housing, sixty days for the hospital, and ninety days to clear up the problems with the police and school. His strident tones and demands alienated the council from the beginning. The two tribal members serving on the board, Midge Morgan and Myrtle Ash, were so offended, they resigned.

Reva Evans ran the story of the march across the front page of the *Gordon Journal* with a picture underneath. She let a hospital administrator respond to the charges and ran a statement from the Human Relations Council chairman. She ended the article in an indignant tone, lamenting Morgan and Ash's resignations: "Midge's and Myrtle's record with working with the community action council speak for themselves."

At the end of the Wounded Knee occupation, Evans ran a two-page photo spread of the destruction AIM left behind. The issue sold out, and she reran the photos the following week. Evans, who rarely reported national stories, made a point of printing any bad news about the movement. And there had been quite a bit to report.

After the remaining three members of the Human Relations Council ruled that Yellow Bird's accusations were unfounded, Evans got busy on her Royal typewriter and started tapping away.

"How sharper than a serpent's tooth it is / To have a thankless child," she began, quoting *King Lear*.

She seemed unaware of her patronizing attitude toward Native Americans. She would never let criticism of Gordon go unanswered. The town had made leaps and bounds toward improving the Indians' living conditions, she wrote. One teacher at the elementary school had been conducting an Indian studies class. Everyone had to wait hours at the hospital when they had a backlog. She also noted that the town was horrified by Yellow Thunder's death and had been equally victimized by the bad publicity. And besides, the majority of the perpetrators were not town residents (the key word being "residents").

Everyone in the Indian community knew where to go to complain about mistreatment: Yellow Bird's house on Ash Street. For activists passing through, their home became a flophouse or a place to pitch a tent. Bob, still intermittently attending classes at Chadron State, worked at a desk in the corner of the living room/kitchen. It was piled high with law and history books and covered in a layer of newspaper clippings. Cigarette butts filled an ashtray to the brim, for Bob was a heavy smoker. A pay phone installed on the wall became a necessity. Since his living room had more visitors passing through than a bus station—every one of them wanting to call someone—that only made economic sense. He'd hauled the mimeograph machine used to publish the first issues of the *Crazy Horse Advocate* to Gordon, and when the mood struck, Bill and he would publish their takes on current events. Each issue was a minor miracle considering all the rambunctious kids—none older than six—running around the cramped house. But they had paid subscribers, and Bob and Bill had an obligation to print their thoughts. Besides documenting injustice in Gordon, they continued their campaign to have Fort Robinson returned to the Lakotas. State Senator Ernie Chambers, the Nebraska Unicameral's only black lawmaker, had sponsored a bill to relinquish the title. It never made it out of committee.

Yellow Bird's march up Main Street to the gymnasium accomplished little besides informing the cops that AIM had returned. To them, the organization was full of notorious "radical Indians" who'd infamously looted the BIA building in Washington, begun a riot in Custer, South Dakota, occupied Wounded Knee, and labeled Gordon as "a racist, redneck town." The affable Bob Case was still chief of police, but Gordon recently began recruiting cops from outside Sheridan County, and few of them treated drunken Indians any better than the untrained cops of yesteryear.

Three months after arriving, the Yellow Birds held a workshop in their backyard on solving racism problems in the Panhandle, and several dignitaries came, including the Nebraska Indian commissioner Robert Mackey. Even Reva Evans dropped by with a pad and pen and remarked in a front-page story about the positive atmosphere. She quoted Yellow Bird in the story: "Anytime an Indian tries to do something, he's considered a radical."

In July, he held a preconvention planning meeting for AIM. He announced that three hundred to four hundred Native American activists would be arriving at Gordon's city auditorium. Only three showed up.

"There has been a remarkable change in Gordon, especially since we got a new mayor," Yellow Bird told Evans, sounding positive despite the miserable turnout.

The new mayor was Jane Morgan, a lifelong Gordon resident and employee of Borman Chevrolet, who had friends in the Native American community. Morgan believed that alcoholism was a root problem in Gordon—for both Indians and whites—that wasn't being addressed. It was hard to argue. Intoxication was still a crime, and police officers still had the right to arrest anyone they believed to be drunk and toss them in jail. If they didn't, drunken Indians would pass out in the gutter on Main Street, the businessmen argued. And they couldn't have that. Especially in the winter when sleeping in a snowbank could be deadly.

But it was funny how no whites were ever arrested for public drunkenness. It was as if no cowboy, farmer, or one of the upright businessmen ever had a drink and walked down the sidewalk. But there were no treatment programs nearby for anyone seeking help. Morgan would try to change that one day. Meanwhile, Bob and Bill began compiling arrest statistics and taking affidavits from alleged victims of police brutality and mistreatment.

One day, a brouhaha broke out at a local store when a clerk accused an Oglala woman of shoplifting. A crowd gathered as the woman declared her innocence. Someone dashed over to Yellow Bird's and fetched Bob, who ran over and whisked the woman away before she could be put under arrest.

"Now what was that all about?" he asked when she was safely in his house.

"I guess they wanted these back," she said, reaching into her bra and pulling out a package of shoplifted underwear.

Everyone busted out laughing. The incident became known as the "Bloomer Riot."

After the Wounded Knee occupation, violence on the reservation became contagious, sweeping over the prairie faster than the smallpox epidemics of old. Stepping into Pine Ridge was like walking into a third-world dictatorship. Everyone had a part to play in America's banana republic. To the left-wing media, AIM played the part of the heroic peasants struggling for democracy against brutal dictators, while the FBI and Wilson's GOON squads played the role of the secret police. A corrupt election was part of the script. Russell Means ran for tribal president against his arch-rival Dick Wilson in early 1974 and lost. Accusations of voter fraud flew from both sides. The Justice Department investigated and found evidence of widespread irregularities, including hundreds of votes cast by outsiders and nonregistered tribal members.

Meanwhile, mysterious deaths and shootings were common occurrences. Both sides employed violence and intimidation. Carter Camp, a member of the Ponca nation, AIM's newly appointed national director and onetime head of security during the Wounded Knee occupation, shot Clyde Bellecourt in the stomach at the Rosebud Reservation. A month later, BIA police shot and killed Wounded Knee leader Pedro Bissonette. The feds said he came out of his car brandishing a rifle, and the BIA cops fired in self-defense. AIM said it was an assassination. His death would remain controversial for decades.

Jess Trueblood, a BIA police officer and first cousin to the Shalds in Gordon, was found dead in the driveway of an AIM activist after blowing holes in the side of the house with a shotgun. Amazingly, the death was ruled a suicide even though the bullet had entered the back of his skull and he had a congenital defect that prevented him from raising his arms above his head. Independent coroners investigating the evidence doubted the suicide ruling. Leonard Crow Dog's sister was found beaten to death in a field. A Wilson supporter, William Steele, was gunned down in a drive-by shooting. The man accused of the crime was shot in the neck and wounded while out on bond. A friend of his was found dead the next day with multiple gunshot wounds in the back. In the first four months of 1975, there were six deaths and sixty-seven assaults on Pine Ridge. Despite the massive presence of FBI agents with the authority to investigate murders on reservations, none of these cases were solved and there were always two versions of every incident. Who to believe?

Banks and Means were brought before a federal court in St. Paul, Minnesota, on charges stemming from the Wounded Knee occupation. Their legal dream team that included famed lawyer William Kunstler got them off. The judge proclaimed U.S. government malfeasance. It was a great victory. But Means and Banks's troubles were just beginning. In March 1975, Means went drinking one night in a bar in Scenic, South Dakota, the reservation's northern version of Whiteclay, Nebraska. He began arguing with a former AIM supporter, Martin Montileaux; then he and a companion, Richard Marshall, followed Montileaux into the men's room. Witnesses heard a gunshot. Montileaux caught a bullet in the neck. He testified on his deathbed that Means did not pull the trigger. A court later convicted Marshall of the crime.

After drinking and fighting in a bar in Fort Yates, North Dakota, on the Standing Rock Reservation, Means and Tom Poor Bear, serving as his bodyguard, had a run-in with a BIA policeman. The cop shot Means in the side. He escaped serious injury, but his friends and enemies began to wonder how many more of Means's nine lives remained.

The dirty war at Pine Ridge reached its darkest day on June 26, 1975, when two FBI agents followed two fugitives into an AIM stronghold near the reservation town of Oglala. As soon as Agents Ronald Williams and Jack Coler left their cars, they were met with a barrage of gunfire. Coler went to his trunk to grab a rifle, but shrapnel from a bullet struck his bicep and severed an artery. He couldn't stanch the flow of blood and soon passed out. After radioing for help—and already wounded by bullets in his side and a foot—Williams hobbled over to help Coler. He recognized the futility of the situation, tossed aside his handgun, and attempted to stop Coler's bleeding. As he did so, the AIM loyalists surrounded the car. Among them was a bodyguard and enforcer for the organization, Leonard Peltier.

Peltier was a part-Lakota, part-Ojibwa from the Turtle Mountain Reservation in North Dakota, who was on the lam after failing to appear for a pretrial hearing on charges of attempting to murder a Milwaukee police officer.

What happened next would be controversial for decades to come. But what is known is that someone fired a bullet from an AR-15 rifle at close range. Williams raised his right hand in a pitiful attempt to protect himself, but the bullet sheared off his fingers and entered his brain. Coler, already passed out and perhaps dead, received a bullet in the head as well.

The dozen or so AIM members nearby escaped after a five-hour shootout with the BIA police and the FBI. One hundred and fifty agents invaded the reservation. The dragnet went on for months as suspects were rounded up all over the country. Banks went on the lam, refusing to turn himself in after his conviction on charges stemming from the Custer courthouse riot. Two men were tried for aiding and abetting the murder, but Kunstler, once again called in to defend AIM, helped secure a "not guilty" verdict. The FBI was convinced that Peltier was the triggerman. A jury later pronounced him "guilty" and he was sentenced to two consecutive life terms. The verdict would be debated for decades. To some, Peltier was the Indian Nelson Mandela, a political prisoner, unjustly jailed for a crime he did not commit. To the FBI, he was a cold-blooded murderer.

The FBI agents' murders heralded the end of AIM's three-year run as a national movement. Banks would spend the next nine years in California and New York avoiding his South Dakota prison sentence stemming from the Custer courthouse riot. He eventually surrendered and served a fourteen-month sentence. Means would also serve time, and continue to feud with the Bellecourts, who retreated to Minnesota.

Whether or not Peltier was wrongly convicted, the FBI agents had been ruthlessly gunned down by someone in AIM, and the movement's already tarnished image among the whites and many Oglalas was sealed. But despite the turmoil within the national leadership, Bob Yellow Bird pressed on.

A half mile west of the Yellow Birds' house, the Hacienda Motel had been billeting marshals and G-men since the occupation. The grand opening in 1973 had been fortuitous for the former grocer and chamber of commerce president Mike Shald and his business partners. They not only enjoyed the cattle buyer and traveler market they'd anticipated when conceiving the business, now they had rooms full of feds who stayed for weeks at a time. By 1974, Mike had opened the Hacienda Restaurant and Lounge, located in the back through a separate entrance. The marshals and FBI agents, though rivals, spent their days doing battle with AIM on the reservation and their evenings unwinding in the lounge, eating prime rib from a recipe passed down from Mike's father, the butcher Ferd Shald. Some of the agents got drunk on their per diem while carousing with local women, both married and unmarried. It wasn't uncommon for the bar to take in four hundred dollars a night. With a 60 percent profit margin, the lounge was a cash cow. When agents and marshals weren't at the Hacienda, they were down at the American Legion club, less than a hundred yards from the Yellow Birds' home.

With the feds in town, the local cops may have thought they had the moral authority to take on AIM's representative. Yellow Bird felt that the dual standard of justice Gordon had imposed on the Indians for decades was still alive and well. The two sides began to go after each other with gusto.

The hope and optimism of late 1974, with Yellow Bird tossing platitudes at Mayor Morgan, was fading under a barrage of nightstick blows. A mini version of the Pine Ridge troubles was well under way in Sheridan County. It was a chicken-or-the-egg situation for Yellow Bird. An AIM council had appointed him Nebraska coordinator in 1974. Right-wingers considered the movement a militant, even a Communist organization. Bob was labeled a "radical" by the local cops. But other than organizing poorly attended workshops, small marches up Main Street, and being a pain in the ass at city council meetings, Yellow Bird had done nothing militant. He did, however, drink to excess and engage in fights at local bars. He was regularly brought to court on assault and battery charges. Most of the time, the charges were dismissed.

Despite his dark side, Bob's activism continued unabated. His right-hand man Bill would watch in amazement as Bob would rally the troops and declare that they were heading over to the county attorney's office to give Mike Smith a piece of their minds. Cross thought Yellow Bird had more courage than all of them put together. Bob didn't need the "liquid courage" to confront anybody.

"Come on guys, it's gotta be done," Bob would say, and the next thing Bill knew he'd be walking into the attorney's Main Street office to watch Yellow Bird and Smith engage in a shouting match.

In late 1975, Dale Mason, a Volunteer in Service to America worker assigned to the Nebraska Indian Commission, and Cathy Merrill, a staff attorney for Panhandle Legal Services, arrived to help Yellow Bird compile statistics and case histories on alleged police brutality to document the dual standards of justice in Sheridan County. The arrest statistics were nothing new. The local papers had been publishing them in January every year. The majority of arrests in Sheridan County were for intoxication, and the majority of intoxication arrests were of Native Americans.

Meanwhile, police chief Bob Case and county sheriff Jim Talbot were forced to recruit officers from out of town; many were of questionable character. One policeman had arrived in Gordon with a South Korean wife in tow. While she lay sick in a Gordon hospital bed, he skipped town, leaving the woman, who barely spoke English, without a penny to her name and a huge hospital bill. Reva Evans spearheaded a fund-raising campaign in the *Gordon Journal* to pay her debts and buy her airline ticket to Seoul.

The town did hire a couple of Indian policemen, but they turned out to be of the Dick Wilson GOON squad variety, at least according to Yellow Bird.

AIM was a youth movement, so Bob and Bill received little support from Gordon's Oglala elders, especially from Bill's father, Frank, who didn't approve of his son-in-law's methods. Bill would still visit his father at his house, but they always argued. When Joann and Bob first married, Frank liked his intelligent and charming son-in-law, but since Bob had moved to town and begun the protests, Frank had soured on him. He told his son hanging around with Bob would lead to trouble. He offered to find Bill a job in another town or to let him stay at his home. Bill tried to explain the civil rights movement to his father. He told him that Indians didn't have to put up with the grief the white man had been doling out for five hundred years.

"Dad, you've been kicked so long by the whites, you don't even know that you're being kicked anymore."

Frank didn't see it that way. There were good people in town, like the Shald family. He wanted to build bridges between the two cultures. This wasn't the way to go about it. He was a teetotaler. He didn't drink or smoke as did his notorious son-in-law. If someone got drunk and had a run-in with the cops, that was their fault. The police were just doing their job, he said.

Bill loved his father, but they were from two different generations.

While Gordon, Whiteclay, and Rushville remained tense, Sheridan County was spared the extreme violence of Pine Ridge to the north.

That all changed in 1976.

It was "standing room only" at the Hacienda Restaurant the night of March 11, 1976. The Nebraska Indian Commission had reserved the spot for an on-site hearing. It was a toothless group that could raise a stink by writing memos. Its members had no real power. But it sounded impressive enough, and the fact that the commissioners had traveled hours from

Lincoln to investigate concerns about Gordon surely meant something. At least they'd temporarily moved the feds out of their favorite watering hole.

Police Chief Bob Case sat in a chair and caught a barrage of flak as accusations came at him faster than a pheasant on the fly. The activists had already scored a major victory that day. For a year, Yellow Bird had been trying to enlist allies in his fight against Sheridan County law enforcement. The American Civil Liberties Union of Nebraska, the Native American Rights Fund, state senators, even AIM sympathizer Marlon Brando. Nobody was interested. Finally, an attorney for the U.S. Civil Rights Commission traveled from Kansas City that week to attempt mediation. Apparently, he rubbed a couple cops the wrong way. A few hours before the meeting, two of Gordon's policemen had resigned. One stated that he didn't agree with the way Sheridan County practiced law enforcement. He'd also been a prime target of AIM's brutality complaints. Case now had two jobs to fill.

Yellow Bird had taken up plenty of police hours. He told everyone that he was the victim of political persecution, but Case and Yellow Bird's friends knew otherwise. He had a drinking problem, a quick temper, and he simply couldn't stay out of the bars.

Cathy Merrill, who'd helped him collect evidence of police brutality, warned him about drinking in the border town dives. "They're dangerous places for you. If you're going to be harmed, that's where it's going to happen."

He'd been arrested eleven times in 1975 for everything from passing bad checks to assault and battery, reckless driving, and intoxication. On six of the charges, he was either found "not guilty" or the cases were dismissed. In March, a jury pronounced him "not guilty" for punching another customer in the mouth at the Western Bar. When Reva Evans asked him how he'd escaped conviction if his assertion that no Indian could receive a fair trial in Sheridan County was true, he said: "It was a fluke. Besides, I was innocent."

While in the Sheridan County jail on one of the assault and battery charges, he'd organized a hunger strike, proclaiming the meal of Swiss steak, mashed potatoes, corn, and dinner rolls "inedible." He demanded real coffee, not "coffee-colored water." As soon as he was released, the hunger strike ended. His luck ended when he received thirty days for resisting an officer in late December.

A few weeks after finishing his sentence, Yellow Bird and his VISTA friends made their first formal accusations against the police, accusing Sheridan County law enforcement of brutality and misconduct. Michael Smith, the FBI, and a committee of eight Gordon residents—hardly a neutral body in AIM's mind—investigated the complaints.

"The charges of police brutality by the Gordon officers have no substance and are totally unfounded," Smith said in a statement.

The attorney's investigation did not quash Yellow Bird's zeal. Now, two months later, with the Nebraska Indian Commission backing him up, he led the harangue against Case. Mercifully for the police chief, the man of the hour arrived, and he was out of the hot seat.

Russell Means strode through the door, out on bond from one of his many South Dakota arrests. He was by then arguably the most famous, or infamous, living Indian in America, depending on one's point of view. Andy Warhol had painted him. He was up there with Marilyn Monroe and Campbell's soup.

It didn't take him long to get warmed up.

"You can only kick somebody so long before they get tired of that kicking!" he said. "Four years ago this month, the American Indian Movement and Oglalas came into Gordon because they were concerned about the law enforcement problem in this area of the state. . . . The town of Gordon has regressed rather than progressed. It is as bad if not worse than it was in 1972. The problem is not really the police force in Sheridan County or Gordon, Nebraska. The problem is the leadership or lack or of it. Specifically the police chief, city manager, and city council. The unfortunate thing is that when these authorities of Sheridan County continue to set the example for the young people with racist policies and ignorance, well, we can't look for any improvement in the forthcoming generation."

Fired up by Means's speech, Yellow Bird and one hundred supporters left the Hacienda to make their way to that night's regularly scheduled city council meeting to level charges of selective policing, brutality, and misconduct. In their hands were twenty-six statements from local citizens. Of the twenty-six, only six were from the Indian community. The rest came from whites.

Yellow Bird stood up in the back of the room, wearing his wide-brimmed Billy Jack hat, holding a rolled-up piece of paper with the complaints in his right hand, a cigarette smoldering between his fingers. He began ripping into Mayor Morgan. The two engaged in a heated argument as a TV crew taped the exchange.

"The police department has continued to brutalize Indians by the sanction of the city council!" Yellow Bird shouted.

Shouting. Demanding. Threatening. This was AIM's modus operandi. Yellow Bird hadn't learned how to win friends and influence people. Morgan was sympathetic to his cause, and even believed that Sheridan County law enforcement had some shortcomings, but when faced with Yellow Bird's fiery accusations, she became embroiled in a heated argument.

At the end of the meeting, the acting director of the Nebraska Indian Commission handed the complaints over to Morgan. She submitted them to Michael Smith the next day.

Smith answered later with a detailed response, which was printed in its entirety in the *Gordon Journal*. Some of the complaints were trivial, seemingly inserted to pad out the list: a man who was angry that he'd been given a ticket for running a stop sign; a minor in possession of alcohol, arrested by Gordon police outside town limits (which they had the right to do). Others concerned cops offering rides to teenage girls and allegedly making salacious remarks. The statements did not come with any corroborating evidence or investigations on the part of the VISTA workers, a fact Smith noted with scorn at the beginning of his letter.

Smith had acquired funding from the county commissioners to hire outside polygraph experts and sent the county sheriffs to find corroborating evidence. They found instances of police misconduct in two cases. In one instance, a white kid was shoved up against a patrol car, and the second case involved an officer shooting an Oglala resident's dog. As far as the teenage girls' accusations, the officers passed the polygraph. They had shown poor judgment by giving them rides, but had committed no criminal acts, Smith said. The fact that so many whites had come forward and complained had to be addressed. The letter had a stinging rebuke for Bob Case's poorly trained officers.

"The extensive interviews and examinations resulted in findings that the officers, to varying degrees, held improper attitudes in dealing with the public and understanding the function of their position," Smith wrote. "One revealing comment came from the private investigators. I shall quote: 'These officers do not seem to feel that they are public servants, but rather overlords whose word is law, and if they give a command it had better be obeyed, and immediately and without question.'"

He called for a more thorough screening process and better training for the Gordon police. He hoped in the wake of the two cops' resignations that more qualified applicants could be found. Chief Case resigned within a few months, tired of all the headaches stemming from Yellow Bird's accusations. Within a year, he would be managing the Hacienda Motel.

The fact that Smith had run the investigation and the sheriff's department carried out the search for corroborating evidence amounted to a "whitewash" in Yellow Bird's mind.

May 4, 1976. Another night of barhopping. Bob, Joann, and a few friends started their night at the Sheridan Lounge, the turn-of-the-century hotel on the corner of Second and Main that had seen better days. At three stories, it was the tallest fixture in town, excluding church steeples and grain elevators. The onetime motel had once hosted traveling businessmen and wealthy ranchers, but its lobby had been gutted and a slop-shoot honky-tonk installed on the first floor. Rooms upstairs were now rented by the month. Bob, Joann, and their cronies began putting away the beers and filling ashtrays as twangy music played on the jukebox in the corner and cowboys and Indians shot pool under soft lights.

The second hop of the night would be their last. They jumped in their car and took the backstreets to the Hacienda Lounge, keeping an eye out for the cops on the way.

Sitting across from them at the Hacienda were three other regulars from the Gordon bar scene, David Gardner, Ronald Zywiec, and Ronald Haag, all in their midtwenties. As Yellow Bird sat at a nearby table, he grew drunker and louder, and started bragging openly about working over a Gordon cop, his nemesis Roger Etzelmiller. The two tables soon began exchanging verbal barbs. Haag challenged Yellow Bird to an arm-wrestling match.

"You guys cool it," said Bob Buchan, the same bartender on duty the night Pat Hare and Butch Lutter pushed Yellow Thunder into the Legion Hall. He told the waitress to stop serving the tables.

Yellow Bird walked up to the waitress: "Why don't you call the cops? I'd like to get Etzelmiller. I got a magnum for him."

When the bar closed, the two groups walked out together. In the parking lot, the spat turned into a shoving match. Gardner and one of

Yellow Bird's friends began to push each other around. Joann, who'd always been a tomboy as a child and never backed down from a fight, smacked Haag on the ear. Haag pushed her to the ground. Bob picked her up, grabbed her by the arm, and pushed her into the car.

"I'm coming back with an equalizer!" he shouted as he sped off. He raced down Highway 20 to his house, ran inside and grabbed a .22 revolver, making Joann stay behind.

Five minutes later, he pulled up to Gardner's truck, jumped out and drew the gun.

"Yellow Bird, put that fucking gun down," Gardner said.

The .22 snapped, no louder than a cap gun. Gardner crumpled to the ground, clutching his bleeding gut. Zywiec turned on his heels, dashing toward the Hacienda Lounge door. He didn't make it. He caught a bullet in the butt; a second struck his arm. Haag dashed unscathed across the highway into a field.

Yellow Bird got out of town while the gettin' was good. He sped north through the reservation, arriving at his younger brother Richard's house in Rapid City within a few hours. Richard drove him to an acquaintance's home on a North Dakota reservation that night. While Gardner spent the next month in the Gordon hospital recovering from his gunshot wound, Yellow Bird wandered the country as a fugitive.

Where was Bob Yellow Bird?

He was having a relatively enjoyable time for someone wanted on "shooting with intent to kill" charges. It was easy to hide out on almost any reservation in the homes of AIM sympathizers. He even made it as far as Philadelphia for AIM's July 4 bicentennial protests. If the cops had been watching the news footage, they might have spotted him there.

But while Bob was attempting to spoil America's big birthday party by reminding it of its mistreatment of the Indians, Joann was having a tough time back in Gordon. She started a fight over the rent with her landlord, and when the Gordon police came and tried to subdue her, she bit one officer on the arm. The cops booked her for disorderly conduct, resisting arrest, and abusing an officer. Soon, the authorities were threatening to take their children away. Joann and Bill played a shell game with the kids, hiding them with friends, keeping them out of the hands of social workers. Fortunately, it was summer and they weren't attending school.

Bob was worried about what Joann was going through. He'd been in contact with AIM attorneys, who'd advised him to surrender. They believed they had a decent chance of winning the case. Since the Wounded Knee trials, AIM's legal defense fund coffers had swelled with contributions from liberals and Europeans. Bob would receive the best defense money could buy, they assured him. Maybe not Kunstler, but pretty damn close.

In late July, he walked into the Gordon police station with Nebraska Indian commissioner Steve Janis and said, "I think I have some business with the chief of police."

Three hours before turning himself in, Bob had given an interview to Reva Evans in her Main Street office. He told a much different story than he would reveal on the witness stand later that year. He claimed that it was all a setup and someone with money had paid to have him assassinated. As he left the Hacienda, the three white men had ambushed him. He didn't have a gun, and therefore had never fired any shots.

His bond was set at five thousand dollars.

The Hacienda shooting was just a prelude. The most tragic night in Indian-white relations in Gordon since Yellow Thunder's death was only weeks away.

Yellow Bird was enjoying a night out with his wife, Joann, and her sister Fern. Bill and Dennis Cross had come along, and they piled into the Sheridan Lounge where they drank longneck beers and shot pool. Joann and Fern were both pregnant—Joann at seven and a half months, more visibly so. It was September 15, and Bob, out on bail awaiting the trial on the shooting-with-intent-to-kill charges, was once again ignoring advice to stay out of the Sheridan County bars.

Dennis Cross sat quietly at a table with his brothers and sisters, waiting for his turn at the pool table. Like his brother Bill, he was a Vietnam veteran. Unlike his brother, he'd seen a lot of action serving in the infantry. He saw things he didn't care to talk about. He had nightmares that sent him bolting up in bed. He came back from the jungle and tried to lead a "normal" life for a while. He held down a steady job, had a home and girlfriend. Bill coped with his Vietnam experience by throwing himself into work, activism, and his studies at Chadron State. Dennis, however, had turned to the bottle. By 1976, he was spending more and more time living on the streets or in the Sheridan County jail.

Around 11:00 p.m., Vinnie Bird Head, another of Gordon's hard-core alcoholics, barged through the front door and rushed up to Yellow Bird as he was lining up a pool shot. He wanted to tell Bob about a run-in he'd just had with the Gordon cops.

"Hey Bird Head! You ain't allowed in here!" the owner Don Brown shouted from behind the bar.

"He's not here to drink; he just wants to tell me something," Yellow Bird said.

Whatever Bird Head had done to be banned from the town's rowdiest bar, it must have been bad. Brown was adamant. So adamant he came out from behind the bar with his wife, Charlene, on his heels. In her right hand, she carried a can of mace.

Yellow Bird and Brown began arguing. Brown pushed him toward the door. About then, Alvin Rawles inserted himself into the fray. The local farmer, who had a passing resemblance to the actor Jack Nicholson, also had a low opinion of the local cops. He butted in as the spat was turning into a shoving match, with Brown and his wife on one side and Bob and the Cross family on the other. As they reached the stairs leading to Main Street, Charlene blasted them with the mace. Fists began flying wildly at Brown as their eyes burned. Red lights were already dancing across the building as the melee spilled out onto Main Street. The police jumped out of their cruisers and converged on the small-scale riot.

Among the policemen responding was Robert Valentine, one of several officers of dubious qualifications the city had hired since the beginning of the year. Since January, newcomers had filled all six positions in the department. Michael Smith's hopes that police officer candidates would be more carefully vetted had gone unheeded. Valentine had been given an undesirable discharge from the army after twice being absent without leave. In his application, he claimed he'd been given an honorable discharge.

Officer Terry Weil also waded in to try to break up the fight. He'd been on the job for only a month. His application failed to acknowledge convictions for resisting arrest and disorderly conduct. Deputy Sheriff Roger Etzelmiller, the target of several of Yellow Bird's complaints, had been convicted of breaking and entering and pardoned, a fact he left off his application form as well.

Rawles, already a bit drunk, inserted himself between the police and Charlene Brown, who was screaming at the officers, demanding they take action.

"Come on now," Rawles said. "Let the Gordon police do what they always do." He paused for comic effect. "Nothing!"

For his smart-aleck remark, Rawles found himself cuffed and set down on the curb.

Seeing the red lights through mace-induced tears, Bob, Bill, and Dennis ran around the corner. Officer Robert Barnes joined Valentine in the chase, catching up to them as they turned the corner into an alleyway.

Valentine pulled out his gun.

"Stop right there!"

The two policemen led the three back to the front of the building.

"Take me to the goddamn police station. I'm swearing out a complaint against Brown!" Yellow Bird said, rubbing his stinging eyes.

Back in front, Brown had already been handcuffed for grabbing a policeman's shirt and screaming obscenities. Charlene was still spewing out epithets at the officers, demanding they release her husband. As the cops, Bob, and the Cross brothers turned the corner, they saw Fern Cross collapse on the sidewalk. Bob pushed Barnes to the side, rushing over to see what was wrong, but he took only a few steps before the cop grabbed him around the neck, applying a chokehold as he fumbled for his cuffs. The riot broke out again. While Bob had the Billy Jack look down, the veteran Dennis Cross had the moves. He karate-kicked one of the policemen, planting a shoe in his eye.

As Barnes continued to choke Bob while struggling to apply the cuffs, Joann came at him, flailing with her hands, screaming "motherfucker!" Barnes's foot went up to meet her. It caught her square in the abdomen. At the same moment, Valentine kicked her on the waist. She staggered back, slamming against a patrol car, slumping to the pavement as she grabbed her stomach, shock and pain frozen on her face.

She felt the baby kick once. She would never feel it kick again.

Seeing their sister helpless on the pavement, Joann's brothers went berserk. Dennis delivered a hard, square kick to Valentine's groin. He collapsed on the pavement clutching his testicles, nearly passing out from the pain. Even the normally quiet Bill went crazy. The battered officers took out their mace and nightsticks to fight for survival. Reinforcements from the sheriff's department finally arrived to subdue the enraged Cross brothers and Yellow Bird.

An ambulance arrived, and the medics led Fern Cross inside, but Joann refused to join her. Instead, Valentine cuffed her and pushed her in the back of his patrol car with two others and lit out for the county jail in Rushville. Rawles, Bill, and Bob were stuffed in a second cruiser with their hands cuffed behind them.

Halfway to Rushville, Valentine began swerving all over the highway. He pulled the car over on the shoulder. His throbbing testicles had him doubled over in pain so bad he couldn't drive anymore. He radioed to one of the deputies in the car behind him requesting that he come take over. He turned to Joann in the backseat.

"I don't know whether to take you out in the country and shoot you or take you to jail!"

"Why don't you go ahead!" she yelled back.

"I would, but I don't want to waste any good bullets." He stepped out of the car to change places with the deputy, pausing to throw up in the ditch.

Joann and the others spent several hours in the holding cells. She would later accuse her jailers of ignoring her requests for medical attention. Later that night, she was taken in handcuffs to the Gordon hospital where doctors determined that she wasn't in mortal danger and sent her off to the Pine Ridge Hospital. None of the doctors there could detect a fetal heartbeat. A few weeks later, she gave birth to a stillborn girl. They named her Zintkala Zi and buried her at Wounded Knee Cemetery.

Bob organized another march down Gordon's Main Street.

"A state of war exists in Sheridan County, and Forces of the American Indian Movement are being mobilized to meet this threat," he declared in a widely quoted press release. He called for an economic boycott of Gordon's white-owned businesses. He demanded that Smith file murder charges against Barnes and assault and battery charges against the other cops.

The incident polarized the town's Indian community and the Cross family. Joann's father, Frank, formed the Sheridan County Indian Association and sent out a press release declaring that "a state of war exists only in the minds of a few individuals of the Gordon community." Coming from the grandfather of the stillborn child, it was widely quoted in the press.

"We believe, with conviction, that justice can be preserved without resorting to violence," the statement ended. He also told a UPI reporter that "Yellow Bird is trying to pull something. I can't prove it, but I know his actions pretty well. I know he knows all the dirty tricks in the book."

Bob cranked up the mimeograph machine and fired back, accusing his father-in-law of being a "paid instigator for the FBI." He said Frank had been promised free housing in South Dakota for his cooperation and that white citizens had written the press release. There were other FBI undercover agents in Gordon, he claimed.

Except for Frank's accepting help with the press release, none of the accusations against him were true.

Reva Evans once again lashed out at the out-of-town reporters writing on her turf, accusing the Associated Press and United Press International of "irresponsible journalism." She banged out another "Reva-lations" column. "The behemoths of the industry fail miserably in truth in reporting, in adherence of ethics—the Hippocratic oath of the journalism field, let us say. If the local press were to take its responsibilities so lightly, it would soon lose all credibility of the people it serves."

What exactly these misrepresentations were, she didn't say.

Smith declined to file charges against Valentine or Barnes. The Yellow Birds, with the backing of the Wounded Knee Legal Offense-Defense Committee, filed an $8 million lawsuit against the Gordon hospital, the city of Gordon, Sheriff Jim Talbot for hiring unqualified officers, Sheridan Lounge owner Don Brown, and the employees of the county jail.

In December, Yellow Bird went on trial on two counts of shooting with intent to kill for the Hacienda Lounge incident. As it was in 1972, Michael Smith was the prosecuting attorney and Judge Moran sat on the bench. This time, Moran had changed the venue to North Platte, a railroad town in west-central Nebraska.

The Fishers weren't there, though. Smith had a tougher opponent—a big-shot out-of-town lawyer paid for by the Wounded Knee committee. Much to Smith's chagrin, Moran gave the defense attorneys plenty of elbow room to prove that Bob was legitimately afraid of a political assassination in the racially charged atmosphere of Gordon. Smith was convinced Yellow Bird's actions had nothing to do with politics. But his attorneys were allowed to paint a portrait of a town "out to get" Yellow Bird because of his activism. Cathy Merrill and Yellow Bird's sociology professor at Chadron State were among those who testified about Gordon's racially charged atmosphere.

At the end of the trial, Bob took the stand. Despite Smith's belief that testifying in one's own defense was almost always a bad strategy, Yellow Bird projected a calm, smooth demeanor. He told the court that he shot Gardner and Zywiec in self-defense. As was the case in almost every Indian-white crime in Sheridan County, there were two entirely different versions of events. The all-white jury believed Yellow Bird's. He was acquitted of both counts.

Yellow Bird had finally scored a victory against his longtime nemesis Michael Smith. And he beat him in the place that mattered to the county attorney the most—the courtroom. It was Smith's first defeat in a criminal trial.

Yellow Bird's next alcohol-fueled fiasco would lead to his departure from Gordon and Nebraska.

By 1978, the hamlets of southern Sheridan County on Highway 2 were "blink and you'll miss 'em" wide spots in the road. Ellsworth's heyday had passed eighty years earlier when it served as a cattle-shipping point for the once mighty Spade Ranch. Antioch, a little farther to the west, enjoyed a brief boom during World War I when European supplies of potash, a vital agricultural resource used for fertilizing cotton fields, were cut off. The Sand Hills' alkaline lakes produced plenty of it, and overnight five processing plants employing hundreds of workers sprouted up alongside the road. The boom turned quickly into a bust when the Great War ended. Almost sixty years later, the potash-processing buildings rusted in the prairie wind.

The town of Lakeside's claim to fame was booze. The bars served beer on Sundays, unlike Rushville and Gordon. And Lakeside was where Bob and Joann headed on April Fools' Day 1978 to go on a weekend bender. Joann's brother Wayne and a couple acquaintances came along. As usual, the children were left home alone to fend for themselves. If they were lucky, maybe a responsible adult would stop by and look in on them. If not, the oldest, Wesley, not yet in his teens, was in charge.

The party began Saturday and lasted into Sunday afternoon when they found themselves driving through the Sand Hills on their way to Marv's Mobile Cafe and Bar. They sat there knocking back the longnecks for four hours, Bob making a point of telling the white woman tending bar that he was *the* Bob Yellow Bird.

As the afternoon light was fading in the west, the crowd became a little too boisterous for the bartender's liking and she announced that she was closing. Wayne grabbed a case of beer for the road, and as the bartender was following them to the door to lock up, Bob turned around and lifted his shirttail, flashing his .22 in a holster around his waist.

"Look what I got," he said.

The brown Pontiac zoomed west down Highway 2 as they drank and tossed empties into the ditch. They were heading to Alliance where Wayne lived, but their final destination wasn't his house.

"Let's go get Mark Monroe," Yellow Bird told the others.

Mark Monroe's skepticism about AIM when it came to Alliance in 1972 for the Hare trial had turned into full-blown hatred. A local chapter left in the trial's wake had been feuding with Monroe over control of the Indian center he'd founded, and Yellow Bird, as Nebraska AIM coordinator, had taken up the cause. Since the trial, Monroe had served on the Nebraska Indian Commission. He'd also fallen off the wagon for three years, but managed to rein in his drinking problem while continuing to organize relief for the Indian community.

Yellow Bird called Monroe a "white man's chief." For AIM, Crazy Horse and Sitting Bull, the rebel chiefs who fought against the white man, were in. Red Cloud and Spotted Tail, the "treaty chiefs," were out. Those who cooperated with the whites, who wanted to work for change within the white system, were "apples"—red on the outside and white on the inside.

Monroe had moved the Indian center from one end of the town to another at his own expense. The center and his residence were the same place, and the city leased the property to him for one dollar per year. Bob accused Monroe of self-aggrandizement. Monroe characterized Yellow Bird and AIM as do-nothing thugs, who had never run any kind of successful Indian assistance program. Bob had gone before the city council several times and asked them to transfer control of the center and its budget to him. When faced with the choice of handing over the building keys to a headline-making member of the notorious AIM, or a local man who'd successfully implemented several projects to help his community, it was a no-brainer for the Alliance town leaders.

At one contentious Indian Center meeting, Monroe's lieutenants had strong-armed Bill Cross out of the building. Now, it was payback time.

Monroe was relaxing in his easy chair as his wife Emma and adult-aged children, Daryl and Hope, were sitting on the sofa watching TV, when he looked up to see someone poking his head around the corner into the living room. Yellow Bird stepped out to reveal himself.

As soon as Monroe stood up, the taller, younger, and stronger Yellow Bird hooked his right arm around Monroe's neck. Joann was right behind him, with her brother Wayne and two other wild-eyed, tough-looking Indians Monroe didn't recognize.

"Come on outside. You and me gotta talk," Yellow Bird said, but Monroe struggled. Bob punched him in the stomach. Monroe, doubled over, stumbled into the hallway, trying to make it to his bedroom where he had a handgun. An unloaded handgun, he remembered.

In the living room, Yellow Bird whipped out his .22 and kept it trained on Monroe's family. He just stared at them, not saying a word. Drunk. Angry.

"Don't, Bob," Daryl pleaded.

Yellow Bird lowered his gun, perhaps sensing that Monroe would be coming back, and ordered an end to the home invasion. They retreated through the front door, with an enraged Monroe on their tails with a now loaded gun. As they pulled away in the car, Monroe began firing, hitting the Pontiac at least once. Monroe ran back into the house and called the Alliance police.

"Handle it yourself," they said. Monroe slammed the phone down. Now he didn't know who he was madder at, the damn cops or Yellow Bird.

Meanwhile, Daryl had grabbed a rifle and was climbing onto the roof just in case they came back. And they did.

Monroe had reached the more sympathetic Box Butte county sheriff, Bill Stairs, at home, and even though he was off duty, he came over in his own car wearing street clothes. While Stairs was inside taking Monroe's statement, they heard shots outside and Daryl returning fire from his rooftop perch.

Bob had returned to Wayne's house, grabbed a rifle out of his trunk, and come back with the others in two cars.

"You let the law handle this!" the sheriff shouted at Mark and Daryl, then jumped in his car to give chase.

The two cars split up, though, and while Stairs chased one of the vehicles, the other car drove by the center again, guns blasting. Five bullets were removed from the facade the following day.

Bob and Joann fled to Martin, South Dakota, in Bennett County, where they had recently secured tribal housing. Bob eventually turned himself in to Nebraska authorities. The trial was held that winter, once again in front of Judge Moran, who once again changed the venue, this time to Scottsbluff, Nebraska. And once again Bob took the stand in his own defense, but without the assistance of the high-priced, out-of-state attorneys. In a case of Indian versus Indian violence, Bob was on his own. He faced a seventy-three-year sentence if convicted of all three felony charges. The jury, of course, wouldn't see Bob's dark side, the angry boy inside who emerged when drinking. They saw only the charismatic, highly intelligent activist.

Before he began his testimony, he held up a Sacred Pipe to the jury. "This pipe is so significant, that (when it is vowed upon) we are speaking from our hearts, we speak the truth."

Bob gave the all-white jury his version of the Alliance shootout, tossing them a bone by admitting he'd punched Monroe in the stomach, but denying he'd shot the building or even had a gun. They believed him. They acquitted him of all felony charges, finding him guilty of misdemeanor assault. Judge Moran gave him a choice: thirty days in jail or treatment in an alcohol rehabilitation program. He chose neither. Bob skipped out on his punishment, and the Yellow Birds left Gordon for good.

The Yellow Birds had one unfinished piece of business with Nebraska. A year and half later in 1979, Bob squared things away with Moran so he could return to North Platte for the Sheridan Lounge civil lawsuit. The big-time AIM attorneys returned carrying in their briefcases extensive background profiles on all the Gordon police officers, who'd since moved on to other jobs. Absent from the proceedings were Michael Smith and Judge Moran.

The judge first dismissed the suits against the Sheridan County Lounge, Sheriff Talbot, the hospital, and the jail, where the Yellow Birds alleged that Joann was denied prompt medical attention. The complaints against the police remained.

The officers denied they'd kicked Joann Yellow Bird. Instead, Valentine and Barnes both claimed they'd extended their legs and she ran into their feet while she was attacking them. Valentine testified that Michael Smith had instructed him not to arrest the richer, white citizens of Sheridan County. He also admitted to threatening to take Joann Yellow Bird out in the country and shoot her.

Defense attorneys during the three-and-a-half-week trial portrayed the Yellow Birds as radicals, anarchists, and agitators. But once again, Bob fearlessly took the stand and made a compelling witness. The jury came back with a judgment against the town of Gordon and Officer Valentine, but not Barnes, who'd kicked Joann in the stomach. They awarded the Yellow Birds three hundred thousand dollars, far short of the millions they'd sought. Vernon Bellecourt, who attended part of the trial and was on hand for the verdict, declared the judgment a "limited victory," but a victory nonetheless. Joann was not satisfied.

The trial ended Bob Yellow Bird's long fight with Nebraska that began the day the small-town cop hauled him off to juvenile detention, changing the course of his life forever. Few knew the source of his anger.

A year after they left Nebraska, Joann swallowed a dose of strychnine. The coroner ruled her death a suicide. She left behind eight children. The Cross family, including Bill, wondered how such a stubborn woman, who loved her kids so much, could do such a thing. They wondered if it was really an accident, that maybe she'd overdosed on acid, which she and Bob were known to use. There was never a thorough investigation. Bill and Bob had a falling out. Bill heard Bob was spending all the settlement money. That was supposed to be for the kids' future.

Bob stayed in Martin, remarrying once, while continuing to attend

AIM meetings and protests. One night in the early 1990s, while drinking in Martin with a group of Vietnam veterans, Bob joined a game of Russian roulette. He lost. The bullet didn't kill him, but it left him paralyzed on his left side.

He died in 1997 at age fifty-two of complications resulting from a lung infection.

Both Joann and Bob are buried at Wounded Knee Cemetery next to their unborn daughter. Their children, many of them activists like their mother and father, sometimes gather to publish the *Crazy Horse Advocate*.

Storeowner John David's car is stuck in the mud on Whiteclay's main street, circa 1945. (Courtesy of Carrie Reeves.)

Little Skid Row on the Prairie

John Brennan couldn't take it anymore.

It was unbearably cold in the reservation office. The entire Midwest was undergoing a severe cold snap. But the entire Midwest didn't have to work in the Pine Ridge Agency office. Brennan was a long-limbed, gaunt man who was easily chilled. The Oglalas, who struggled with pronouncing outsiders' names, called him "Longneck" because of his wiry frame. And his long neck was cold. He called in his assistant to take some dictation. A strongly worded letter was in order.

Pine Ridge Agency, S.D.
January 26, 1904
    Hon. Commissioner of Indian Affairs
    Washington, D.C.

Sir:—

TWENTY-FIVE BELOW ZERO HERE TO-DAY.
DISAGREEABLY COOL IN THIS OLD SHACK OF AN
OFFICE. FOOT WARMERS CALLED INTO USE!!!

The agent hoped the capital letters would do some good.

They probably wouldn't, though. The last time he'd taken up the matter with Commissioner William Jones was the previous month when he'd traveled to Washington. Not that lodging the complaint so late in the winter would do him any good. But promises were made last summer about building some kind of habitable office. And not a thing had been done!

The cold weather, however, was the least of his problems.

He'd been telegraphing the commissioner about the Extension for several weeks, attempting to head off a potentially violent confrontation between the Oglalas and the settlers in Sheridan County. Something was afoot in Washington, and trying to find out what was going on from the middle of the prairie was impossible.

Meanwhile, twenty-five miles down the road, Judge William H. Westover in Rushville had been calling for an illegal takeover of the ten-by-five-mile strip of land, threatening to let settlers stake claims there under the protection of county sheriffs. Westover was one of the most influential and powerful men in Sheridan County. He was one of the area's original settlers, who'd arrived in 1885 as a country lawyer, risen to county prosecutor, and then gained an appointment as a circuit court judge. He was well connected in the Democratic Party and a member of the Masons, the Elks, the Knights of Pythias, and the Modern Woodmen of America. He was also trying to provoke bloodshed as far as Brennan was concerned. The Indian police were patrolling the Extension, and the possibility of violence couldn't be ignored.

The land had been given to the Oglalas for their own protection. It was created by executive order in 1882, and enshrined in the Treaty of 1889: "That the said tract of land in the State of Nebraska shall be reserved, by Executive Order, only so long as it may be needed for the use and protection of the Indians receiving rations and annuities at the Pine Ridge Agency."

A Nebraska circuit court judge did not have the right to take it away. And neither could the Nebraska Unicameral. Only a president of the United States could reverse the order, as long as he determined that it was no longer needed as a buffer zone between the Oglalas and the whiskey ranches. And both Brennan and the Oglala elders believed it was still needed.

The residents of Sheridan County had been trying to grab that patch since arriving in 1885. They called it "No Man's Land," and it was. After the Ghost Dance troubles in the early 1890s, traders, white husbands of Oglala women, and other mixed-blood squatters tried to put down roots there. The residents weren't quite Indian, and not quite white. Kind of like the Extension itself: not quite the reservation, not quite Nebraska. But some of the squatters were bootlegging, defeating the purpose of the strip, so the army had them removed for good. For the past twelve years, the land had remained unoccupied, a fact that was driving the nearby settlers insane with land lust. The thought of rich farmland, good pastures, and groves of trees along the creeks not being put to use was an outrage to them. Brennan's Indian police officers were constantly shooing cattle off the land and kicking out timber thieves.

For many white settlers, any land belonging to an Indian was wasted land. The thought of a "savage" occupying a single acre of Nebraska was maddening to some. Nebraska politicians had unsuccessfully agitated for the removal of the Winnebagos and Omahas in the 1870s, but they had managed to illegally boot the Poncas out of the state, exiling them to Indian Territory as soon as it became politically expedient. These tribes were peaceful, had never fought the United States, and were on the road to assimilation when the land-hungry settlers set their sights on their rich soil.

Nebraskans were still after what remained. For years, the state's congressmen had been trying to open up the Extension for homesteading. Brennan believed the Sheridan County agitators wanted the land to move their bootlegging operations right up to the state line, where they could make a tidy profit selling whiskey.

In truth, it was nearly impossible to keep booze out of the Oglalas' hands. For those who could make it to Rushville, there was always someone in town willing to sell them a bottle. Brennan had waged a war of words with Judge Westover in the local newspapers, claiming Sheridan County law enforcement did nothing to stop the illegal sale of alcohol to Indians. The churchgoing Gordon citizens recently voted to impose prohibition in their town, but Oglalas on the east of the reservation simply made their way to Merriman in Cherry County to acquire their whiskey (as did many Gordon citizens). Brennan managed to have a saloonkeeper there fined two hundred dollars and sent to prison for a year for bootlegging to Indians, but keeping John Barleycorn out of Oglala mouths was a losing battle.

For those who couldn't make it to the border towns, smuggling was rampant. The contractor who brought the mail to the agency from Rushville and his boy were two notorious culprits. They hid whiskey in the mail wagon and delivered it to middlemen on the reservation until Brennan grew wise to their scheme. However, they simply began dropping their shipments off at a designated point just outside the Extension so cohorts could pick them up later.

Brennan's first hint that the Extension was at risk came from an article in the January 16 *Sioux City Journal*. Commissioner Jones was considering opening up the Extension for settlers, the newspaper claimed. A copy of the article arrived in his freezing office only hours after he'd mailed a letter to the commissioner asking him to respond to another four-page missive from Judge Westover. Once again, the judge had been attacking the Oglalas' right to keep the land.

Why did he have to hear about this from a newspaper? This demanded a telegram. Brennan sent it off to the commissioner right away. "Dispatch from Washington in today's *Sioux City Journal* says Commissioner Jones recommends throwing open for settlement the extension to this reservation. Considerable excitement. See my letter today. Is report true or not."

The Oglala elders were up in arms when they heard about the proposed land grab. They signed a petition asking that the tribe be allowed to buy the land at $1.25 per acre to be paid out from their trust fund, money acquired from the sale of treaty land to South Dakota settlers. Brennan also pointed out to the commissioner that the tribe had developed an irrigation ditch and pasture for the nearby boarding school that extended into the strip. The land was being put to good use no matter what the settlers claimed. Brennan finished his letter with a warning. "Definite action should be taken on this matter immediately in order to head off or prevent possible trouble that might arise through fool advice and bad [counsel] given to the people of Sheridan County, Nebraska, by their, his honor, Judge Westover."

Commissioner Jones did take action. In fact, the day before Brennan sent his letter complaining about the cold office, the commissioner, at the behest of Nebraska Congressman Moses Kinkaid, went to see President Teddy Roosevelt for a private meeting. After Jones left the Oval Office, Roosevelt signed an executive order opening the Extension to settlement. What kind of backroom deal was cut would remain unknown. The Oglalas were not consulted, nor was evidence presented that the strip was no longer needed for their protection. In fact, no one in Washington bothered to inform Brennan.

On February 5, an Indian policeman barged into Brennan's office and reported that surveyors and white settlers were swarming over the Extension. Brennan rode the two miles to see for himself. He was shocked to find two white reservation traders staking claims on two prime spots. They insisted that the Extension was now open for settlement. Blasted if he wasn't the only white man on the whole prairie that didn't know what was going on!

He returned to Pine Ridge and had his clerk send an urgent telegram to the commissioner. "I desire to be informed at once whether I am to maintain control over this strip or withdraw our police from patrol duty there."

The next day, the commissioner replied in a terse telegram.

By executive order dated Jan. 25, 1904 the Executive
addition of Pine Ridge was restored to Public Domain.
You have, therefore, no further jurisdiction or control
there and should withdraw your police force.
    W. A. Jones.

The Extension was lost.

Meanwhile, it would be another two winters before the bureaucrats in Washington sent the funds to build "Longneck" Brennan a new office.

The winner of the Extension sweepstakes was the trader William Jacobs. He'd arrived in Sheridan County with the first wave of settlers in 1884, and first homesteaded west of Rushville. Later, he moved north near the agency, where he also owned a Pine Ridge trading post. When the Extension was flung open to settlement, Jacobs grabbed two of the best sites for his daughters. Caroline, his eldest, was given the section directly south of Pine Ridge bisected by the dusty road to Rushville. His daughter Sarah took a large plot directly east, and he took a couple of sections between them for himself.

Judge Westover's constant agitation for the Extension's return paid off handsomely. He claimed 320 acres along its southern edge and later sold the parcel for two thousand dollars.

In 1906, twenty-three-year-old Caroline Jacobs married thirty-nine-year-old farmer Tom Dewing, and they settled on the farm south of Pine Ridge. They were both good Presbyterians, and neither was interested in opening a whiskey ranch or an all-night dance hall similar to the ones that sparked the creation of the Extension more than twenty years before. Caroline played the piano and became the Extension's first schoolteacher, while Tom tilled the soil and kept an interest in a small general store.

After seven years, Caroline applied for her patent, and the land was now hers to do with as she pleased. Tom began laying out individual plots on the west and east sides of the road, just over the state line. Merchants snapped up the plots in the new town called "Dewing" for prices ranging from four hundred to one thousand dollars, the most expensive sites being the ones closest to the state line—good spots since many Indians still arrived on foot.

The Dewings made a killing.

The original town of Whiteclay sat on White Clay Creek two and a half miles southwest. It was never much, just a few houses, a church, a graveyard, and a post office. The first Whiteclay became a ghost town as residents flocked to the prime pieces of real estate. If a merchant went belly-up, Caroline would often reacquire his plot and resell it to the next entrepreneur. Caroline donated a small piece of land to the federal government for a new post office. She was most displeased when the Washington bureaucrats refused to change the post office's official name to "Dewing." Despite her protests, the Whiteclay name stuck.

J. W. Hanks unlocked the door, opened the shades, and let the cool April air into his wood-frame general store, less than a hundred yards from the state line. He checked his till, put things in order, and scanned the shelves to see if he was low on anything.

He'd spent eighteen years in the traveling circus business, eventually becoming an owner. But he'd cashed out in 1915 and given up that nomadic life to become a shopkeeper. And a wise investment it was. He had both Indian and white customers. The nearby farmers and ranchers who didn't want to make the long trip to Rushville bought their goods there, as did agency bureaucrats. And when the Indians had some change in their pockets, and the means to make the trip, they hitched up their teams and took their business to Whiteclay, where prices were lower than the reservation traders'.

Hanks with his feather duster began sweeping off the cans and bottles. His little store had everything. Beans, flour, bolts of cloth, tobacco, coffee, sugar, salt, hammers and nails. Horse tack. Farm implements, block and tackle. Shovels, pitchforks, barbed wire. And vanilla extract. Lots of vanilla extract. In fact, it was his most popular item. It was said he sold more of it in his store than the whole state of Nebraska put together. An exaggeration most likely, but there was no exaggerating the profits.

An old Indian gentleman came through the door. A regular. The first customer of the day.

"I'll take a bottle of that," he said, motioning to the vanilla extract on the shelf. He opened his hand, and peered at the Indian Head pennies in his palm, counting each one out. Hanks handed him the bottle, and the old man walked out without another word.

Another regular walked through the door. He nodded to the vanilla extract.

Although selling alcohol throughout the United States was illegal, supplying the alcohol-laced extract was not. Nor was peddling white shellac. Hanks sold plenty of that, too. The trick was to filter it through a piece of bread into a cup. The alcohol left in the bottom was diluted with soda pop. Reportedly, it had some kind of kick.

Hanks watched the second man walk out the door and duck behind the building where he joined his friend to get drunk.

Later the Smiths, the Lehmans, the Lawrences, and longtime residents the Reeves joined Hanks as Whiteclay merchants. When automobiles began plying the roads, nearly every store had a gas pump out front. While the all-night rowdy whiskey ranches Brennan predicted never materialized, the hamlet became a primary source of alcohol for Pine Ridge. It wasn't long before two saloons opened their doors. Their legal customers were the nearby white ranchers and farmers. But plenty of booze went out these establishments' back doors to the bootleggers. That was where the real money was made.

When Prohibition came, it made things difficult, but not impossible. In a valley near the Pine Ridge razorback hills south of the Extension, moonshiners set up a still. When a southerly wind blew, the locals could smell the mash wafting across the cornfields. Many Extension farmers made extra money by taking wagonloads of produce up to the agency to sell, so the bootleggers hid the moonshine in an egg cart and made the rounds.

The Depression was tough for everyone. Some general stores went out of business. Transients showed up in town, perhaps lured by the prospects of jobs on the reservation with the Civilian Conservation Corps, President Franklin Delano Roosevelt's plan to put men to work. The hard times sent some Oglalas to Whiteclay where they lived in shacks. Disease swept over the reservation several times. Suffering, grief, and misery followed. Indian Commissioner John Collier's New Deal had lightened the penalties for drinking. Being caught with liquor used to land an Oglala in jail for up to a year, but those days were gone, and the bootleggers found more customers than ever. The alcoholism plague spread to the women, which was unheard of in the old days. Meanwhile, alcohol sales out Whiteclay's back doors continued. The town was a lawless place, under the jurisdiction of the rarely seen county sheriffs, twenty-five miles away in Rushville. Even after the automobile age arrived, it was still a long trip on the rough, unpaved road.

In the 1950s, Hanks's day had come and gone, and a third generation of merchants began trading in Whiteclay. Kelley Coomes arrived in the late 1940s and opened a general store. Roy Smith sold hardware, clothing, groceries, and gas, and ran a regional vending machine business from his shop on the north side of town. Howard Reeves, the son of Whiteclay grocers, met wife Mildred, a nurse from Norfolk, Nebraska, who was working at the Pine Ridge Hospital when they married. They took over the Gambles Hardware store, and would later run a pool hall, bowling alley, furniture store, then apply for a license to sell beer, opening the H&M Mini Store. Randy Thies met his wife, Donna, another Pine Ridge nurse, then moved to Wyoming so he could finish his degree. They returned to Whiteclay when his mother became too ill to run her grocery store. It was only supposed to be temporary, but they stayed for nearly forty years.

Maurice Eckholt was working as a carpenter in Oregon when his sister Mildred Reeves asked him to come to Whiteclay and run the Gambles store for her. His wife, Mary, a Southern Californian who hated the rainy Pacific Northwest, readily agreed. The Eckholts would remain in the small town for the rest of their lives.

The young couples started families, and their baby-boomer children grew up together in the tiny town. Some Oglalas also settled there, and Indian and white kids played together, went to the small Extension school west of town until eighth grade, then attended high school in Rushville. Whiteclay began to resemble the brief period in the 1890s when the Extension was neither completely white nor completely Indian.

It wasn't as if no one noticed the illegal liquor sales in Whiteclay. The Nebraska Liquor Control Commission suspended the license of one bar owner in early 1953 for bootlegging and rowdiness. The grocery and hardware store owners who didn't profit from alcohol sales complained of brawls, intoxicated Indians walking into their homes, and public urination. The bar reopened under new ownership, which was suspected of being a front for the former license holder. That brought the liquor commission to Rushville for a special hearing. Residents of Whiteclay and the law enforcement officers of Pine Ridge and Sheridan County appeared at the courthouse to testify against the granting of new licenses. The records showed that the new operation had once sold sixty cases of beer to one person, and the new owners were spending almost no time at the bar. Other Whiteclay residents spoke out in favor of alcohol sales. Kelley Coomes, the general store owner, testified that he'd seen no public intoxication, brawls, or evidence of bootlegging.

In 1953, the U.S. government ended the law making it illegal to sell alcohol to Indians. Individual states and municipalities were free to keep such laws on the books, but one by one their ordinances, including Nebraska's and Sheridan County's, were also repealed. Almost immediately the Oglala Tribal Council voted 13-12 to lift the alcohol ban on the reservation. Twenty applications for liquor licenses arrived within days at the council's door. It had the authority to lift the ban, but pressure mounted for the matter to be put to a referendum. Two months later, the voters rejected alcohol sales 665–484.

Kelley Coomes was proud of his new bar. It was a brand-new day in Whiteclay. No more selling beer out the back door to bootleggers and Oglalas. Pine Ridge was dry. Sheridan County was not. It was simply a matter of supply and demand. The only complication was the "beer only" law. So the backdoor sales wouldn't completely end. Many old-timers still had a taste for whiskey and fortified wine.

Coomes sent out a press release, reprinted on the front page of the *Sheridan County Star*, to announce his bar's grand opening:

> 'Kelley's Cove' opening Friday in White Clay will be one of the most modern and attractive bars in Northwest Nebraska.
>
> The Interior of Kelley's Cove is most attractive and colorful and the last word in modern fixtures. A color scheme of rose and green has been effectively worked out. The booths are leather upholstered in a shade of rose with dark green semi-circular shape seating about eight persons . . .

Mr. Coomes has invited all members of the Rushville Chamber of Commerce and their wives to be his guests opening night.

Whether any of Rushville's business elite drove the twenty-five miles to celebrate the grand opening has been lost to history, but plenty of Oglalas began driving or walking the two miles to drink there. Soon, Kelley's Cove and the Jumping Eagle Inn became infamous as two of the rowdiest dives in Nebraska. Even matching color schemes wouldn't draw a crowd from Rushville.

Fights. Hollering. Hell raisin'. Bottles smashed on the highway. Puking in the weeds. Deadly car crashes on the curvy two-mile road between Pine Ridge and Whiteclay. The occasional pop of a gunshot in the air. Residents hoped it was in the air, anyway.

It was an odd place for the merchants' baby-boomer children to grow up. Once a year, a carnival came to town and set up in an empty field on the north end, drawing both Whiteclay and reservation kids. A down-and-dirty rodeo was also an annual event. It attracted riders from the reservation and Sheridan County alike. It was so low budget, the organizers couldn't afford proper fencing and the bulls would sometimes escape the "arena," causing spectators to jump up on their car hoods to avoid being trampled as the ornery beasts headed down Main Street. Sometimes the beer and testosterone would overwhelm the cowboys, and fights would break out.

Whiteclay's other citizens, the grocery and general store owners, waited for the day when everything would settle down. They thought the Oglalas needed an adjustment period to become accustomed to drinking in public houses. But the situation never improved. When the liquor commission arrived in Rushville for a hearing in 1956, tribal leaders lodged complaints about Kelley's Cove.

The law enforcement situation hadn't changed. The county sheriffs were still twenty-five miles away, and once the sun went down, Whiteclay turned into the Wild West. One crackdown in 1956 resulted in twenty-six arrests in a forty-eight-hour period. All were for drunk driving or public intoxication. The sheriffs, however, didn't hand out a single citation to the drinking establishments.

Josie Smith had married into the respectable and well-liked Smith family, who ran the general store and vending machine company on the north end of town. She divorced her husband, Albert, in 1960, but remained in Whiteclay, running a dingy, rarely opened café, which served as a front for her backdoor business.

For Josie was the "queen of the Whiteclay bootleggers." Her reign would last for decades, and it's doubtful that any illegal wine seller would ever top her sales volume. She sold only fortified wine, which she bought wholesale in Rushville. Her customers would knock on a wooden sliding window at the back of her house, and she would retrieve a bottle of muscatel from underneath loose floorboards covered by a throw rug.

She was a kindly old woman and a soft touch for those in need. If one of her customers complained of being hungry, she would fix him a sandwich. Her business was so well known that after Maurice and Mary Eckholt bought her house in the 1980s, former customers knocked on the back window for the next ten years. Most of them expressed disbelief when the Eckholts insisted that they didn't sell wine. Occasionally, a hungry street person would come in to ask for a sandwich. Maurice, a born-again Christian, usually accommodated them.

A drunken Oglala man once walked in and declared that he was hungry, wondering if he could have something to eat. Maurice found some bread and cheese in the refrigerator, but he didn't have anything else.

The man looked at the sandwich and said, "What, ain't you got any lunchmeat?"

"That's it! No more free sandwiches!" Maurice declared.

Even a born-again Christian could only be pushed so far.

Relative peace and tranquility arrived in 1962 in the form of Jim Talbot.

That year, the Nebraska Unicameral allocated funds for three deputy sheriffs, one in Whiteclay and two in Pender next to the Omaha-Winnebago reservations in eastern Nebraska. The man for the job in Whiteclay was Talbot. He was born and raised on a nearby farm, had run a filling station in Whiteclay, and knew just about everybody on both sides of the border. One of his aunts and two of his uncles had married Oglalas, so he had cousins all over Pine Ridge. He and his young family lived in town, and it was his job to keep the peace twenty-four hours a day.

He was by all accounts one of the most evenhanded lawmen to ever wear a badge in Sheridan County. He broke up fights, sent drunks home, made sure no one passed out in a snowbank when it was cold. He noted every incident in a daily diary, scribbled down in his left-handed scrawl. But not everybody liked Talbot. One day, a disgruntled teen from the reservation whom he'd kicked out of town came back and blew a hole in the side of the lawman's house with a shotgun.

Talbot wasn't perfect. He turned a blind eye to Josie Smith's bootlegging. He knew the old woman had few resources, and she had to make a living. Her wine bottles left a trail from Whiteclay to Pine Ridge, but she was arrested only twice during her two-decade reign, and never during Talbot's tenure. Her first arrest came in 1960 for selling alcohol without a license, but those charges were dismissed. Eighteen years later, the police decided to launch a sting operation. It didn't take them long to spot one of her customers walking up to the back window. They raided her house and found, along with the cases of muscatel, stacks of U.S. government commodities distributed to impoverished Oglalas. She claimed she'd only been storing the food for friends, so the prosecutors never filed any charges for her ill-gained government cheese. However, they convicted her on two counts of selling alcohol without a license. The judge fined her $150 on each count, with no jail time.

Perhaps because they felt good about the Unicameral arranging full-time law enforcement, the Liquor Control Commission in Lincoln eventually approved licenses for two additional Whiteclay beer sellers. Now, there were four. But in 1974, lawmakers cut off funding for Jim Talbot and his Pender counterparts. He'd done a good job there, most agreed, and was well liked and respected. The Sheridan County voters later elected him sheriff, and he moved to Rushville. However, the four liquor licenses remained.

With no full-time law enforcement and the FBI-AIM dirty war spilling over into the nearby drinking establishments, the county finally shut down the rowdy bars. Beer-to-go was permitted, so the drinking was now done on the street. Fights, robberies, and burglaries occurred regularly. Every few winters, someone would pass out in the cold and die of exposure.

Whiteclay soon became the Little Skid Row on the Prairie.

However, nothing would top October 27, 1978, for sheer mayhem.

It was Friday night in Whiteclay and business was good at the Jaco's Off Sale Bar. The grocery and hardware stores were long closed, but cars were streaming down from the reservation to load up for a weekend of drinking. If alcoholism was a disease, it was now an epidemic on the reservation, as devastating to society as the smallpox in the 1800s. But unlike the contagious diseases, this one never ran its course and disappeared. While the AIM-FBI dirty war was coming to an end, poverty and its symptoms remained. Domestic violence, diabetes, chronic unemployment, underfunded schools, government corruption, high infant mortality rates. Drugs and alcohol to deaden the pain.

And Jaco's Off Sale Bar reaped the profits. This wasn't street-drunk business. Although single-can sales were allowed, no one made money off the chronic alcoholics who hung around the town all day, panhandling from the grocery store customers. They were lucky to scrounge up enough change to buy a couple of Colt .45s. No, the money was in selling cases. Customers usually bought two or three at a time to hide in their trunks and take back to the reservation.

Terry Frohman had owned the bar, now an off-sale package store, for eight months, and nights like these confirmed that it was a good investment. Business was so brisk, he'd hired a white schoolteacher, Larry Miller, to help him on the weekends. The building had once housed the raucous Kelley's Cove, and the L-shaped bar remained, although no one was allowed to stand there and drink. Six customers, five young adults and one older man, a regular, waited their turns. One of the customers was clearly underage, but what the hell.

Selling to minors? Against the law. But this was Whiteclay. No law. Customers drinking outside the doors and in the parking lots? Against the law. Selling to intoxicated customers? Against the law. But again, this was Whiteclay. No law. No problem. The county sheriffs were twenty-five miles away. The Nebraska Liquor Control Commission, four hundred miles away in Lincoln.

Buying in Whiteclay wasn't a problem for Gerald McLaughlin, an eighteen-year-old Oglala teenager Miller knew well enough to call by name. Miller had taught at the Shannon County public schools for six years and knew several of the kids. He didn't bother asking McLaughlin for ID when the teenager ordered a case of Budweiser tallboys. Meanwhile, his fourteen-year-old white buddy, Gilbert Cuny, waited outside in the car, though being fourteen inside this liquor store wasn't really a problem. Not in a Wild West town. Cheryl Chase, a ninth grader at Pine Ridge High School, had spent the evening cruising around Pine Ridge with some older boys—men really—all in their early twenties. She tagged along as they went in Jaco's to nab some beers.

McLaughlin paid for the case, hoisted it up, and turned around to leave. He'd forgotten he needed to pick up a six-pack for someone else, though, so he laid a few more bills on the bar as Miller set the bottles on top of his load. When McLaughlin turned to leave again, he faced four masked men, three with revolvers and one with an M-1 rifle, standing silently, pointing their guns at Miller and Frohman.

No one said a word. Not even the robbers.

Frohman ducked behind a doorway that led to the backroom where his wife and children slept. Miller made for the cash register in a side room, where a .30-caliber rifle stood.

The four men unloaded their guns, blasting the back of the bar, sending bullets through the drywall. McLaughlin and the other customers hit the floor. Chase crawled to the phone booth, covering her head. Miller in back tried to load a round into the rifle, but he was shaking so badly he ejected the bullet onto the floor. When he poked his head around the corner, the four men were gone.

McLaughlin and the other customers slowly stood up to find Miller pointing a rifle at them.

"Don't shoot," McLaughlin said. "They're gone."

The boy picked up the case and turned to leave, only to find the body of one of the masked men sticking halfway out the door with his head outside. Blood was pulsing out of his temple like a longneck beer bottle tipped on its side.

"They shot one of their own, and by God, he deserved it!" the older customer declared.

As Frohman's wife in the back called the police, McLaughlin set the case of beer back down on the counter. Miller gave him his money back. The cops would be there soon. No need to bring an underage rap into this. McLaughlin stepped over the body and made a quick exit. Chase and her friends had already made good their escape.

Randy Thies, owner of Randy's Market next door, came to look over the body. His daughter, a registered nurse, followed. She felt for a pulse. Nothing.

Duane Morgan was dead.

Wade Vitalis, a nineteen-year-old mixed-blood Lakota, had inadvertently shot his twenty-five-year-old friend Duane Morgan in the head, but he didn't flee the reservation. After all, he was wearing a black bandana over his face. How could there be any witnesses?

The problem was that he, Morgan, and the two other accomplices, all AIM members, were drunk and whacked out on drugs when they cooked up their ill-fated plan to rob Jaco's. They'd forgotten to yell "freeze or I'll blow your head off," when they barged into the package store. They also forgot to demand money. And after they shot up the joint and left the bar in a panic, Vitalis forgot Morgan was behind him when he turned to fire two more rounds. One of them entered Morgan's skull above the right ear. Vitalis made a failed attempt to drag him out, but realized it was too late. He left Morgan face down in a widening pool of blood.

Within an hour, Sheriff Talbot greeted state patrol investigator Max Ibach and two patrolmen, who took charge of the crime scene. Ibach by this time knew Sheridan County well. He'd investigated Raymond Yellow Thunder's death, Bob Yellow Bird's Hacienda shootout, and the Sheridan Lounge riot. Now he was in Whiteclay for the latest alcohol-fueled tragedy, and bending over Morgan's corpse, which was covered in a white sheet.

By 2:30 a.m., two state patrol investigators arrived in the mobile crime lab after a three-hour trip from Sidney. After taking all the necessary pictures and measurements, they flipped the body over to find a still-cocked .38-caliber revolver in Morgan's hand. Talbot was then called away to answer a call for assistance in Gordon. Ibach and another patrolman left for Pine Ridge to seek potential witnesses. The two crime lab technicians and a deputy sheriff remained. They made measurements, drew sketches of the floor plan, pried bullets out of holes, bagged shell casings, checked the gun Miller had taken from behind the counter to see if it had been shot. It hadn't.

Outside, they heard car doors slam. During the past three hours, a rumor had spread through the reservation that a bartender had shot Morgan. Now, about thirty of his angry friends and relatives were there seeking justice.

"Why are you leaving him lying there like a dog!"

"If he were a white man you wouldn't do that!"

"The bartender shot my brother!"

The technicians quickly loaded the body into the van, which the deputy drove to the Rushville mortuary, and the crowd dispersed.

At 5:00 a.m., the technicians heard cars outside screech to a halt. Five carloads of angry Oglalas were outside Jaco's trying to push their way in. One of the men tried to radio for backup from a patrol car, but a member of the mob ripped off the antenna. The enraged crowd jumped back in their cars and sped south toward Rushville declaring that they were going to recover their cousin's body. In Lakota culture, the side of the family that takes possession of a deceased loved one's body has the right to perform funerary services. Disputes over dearly departed corpses were common in border town funeral homes.

The patrolman telephoned the mortuary. Expect trouble. Twenty minutes later, Morgan's friends and family were at the mortuary door. Sheriff Talbot had only enough time to call two deputies and two patrolmen for backup. The mob busted down the garage door, and one man socked Talbot on the cheek, opening up a gash. The Morgan family flooded in, and the nightsticks began flying. After a few minutes, the five lawmen beat back the crowd, and the assailants sped out of town.

As the sun rose on Whiteclay an hour later, Howard Reeves was about to step into his pickup when four cars came roaring through town from the north, guns blazing from their windows, shooting up the buildings and cars on the east side where Jaco's sat. He ducked behind his truck just in time. Two bullets plunked his fender.

The drive-by shooting ended the night's death and destruction.

Wade Vitalis was arrested for murder, which was the charge in Nebraska when a death occurred during an armed robbery, then released on bond. He'd been so high when he entered Jaco's, he hadn't noticed the half-dozen bystanders outside watching him put the bandana over his face. Two women gave statements to Ibach identifying Vitalis, and the Sheridan County assistant prosecutor was ready to go to trial. But when the court date arrived, they had nothing. The judge had granted a motion to have the identities of the witnesses sealed, but that was a futile gesture. In the small, tightly knit Pine Ridge community, everyone knew everyone's business. Their identities weren't a secret. One of the witnesses had fled the reservation. Whereabouts unknown. The other told investigators she'd been shopping at a grocery store in Rushville when four Oglala women surrounded her and threatened to kill her if she testified. She didn't show up for the court date, either.

Wade Vitalis would never stand trial for accidentally putting a bullet in his buddy's brain and died several years later in a car accident.

However, the Wild West town's wildest night never made headlines beyond Rushville. Whiteclay continued to sell groceries and gas—along with millions of cans of beer every year—to the reservation, an ignored, remote speck in a remote county, in a remote part of the state.

That would change twenty-one years later.

Deanna Clarke took one look at Whiteclay and thought she would never agree to live there. No way, she thought as she sat in her car.

By 1992, the town was a dump. Abandoned, unpainted stores lined the streets. The Smiths' general store and vending machine company had long since gone out of business, but they'd held on to their properties, allowing them to fall into ruins. A brick house on the south end of town was an empty red shell. The curvy blacktop from the border to Pine Ridge had been straightened out, but on the Nebraska side it was the end of the road—the last place to be plowed in the winter. The last place anyone would dispatch a crew to fix potholes. The pavement was cracked. Beer cans littered the parking lots.

Street people, as rough looking as the buildings' facades, eyed Deanna's car while her three young boys sat nervously in the backseat. Her husband Vic had left them and walked across the road to check out the potential competition. Whiteclay had two medium-sized grocery stores remaining, and one of them was for sale.

The Clarkes had driven up for the day from Brush, Colorado, to look into buying Randy's Market, Donna and Randy Thies's grocery store. It was a Sunday, and Vic hadn't realized that it would be closed and the Thieses gone for the day.

The street people were circling her car, eyeing the blonde white woman and her three fair-haired, pre-teen boys. Finally, one tapped on the window.

"You think you could spare fifty cents?"

She fished around in her purse for some change, handed some coins out to the man and a few of his buddies, then rolled up the window.

Vic had a dream to be his own boss. He'd been a grocery man all his life, working for Safeway all over the region, moving from town to town as frequently as a military family. He'd wanted to run his own store for a long time and thought he'd achieved that dream the previous year when he'd entered a partnership to open a supermarket with three other businessmen in Colorado. Six months after the new grocery store opened, his partners decided they'd learned enough from Vic and voted him out of the corporation. He had heard about Randy's being for sale, and he couldn't wait to drive up and see it for himself. He came out of the Jack and Jill across the street all fired up. Vic was a short but hard-charging man, ambitious with a Type A personality, and he knew the grocery business. By the time he jumped back in the car, he'd made up his mind.

"If we can get even half the foot traffic as the Jack and Jill, we could make a go of it."

Deanna didn't think she'd ever agree. She didn't have a problem living near Pine Ridge. She'd grown up near the Cheyenne River Reservation in South Dakota, where the Hunkpapas and other Lakota tribes lived. Her father was a teacher in a reservation day school and her mother the cook. Her uncle had married a Yanktonai tribe member, so she had first cousins who were Sioux. She just didn't like the look of the place. It was a dirty small town.

At Vic's insistence, they drove back to Whiteclay a few weeks later to meet Randy and Donna. The Thieses were a throwback to the small-town merchants of yesteryear whose homes and businesses were in the same building. Deanna loved the two-story residence found behind the back doors of the small grocery store. Donna told them they'd raised seven children there, and Deanna began to believe that moving to Whiteclay might work.

The Thieses' business had thrived for four decades. Despite Whiteclay's reputation as a source of alcohol, it had always been a spot to buy groceries. The small general stores in Pine Ridge usually had slightly higher prices, and the Thieses had kept their prices lower and prided themselves on keeping a selection of meats, fruits, and vegetables. Donna's philosophy was to treat everyone with respect, no matter how down and out they looked. All her children had worked in the store as they were growing up. The Eckholt kids who lived across the road worked there, too.

In 1968, the era of the small general store at Pine Ridge ended with the opening of the Sioux Nation supermarket. Although the new store to the north was more spacious and could carry a larger selection of goods,

Whiteclay managed to keep its two groceries. Sioux Nation did not belong to the Sioux. It provided much-needed jobs, but the profits went to white businessmen who didn't even live on the reservation. Whiteclay grocers could extend credit if they knew the customer, unlike the managers at Sioux Nation. The independent Whiteclay merchants could cut deals on bulk orders on the spot. And they kept their prices lower. And of course, some people shopped on the way back from picking up beer.

President Lyndon Johnson's Great Society brought new welfare programs to the impoverished—Food Stamps, Aid to Dependent Children— all good news for anyone selling groceries near the reservation. Millions of dollars from welfare programs flowed into the local economies, and the border town grocery stores grabbed big pieces of the federal pie. When the checks came in, cash registers at Whiteclay, Rushville, and Gordon had lines ten customers deep. Adding to the boom was the lack of a bank on the reservation. For those who received BIA or tribal pay-checks, they had to cash them in a border town bank or a grocery store. Naturally, they stopped to shop before heading back. Whiteclay didn't have a bank, either, but the grocers were happy to cash checks for their regulars. And when times were rough, when there were mouths to feed and days before the next check arrived, they could head to Whiteclay, or see Pat Shald in Gordon (a well-known softy), and have a quiet word with the merchants in the back room to explain the situation. Maybe they'd extend a bit of credit and those hungry mouths could be fed until the next check arrived.

The Clarkes bought Randy's Market, changed the name to VJ's, and settled into life at Whiteclay. Vic and his three sons were all sports nuts, with summers revolving around baseball, falls devoted to football, and winters to wrestling. Vic also coached Rushville's American Legion base-ball team. There was little to separate their backyard from anyone wishing to hop over, just a white picket fence. Between their back window and the prairie, an old dirt road laid out by Tom Dewing almost ninety years ago still saw an occasional car. The road didn't really lead anywhere, but vehicles would still pass by when drivers wanted to maintain a low profile. One night during spring prom at Pine Ridge, a limousine pulled up, and a boy in a tuxedo stepped outside to take a leak. He didn't know, or may not have cared, that the Clarkes had a clear view of him as they ate dinner.

One day, Deanna was cleaning up some garbage that had blown out of their backyard incinerator when she found several old needles, some of them wrapped in tape as if addicts had used them over and over. The Clarkes, with the agreement of their neighbors, had the road blocked off. Vic installed a tall chain-link fence.

The fence didn't stop Ronnie Hard Heart from coming back one day to join the kids in a game of catch. As the Clarke boys practiced pitching, Ronnie squatted down to catch, but he was so drunk he kept falling over or missing the ball entirely. The boys were ticked off, but Deanna, watching the whole comical scene from the back window, had to laugh.

Whiteclay attracted a steady group of street people, and Hard Heart was one of the regulars. Every day, men and women wandered down from the reservation, panhandled from customers, and tried to pool their money to buy beer and cigarettes. Sharing remained a big part of Lakota culture, and when the street people spotted relatives, they would hit them up for some small change or a can of beer from their newly purchased case.

For most of the 1990s, Ronnie Hard Heart was a fixture in Whiteclay. The slight man with no meat on his bones was the son of a medicine man, Edward Hard Heart. When he was young he wanted to follow in his father's footsteps. But his father died young, and Ronnie lost direction. He was baptized into the Mormon Church when he was twelve years old, and went to Idaho to attend a Mormon school and live with foster parents, but he became homesick and returned to Pine Ridge when he was thirteen. He joined the Job Corps program, which sent him to Montana, but he once again began to miss Pine Ridge and hitchhiked back. He never graduated from high school. Soon, he began getting into trouble with the law. He spent two years in a South Dakota prison for grand theft, then two more years in the Nebraska penitentiary for selling ditch weed, the low-grade marijuana that grew wild in the area, to an undercover cop.

Whiteclay became Ronnie's world. Some of the street people had homes to go to at night, but he preferred to live in abandoned houses, and many nights slept in a dried-out well. All the storeowners knew him and liked him. He would often come into Mary Eckholt's gift shop across the road from VJ's, attempting to sell her old flowerpots he'd stolen from the Whiteclay cemetery southwest of town. When Deanna saw Ronnie playing catch in the backyard, she wasn't worried at all. He was harmless.

Mildred Reeves at the H&M Mini Store knew him best. After her husband, Howard, died, she sold the store to her daughter and son-in-law. After twelve years, they were about to go out of business, and she bought it back in 1994. From then on, Ronnie was Mildred's right-hand man. He would do odd jobs for her without asking for money. He called her "Mom." Because of his size, some of the storeowners thought the bigger guys took advantage of him. The bullies would make him go inside the stores to beg for change or force him to sell stolen goods. Arguments and fights were a common occurrence among the Whiteclay regulars, and Ronnie was on the receiving end of more than a few beatings. Later in the day, he'd be spotted with the same men who'd whipped him, sharing a beer and a cigarette.

No one was sure why Wilson "Wally" Black Elk began hanging around Whiteclay the summer of 1999. He'd taken a much different path to the prairie skid row. Wally was Ronnie's cousin, but they didn't hang out together as kids. He graduated from Pine Ridge High School and went to work as an itinerant mason, traveling from job to job until he became a BIA policeman, serving on the Pine Ridge force in the 1980s. He quit that and moved to Montana, where he married and started a family. He spent about seven years there, until the marriage ended and he returned to South Dakota, working construction for a time in Rapid City. He returned to Pine Ridge for good, making a living doing odd jobs, crashing sometimes at his half brother Tom Poor Bear's house, baby-sitting his nephews to help out. One day, he became a born-again Christian and that was all he talked about. He'd always been a spiritual man, living on the straight and narrow, going on an occasional bender while pursuing an aimless life. And maybe that was what first brought him to Whiteclay. Maybe he was there to save souls on behalf of the church. Whatever the reason, someone somewhere in Whiteclay gave him a beer, and it made him feel good. Before long, the border town became his world, too.

There are plenty of theories about the high rate of alcoholism among Native Americans. Some say it's the U.S. government-issued commodities, white flour and sugar, for example, that act to heighten the booze's effect. Some say it's the fact that it was outlawed for so long. That Indians never learned *how* to drink, guzzling it secretly to escape detection. Some say it's because alcohol didn't exist in their diet prior to the white man's arrival. That their metabolism just can't handle it. Then there's the gene. The Indian-alcoholism gene. A gene that natives have carried in their DNA code from the day their ancestors first crossed the Bering Sea—the gene that has never been found or proven to exist. Some respectable researchers believe that the mystery gene causes an enzyme deficiency in the Native American liver, an enzyme needed to break down alcohol.

But don't forget poverty, hopelessness, and grief. There's no disputing their existence. No gene ever forced a bottle to a man's lips. No genes ever circled a man attempting abstinence like hungry wolves, pushing a bottle in front of him. Cajoling him. Making him feel bad for not joining his friends for a taste. No gene ever forced a driver to guzzle a can of malt liquor in the parking lot outside a Whiteclay off-sale while his carload of impressionable children watched. No gene handed a twelve-year-old a beer, the average age when an Oglala has his first drink.

Whiteclay and booze sucked Wally in like Niobrara River quicksand. His sisters, friends, and cousins spotted him in the summer of 1999 hanging around town with Ronnie. One day in early June, the pair stumbled in front of Ronnie's sister's car as she was driving through Whiteclay. They were both so drunk, they didn't even recognize her. It was the last time she would see her brother and cousin alive.

On Saturday night, June 6, a vicious summer storm swept over the town, and Mildred let Ronnie and a few other street people stay in the H&M store until it passed. He said "thanks Mom," and walked out into the night. "Mom" never saw her right-hand man again.

A few days later, in the ditch along the unadopted road, where thousands of empty, shredded beer cans, muscatel bottles, and whiskey flasks lay just beneath the surface, among the tall summer grass, Ronnie and Wally's bodies were found—bloody and beaten to death.

The vicious storm that pounded Whiteclay also spawned a deadly tornado that had cut through the village of Oglala on the west side of the reservation. Tom Poor Bear was unloading donations for the storm's victims when he heard about the discovery of the two bodies. If the reservation and Sheridan County had one thing in common, it was this: bad news traveled fast.

Poor Bear was the sergeant at arms for the tribal government, so he dropped what he was doing and drove to the state line to check out the situation. As he pulled up on the shoulder and looked down into the steep ditch, he was shocked to see a host of Whiteclay street people walking near the bodies, twenty to thirty people poking around. Most of them had no business being there. There was no security, and the crime scene had already been corrupted. The bodies lay under blue tarps, so he had no way of knowing the victims were his brother Wally and cousin Ronnie.

Later that afternoon, the police asked him to go to the hospital and identify Wally's body. That was when he found out. At first, he couldn't believe the corpse in front of him was his brother. His body was blackened. The denial turned to grief, the grief to anger.

He made a call to Minnesota. Poor Bear had been a proud member of AIM his whole adult life. He was in high school in 1972 when he skipped classes to march on Gordon. It was there that he first saw Means, the Bellecourts, and Banks speak. He was seventeen years old when he joined the Wounded Knee occupation. After that ended, he became one of Means's bodyguards. In 1975, Poor Bear was on the border of the Standing Rock Reservation in North Dakota when a BIA cop shot Means.

Like many AIM members, Poor Bear had a falling out with the movement's most controversial leader. By 1999, AIM had posted a press release on its Minnesota-branch Web site declaring Means a former member. Poor Bear was among many in the movement who'd had enough of his camera-hungry ways. Many said he'd gone "Hollywood" after starring alongside Daniel Day-Lewis in the hit movie *Last of the Mohicans*. Lately, some said he cared more about his acting career than his people. Despite "going Hollywood," Means lived part-time in Porcupine, the heart of the so-called traditional side of the reservation, about as far from Beverly Hills as one could go in America.

Poor Bear wanted to organize a "walk for justice" for Ronald and Wally. He called Banks. He called the Bellecourts. He never called Means. But the mercurial activist/actor showed up anyway.

June 26, 1999, at Billy Mills Hall. Twenty-seven years after they'd taken over the multipurpose gymnasium to energize their followers before marching on Gordon, AIM's leaders returned. Tom Poor Bear and Clyde Bellecourt spoke first.

Then Banks stood and whipped up the crowd.

"We're up against people who think it's OK to kill Indian people. They think it's okay because they'll get away with it. . . ."

"We'll go after these people who killed these people. And when we find them, we're going to get justice. . . . I believe we're looking at some hate crimes and I think the members of the Klan are involved. AIM is going to start something."

"We came in '72 and said we were sick and tired of the abuse. Now, again, we have to rise up and say we're sick and tired of this treatment, of this abuse! STAND UP IF YOU'RE SICK AND TIRED OF THIS ABUSE!"

The crowd jumped up from their bleacher seats and roared.

The others hadn't invited Means, but he was still the star of the show and their best speaker. He evoked the name of Raymond Yellow Thunder. He told the audience, filled with teens and some adults too young to remember, how AIM marched into Gordon to demand justice.

"I was here in 1972 to stop this stuff so my grandchildren wouldn't have to go through it! All those people we taught a lesson to in 1972, they've all died or retired. So we've got a whole new generation of racists growing up!"

There was one difference between 1972 and 1999.

Now, there were no Hares.

That didn't bother the AIM leadership. They simply blamed the murders on nefarious white people and repeated the rumors that had been flying around during the past week. White supremacists. A deputy sheriff named Randy Metcalf. Or an evil beer store owner. AIM knew who killed Ronnie and Wally. Later, Banks and Means told one reporter that it wasn't the Ku Klux Klan but a law enforcement officer. A niece of Wally Black Elk told a *Rapid City Journal* reporter she was in a car with her uncle when a white bar owner pulled him out of a car and demanded that he pay a ninety-dollar bar tab or "the sheriff and the boys would handle it."

Of course, there were no bars in Whiteclay. And probably no package store owners who would lend that kind of money to Wally or Ronnie.

Back in Whiteclay, two state patrolmen were monitoring the fiery speeches and thunderous applause broadcast live on KILI radio. Sitting in the next car was Sheriff Terry Robbins, known to all as "Homer." He was the epitome of the country sheriff—potbelly, thick arms, sideburns, and mustache, topped off with a cowboy hat.

Robbins had grown up on a farm in Bennett County, South Dakota, the quarter of the reservation with good wheat-growing land that had been allowed to secede from the reservation after being overwhelmed by whites in the early part of the twentieth century. He'd grown up among the Oglalas because some of Bennett County's land remained in a tribal trust and his family leased their farm from an Indian family. The vitriol coming from up north saddened him. Only two weeks ago, after the tornado ripped through the village of Oglala, he and two deputies, including Randy Metcalf, had volunteered their time to help the tribal police cope with the disaster. They pulled two shifts, worked throughout the night, helped with traffic control and took missing persons reports. Now, Metcalf was being accused of murder, Sheridan County law enforcement of racism. That's the way it went in his line of work. You were a hero one day and a heel the next.

What Banks, Means, and the others didn't know was that Ronnie Hard Heart was one of Sheriff Robbins's best informants in Whiteclay. Because of his police record and chronic alcoholism, he couldn't use him as a witness in a trial, but the information he provided usually checked out. Ronnie would approach his cruiser alone pretending to panhandle, and Homer would fork over some change or small bills to keep up appearances as Ronnie filled him in on the latest Whiteclay crimes. Despite the sheriff's best efforts, it was a poorly kept secret in the tiny town. Did someone seek revenge on Ronnie for being an informant? It was a possible motive for the crime and something his family and AIM wouldn't want to hear.

The patrolmen next to Homer were receiving intelligence from the reservation that some of the vehicles had guns, and out-of-state youths were there looking to cause trouble. An emergency service team—the gentler term for what was once known as SWAT (Special Weapons and Tactics)—had been cobbled together from about twenty Panhandle state patrol officers and was stationed out of sight south of town along with a Rushville Volunteer Fire Department truck. Even with the team in place, the state patrol was woefully understaffed. Twenty men wouldn't be enough. Robbins and the patrolmen fanned out to tell the handful of residents remaining in town that they recommended an immediate evacuation.

It had already been a trying week for Deanna Clarke.

First, her father-in-law had been diagnosed with colon cancer, then she received bad news from her doctor. She had breast cancer. She was working up front in the store, trying to keep her mind off all the bad news, oblivious to the gathering storm two miles north. Vic had been telling her all week that the march wouldn't amount to anything.

"Don't worry about it," he kept repeating. He was so unconcerned that he'd left that morning with their three boys for a baseball tournament in Gordon.

Suddenly, Homer came in. He recommended that she close up the store and leave town.

Immediately.

"I cannot guarantee your safety," he said.

Deanna couldn't believe what she was hearing. She sent the employees home and ran back into the house. She frantically looked around, threw some family pictures in a suitcase. The Clarkes kept a house in Rushville so the boys had a place to stay on school nights during winter. She took her dog, Peewee, jumped in the car, and headed south.

Mildred Reeves closed up the H&M Mini Store, retreated to her home south of town, and turned on her police scanner. Mary Eckholt heeded the evacuation order, too. She left to stay with friends a few miles away. If Maurice hadn't passed away, she would have stayed.

But not Gary Brehmer. A lifelong resident, he owned a car repair business next to the abandoned Jaco's package store. He and his two teenage sons weren't going anywhere. Maybe the sheriff couldn't guarantee their safety, but his boys and his guns could! Brehmer was an avid hunter and had plenty of firearms around. They locked themselves inside the shop, which was surrounded by a chain-link fence topped with barbed wire. His son Danny grabbed a camcorder, put in a tape, and let it roll.

Down from the reservation came one thousand marchers. Some came in pickups. Some on horseback. Some came pushing baby carriages. For the first time since 1972, Clyde Bellecourt, Means, and Banks were leading a protest into a Nebraska border town.

The Black Elk and Hard Heart families stopped and climbed down into the tall grass to pray at the site where their loved ones' bodies had been found. After the ceremony, the protesters continued until they crossed the state line. Some marched past the businesses with their fists in the air. One man shouted "burn it down," but no one took him seriously.

Kids ran alongside the marchers. Some mothers carried their babies. They stopped in the street in front of Mike Coomes's Pioneer Package Store and began to sing, accompanied by a thunderous drum. The wind swept brown prairie dust into their faces as the song grew in intensity. They turned back north, where a flatbed truck and a public address system waited. The AIM leaders weren't done making speeches. This time they evoked the General Allotment Act of 1887 and the Treaty of 1889. Whiteclay was their land! Teddy Roosevelt had illegally nabbed it from them in 1904. The Extension belonged to the Oglalas.

Poor Bear first made the suggestion. Then Banks.

"We're going to take that 'Welcome to Nebraska' sign and move it two or three miles south!" He said it several times, but no one took him seriously. Besides, they weren't going anywhere until Means had his say.

"We're here today to tell Nebraska, all the way to the governor, that this is our land!" Means shouted.

"TEAR THAT SIGN DOWN!"

When Means said it, it happened.

The angry young men leapt into action. The time for speechmaking, singing, and praying was finished. They attacked the sign, pushing the wooden poles back and forth until they snapped. As soon as the sign came down, Banks, Bellecourt, and Means—the angry men who'd once staged an armed occupation of Wounded Knee—turned their tails and headed back north.

About twenty protesters hoisted the sign over their heads, parading it through town as rocks and bottles flew at the buildings, smashing against sidings. They dumped the sign in front of Sheriff Robbins and the two patrolmen, who sat uneasily in their cruisers. The young men spat on it, gave the cops the finger, and launched a few bottles their way for good measure. The emergency service team, standing by south of town, continued to "stand by."

Seeing that there would be no interference from law enforcement, a mix of drunken Whiteclay street people, outside agitators, and Pine Ridge residents set out to see how far they could go. The cherubic cartoon kids on the Jack and Jill sign smiled down on them as the mayhem began.

Gary Brehmer stood in his auto-repair shop with his boys, wondering if he should grab one of his guns. "Don't go out there," he told his boys as rocks hit the side of his building. "You might be able to whip a couple of them, but you can't whip 'em all."

The mob went after Mildred Reeve's H&M store first, but a couple of her Oglala employees stood in front, blocking their way. The rioters tried to bust into the package stores, but the heavy grilling covering their windows and steel doors withstood their best shots. One chunky teenager in a black shirt tried to kick in the Jack and Jill door, but it wouldn't give.

VJ's Market had flimsy doors, though, and no Oglala employees around to throw their bodies in front of the assailants. A couple of boys busted down the door, opening it to a flood of looters. Inside, they grabbed the most valuable item available: cigarette cartons. They were as good as cash on the rez. Less valuable items flew through the smashed window. Watermelons and soda pop cans exploded onto the street. The looters took out their lighters and tried to torch the place. A news photographer, inexperienced with covering riots, ran up to VJ's door and started snapping away. One of the angry young men stripped him of half his equipment. Inside, another rioter lit Vic's hard plastic cash register on fire, but the black, acrid smoke coming off it sent the invaders scurrying out.

The troopers called in the emergency service team and requested assistance from the Pine Ridge police. Six cruisers began inching their way up the street from the south, meeting a barrage of unopened soda pop cans.

A muscular man in a white sleeveless shirt stood alone in the middle of the street screaming at the patrolmen.

"YOU GUYS PULL YOUR FUCKING GUNS OUT! AND I'LL GO HOME AND GET MINE! USE YOUR FUCKING GUNS! COME ON!"

But Robbins and the troopers refused to take his bait. The rioters fell back, and Brehmer and his boys went over to assess the damage at Vic's. They looked inside the window and saw the cash register smoldering; at first glance the damage didn't look so bad. He told his boys to fill some buckets with water. By that time, the cruisers had pulled up next to VJ's. Brehmer asked Robbins for a fire extinguisher, but Homer declined to get out of the car. Stepping outside would only aggravate the situation, he believed.

"The fire department should have been here, Homer!" Brehmer shouted. "You fucking guys look real good sitting in your cars!"

The antiquated fire truck finally arrived, sirens blaring and its ancient diesel engine roaring like an old tractor. However, the mob was within firing range. A fusillade of rocks and bottles greeted the firefighters. The volunteers stepped out under the withering projectiles, made a move to unravel their hose, then abandoned the truck, running to the south of town behind the troopers' retreating squad cars. Unfortunately, they left the keys in the ignition. As black smoke spiraled out of the grocery store, one rioter jumped up into the fire truck cab, and drove it off toward the reservation.

The mob turned its attention to the reporters. One TV soundman was socked in the mouth and fell to the ground. He quickly stood back up, apparently unhurt, and fled. The hapless news photographer who'd had half his gear stripped was mugged again. This time they took off with the rest of the equipment.

Twenty-five miles south, Deanna received a call at the Rushville house from her bread distributor who'd been listening to the whole mess on his police scanner.

VJ's was on fire.

Deanna freaked out. She didn't know what that meant. Was it completely gone? He wasn't sure. She envisioned her entire home burned to ashes.

The emergency service team made a line on the north edge of town. The rioters formed their own line, taunting them, daring them to come over. The troopers weren't biting. They knew any such move would just create more trouble. The cavalry arrived in the form of the tribal police. They inserted themselves between the two sides. One of the agency policemen had to smack a bare-chested protester with his baton to make him back off. Once the other toughs saw that, they retreated to the state line.

A Good Samaritan from the reservation kindly returned the fire truck, and the Rushville volunteers went back to putting out the flames, which fortunately had not engulfed the building.

Chief Oliver Red Cloud, the great-great-grandson of the Oglala chief, arrived with former councilman Milo Yellow Hair. They put themselves in front of the mob and convinced them to return north. But first, six representatives from the rioters' side asked to parley with Sheriff Robbins. They met him on the pavement in the middle of the road as the two sides faced off.

"You tell Governor Johanns to meet us here next week, or we'll be back to finish the job!"

As promised, Means, Banks, and Bellecourt returned the following week. But instead of the governor, 150 troopers and tribal police were there to greet them.

Protesters square off against the Oglala Tribal Police and the
Nebraska State Patrol on July 3, 1999. (Photo by author.)

The Battle of Whiteclay

The angry young men slammed against the line of plastic shields. Spitting. Cursing.

As promised, AIM and one thousand supporters had returned to Whiteclay the Saturday after the riot. This time, dozens of print and television reporters were there. "Get out! You're on our land!" a protester hollered.

"Let's take Whiteclay NOW!"

The photojournalists gravitated to a spot against a pale gray prefab building where they tried to take pictures of the young men pushing against the riot shields. A short Indian woman, as wide as she was tall, tried to block their view.

"You're not supposed to stand there!" she said, trying to move the photographers back to where they couldn't see. "We had an agreement with the state patrol. All press is supposed to stand here!" She pointed to a spot five feet away.

"We didn't agree to that. Nobody told us anything about it," one reporter said.

"You better watch your mouth, mister, or we're going to confiscate your camera!" a second woman said, pushing herself in front of the reporter, who was still trying to squeeze off shots of protesters spitting on the plastic shields.

"You're here to exercise your First Amendment rights. What about our rights?" the reporter said. With that, the short woman nudged her way in front of him, raised her fist in the air in an "Indian power" salute, then moved him back with her considerable bulk. He gave up and went to the other end of the line where no one bothered him again.

"This is the Nebraska State Patrol; you are in violation of Nebraska statute," the cop with the bullhorn said without emotion. "If you do not disperse, enforcement action will be taken."

The thirty tribal police on the west end of the line received the most abuse. Gobs of spit trickled down their shields. A plastic water bottle flew over their heads, landing harmlessly behind the line.

After the scuffle began, Allen Sheppard, the Ojibwa who'd earlier demanded that the police move so they could enter the town, was the first to walk through the line in an act of civil disobedience. He collapsed to the pavement as two troopers handcuffed his wrists. The troopers loaded him into a yellow and black school bus.

Next came Russell Means, who strode through with his head held high, shoving aside the plastic shields, parting them like a swimmer doing the breaststroke. One by one, the others walked through the police line. Tom Poor Bear was next. He was mad as hell with Means, the man he called a friend twenty years ago. Clyde Bellecourt and Poor Bear had made an agreement with Colonel Tom Nesbitt the night before to keep the demonstrators away from the village. People could have gotten hurt when Means egged on the marchers to charge the line. It was still a volatile situation. But now that the civil disobedience had started, he couldn't watch while the cops carted the others away. He stepped through and a trooper applied the cuffs. Poor Bear, former tribal president John Yellow Bird Steele (Bob Yellow Bird's first cousin), and five others joined Means and Sheppard. Patrolmen loaded them into the bus, cuffing their hands, taking Polaroids for future identification. Sheppard smiled for the camera.

Still, the angry young men pushed and shoved. Others wanted to cross the line to stand up for their right to assemble, but Bellecourt told them to calm down. The protesters continued to chide the tribal police for assisting the Nebraska State Patrol. One middle-aged man in a black T-shirt took it upon himself to be their chief tormentor.

"What's wrong with you? You live on the fucking rez! These people are keeping us down! Turn around and walk with us. Come over to this side. Come on. Come and pray with us."

Meanwhile, a skinny protester wearing a red bandana asked a beefy tribal policeman for a bottle of water, which he handed over with a look of amusement.

The bus driver turned the ignition over and started down Highway 87 with his load of passive resisters, the jeering of the crowd sending them off.

Back at the skirmish line, Bellecourt, Banks, and Chief Oliver Red Cloud were already starting to negotiate their release. Red Cloud motioned for a lieutenant to come over to the line.

"I want you to tell the governor that we want our land back," the elder
said.

"I will pass that message on to him, sir. But right now you need to
honor your agreement and move your people back to the parking lot."

Red Cloud borrowed the state patrol's bullhorn and asked that
everyone move back from the line. Some obeyed the hereditary chief, but
others didn't. Bellecourt borrowed the loudspeaker next.

"We keep our agreements; they break their agreements. Let's not be
like the white people."

Banks and Bellecourt were escorted through the line, where Colonel
Nesbitt agreed to release the nine on their own recognizance with a $250
bond, but only if the demonstrators returned to Pine Ridge. After Bellecourt announced the deal, the protesters started slowly shuffling back
toward the reservation. The angry young men were no less angry. Many hung
around to see if the state patrol would honor their end of the agreement.

The "Whiteclay Nine," as they would call themselves, were cited for
"failure to obey a lawful order" and driven back to the police line. The
dejected demonstrators walked back up the highway carrying their protest
signs limply in their hands, past the spot where Black Elk and Hard Heart's
bodies were found, back along the trail of empties. They knew deep in
their hearts that not a damn thing would change.

Back at Billy Mills Hall, Means took the microphone again. The old rift,
the progressives versus the traditionals, was alive and well, and the tribal
police, who'd stood with the Nebraska State Patrol, bore the brunt of his
anger. He likened them to World War II Nazi soldiers who claimed they
were "only following orders."

"I want to tell you about one of the saddest sights I've ever seen.
You know I wasn't around in 1890, believe it or not. I wasn't around in
1890 when the tribal police killed Sitting Bull. I wasn't around before then
when the Indian police killed Crazy Horse. I wasn't around on the highway
when the tribal police killed Pedro Bissonette with a shotgun blast, not one
shotgun blast, but many shotgun blasts. And I wasn't around today after
I was handcuffed and put in that van. I watched [the tribal police] under
orders! UNDER ORDERS to do everything and anything they could
against their own people.

"And that's a sad sight. I know they have families. What does that patch say on their uniform? Oglala Sioux Tribe. WE have families! What about our families? What about us? Someone has to get something straight. And you and I know it, that we are the poorest of the poor in this entire country. We have a higher infant mortality rate on Pine Ridge than in any other country in the Western Hemisphere. Higher than Guatemala. Higher than any Central American or any other third-world country. More of our young people go to prison than any other ethnic race in America.

"This first step we took today was because of our heritage and our future is why we're out there today in that hot sun walking two miles. We were there because not only do we work for heritage and freedom of being free. We want our heritage and our FUTURE to be free. We have the RIGHT to become a free people. And you and I know, on this reservation, NOTHING has changed for us. So what happens to our people? So what happens on this reservation? Most of our people leave the reservation. Why? For opportunity. So all the Indian people in America will be off the reservation. Whether it's Minneapolis, or anywhere else. Rapid City. It's because they are refugees. Because there is oppression, repression, and suppression on the reservation! Because they have no opportunity and we have no protection. . . .

"Now this march can't happen every Saturday, I know that. Arrests can't happen every Saturday, I know that. But what can happen is that a concerted effort, this people power that we exhibited last Saturday and today, is not wasted."

Means promised to hold an all-Indian grand jury to look into human rights and unjust judicial systems in the towns of Gordon, Whiteclay, and Rapid City. He said he would build schools and a health clinic.

"We will continue building these institutions until we are a free people. And this kind of genocide stops."

He stopped to let the crowd applaud.

"If things don't change for us, then we have to change. Understand the process of decolonization. All I'm saying is we are no longer going to accept what we have and we are no longer going to accept people like Clinton. Now I was told by one of the staunchest AIM grandmothers that we have that her grandchildren wanted to see Clinton when he comes. And I said WHAT? That man cheated on his wife. . . .

"We have two choices in life: we can be happy or we can be unhappy. If we choose happiness, then that means we're going to start decolonizing

ourselves, and we're going to start acting like our heritage as Oglala, as
Lakota . . . and we will change our FUTURE!"

The audience filed out of Billy Mills Hall into the late afternoon heat.
It was a great speech.

But not a damn thing changed.

Four days later, President Clinton and his entourage swooped into the
Pine Ridge airport in helicopters; pulsing rotary blades echoed with the
thumping Lakota drums.

On the president's heels was another of the nation's great orators,
the Reverend Jesse Jackson. Housing Secretary Andrew Cuomo and Agri-
culture Secretary Dan Glickman followed. Five CEOs from Fortune 500
companies came along. Lakota singers greeted the entourage with an honoring song. Clinton was the first sitting president to visit a reservation since
Franklin D. Roosevelt made a brief stop at a Cherokee reservation in North
Carolina sixty-three years ago. And FDR was on vacation at the time.

Clinton wasn't the first president to visit Pine Ridge. President Calvin
Coolidge and his family had dropped by in 1927 while visiting the Black
Hills for the summer. Men dressed in war bonnets had greeted him as well.
They gave him a Lakota name: Chief Leading Eagle.

In front of thousands of Lakotas on a hot August day, Coolidge delivered a long speech.

Representatives from the eight Lakota tribes gave Coolidge something
beside the Oglala name: a petition asking for the return of the Black Hills.
Or $850 million. Whichever was more convenient.

Ever since the white man had nabbed the Black Hills, white-owned
companies had hauled out billions in gold, minerals, and timber. But there
were new fortunes to be made. Coolidge's vacation in the Black Hills was
no accident. He relocated the White House there for the summer to pro-
mote the spot as a tourist destination. Before departing for Washington,
he would approve the sculpting of a mountain face and stand at its foot for
the dedication ceremony. The "Great White Fathers" would be carved into
the side of one of the Lakotas' sacred mountains.

Coolidge accepted the petition, but of course took no such action. The
beautiful Black Hills became the tourist attraction envisioned. Mount
Rushmore became an icon. The Reptile Gardens. Deadwood casinos.

Flintstone Village. The Lakotas would spend the rest of the century waging a legal battle to win back the Paha Sapa. Meanwhile, the only Indians to see a cent were those who wore war bonnets and posed for tourists.

Seventy-two years after Coolidge's visit, the paved streets of Pine Ridge looked scrubbed clean, and the embarrassing Whiteclay beer stores were temporarily closed down. Protesters were few and far between. President Clinton was there to tout economic development for the reservation, and no one wanted to screw that up. One hundred tribal chairmen from across the nation congregated for the momentous occasion. The South Dakota congressional delegation made an appearance as well. But this was the Oglala Tribal President Harold Salway's show. He was there to greet the president—one sovereign nation to another. One wealthy, booming superpower to a tiny reservation many compared to a third-world nation. Outside the rez, the nation's economy was on the tail end of an eight-year upward spiral. Inside the Pine Ridge border, it was the same old, same old. Grinding poverty. Not enough housing. Virtually no jobs or prospects for jobs. Eight-five percent unemployment. Teenage suicide rates triple that of the rest of the country. Diabetes rates through the roof. Alcoholism. Meth. Gangs. Salway could talk all day on the evils of booze. He'd lost two older brothers to alcohol-related deaths. But that wouldn't be on the president's radar screen that morning. He had no intention of bringing up booze, or Whiteclay. It was all about jobs. And no one wanted to give jobs to drunks.

No Indian leader in recent memory had enjoyed three hours of face time with a president, and Salway intended to make good use of it. There were decent, hard-working people on the reservation. Not all of them were "drunk, lazy Indians." There were smart people there, good, churchgoing Americans who wanted opportunities and a better way of life. Seventy-five percent of the adults were out of work, according to Clinton. Closer to 85 percent, according to the tribal government's figures, but Salway wasn't about to correct him.

Dennis Banks, Russell Means, and the other AIM firebrands were nowhere to be found; even they didn't want to scare off the president and mar this historic day. Seven thousand people were expected at the school to hear the president's speech, which was six thousand more than the Walk for Justice attracted on Saturday.

Not that there wasn't any dissent. The Taco John's franchise had changed their sign to "Forked Tongue Special $2.00." Someone hung a "Free Leonard Peltier" banner along the motorcade route.

Clinton would have the chance to do just that in the waning days of his presidency. But five hundred Justice Department employees and FBI staff left their desks and marched up Pennsylvania Avenue to make their feelings known about a potential pardon for the man convicted of killing FBI agents Coler and Williams. The pardon never came, and Peltier would remain in prison.

The entourage arrived at the school to the sound of thousands of cheering Lakotas.

Clinton gave them his speech of hope as the late morning sun beat down on his head.

"We have in America almost nineteen million new jobs. We have the lowest unemployment rate ever recorded for African Americans and Hispanics. For over two years our country has had an unemployment rate below 5 percent. But here on the reservation the unemployment rate is nearly 75 percent.

"That is wrong. We have to do something to change it and do it now.

"I asked you today, even as we've remembered the past, to think more about the future. We know well what the failings of the present and past are. We know well the imperfect relationship that the United States and its governments have enjoyed with the tribal nations. But I have seen today not only poverty but promise, and I have seen enormous courage.

"We are coming from Washington to ask you what you want to do and tell you we will give you the tools and support to get done what you want to do for your children and their future.

"Good people are living in Indian country, and they deserve a chance to go to work.

"This is not about charity. This is an investment . . . the new workers of tomorrow are the unemployed of today, the new consumer markets of tomorrow are here today. There is business to be done.

"My neighbors and friends, we are all related.

"There's opportunity to work, and if you work, we will work with you."

In the back of the crowd, a few scattered protesters hoisted signs above their heads.

GIVE BACK THE PAHA SAPA.

Clinton made a lot of promises about the New Markets Initiative that day. He had many good ideas. He wanted to seize the vast potential of tourism and build a Lakota Sioux Heritage Center. He wanted to set up a wind and solar energy farm. He wanted to upgrade the telecommunications lines to bring in "twenty-first-century jobs."

The president waded into the crowd to shake hands. One protester walked up with a cloth sign reading, "Stop Lakota Ethnic Cleansing." Jesse Jackson and Clinton both autographed it.

The president and his entourage climbed back in their helicopters and flew away. It was an exciting day. A great speech.

But not a damn thing changed.

Tom Poor Bear raised a tipi near the spot where Hard Heart and Black Elk were found. He said he would march on Whiteclay every Saturday until Governor Johanns answered him.

But as the weeks passed by, Poor Bear marched with dwindling numbers, and the state patrol sent dwindling numbers of officers to make sure nothing got out of hand.

On July 31 someone posted a notice on the doors of the four beer stores:

EVICTION NOTICE

All alcohol establishments in White Clay have exactly seven (7) days to cease and desist from the sale of alcohol.If you fail to comply, we will take legal remedies,

—Walk for Justice

JULY 31, 1999

Soon, the Walks for Justice ended.

Poor Bear kept the victims' memory alive by marching on the first Saturday of June every year. In 2001, Governor Johanns even traveled to Pine Ridge to hold a summit with tribal leaders over Whiteclay. Everyone walked out of the meeting expressing optimism that something would be done.

But still, not a damn thing changed.

The only battle the seven Lakota tribes won after Custer's Last Stand was in court. The Supreme Court in 1980 upheld a lower court's ruling that found the U.S. government had in fact illegally taken the Black Hills in 1876 and owed the tribes $106 million. But the Lakotas saw the judgment as a hollow victory. They wanted the Paha Sapa back, not the money. And so the millions sit in a U.S. government account, unclaimed, accruing interest, the account growing fatter by the day. So fat, the Oglalas' share alone would be enough to invest the money and give them $20 million per year without touching the principal. Enough to do a lot of good, if spent wisely. But the sacred Black Hills are not for sale.

The number of Oglalas in favor of accepting the money and relinquishing their claim to the land are as scarce as gray wolves. And the ranchers got rid of wolves a long time ago.

Meanwhile, up in the Black Hills, a privately financed endeavor to right the wrong called Mount Rushmore continued as the descendants of its sculptor blasted a mountain into a representation of Crazy Horse. Enough of its shape had emerged to create another roadside attraction.

By 2003, the jobs Clinton spoke of were nowhere to be found. The border town boycotts Means promised hadn't materialized, either. The economic expansion of the Clinton years was a distant memory. All the hi-tech jobs brought about by better telecommunications the president envisioned did go to Indian country. Bangalore. New Delhi. Bombay. Wrong kind of Indians.

Whiteclay continued to do business as usual. Mildred Reeves closed the H&M store. She blamed former employees for breaking the liquor laws while she was gone. She couldn't fight the citations, pay the fines, and stay in business. She opened up the building again only once. In 2001, Chris Eyre, the Cheyenne/Arapaho director of the acclaimed movie *Smoke Signals*, adapted the Adrian C. Louis novel *Skins* for the screen and used the store and Whiteclay's decrepit backdrop in several scenes. The movie portrayed the life of a Vietnam veteran and hardcore alcoholic, Mogie Yellow Lodge, who spends his days waiting for a drink to come his way. His younger brother Rudy, a tribal policeman, becomes a part-time vigilante, and in a night of frustration torches a Whiteclay package store.

The auto-repair shop owner Gary Brehmer purchased Reeves's off-sale license for his sons, and they opened State-Line Liquor. Customers streamed in all day to buy cases of beer as he tinkered with cars in the shop next door.

Vic Clarke had reopened VJ's by the end of the summer of 1999. It wasn't long before his regular customers returned and his business began to thrive as never before. After the riot, a rumor swept the reservation that the store was attacked because the Clarkes were white supremacists. It was a story that had no basis in fact. For Deanna, who'd grown up on a reservation, the rumors were particularly hurtful. Other storeowners maintained that the mob targeted VJ's because Vic aggressively called the county sheriffs whenever the street people created trouble. In fact, the mob attempted to kick in the doors of all stores. They were either blocked by sympathetic protesters, as was the case with Mildred's H&M store, or the doors wouldn't budge. VJ's simply offered the path of least resistance.

On June 6, 2003, protesters marched into Whiteclay again. But this time it was different. The phalanx of state troopers was absent. There were no police dogs, "armed observers," or helicopters thumping above. Four years after the first marches, the atmosphere had changed. A group of liberal concerned citizens, Nebraskans for Peace, marched from the south, and friends and family of Hard Heart and Black Elk came from the north. In the center of the dirty road, the two sides met. Not only were the marchers allowed to enter Whiteclay, Colonel Nesbitt, decked out in civilian clothes, along with Nebraska's attorney general, John Bruning, were there to greet them. Clarke offered free coffee and doughnuts to anyone who ventured into VJ's.

After four years, there seemed to be slightly more political will in Lincoln to do something about Whiteclay. A Winnebago activist, Frank LaMere, was one of the "Whiteclay Nine" who'd been arrested in 1999. He was by then the vice president of the Nebraska Democratic Party and had been tirelessly keeping the issue alive in the halls of the capitol. Three separate pieces of legislation seeking ways to help clean up the hamlet had been introduced in the Unicameral.

On March 1, 2003, Nebraskans for Peace had organized a meeting at the University of Nebraska–Lincoln campus, and Vernon Bellecourt was the honored guest. In a study room at the student union, walking with a cane, dressed in Ojibwa jewelry, his long gray hair tied in a ponytail, he addressed the crowd during a panel discussion.

"The Oglala Lakota people have been patient. We can't question their patience, but time is running out. We're beginning to get a little bit impatient with how Nebraska authorities are handling this cancer; and that's what this is, a cancer. I don't know the people who run those businesses there; they're probably decent people, but they found a way to exploit a sickness, a cancer of the people. I would think Nebraska would be embarrassed about this. . . ."

Byron Peterson, a Nebraskans for Peace member on the panel, said three people who'd been drinking in Whiteclay died from exposure that winter. The statement was completely false. No one had died of exposure in Whiteclay that winter, although deaths from exposure had occurred in Whiteclay in the past. Harking back to the Yellow Thunder rumors printed without question by the press in 1972, the false statement went over the Associated Press wire and ran in the *Lincoln Journal Star* and the university's student newspaper.

Colonel Nesbitt, there to take the flak for the entire state of Nebraska, said the state patrol had tried several tactics to stop the problems in Whiteclay. He came armed with facts and figures in his defense. There are 640 liquor licenses in 272 communities that don't have law enforcement, he said.

"I hear from people in those communities, too."

He just didn't have the manpower to cover every liquor store in every unincorporated town, village, and hamlet. The state patrol tried undercover operations in Whiteclay, a Crime Stoppers reward campaign, and once set up a table on the streets of Whiteclay asking for those with information to come forward on the unsolved murders. No one did. He said the patrol was short of officers, and he didn't have the manpower. There was a war brewing. Many of his troopers had already been called up for active duty, and once the bombs started falling on Baghdad, he'd lose even more.

LaMere didn't accept any of it.

"It is the nature of law enforcement that when you shut down a crackhouse because of the illegalities, they are going to open up across the road. And when you shut them down across the road, they're going to move across town. It is the nature of law enforcement that you will then go there and shut them down. Then they might even move to the next county, and it is the nature of law enforcement that you go there and shut them down. You deal with illegality fairly wherever you can. Whenever it's appropriate. But we don't do that in Whiteclay. . . . Think about the double standard. It means we feel that there are two classes of citizens in this state. . . . Would we allow the things in Whiteclay in western Omaha or southeast Lincoln? I don't think so!"

He continued, his voice rising with every sentence.

"Scores of our young people are victimized, and many of our people are murdered. God forbid that one young white woman or one young white man dies in Whiteclay tonight; we'd shut the damn thing down in the morning!"

LaMere announced that March 1, 2003, through March 1, 2004, would be the Year of Atonement. The state of Nebraska had twelve months to solve the Whiteclay problem.

Or what?

AIM would return to Whiteclay in full force, Bellecourt promised.

By the time of the June 6 march four months later, only one of the proposed laws seemed to have much of a chance. Cross-deputization. Mostly because it was cheap. Nebraska, like many of the states suffering in the Bush recession, was undergoing a budget crisis. Taking the tax revenue from beer sales and giving it to the state patrol to provide twenty-four-hour law enforcement wasn't going to happen. The approximately $170,000 wouldn't be enough to pay the salaries and expenses for three full-time cops anyway. The days when you could hire a local like Jim Talbot to keep an eye on things were over.

Cross-deputization would give the tribal police authority to issue tickets for liquor violations and was something the state could live with. The idea had enough momentum to catch the interest of Bruning, who took the microphone during the 2003 Walk for Justice to address the crowd spread out in a circle in the middle of the road.

"I'm here—probably the first attorney general in Nebraska history to stand in this spot—I'm here because I care. I care about the American Indian Movement. I care about Pine Ridge. I care about the people in Pine Ridge. I'm here because I care. The same reason you're here. I wanted you to know that I want to make a difference. I want to make things better here. We're going to work to do that. I applaud you for the peaceful way in which today was conducted. It hasn't always been that way. A grocery store was nearly burned to the ground several years ago."

"Yeah!" shouted an arson supporter from the crowd. Bruning ignored him and went on.

"I'm here to applaud you that that kind of thing didn't go on today. If you want change, you gotta go about it the right way. . . ."

"Shut it down!" someone else yelled.

Sprinkles began to fall, just enough to put splotches on the dusty road. Tom Poor Bear made a joke about someone doing a rain dance. Protesters held up their signs.

> Whiteclay: 11,000 cans of misery each day
> Serve Justice Not Beer

Poor Bear ignored the issue of alcohol and focused on the unsolved murders.

"I have a lot of anger in me, but I turn that anger into something positive, and that is to unite the people. Wally and Ron were not murdered in Camp Justice; they were murdered somewhere here in Nebraska, Sheridan County. I really feel that the law enforcement of Nebraska should get involved with the murders of our people. . . ."

Vernon Bellecourt threatened to bring AIM back and form a blockade.

The protesters adjourned to Camp Justice to share a meal of buffalo stew with the Nebraskans for Peace. It was a remarkably different day from the troubles in 1999, and it ended with a sense of optimism.

But the optimism was unfounded, for not a damn thing would change.

In December 2003, the tribal government came up short. It was broke. The reservation's largest employer had to lay off hundreds just as the holiday season approached. For the first time in decades, the tribal council brought up legalizing alcohol in Pine Ridge. Not as a way to raise money for drug and alcohol rehabilitation services, but as a way to put some money in its own coffers. Because council meetings were broadcast live on KILI radio, several elders heard what they were up to and jumped in their cars to put an end to the debate. The council had the legal authority to end prohibition, but not the moral authority, so it would have to be put to a referendum. Those in favor said the funds raised would pay for rehabilitation services, but in fact, there wasn't a word in the proposal to guarantee they would. The council members were told to go to their districts and gauge their constituents' feelings on whether to hold a referendum.

The council held its meeting in Manderson on February 6, 2004. The antibooze forces arrived in overwhelming numbers. Elders, clergy, and children all stood up to speak out against it. The kids held up signs in back.

Alcohol = death

Remember our children / Vote no to beer

Beer money is bad money

The proposal to have a referendum was defeated ten to two. The status quo remained, and the bootleggers and Whiteclay beer store owners could conduct business as usual.

Means was on the reservation and attended the meeting briefly, but didn't stay for the vote. On KILI radio later that day, he went after John Yellow Bird Steele for supporting the proposal. Bob Yellow Bird's first cousin had replaced Harold Salway as tribal president.

"When John and I were arrested four years ago in Whiteclay, he told me if he ever got to be tribal president again, he would shut down White-clay. He didn't say that he wanted to move it to Pine Ridge!"

Means was in the area to attend the trial of Arlo Looking Cloud. The Whiteclay march in 1999 was the last time Banks, the Bellecourts, and Means worked together. In November that year, Means called a press conference on the steps of the federal building in Denver. He accused two former AIM members, Arlo Looking Cloud and John Graham, of murdering AIM member Anna Mae Pictou-Aquash on the orders of his rival AIM leaders because they suspected her of being an FBI informant. Banks, Vernon, and Clyde Bellecourt denied the charges.

History was not being kind to AIM. Evidence mounted that the leadership in the 1970s was even worse than its critics imagined. Banks and the Bellecourts could rightfully counter that the FBI had a secret campaign to discredit them. It had successfully infiltrated their group with agents provocateurs, but that did not excuse cold-blooded murder. A devastating book by journalist Steve Hendricks, *The Unquiet Grave*, thoroughly documented both the FBI's abuse of power and AIM's culpability in Aquash's death. It described the possible death of a black activist, Ray Robinson, who was smuggled into Wounded Knee, then allegedly shot in the knee. Eyewitnesses suggested that he both annoyed AIM leaders with his message of nonviolence and raised suspicions that he was working for the feds. He was led to a makeshift AIM clinic, then never seen again. Rumors have persisted for three decades that his body is buried among the same gullies where the victims of the 1890 massacre fled.

Pictou-Aquash had been the subject of a book and documentary, both of which suggested the FBI had been involved in her death or in some kind of cover-up. But decades later, it was apparent that AIM had killed one of their own. While left-wing journalists and authors at first championed AIM leaders as heroes fighting an overreaching FBI, it was becoming apparent that there were no "good guys" in the 1970s dirty war.

A South Dakota jury eventually convicted Looking Cloud. Means, unhappy that the federal government hadn't arrested the leaders who ordered the killing, called the verdict "racist." He unilaterally declared that the American Indian Movement was finished.

Mention Russell Means's name to anyone old enough to remember him in the Nebraska border towns and you will get an opinion. Almost always negative. White, Indian, mixed blood, even those who are sympathetic to the Oglalas will call him a "shit-stirrer." They'll tell you he's just a self-promoter in it for himself. A long string of curse words describing him usually follows. But then they'll add, "Did you see him in *Last of the Mohicans*? Man, he was good in that!"

Some folks on the reservation do still think highly of him. In 2004, he ran in the election to replace John Yellow Bird Steele as tribal president. He campaigned on a platform of self-reliance. He wanted to open a bank in Pine Ridge. He wanted to oust the BIA from the reservation, and most of all he wanted to scrap the tribal constitution, which had been in force since the Indian Reorganization Act of 1934. They were some of the same demands he made during the Wounded Knee occupation in 1972, and not completely bad ideas. He came in first place in a slate of thirteen candidates after the first round of voting, even though he'd recently shocked the heavily Democratic constituency by declaring his support for a Republican U.S. Senate candidate. The runoff promised a historic outcome, for his second-place opponent was a woman, fifty-eight-year-old grandmother and health-care specialist Cecelia Fire Thunder. And no woman had ever served as the tribe's president.

As for his detractors who remembered him from the turbulent 1970s, he told a television reporter: "The people have long memories. But there are very few of them left. Our life expectancy makes sure of that."

Means lost the runoff election by five hundred votes. He later protested the outcome in court, claiming Fire Thunder lived in Martin, South Dakota, not the reservation, and was therefore ineligible. It seemed a petty claim considering a good chunk of Bennett County is still tribal trust land, and the remainder, where Martin sits, was practically stolen from the Oglalas under the hated General Allotment Act.

Within months, a movement to toss Fire Thunder out of office would be well under way, underscoring Means's point that the constitution and government imposed on the Oglalas was dysfunctional and needed to be scrapped.

Vernon Bellecourt was the first of AIM's top leaders to pass away. He died at age seventy-five in Minneapolis on October 13, 2007, of complications from pneumonia. Vernon and Means had never stopped sniping at each other. Bellecourt told a reporter in 2004 that Means's autobiography, titled *Where White Men Fear to Tread*, was so named "because they don't want to step in the buffalo shit."

Means had the last word when he accused Bellecourt of having a hand in the Pictou-Aquash murder, and that his death meant that he had escaped justice. "I wanted him to live long enough to be indicted and go to jail for Anna Mae's death," he told a journalist.

At his home in the country in the northeast corner of the reservation, Tom Poor Bear sat at his kitchen table and pulled out a letter from his attorney. The previous year, an Omaha-based lawyer helped him file a civil rights lawsuit against Colonel Tom Nesbitt and Sheriff Terry Robbins, accusing them of depriving him of his rights to free speech, assembly, association, and the free exercise of his Lakota religious practices when they arrested him for crossing the police line in July 1999. The lawsuit also sought the enforcement of the 1882 executive order, which declared the Extension a buffer zone to protect the Oglalas from the sale of alcohol. It accused the Nebraska Liquor Control Commission of failing to enforce the law.

Poor Bear still hadn't paid his one-hundred-dollar fine for failing to obey a lawful order. He was angrier than ever at Means for copping a plea, paying the fine, and leaving the others to continue the fight. The letter from his attorney informed him that the lawsuit had been dismissed.

Some marched in 1999 to end liquor sales, others to get the land back. For Poor Bear, it was always about justice for Ronnie and Wally. He remained convinced that white people killed them. He claimed Wally died from dozens of puncture wounds. Only those with hatred in their hearts could carry out such a crime, he says. People who hate Indians. "I'm going to keep marching every year. As long as I'm alive I won't stop demanding justice."

Ask folks in Sheridan County and Whiteclay, and they'll say Indians were the killers. Ask folks in Pine Ridge, and they'll say racist whites were responsible. These are the attitudes of people who want to believe the worst of each other.

Dennis Yellow Thunder at the resting place of his uncle Raymond Yellow Thunder, near Porcupine, South Dakota, December 2003. (Photo by author.)

Another Saturday Night in Gordon

A pair of teenage white boys cruise up and down the streets in their black Pontiac Firebird, passing other high schoolers in pickup trucks and Stingrays, each vehicle polished like a mirror. They drink beers, toss their empties into the gutters, and play cat and mouse with the town cops while searching for girls driving less glamorous Ford Tempos. They crank up their woofers loud enough to vibrate picture glass windows in the dimly lit houses along the otherwise silent streets. The formless pounding annoys the old ladies sitting in their homes. Exactly the desired effect.

Toby Bayliss's Ford Custom never had a sound system like theirs.

They pull up at the truck stop on the corner of Highway 20 and Main Street to talk with some other teens loitering on the north side of the station, out of the view of the low-paid clerks inside. A boy old enough to buy tobacco walks in the store to purchase five packs of cigarettes and several cans of snuff. Outside, he hands the contraband out to the teens.

The boys slide back into the Firebird, stick the chew between their cheeks and gums, then head north up Main Street, taking a right along the railroad tracks. They turn north again, passing the laundromat where Les Hare tossed Yellow Thunder his clothes after abducting him twice. Four cars with South Dakota tags sit in the gravel parking lot. Inside, Oglala women wait for their clothes to dry just as Yellow Thunder's sisters did thirty-one years ago as their brother lay dying in an old truck across the street. Borman Chevrolet's used-car lot is now a self-storage business. The dealer's showroom is a mortuary.

The boys in the Pontiac Firebird continue north, blasting music out their windows, spitting tobacco juice into empty plastic pop bottles until they reach the end of the town where the backyards meet the pastures. They then take a left, crossing Main Street to make a U-turn at the Family Dollar parking lot, once Shald's Jack and Jill. Avoiding the main drag where they might encounter the cops, they head south down Oak Street past the high school.

The car passes over a spot on the cement where a Gordon police officer shot Dennis Cross in 1992.

Dennis Cross, the brother of Joann Yellow Bird and Bill Cross, never conquered the drinking problem that consumed him after returning from Vietnam, although he mellowed a bit as he grew older. By the early 1990s, he was spending most of his time on the reservation restoring a log cabin near Porcupine, but every once in a while he would appear in Gordon and go on a bender.

On one such night, February 4, 1992, he stole a rifle out of a resident's garage. He was walking down the street when he encountered a neophyte police officer. The rookie said he asked Dennis to halt, and when he didn't, he shot him dead.

There were no witnesses to the shooting, and Bill, who'd had more than his share of grief over the years, asked Russell Means to help. Means said local AIM members were capable of handling the matter themselves. Bill was still a supporter of the movement even though he'd lived a quiet life since the turbulent 1970s when he and Yellow Bird fought against the county's dual standard of justice. In truth, he was too distraught over his brother's death to be of much use. Tom Poor Bear came down from the reservation to help him organize a small prayer ceremony at the spot near the high school where Dennis fell.

Afterward, they walked down the hill to the city auditorium where town leaders, a Justice Department mediator, and the Human Relations Council waited to hear their grievances. The board, organized at AIM's insistence after Yellow Thunder's death in 1972, had survived for two decades, although it was rarely convened.

Although the crowd assembled to speak out against Dennis's death was smaller than 1972's, they were equally upset. However, Gordon had changed. Fred Hlava, Jr., the city manager, called in the Justice Department mediator from Kansas City. Hlava traveled to the reservation at the invitation of Tom Poor Bear to address an AIM meeting and discuss the shooting, a first in white-Oglala relations. Hlava was a Gordon native, a Vietnam veteran, and a former businessman who preferred to nip potential racial problems in the bud by dealing with them before they made it to the Human Relations Council.

The Gordon Police Department had changed as well. It was no longer the poorly trained, dubiously qualified force of the past. They were police academy graduates who completed Justice Department sensitivity training workshops and even had a few hours of Lakota language lessons.

Still, an Oglala was dead. Unlike with the Broken Rope shooting in 1954, where a panel of white businessmen "investigated" the incident and declared Police Chief Sailor Lane innocent of any charges, Nebraska law now required a grand jury investigation. And the grand jury had found the officer acted properly. That wasn't good enough for the Oglalas assembled in the auditorium.

Bill took the microphone. He was never the one to make speeches back in the 1970s; that was his brother-in-law Yellow Bird's role. Although wracked with grief, he had to speak up for his lost brother. He told the audience about the man the white folks of Sheridan County never knew. Not the alcoholic whom local officers had arrested more than eighty times for intoxication and petty crimes, but the Vietnam War infantryman who fought for his country and came back with wounds that wouldn't heal. He told them about their sister Joann, who lost her child after a Gordon police officer kicked her, and how that incident also brought residents together to talk about injustice.

"We are told that there's been an in-depth investigation—police investigation. We are told that a grand jury met; there was no compromise. We are told that everything was fair and square and that the officer was cleared. He's back on duty. But as Indian people who suffer from so much injustice from the system, we have to stop and question very seriously, very objectively. We have to stop and say 'I don't think that's so because the system is stacked against us as we all know.' We have to admit that. It's not rhetoric. The system is stacked against Indians: as a minority; Indians as historical enemies; Indians as poor people; oppressed Indian people as a pain-in-the-side because of treaty; because of history; because of land; because of jurisdiction; because of poverty. All those things come to be a part of our condition today when it comes to the legal system. We do have to consider those things. So once again, we lose a fellow Indian. A brother. Back in '72 Raymond Yellow Thunder; same thing happened. Indian people stopped. They said, 'No. There's got to be more to this.'"

One by one, AIM members spoke. They wondered why the officer didn't call for backup, why he used deadly force. They called for a boycott. They called for a new investigation. But none of this came to pass.

The white boys in the black Pontiac continue cruising south, oblivious to the history around them. Past the city auditorium, past the park across the street, they drive by the Kut and Kurl Beauty Salon. Pat Shald, now retired from the grocery business, rents a room adjoining the beauty parlor. He sits in a reclining chair, smoking cigarettes, drinking Pepsi, and watching Fox News until the late hours. He's still the town liberal who likes to pick arguments with the local hardcore Republicans. But when no one is around to indulge him, he watches Fox just so he can wage arguments in his mind with the conservative network's commentators.

Shald once invited himself to a Sheridan County Historical Society meeting where the topic of the week was the life of Mari Sandoz.

"I think it's pretty interesting that Mari Sandoz was gay," he interjected.

The Historical Society crowd, mostly made up of churchgoing elderly ladies who revered the author as the town's only claim to fame, stared back, silent as stones.

"Well, she was," he continued, sharing his theory with the unwilling listeners. Once, while his girlfriend Norma and he were visiting Mari's last living sibling, Caroline, he was allowed to go through Mari's letters, filed away in a cabinet. While Norma and Caroline had coffee, Shald claimed that he found some love letters written to Lawrence Bixby's first wife. Bixby was the rancher who bought what remained of the Spade Ranch from Bartlett Richards after his empire collapsed. The history books say Mari ran off to Lincoln with her first cousin. The whisperings in the Southhills said she left with her lover. Undoubtedly, many of those in attendance that day had heard the same story. But you just didn't talk about those things at a historical society meeting! Unless you were the town gadfly, Pat Shald.

During her lifetime, Mari was continually scandalizing the townspeople of Gordon. Now, they embrace her. A fading sign east of town says,

HOME OF MARI SANDOZ: STORY CATCHER OF THE
PLAINS: OLD JULES COUNTRY

The grizzled face of the Swiss immigrant is now featured on postcards.

The black Firebird takes a left on Second Street, past the law office where Michael Smith practices. While balding and gray, and a little paunchier, he still dresses in business attire even on days when he never leaves the office, and he still wears many hats in town. He's now an assistant county attorney, leaving to a younger partner the job of the county's top law enforcement officer. He believes justice was served to the Hares and Bayliss and talks openly of his doubts that the beating Yellow Thunder endured in the used-car lot led to the injury that killed him. But he believes their actions—possibly when Yellow Thunder was shoved in the trunk—led to the injury. And that's proximate cause, as defined by the law. The Hares needed to serve time, and they did. And that's that.

"That jury found a way to convict them. Let's put it that way."

Thirty-one years later, he's still irked by the accusations AIM made against him, the sloppy reporting, the portrayal of Gordon as a racist town. And he's still irked about the defeat Bob Yellow Bird handed to him in North Platte.

The Pontiac Firebird pauses at the stop sign at the corner of Second and Main, between the First National Bank of Gordon and the Italian Inn. The two boys check for cops before pulling out.

On the two corners sit Gordon's two downtown bars. The Italian Inn, co-owned by Les and Pat's half brother Vern, serves pasta and hamburgers and Busch Lights to a steady clientele of ranchers, farmers, and out-of-town businessmen. The Sheridan Lounge, the tragic scene of Joann and Bob Yellow Bird's fight with Sheridan County law enforcement, is still open and is still a dive. Indians do occasionally stop for a drink at the Italian Inn, despite false rumors believed by some that Yellow Thunder's killers own it. White folks walk across the street to the roomier "Scrounge," where they can shoot pool. But basically, the Inn is the white bar and the Lounge is the Indian bar. White or Indian, the Sheridan Lounge is a place where customers of any race can get sloppy drunk and play loud rock 'n' roll or country on the jukebox.

A half block up the road is the newspaper office. The *Gordon Journal* is now the *Sheridan County Journal Star* and under new ownership. Reva Evans passed away in 1989. Long after her employees had switched to word processors, she continued to use her Royal manual typewriter. She served as publisher and editor until a week before her death, but not before being inducted into the Nebraska Journalism Hall of Fame. She was so secretive about her age, her tombstone doesn't include her date of birth. It reads:

Reva Rosseter Evans
Loving Mother of Susanne and Morris
Editor and publisher Gordon Journal 1949–1989

Across the street from the Italian Inn sits the First National Bank of Gordon. In 1970, the Oglala tribal government began depositing its money there, and it has been a loyal customer ever since. There are banks in Gordon, Rushville, Martin, and Rapid City that could take their business, but the bank remains the strongest manifestation of the symbiotic economic relationship between the reservation and the county. Aside from the tribal government, federal programs administered on the reservation, schools, and Oglala individuals also park their money there.

Sheridan County ranchers, farmers, and small businessmen borrow and keep their savings there as well. By the end of the century, as farms and ranches consolidated, that part of the business began to shrink, and the bank's ties to the reservation grew stronger. Soon, a blue and red Oglala tribal flag stood in the doorway next to the Stars and Stripes. When the end of the month came, reservation residents flocked to the bank to deposit their checks and do some shopping on the way out of town. Small personal loans were part of doing business. When someone died or graduated from high school, when a customer was a little short at the end of the month, or needed to buy or repair a car in a hurry, he could go to a loan officer. The small loans made little money for the bank; they were just part of doing business.

And it wasn't just individuals who came to the loan officers. When the tribal government came up short, the bank tided it over so it could make payroll. When federal dollars were disbursed late, the bank filled the gap. Meanwhile, no bank would ever open its doors on the reservation. Banks need commercial loans to stay afloat, and the reservation could never attract enough small businesses to keep its money circulating.

In the 1990s, direct deposit lessened the need to make weekly trips to the border towns. Then a Rushville bank began sending a van every Friday to service its customers at Pine Ridge. It was a convenience for the Oglalas, but the beginning of the end for Rushville's retail stores. Not needing to cash one's check down south meant not stopping to pick up groceries on the way home. The town lost both its high school and its newspaper when they consolidated with their counterparts in Gordon. If it weren't for the courthouse, Rushville would have little need to exist.

When Indian-white relations sour, as they did in 1972, calls emerge for the tribal government to withdraw its money from the bank. But this has always been bluster, because it's an institution that readily accommodates the tribe's unique needs.

The Justice Department busted the bank in 1996 for charging higher interest rates to its Indian customers. It got socked with a $275,000 fine, which was used to compensate the victims and hire Indian loan officers. Bank officials, and their attorney Michael Smith, protested, claiming the small consumer loans were unprofitable and were provided as a convenience to the Oglalas, but the fine stood. If the tribal government or the individual Oglala customers were upset about the conviction, they didn't show it. Their money remained in Gordon.

As the two teen boys in the black Pontiac Firebird continue south down Main Street, they pass by four storefronts owned by the grandchildren of the Syrian immigrant Sam Hinn. The family has mostly abandoned Rushville's dying Main Street. In Gordon, Sam's descendants own two furniture stores, an auto-parts franchise, and a clothing store.

Their father, Charlie Hinn, remained in Rushville and ran the True Value Hardware store, claiming he would never retire. His children believed he would die behind the hardware store counter. Charlie Hinn loved running a small-town business and passed his enthusiasm on to his children. He put them to work in his store as soon as they were tall enough to look over the counter.

"If you don't take of your business, you won't have to worry about it. It will be long gone," he often said, passing on wisdom learned from his father. The Hinns now own ranches, farms, two auto-parts stores, a mobile home dealership, and residential property all over the county. In 2004, he would pass away, not behind the counter, but at the Gordon Memorial Hospital, at the age of seventy-eight.

Over the railroad track and out to Highway 20, the Firebird takes a right, leaving behind the Legion Hall. The old log-cabin-style building is long gone. In 1978, a tornado swept out of the sky from the west, cutting a path through town, destroying Otto and Mickey's Cafe before it plowed into the Legion, scattering the wood like Lincoln Logs on a four-year-old's bedroom floor. The new building still hosts dances on Saturday nights. And a sign near the door still asks gentlemen to remove their hats, but no one bothers with that anymore.

The teenagers end their tour as they reach the western edge of town. The truck stop where Les Hare bragged openly about shoving Raymond Yellow Thunder into the Legion Hall still marks the end of Gordon. It looks about the same, although the owners don't. Gordon is entering a new era. The Gordon hospital employs a Nepali doctor. Hasidic Jews purchased the meatpacking plant, where they produce kosher meat. And a Chinese family bought the café, where the locals sip coffee on stools along the counter. Gordon isn't changing as much as reverting. One hundred years ago, census figures showed Chinese, Japanese, and black families living in Sheridan County.

In a corner booth, Les sits down to talk with a journalist, the first interview he's given to a member of the media. He no longer lives in Gordon, but he stops by from time to time to see Vern and an adopted brother. His face is weatherworn and long. He wears a wide-brimmed hat and a green hunting jacket. At age fifty-nine, he's not the wild boy of the Sand Hills anymore. He quit flying because it grew too expensive, and he believed that by never experiencing a crash he was pushing his luck, a sentiment the younger Les Hare would not have considered for a moment. He walks with a limp and has a bad back. He's spent postprison life as a truck driver and has never had much money.

Les is very bitter. Pat even more so.

Pat moved to California, returning to Gordon only in 1980 for Dean Hare's funeral. Since then, he doesn't want anyone in Gordon to know his whereabouts. He legally changed his name and believes enemies in Gordon will attempt to track him down and ruin his life. When his mother flies out to see him, and her friends innocently ask her what part of California she visited, she refuses to tell them. Norma is a staunch defender of her boys and will tell anyone willing to listen that there was a miscarriage of justice.

Les says he and his brother are innocent of the manslaughter charges.

He admits to everything except beating Yellow Thunder. He does back off the "humanitarian defense" tale Pat spun on the witness stand in Alliance—a story other members of the Hare family still cling to.

"It was a sick joke, all right," he says testily when asked why he did it. He wants to tell his side of the story.

"I had previously got in a fight in the Legion club with the guy who runs it, and ended up being barred where I couldn't go in there. So that night this was supposed to have happened we were riding around drinking and they was having a dance down there, but I couldn't go, so we found this Indian guy walking around, got him out of a car, and we took his pants off of him and we took him down to the Legion club and put him in the Legion club, and we started to leave. I bet he wasn't in there ten seconds and they throwed him out as we was leaving the parking lot. So I told Toby 'it's cold you know, we'd better pick him up, help him get dressed,' so we did. We went back and picked him up, took him up to the laundromat, went across the street to where we taken his pants off. I helped him get dressed, he was starting to sober up after all that, so I apologized to him and gave him a can of beer. He was still in the laundromat, and we left, and that's the last time I ever seen him.

"But it isn't anything that hasn't been done to me. I mean in them days, crap like that went on all the time. And it wasn't just because he was an Indian, you know. I think it was political, or something like that. We pretty much proved we was innocent in court, and they still took us down the road.

"But we did not hurt that Indian."

Les is unaware that Michael Smith told a Chadron State history professor who published a book on the Wounded Knee occupation that he didn't think Yellow Thunder died as result of a beating. He doesn't read a lot of books, he confesses. But he's also unaware that in two statements given to state patrol investigator Max Ibach, his friend Toby sold him out and described him beating up Raymond.

The Hares have held on to two appellant briefs for the past thirty-two years. One the Fishers filed reached the Nebraska Supreme Court, which upheld the verdict. In this document, Charles Fisher argues that pathologist W. O. Brown's testimony proves that the injury was sustained several days after February 12. The pathologist's testimony was confusing and vague on the time frame. Fisher bases the argument on the supposition that George Ghost Dog saw Yellow Thunder alive the second time he came across him on Friday, February 18. However, Ghost Dog did not linger at the used truck long enough to determine whether Yellow Thunder was alive or dead. He testified that he "thought he was sleeping." In fact, he saw him lying against the door in the exact same position as he'd seen him on February the 13th. He was likely already dead.

Pat wasn't always so reclusive. In the early 1970s, he was keen to tell his side of the story. While serving his nine months in prison, he wrote a seven-page letter to *Penthouse* magazine detailing the conspiracy that put him and his brother in prison. After reading an interview in the magazine with Vernon Bellecourt, he thought the editors should know the truth about what happened. The people of western Nebraska were so terrorized by AIM that they conspired to sacrifice two innocent men, he wrote.

"So I have decided to give the public the truth about this case, so that the people of America will know what can happen to you because of terrorist groups who blackmail people into using the court system to gain their fame and power. . . . I have only touched on the whole story in these pages.

"How do I know these things? Because my name is Melvin Hare. I am not guilty. I proved it. But still I am in prison," he ended his missive. *Penthouse* didn't print his letter or accept his offer of an exclusive interview.

The Hares blame AIM. They blame the people of Gordon. They blame Butch Lutter. They blame the prosecuting attorney, Smith. They blame their defense attorneys, the Fishers. In short, they blame everyone but themselves.

George Ghost Dog lives on the streets in Rapid City.

He is now in his forties and still skinny. His face is scarred and his nose malformed from street fights. Like many men living on skid row, he claims to know martial arts. He's struggling with an alcohol problem, and he's in and out of jail and detox. People who know him warn that he can be a belligerent drunk. He's been banned from several Rapid City stores as well as the Open Door Mission. He rides a bicycle downtown and keeps all his possessions in a book bag.

He's found at 9:30 in the morning before he's scrounged up enough money to begin drinking. When sober, Ghost Dog is not the violent man described. He's smart and has a good memory for details. He's told some of the other homeless Lakotas that he was a part of the Yellow Thunder case, but they think he's full of it.

The story he relates as he sits in a fast-food restaurant drinking coffee and eating breakfast sandwiches is almost identical to what he said in the trial. When he asked Yellow Thunder what had happened, he said four white boys roughed him up. One Indian speaking to another, and the story was unchanged. It is the same thing Yellow Thunder told Bernard Sandage, John Paul, and the magistrate at the police station.

John Paul left law enforcement and works for the county. Now in his sixties, he's still an imposing man. At the Italian Inn, with a drink in one hand, he brushes off inquiries. "A lot of accusations were made about me that weren't true. An investigation cleared me of all charges. And that's all I have to say about it."

Other than that, he refuses to discuss the case. However, there's no evidence the town of Gordon investigated the charges of molesting Indian women AIM leveled at him. And no evidence that they were ever true.

Max Anderson, the nineteen-year-old meatpacking plant worker who watched as the Hares and Bayliss stuffed Yellow Thunder in the trunk a second time, is no longer alive to tell his side of the story. Ten years after the incident, he constructed a homemade boat from a cement truck slough. He and a buddy took it out on a Sand Hills lake with their children. It didn't float. Anderson and his friend drowned. Fortunately, the kids made it to shore.

Anderson, and Jeanette Thompson, who lives west of town and works with her husband driving long-distance trucks, were never convicted of any crimes. And their involvement is all but forgotten.

Gordon in 2003 is not the Gordon of 1972. Back then, there were few Oglala clerks in the stores, while there are many working in town today. They have the same low-wage, dead-end jobs as the whites. But they're jobs, and those are hard to come by in a town of eighteen hundred in the middle of nowhere. At one time, Indians weren't welcomed as members of the Gordon Country Club. Now golfers from the reservation are keeping the place afloat.

Bill Cross still lives in Gordon. He still sees prejudice. He still sees whites holding on to the better-paying jobs at the schools and the hospital. Three of his siblings died in Gordon, and his sister Joann lost her unborn child there. People tell him he should move away for his own safety, but he stays. He lives a quiet life, commuting to the reservation every day where he serves as a social worker for the tribal government. Most who remember him from the 1970s don't even realize he lives in town. He talks about the legacy of AIM in the Nebraska border towns: "Indian people regained their identity. Gave them back the sense of who they are." He's not alone in these thoughts. The Oglalas, for the first time, could raise their heads high as they walked through town.

When asked if AIM did more to harm white-Indian relations in the border towns than to help them, he answers that AIM was not meant to be a "bridge builder."

"It was a polarizer and that was its function. The war never ended. It's still going on. It wasn't like 'be good and live side by side.' It was, 'Hey, we're a sovereign nation. We got rights. Let's assert them. Let's get all the white people off the reservation.'

"We'll never live together. Physically, we will, but we'll never share. We're living in [the white culture] but we're not part of it. That's something we choose ourselves, I think."

Jane Morgan, the former mayor who engaged in heated arguments with Bob Yellow Bird at city council meetings in the 1970s, always felt that alcohol was a root problem. At that time, the men and women who hung out on Gordon's streets had few options for treatment. She set out to bring a rehab center to Gordon, which opened in 1990. She's now the executive director of the North East Panhandle Substance Abuse Center, which sits in the southeast section of Gordon—still referred to as "Indian town."

She admits that Yellow Bird was right. Gordon had some bad cops in the 1970s. His strident, often belligerent words just turned people like her off. She has few charitable words to say about her onetime adversary. She believes that Indian-white relations have improved, but bigotry and misinformation still exist.

"We have farmers and ranchers who are part of a survivalist culture. . . . They are always at the mercy of the weather. It takes a different breed to continue to plant after they've been hailed out. And when you take that survivalist culture and put it against some of the issues over there [on the reservation], which receives so many federal dollars. And that has always rubbed the ranchers and farmers the wrong way because they felt they had to do it for themselves. Of course, you can always argue that they receive farm subsidies, but they don't look at that as the same as what is going on up there."

The Lakota Red Nations Sixth Annual Thanksgiving Powwow begins in the Gordon City Auditorium with an afternoon of dancing for the children. When it's too cold for traditional gatherings outside, hundreds come down from the reservation to celebrate their culture in the building AIM occupied in 1972.

The jingle dancers, girls wearing dresses festooned with aluminum snuff-can lids bent in the shape of bells, put on their clinking garb in the stands. Boys with plumes of dyed feathers spread out from their back make last-minute preparations for the fancy dancing. Their mothers help straighten their headdresses.

Robert Two Crow, the Vietnam vet who wandered the streets of Gordon in 1972, offers a prayer in Lakota. Then he says a few words in English. Gordon has come a long way since AIM took over the auditorium in 1972, he tells the audience full of kids, all of them too young to remember.

Two Crow has come a long way, too. He is one of the few who survived the border town drinking lifestyle and remembers sitting in a bar next to "the quiet man" Raymond Yellow Thunder. He left Gordon in the late 1970s, moved to Lake Wakpamni to a house just east of Russell Yellow Thunder's place, and straightened out his life. He found a job with the Shannon County Public Schools, eventually earning his master's degree in education. Dressed from head to toe in a traditional Lakota dress, he joins the children in a dance.

The Porcupine Singers, the departed Severt Young Bear's old troupe, begin to pound on the same drum used in 1972 during the celebration after the end of the city auditorium occupation. The singers lift their voices, and the dancers begin to spin around the auditorium.

After the Oglala children finish the afternoon dancing session, everyone goes into the basement to feast on buffalo meat donated by the Turner Foundation. CNN founder and billionaire Ted Turner has been buying ranches all over the Sand Hills for the past ten years, allowing buffalo to graze the grasslands instead of cattle. A few weeks before the powwow, he purchased two more ranches in Sheridan County. Critics complained that the family-owned ranches were disappearing. The little guy was losing out to the corporations. When corporations buy and consolidate ranches and farms, more families disappear, and they fear the businesses and towns will go with them. Turner still didn't own anywhere near the amount of Sheridan County acreage that Bartlett Richards did a century ago. Not yet, anyway.

As the clock reaches 10:00 p.m., the emcee and organizer of the powwow, Kelly Looking Horse, calls for a communal dance. Everyone is welcome, Indian or white, wearing traditional dress or not. The men and boys dance around the outside as the women and girls move in an inner ring. The stands are full by that time. Looking Horse started the annual Gordon powwow to serve as a cultural bridge. Gordon businesses sponsor the prize money given out to the top dancers. A few locals like Charlie Hinn's son Charles and his children had come by to watch that day, but most of the white residents are gone by now. Only one white family remains. Doyle Bixby and Susan Phillips, the two Shald family sisters who'd attended the Yellow Thunder protests three decades ago, sit with one of their nephews, who is experiencing his first powwow. As the last song grows in intensity, the dancers continue to circle. A microphone sticks out of Severt Young Bear's drum, but artificial amplification is unnecessary. It can still shake the walls.

"Wow, we haven't seen that kind of spirit in here since 1972," Looking Horse says. "Who was here in 1972? Let's see your hands."

Only the two white women, Susan and Doyle, raise their hands. No one else in the mostly younger crowd can do so. Even the children's parents are too young to remember Yellow Thunder. The Shalds were always a family willing to serve as one of the rare cultural bridges between the two peoples. But only Pat, Mike, Doyle, and Susan remain in the county. Almost all the grandchildren of Gladys Shald have moved to bigger cities in search of opportunities. Along with stories of prejudice and hatred in the Nebraska border towns, the Shalds prove that there are less sensational stories of friendships and respect.

Arlene Lamont, remarried and living in the picturesque Black Hills town of Hot Springs, South Dakota, sits in her living room and remembers the Gordon of yesterday. Once, after she remarried, she had her new husband drive them through Gordon. It was her first time back after living for many years in Denver.

Thirty-two years later, she still feels the ambivalence toward Gordon that overtook her in the city auditorium. She maintains that she felt no prejudice directed toward her in Gordon when she was growing up in the 1950s.

She begins to cry as she remembers what she lost.

"I don't know. Was I blind? Maybe I was living in a fantasy world."

As for the Hares, she isn't very forgiving.

"I have great hatred for those people. I will probably bring it to my grave."

Dennis Yellow Thunder lives in his parents' former house across the road from Lake Wakpamni, threading tiny colored beads. He spends his days doing the painstaking work, putting traditional Lakota designs on pens and hats to sell to tourists. He never wears a shirt while he works. Scars from Sun Dance piercings dot his chest. It's tedious work, but on the reservation, cottage industries such as these are one way to pay the bills. Behind his desk, a picture of his uncle Raymond, only one of two pictures of him known to exist outside of his crime scene photos, hangs on the wall. He has a stack of videos he plays while he works. One of them is *Billy Jack.*

His parents, Russell, and Amelia Yellow Thunder live in a trailer house next door. They talk about their brother, remembering the gentle man they lost, laughing at some of the cattle-rustling jobs he pulled off as a young man.

Dennis has an education degree from the University of South Dakota, and once taught art, but he left the classroom. He had some hard deaths in the family, including his brother, and some at the school complained about his teaching methods, so he resigned. He'd inherited his family's drinking problem, but he quit alcohol altogether twelve years ago. He is a talented artist, something his uncle once nurtured in him, but paintings aren't as easy to sell as Bic pens covered in beads, so this is what he does. He dreams of starting a nonprofit art gallery and naming it after his uncle. He has the paperwork done, and now he's looking for the funding. He sees it as a place where all the local artists, Indian or white, could display their work.

After his uncle's death, anger and hatred consumed Dennis. He would fight any white kid he came across. The anger led to drinking and drugs, and he was heading down a road leading only to two places: an early death or prison. Then a medicine man, Dawson Has No Horse, saw what no one else could. That the anger over his uncle's death was eating away at his soul. Has No Horse offered him the Sacred Pipe, the Lakota spiritual path, and made him see why he was so angry at the world. Dennis let the hatred go. He credits the medicine man for saving his life.

He thinks about his uncle and the men who were held responsible for his death.

"Why would you want to put somebody through that kind of pain? Maybe they got enjoyment out of it at that time, or whatever, but they didn't know that there was a little boy sitting waiting for him. They didn't know that. My prayers are with them. In our culture, and the Way of the Pipe, we pray for our enemy so they don't do it again. Because nobody wants to go through that kind of pain."

ACKNOWLEDGMENTS

There are two women I met during my time in Gordon whom I would like to thank.

First, there was the white woman at the Italian Inn who had married into a grocer's family. As many did when meeting an out-of-towner in the local watering hole, she asked me what I was doing in Gordon. I told her I was writing a book about the shared 130-year history of Sheridan County and the reservation. She expressed her doubt that an outsider like myself could ever hope to understand the situation. She was born and raised in Gordon, and unlike many in her generation, decided to stay instead of moving to a larger city. I asked her to explain it to me. "Haven't you driven up there and seen how those people live?" She told me that they were all living off her tax money, most of them were drunks and beggars, they had every opportunity she had, and they threw these opportunities away. In short, she had no respect for the Oglalas. She insisted that without the Oglala trade, the grocery store her family ran would still survive.

I asked her how much she knew about the history of the reservation between the first and second Wounded Knee incidents (giving her credit for knowing about these two events). She simply replied: "Nothing."

I launched into a rambling speech about land acquisition, the Indian Reorganization Act, and how the once self-sufficient Oglalas had been forced into dependency. Midway through, she interrupted me. She said I had lost her.

The second woman was an Oglala in her midthirties I met across the street at the Sheridan Lounge about a week later. She lived in Rapid City, but had come to Gordon to visit her uncle. She too asked me what I was doing in Gordon. She was an AIM supporter and said she was related to Leonard Peltier. She asked me if I had read Peter Matthiessen's *In the Spirit of Crazy Horse*. I said I'd read enough to know that I didn't care for it. Its outrageously inaccurate portrayal of the Yellow Thunder incident caused me to doubt its reporting. We then got into a heated argument over the circumstances of Yellow Thunder's death. She not only insisted that Yellow Thunder had been tortured and forced to dance Indian style, but that he had died in the American Legion Hall. When I told her that AIM had paid for a second autopsy and it showed no signs of torture, she refused to believe me. When I told her she was relying on "oral tradition," not facts, she said I was "full of hate" and a "racist."

These two women gave me a renewed sense of purpose. I decided that I didn't want to write a *New York Times* best-seller anymore. I just wanted to write something people north and south of the border would read.

I would also like to thank the people who gave me their support. When I started this project, I was coming off a year of freelancing in Los Angeles and had little money to show for it. To fund the research phase, I spent seven weeks working in a salmon-canning factory in Ketchikan, Alaska. But completing a book of this nature takes more than money. It takes the support of friends and family. First of all, without my Grandmother Bernice Magnuson's unconditional support while letting me pound away at the first draft in her basement for two months, this book would not have been possible. My mother, Julie Strnad, and stepdad, Charlie, also loaned me their basement and gave me some funds to keep the repo man from taking away my car. Zia Rawish and Jon Rothenberg helped me get back on my feet here in the Washington DC area. Jon's computer wizardry helped with collecting photos and building my Web site.

Mark Edison, Rick Vosik, Peter Atkinson, David Hubler, Warren Ferster, and members of my writing group, Katie Rossner, Nancy Ruth Davis, Mary Kalfatovic, and Jamie Yesnowitz, gave me feedback on my early drafts. My fiancée, Nioucha Homayoonfar, helped me ready the final draft. Thanks to *National Defense Magazine*'s ace graphic artist Brian Taylor for his assistance making the map. My thanks to series editor John Wunder and to Judith Keeling at Texas Tech University Press for believing in the value of this work. I'm also grateful to editor John Mulvihill for both fine-tuning the writing and catching several factual errors.

One day in the spring of 2003, Pat Knapp, a law professor at the University of Nebraska–Lincoln, gave me a stack of state patrol documents and a videotape of the second march on Whiteclay. That was the day I decided to take this project off the back burner and devote the next year to the research.

Pat Shald at the site of
Camp Sheridan, July 2004.
(Photo by author.)

In Gordon, I would like to thank Jerry and Marilynn Halverson, Norma Burnham, and Pat and Susan Phillips for their hospitality. Thanks to Pat Shald, who argued every point I ever brought up. He challenged my thinking, and the book is better for it. Too many to list here are the dozens I need to thank who agreed to sit down for interviews.

Thanks to Matt Pearsol at the Nebraska Historical Society in Lincoln; Joel Minor, former archivist of the Oglala Community College; the staff of the Gordon Public Library; and Sheridan County district court clerks Eloise Kampbell and Sharon Engel for digging out those ancient court records. I'm grateful for the assistance of Gayle Davis, the editor of the late *Sheridan County Star*, and Tom Shall, editor of the *Sheridan County Journal Star*, for allowing me to search for seemingly endless hours through back issues and for giving permission to reprint photos and the Reva-Lations column in its entirety.

On the reservation, Dennis Yellow Thunder was always generous with his time. I know I slowed down his beadwork, but he always welcomed me

Acknowledgments

in his home. On the other side of the fence, the Hares could have told me to take a flying leap, but two members of the family didn't. Les went out of his way to tell me his side of the story, and I thank him for that.

Lastly, we all owe a debt of gratitude to the storytellers. Mari Sandoz suffered through the Depression and lived the life of a "starving artist" as she submitted stories of the Sand Hills to magazines that answered with rejection letters. A fellow Omaha native, George Hyde, with an eighth-grade education, deaf and legally blind, spent his life writing three seminal histories of the Oglalas and Brulés. Amos Bad Heart Bull spent untold hours under dim kerosene lanterns drawing his pictographs. Will Spindler, a Pine Ridge educator, self-published several history books on the reservation and Sheridan County. I don't know how many copies he sold in his lifetime, but his softcover books made their way to the Library of Congress, which is where they belong. These self-taught historians inspired me every step of the way, and this book would not be the same without their contributions.

ABBREVIATIONS

ADT	*Alliance Daily Times*
AP	Associated Press
BIA	Bureau of Indian Affairs
BYB	Bob Yellow Bird Steele
CR	*Chadron Record*
DMR	*Des Moines Register*
GJ	*Gordon Journal*
LAT	*Los Angeles Times*
LJ	*Lincoln Journal*
LJ/S	*Lincoln Journal Star*
LS	*Lincoln Star*
NPT	*North Platte Telegraph*
NSP	Nebraska State Patrol document
NYT	*New York Times*
OWH	*Omaha World-Herald*
RCJ	*Rapid City Journal*
RNS	*Rushville News Star*
RYT	Raymond Yellow Thunder
SCN/S	*Sheridan County News/Star*
SCS	*Sheridan County Star*
SSH	*Scottsbluff Star-Herald*

PROLOGUE

🏛 The bulk of this chapter is derived from the author's observations, tapes, and notes. Other sources include: interview with Tom Poor Bear, Wanblee, South Dakota, February 21, 2004; interview with Col. Tom Nesbitt, Lincoln, Nebraska, January 7, 2004; NSP file E99-5424-21213; NSP videotape of march in possession of author; and *OWH*, July 4, 1999.

A COLD NIGHT IN GORDON

🏛 Primary sources for this chapter, unless otherwise noted, are: district court records, Rushville, Nebraska, *State of Nebraska vs. Robert Richard Bay-*

liss, case nos. C-1287, C-1275; NSP interview reports, file 0110034; telephone interview with Bernard Lutter, October 19, 2003. FBI file: memo from Omaha to Minneapolis bureau, July 2, 1999, Case ID 198A-MP-52976, in author's possession.

🏠 Jerene and Les's marriage: from several off-the-record interviews with former classmates, and correspondence with former classmate Max Grimes, November 2, 2003.

🏠 Leslie Hare's wild teenage days documented in several interviews; also confirmed in interview with Leslie Hare, Gordon, Nebraska, November 25, 2003.

🏠 Details of Jeannette Thompson's marriage: from Sheridan County court records, *John L. Thompson vs. Jeannette Thompson*, case no. 6145, March 1, 1971.

🏠 Bayliss background and feelings about father: from district court records. Death of father: from *GJ*, August 11, 1971. Insights into Pat Hare: from a former wife, who prefers not to be named, November 23, 2003.

🏠 Information on Dean Hare: from numerous sources including interviews with unnamed Hare family member. Description of bunkhouses: from Jerry Krasomil, interview, Gordon, Nebraska, October 23, 2003. A more positive portrayal of Dean Hare: from first cousin Max Dykes, interview, October 22, 2003. Dean Hare wife beating: from Sheridan County court records, *Norma Lhee Hare vs. Dallas Dean Hare*, case no. 5054, January 23, 1947; correspondence with Hare family member. In his lifetime, Dean Hare made no secret that he doubted Pat was his son; confirmed in interview with Dykes. Hare family's passion for coyote hunting and description of methods: from interviews with Lutter, Les Hare, Dykes. Description of dispute with Bernard Sandage at Legion Hall: from *GJ*, March 15, 1972; also interview with Sandage, Gordon, Nebraska, October 17, 2003; dispute confirmed in interview with Les Hare.

THE STORY OF JOHN GORDON

🏠 John Gordon's second trip to the Black Hills: from Jeffrey L. Patrick, "To the Black Hills Gold Fields: The Letters of Samuel M. Zent, Hoosier Prospector, 1875–1876," *Indiana Magazine of History* 91, no. 3 (September 1995): 262–87; Erik M. Eriksson, "Sioux City and the Black Hills Gold Rush 1874–1877," *Iowa Journal of History and Politics* 20 (July 1922): 319–47; Brigadier General Anson Mills, U.S. Army, *My Story* (Washington, DC: self-published, 1918), 156–57; correspondence describing incident: Mills to Gen. George D. Ruggles, adjutant general, Dept. of the Platte, May 23, 1875, Letters Received, Records of the Adjutant General's office, 1780s–1917, RG94 (National Archives); Grant K. Anderson, "The Black Hills Exclusion Policy: Judicial Challenges," *Nebraska History* 58, no. 1 (Spring 1977): 1–24; also, *NYT*, March 1, 3, 13, and May 24, 1874.

🏠 After the Civil War, the military did not need as many command officers, so most were decommissioned. In 1866 George Armstrong Custer was required to revert to his previous permanent rank and begin the small regular army's slow promotion process. His official rank thereafter was Lt. Colonel. However, he continued to be known as General Custer to his men and to the public.

🏠 Gordon's first trip to the Black Hills, its organization and camp life: from Annie D. Tallent, *The Black Hills or Last Hunting Ground of the Dakotas* (Sioux Falls, SD: Brevet Press, 1974), 15–32; and David Akens, *Pioneers of the Black Hills or Gordon's Stockade Party of 1874* (1920); Watson Parker, *Gold in the Black Hills* (Norman: University of Oklahoma Press, 1966), 28–33. Report of second party's fate: from *NYT*, October 18, 1874. Also consulted: Lesta Turchen and James D. McLaird, *The Black Hills Expedition of 1875* (Mitchell, SD: Dakota Wesleyan University Press, 1975); Thomas R. Buecker, "History of Camp Sheridan, Nebraska," *Periodical: Journal of America's Military Past* 22, no. 4 (1995): 55–73.

🏠 Sand Hills geology and archeology: from *Sand Hills Archeology*, Nebraska State Historical Society (1999); Charles Barron McIntosh, *The Nebraska Sand Hills: The Human Landscape* (Lincoln: University of Nebraska Press, 1966). Note: Most maps spell "Sandhills" as one word. The author sides with those who believe the Sand Hills rival the Black Hills in both beauty and geological uniqueness, and therefore both words should be capitalized.

WHERE IS UNCLE RAYMOND?

🏠 Arlene Lamont's point of view in this chapter: from interviews with Arlene Hepner (Crazy Bear-Lamont), Hot Springs, South Dakota, June 5, 2003, and phone interview January 21, 2004.

🏠 Interview with Pat Shald, Gordon, Nebraska, October 3, 2003.

🏠 RYT's final day: from interview with Jerry Matula, November 2004. RYT's life on the ranch: from interview with Jim "Bucky" Rucker, August 2, 2005. Seger's Cafe incident: from district court records, *SoN vs. Bayliss*.

🏠 For RYT's early life prior to death, see Richard La Course, "Yellow Thunder: Violent Death of a Silent Man," *Oglala Nation News*, March 27, 1972; *OWH*, March 19, 1972; also interviews with Dennis Yellow Thunder, Lake Wakpamni, June 2003; Ray Lamont, Gordon, Nebraska, November 10, 2003; and Hepner. Russell and Amelia Yellow Thunder oral history: tapes recorded by Dennis Yellow Thunder in 1998 and interview with author, July 30, 2005.

🏠 George Ghost Dog's point of view: from interview with Ghost Dog, Rapid City, South Dakota, November 21, 2003; also court testimony.

🏠 John Paul's rough handling of intoxicated Indians was witnessed by many in town. Interviews with Pat Phillips, December 2, 2003, Gordon, Nebraska; former mayor Bruce Moore, Gordon, Nebraska, November 15, 2003; several other off-the-record interviews. John Paul declined to be interviewed for this book. Paul's point of view: from court testimony. The inaction of the Gordon Police Department was revealed in Paul's own testimony under examination by Smith during the Bayliss trial.

Laundromat scene: from interview with Elizabeth Young Bear, RYT cousin, Porcupine, South Dakota, June 2003.

Interviews with Michael Smith, Gordon, Nebraska, October 28, 2003, December 15, 2003, and August 2005. Smith does not remember hearing about the Legion Hall incident prior to discovery of RYT's body or recall conversation with Lamont. However, a 1983 interview suggested he did know beforehand. See Rolland Dewing, *Wounded Knee II* (Chadron, NE: Great Plains Network, 2000), 30.

Max Ibach point of view and investigation details: from NSP report, case file 0110034, February 24, 1972. Report shows that Ibach was handed a list of four suspects immediately upon arrival, indicating Sheridan County law enforcement knew the perpetrators ahead of time. A Seger's Cafe customer was incorrectly identified as a suspect instead of Lutter.

Birgil Kills Straight point of view: from phone interview, December 12, 2003.

Biographical information on Russell Means prior to RYT incident: from Russell Means, *Where White Men Fear to Tread: The Autobiography of Russell Means*, with Marvin J. Wolf (New York: St. Martin's Press, 1995), 1–193, and David R. Edmunds, ed., *The New Warriors: Native American Leaders since 1900* (Lincoln: University of Nebraska Press, 2001), 144–69.

Rancor at Omaha meeting: from *LJ/S*, May 28, 1972; *OWH*, March 5, 1972; and UPI, March 5, 1972. Severt Young Bear POV: from *Voices from Wounded Knee, 1973: In the Words of the Participants* (Rooseveltown, NY: Akwesasne Notes, 1974), 13. Clyde Bellecourt background: from Dewing, *Wounded Knee II*, 25–26. Banks's background and first meeting with Bellecourt: from Dennis Banks and Richard Erdoes, *Ojibwa Warrior: Dennis Banks and the Rise of the American Indian Movement* (Norman: University of Oklahoma Press, 2004), 12–63. Means's vow to march on Gordon: from *OWH*, March 5, 1972.

THE OGLALAS' LONG JOURNEY TO PINE RIDGE

Bull Bear story: from R. Eli Paul, ed., *Autobiography of Red Cloud: War Leader of the Oglalas* (Helena: Montana Historical Society Press, 1997), 64–70.

For pre-plains and early history of the Sioux nations, see Guy Gibbon, *The Sioux: The Dakota and Lakota Nations* (Malden, MA: Blackwell, 2003), 47–53; Catherine Price, *The Oglala People, 1841–1879: A Political History* (Lincoln: University of Nebraska Press, 1996), 1–21; Richard White, "The Winning of the West: The Expansion of the Western Sioux in the Eigh-

teenth and Nineteenth Centuries," *Journal of American History* 65, no. 2
(September 1978): 319–43; Pekka Hämäläinen, "The Rise and Fall of Plains
Indian Horse Cultures," *Journal of American History* 90, no. 3 (December
2003): 859–62. Black Hills carvings and archeology: "Black Hills Art May Be
5,000 Years Old," *Sioux Falls Argus Leader*, July 23, 2004.

On alcohol and its influences: William E. Unrau, *The White Man's Wicked
Water: The Alcohol Trade and Prohibition in Indian Country, 1802–1892*
(Lawrence: University Press of Kansas, 1996).

Rouleau family history: from Judy Kienzle, "Kola Oyate," a college research
paper in possession of author, December 9, 1989.

Bozeman Trail war: from Dorothy M. Johnson, *The Bloody Bozeman* (New
York: McGraw-Hill, 1971), 233–37; Kingsley M. Bray, "Spotted Tail and the
Treaty of 1868," *Nebraska History* 83 (Spring 2002): 19–35; Dee Brown,
*Bury My Heart at Wounded Knee: An Indian History of the American
West* (1971; repr. New York: Henry Holt, 1991), 122–46; Rex Allen Smith,
*Moon of Popping Trees: The Tragedy at Wounded Knee and the End of the
Indian Wars* (Lincoln: University of Nebraska Press, 1975), 36–45.

Description of Red Cloud's trip to Washington and speech: from Olson, *Red
Cloud*, 96–113. Events leading to war of 1875–76: from Thomas R. Buecker,
Fort Robinson and the American West: 1874–1899 (Norman: University of
Oklahoma Press, 1999), 77–78; George Hyde, *Red Cloud's Folk: A History
of the Oglala Sioux Indians* (1937; repr. Norman: University of Oklahoma
Press, 1975), 231–33; Brown, *Bury My Heart*, 276–313; Mari Sandoz, *The
Great Council* (Crawford, NE: Cottonwood Press, 1970); Mills, *My Story*,
167–69; Smith, *Moon of Popping Trees*, 53–54. Grant's secret order: from
Edward Lazarus, *Black Hills/White Justice: The Sioux Nation Versus the
United States* (New York: HarperCollins, 1991), 83.

For Nebraska reaction to the agencies, see Buecker, *Fort Robinson*, 118;
also, David J. Wishart, *An Unspeakable Sadness: The Dispossession of the
Nebraska Indians* (Lincoln: University of Nebraska Press, 1994), 188.

Death of Crazy Horse: from Mari Sandoz, *Crazy Horse, Strange Man of the
Oglala* (New York: Hastings House, 1942); also, Brown, Buecker, Bad Heart
Bull, and Blish.

Oglalas' choice of Pine Ridge: from Everett Leslie Marley, "History of Pine
Ridge Indian Reservation" (master's thesis, University of Nebraska, 1935),
14–21, and Hyde, *Red Cloud*, 299–303.

THE WHITE FOLKS' JOURNEY TO SHERIDAN COUNTY

Mari and Jules Sandoz: from Helen Winter Stauffer, *Mari Sandoz: Story
Catcher of the Plains* (Lincoln: University of Nebraska Press, 1982), 32;
Mari Sandoz, *Old Jules* (Lincoln: University of Nebraska Press, 1935).

Dahlman and Irwin story: from Dick Everett, *Conquering the Great American*

Desert (Lincoln: Nebraska State Historical Society, 1975), 272; Bartlett Richards, Jr., *Bartlett Richards: Nebraska Sandhills Cattleman*, with Ruth Van Ackeren (Lincoln: Nebraska State Historical Society, 1980), 55; J. R. Johnson, *Representative Nebraskans* (Lincoln, NE: Johnsen Publishing Co., 1954), 60–61; Mari Sandoz, *The Cattlemen: From the Rio Grande across the Far Marias* (New York: Hastings House, 1958); Fred Carey, *Mayor Jim* (Omaha, NE: Omaha Printing Co., 1930), 31–35. Note: most accounts have this story taking place in 1878. This is illogical since the agency and the Newman ranch were established in the spring of that year. Dahlman's account in *Mayor Jim* places the incident in April 1879.

Extension history: from annual reports of Pine Ridge Agency, October 15, 1879; September 1, 1881; August 27, 1889; Julia B. McGillycuddy, *Blood on the Moon: Valentine McGillycuddy and the Sioux* (Lincoln: University of Nebraska Press, 1990), 137.

Scamahorn party and early Gordon: from Grant L. Shumway, ed., *History of Western Nebraska and Its People* (Lincoln: Western Publishing and Engraving Co., 1921), 417–18; Harold Hutton, *Doc Middleton: Life and Legends of the Notorious Plains Outlaw* (Chicago: Swallow Press, 1974), 163–74; Sandoz, *Old Jules*, 20–34.

Bartlett Richards history: from Richards, *Bartlett Richards*.

Beef issues and Coon history: from Will H. Spindler, "Pioneers Recall Early Day Beef Issues," *GJ*, August 30, 1950; *Gordon Nebraska: Our First One Hundred Years* (Curtis Media Corp., 1984), 240. Other accounts of beef issues can be found in Charles W. Allen and Richard E. Jensen, *From Fort Laramie to Wounded Knee: In the West That Was* (Lincoln: University of Nebraska Press, 1997), 52–53, and McGillycuddy, *Blood on the Moon*.

A NEW WORLD

Charley Allen point of view and Red Cloud July 4 speech: from Allen and Jensen, *From Fort Laramie to Wounded Knee*, 140–81.

Crook commission: from Jerome A. Greene, "The Sioux Land Commission of 1889: Prelude to Wounded Knee," *South Dakota History* 1, no. 1 (Winter 1970): 41–72; Olson, *Red Cloud*, 306–19; George E. Hyde, *A Sioux Chronicle* (Norman: University of Oklahoma Press, 1956), 203–28; Smith, *Moon of Popping Trees*, 71–75, 146–60.

Primary sources on the life of Wovoka, Ghost Dance, Pine Ridge reaction to and stories of Sitting Bull and Big Foot: James Mooney, *The Ghost-Dance Religion and the Sioux Outbreak of 1890* (1896; repr. Chicago: University of Chicago Press, 1965); Michael Hittman, *Wovoka and the Ghost Dance Religion*, ed. Dan Lynch (Lincoln: University of Nebraska Press, 1997); Smith, *Moon of Popping Trees*, 71–75, 146–60. Description of Ghost Dance: adapted from William S. E. Coleman, *Voices of Wounded Knee* (Lincoln:

University of Nebraska Press, 2000), 36–38, and Mooney, *The Ghost-Dance Religion.*

🏠 Allen's feelings about Cressey and Kelley and editorial: from Don Huls, *The Winter of 1890 (What Happened at Wounded Knee)* (self-published, 1974), 21–22. For descriptions of the reporters at Pine Ridge Agency, see George R. Kolbenschlag, *A Whirlwind Passes: News Correspondents and the Sioux Indian Disturbances of 1890–1891* (Vermillion: University of South Dakota Press, 1990), 19–21.

🏠 Role and reaction of Nebraska border towns: from Sandoz, *Old Jules,* 129–31; Carl Lockman, *The Years of Promise* (self-published, 1971), 52–53; Elmo Scott Watson, "The Last Indian War, 1890–91: A Study of Newspaper Jingoism," *Journalism Quarterly* 20, no. 3 (September 1943): 205–19; Thomas Henry Tibbles, *Buckskin and Blanket Days* (1957; repr., Lincoln: University of Nebraska, 1969), 309–16; Nebraska National Guard, "Adjutant General's Report," January 24, 1891.

🏠 Border town panics and Fort Nendle: from Will H. Spindler, *Tragedy Strikes at Wounded Knee* (Rushville, NE: News/Star, 1955), 8–10; Spindler, *Centennial Prairie* (Gordon, NE: Gordon Journal Publishing Co., 1965), 60; John Coleman, "The Indian Uprising of 1890–91 Culminates in Wounded Knee," *Hay Springs News,* March 16, 23, 1928.

🏠 Rough Feather story: from James H. McGregor, *The Wounded Knee Massacre: From the Viewpoint of the Sioux* (1940; repr., Rapid City, SD: Fenwyn Press Books, 1969), 99–101.

INDIAN SCARE

🏠 FBI teletypes: from FBI, file 105-203686, sec. 3.

🏠 The following eyewitnesses to the march and occupation were interviewed for this chapter: Means, Smith, Vernon and Clyde Bellecourt, St. Paul, Minnesota, March 19, 2004; Susan Phillips, Gordon, Nebraska, October 21, 2003; Pat Shald; former mayor Bruce Moore, Gordon, Nebraska, November 15, 2003; Arlene Hepner (Lamont); Robert Two Crow, Lake Wakpamni, South Dakota, February 17, 2004; Elizabeth Young Bear, Severt Young Bear, Jr., Porcupine, South Dakota, June 2003; Gerald Big Crow, Pine Ridge, South Dakota, December 13, 2003; Ghost Dog; Ed Hollstein, Rushville, Nebraska, October 24, 2003; Vern American Horse, Gordon, Nebraska, November 4, 2003; Billy Gibbons, Gordon, Nebraska, November 23, 2003; Noah No Leaf, Gordon, Nebraska, November 4, 2003.

🏠 Smith interview with AP writer: printed in *ADT,* March 3, 1972; also correspondence from Bordeaux to Smith, February 28, 1972; Ibach and state patrol movements found in NSP supplemental report, Max B. Ibach, March 20, 1972.

🏠 Crow Dog background: from George E. Hyde, *Spotted Tail's Folk: A History of the Brulé Sioux* (Norman: University of Oklahoma Press, 1961), 335–42; Leonard Crow Dog and Richard Erdoes, *Crow Dog: Four Generations of Sioux Medicine Men* (New York: HarperCollins, 1995) 166; Means, *Where White Men Fear to Tread*, 175.

Means quotations: "We came here today . . . ," *CR*, March 9, 1972; "I am like a rubber band . . . ," *OWH*, March 8, 1972; "No. It's about time . . . ," *DMR*, March 12, 1972; "The only weapon . . ." and "Indians don't have to . . . ," March 9, 1972; Means called him a "bellboy . . . ," *OWH*, March 8, 1972; Means's demand that John Paul come to auditorium, *CR*, March 9, 1972.

Hollstein incident: from *CR*, *OWH*; Hollstein interview; district court records. Arlene Lamont quotations: from *NYT*, March 20, 1972.

Sources for Reva Evans include: interviews with former employees; Errol Brakeman, phone interview, October 23, 2003; Neil Ziller, Gordon, Nebraska, October 2003; *Gordon, Nebraska*, 187; *DMR*; "Reva-lations," *GJ*, March 15, 1972; *Washington Post* article reprinted in *LAT*, March 5, 1972.

Other news sources: most inaccuracies from the AP originated in the Rapid City bureau and were reprinted in the *Rapid City Journal*. The legendary *Omaha World-Herald* reporter Tom Allen did a good blow-by-blow account of the march; however, his paper's Washington bureau reporter did repeat the "forced to dance Indian style" rumor in a March 14, 1972, article. Other media outlets like the *Kansas City Times* (March 9, 1972) said he had been stripped and pushed onto the dance floor. Technically, this is correct since the American Legion dance floor went right up to the front door, but the implication that he had been brought in and pushed into the middle of the dance is untrue. Whether it was a result of Reva Evans's call to his editor or not, the *Des Moines Register* reporter Dan Piller produced one of the more balanced, in-depth stories of the march.

Local Oglala attitudes toward march: from interviews with Gibbons, American Horse, No Leaf, Ghost Dog; also many of Gordon's Oglala community were quoted in the press as welcoming the occupation and said they were interested in what AIM had to say.

"Evans told an outside reporter . . .": AP story reprinted in March 9, 1972, *RCJ*.

Negotiations for end of occupation: from interviews with Means, C. Bellecourt, Smith; also Means, *Where White Men Fear to Tread*, 198–99. Means declares "complete victory": *OWH*, March, 9, 1972. AIM song: Severt Young Bear and R. D. Theisz, *Standing in the Light: A Lakota Way of Seeing* (Lincoln: University of Nebraska Press, 1994), 155–57.

Autopsy press conference: from *RCJ*, March, 11, 1972. A haughty editorial in the *RCJ* entitled "Now, maybe the next set of rumors will be harder to sell" (March 12, 1972) took AIM to task without naming them specifically for spreading the rumors, but only two days before its reporter wrote without attribution that RYT "was ordered to dance Indian style" (March 10, 1972).

𐋇 American Legion investigation: from *GJ*, March 15, 1972; statement by May-
nard Jensen, commander, American Legion, in undated Legion newsletter.
Sandage repeated in 2003 interview that he did not call police.

𐋇 Note: The most egregiously inaccurate descriptions of Yellow Thunder's
experience inside the club are found in Peter Matthiessen, *In the Spirit of
Crazy Horse* (New York: Viking, 1983), 59–60, and Banks and Erdoes's
Ojibwa Warrior. Means in his 1995 autobiography maintains that the autopsy
was wrong and RYT was mutilated, despite the fact that two neutral pathologists, one paid by AIM, said otherwise. He maintained in the book that RYT
was forced to dance to the delight of the crowd. In a 2003 interview with the
author, he backed down from those claims and said he believed the sequence
of events stated in the trial, but said someone yelled out "dance you damn
Indian" after Yellow Thunder was pushed into the hall. Banks topped both
Means and Matthiessen in 2004's *Ojibwa Warrior* by claiming the townspeople gathered around to take turns beating up RYT.

TWO PATHS

𐋇 Charley Allen and writing of Red Cloud autobiography: from Paul, *Autobiography of Red Cloud*, 8–28; Allen and Jensen, *From Fort Laramie to
Wounded Knee*, xiii–xix.

𐋇 Spade ranch trials: from Richards, *Bartlett Richards*.

𐋇 Hare and Yellow Thunder histories: from interviews with Russell and Amelia
Yellow Thunder tapes and interview; unnamed Hare family member corre-
spondence in author's possession. Death of Andrew Yellow Thunder: from
Bennett County Booster, June 29, 2005, reprint of June 23, 1945 article.

𐋇 History of Sheridan County and immigrant communities: from James C.
Olson, *History of Nebraska* (Lincoln: University of Nebraska Press, 1966);
Stanley B. Parsons, *The Populist Context: Rural versus Urban Power on a
Great Plains Frontier* (Westport, CT: Greenwood Press, 1973); Helen Winter
Stauffer, ed., *Letters of Mari Sandoz* (Lincoln: University of Nebraska
Press, 1992), 103–4; Caroline Sandoz Pifer, *A Kinkaiders' Child* (Gordon:
Ad Pad, 1995); Caroline Sandoz Pifer and Jules Sandoz, Jr., *Son of Old Jules:
Memoirs of Jules Sandoz, Jr.* (Lincoln: University of Nebraska Press, 1987);
Sandoz, *Old Jules*; Sandoz, *The Cattlemen*; Stauffer, *Mari Sandoz*.

𐋇 Description of Arab peddlers: from Will H. Spindler, *Yesterday's Trails*
(Gordon, NE: Gordon Journal Publishing Co., 1961), 47–49.

𐋇 Destruction of Lakota cattle industry: from Paul Robertson, *The Power of
the Land: Identity, Ethnicity, and Class among the Oglala Lakota* (New
York: Routledge, 2002).

𐋇 Death of Old Jules and Sandoz career: from Stauffer, *Mari Sandoz*.

𐋇 Indian Reorganization Act: from Thomas Biolsi, *Organizing the Lakota:*

The Political Economy of the New Deal on the Pine Ridge and Rosebud Reservations (Tucson: University of Arizona Press, 1992); Kenneth R. Philp, *John Collier's Crusade for Indian Reform, 1920–1954* (Tucson: University of Arizona Press, 1977); Robert M. Kvasnicka and Herman J. Viola, *The Commissioners of Indian Affairs, 1824–1977* (Lincoln: University of Nebraska Press, 1979); Richmond L. Clow, "The Indian Reorganization Act and the Loss of Tribal Sovereignty," *Great Plains Quarterly* 7, no. 2 (Spring 1987): 125–34; Akim D. Reinhardt, *Ruling Pine Ridge: Oglala Lakota Politics from the IRA to Wounded Knee* (Lubbock: Texas Tech University Press, 2007); Price, *The Oglala People.*

Norma and Dean marriage: from correspondence with Hare family member; Sheridan County, *Hare v. Hare* divorce court records.

Red Hawk and Broken Rope incidents: from *CR*, March 25, April 1, 1954; *SCS*, March 11, March 18, May 6, 13, 1954; *GJ*, March 10, 17, 24, 1954.

Death of Blish, Mari Sandoz: from Bad Heart Bull and Blish, *A Pictographic History*; Stauffer, *Mari Sandoz.*

THUNDER IN THE COURTHOUSE

Dennis Yellow Thunder point of view: from interviews with Dennis Yellow Thunder.

Hares under siege: from Box Butte County district court records, case N. 9092, *SoN vs. Melvin P. Hare; Leslie D. Hare.* Also off-the-record interviews and correspondence with a member of Hare family; Pat Vinton story is oft repeated in Gordon, and most details confirmed in interview with Les Hare.

Moran background: from interviews with Smith, telephone interviews with former court reporter Don Gilbert, November 22, 2003; Charles F. Fisher, October 21, 2003.

AIM after Gordon march: from Dewing, *Wounded Knee II*, 33; Means, *Where White Men Fear to Tread*, 20–27. For AIM's attitude toward trading post, see Paul Chaat Smith and Robert Allen Warrior, *Like a Hurricane: The Indian Movement from Alcatraz to Wounded Knee* (New York: New Press, 1996), 118. For an alternative point of view on the Gildersleeves, see Tim Giago, "Thirty-Year-Old Ghosts of Wounded Knee Soon Might Talk," *OWH*, September 2003. AIM's declaration of 15,000 to 30,000 protesters: *RCJ*, March 12, 1972.

Mark Monroe background and recollections: from Mark Monroe, *An Indian in White America* (Philadelphia: Temple University Press, 1994). Descriptions of Alliance: from Monroe and from Leslie Francis Durham, "Nowadays We Call It South Alliance: The Early History of a Lakota Community," master's thesis, University of Arizona, 1997; Kenneth Lincoln, *The Good Red Road: Passages into Native America*, with Al Loan Slagle (San Francisco, Harper and Row, 1987).

᭤ Description of the trial atmosphere: from interviews with Smith, members of Hare family, Fisher, Gilbert, jury foreman Robert Neely, telephone interview, October 30, 2003; also *ADT, OWH, SSH, GJ*; Means, *Where White Men Fear to Tread*, 213–15; Hugh Bunnell, managing editor of the *ADT*, "The Yellow Thunder Case," a detailed unpublished account of the trial in author's possession. Haller recollections: from John D. Haller, telephone interview, October 29, 2003.

᭤ Banks quotations alleging court racism: from *ADT*, May 24, 1972. Means quotation on park and declaration on press conferences, state of mind: from *SSH*, May 25, 1972; Means, *Where White Men Fear to Tread*, 214; V. Bellecourt's life threatened: from ibid.; confirmed in interview with V. Bellecourt; biographical details, *Minneapolis Star-Tribune*, October 14, 2007.

᭤ Two copies of the Bill of Exceptions (trial transcripts) have been missing since 1975. Court proceedings have been reconstructed from articles in the *OWH, SS-H, ADT, GJ, AP*, and Brief of Appellant, no. 38762, Supreme Court of Nebraska, *SoN vs. Melvin P. Hare*, Bunnell report. Ghost Dog interview; threatening AIM press release: *ADT*, May 25, 1972. Anderson's location during incident: from *NSP* records, statement by Max Anderson to Max Ibach; interview with Doyle Bixby, Spade Ranch, Sheridan County, Nebraska, October 3, 2003.

᭤ Means's plan to attack, from Means, *Where White Men Fear to Tread*, 214–15. V. Bellecourt doubts story, but the numbers of undercover officers indicates law enforcement believed something was afoot. Presence of officers noted by court reporter Don Gilbert and wife, Gwen, who knew many of the men from working at local trials. Yellow Thunder family reaction to verdict: from *OWH*.

BILLY JACK GOES TO GORDON

᭤ Bob and Richard Yellow Bird story and BYB's early years: from interview with Richard Yellow Bird Steele, Pine Ridge Reservation, February 21, 2004.

᭤ Hare sentencing: from district court records, Box Butte County. AIM reaction: Teletype, Omaha to Acting Director, FBI, August 24, 1972, Bureau file 105-203686, sec. 4.

᭤ Bayliss trial: from district court records, Sheridan County; *GJ*, November 8, 1972.

᭤ The Trail of Broken Treaties and BIA occupation: from Robert Burnette and John Koster, *The Road to Wounded Knee* (New York: Bantam Books, 1974), 195–219; Smith and Warrior, *Like a Hurricane*, 141–68. Custer courthouse riot: from Dewing, *Wounded Knee II*, 40–45; Smith and Warrior, *Like a Hurricane*, 183–86.

᭤ BYB, Joann, and Bill Cross early activism: from interviews with Bill Cross;

Notes

W. Dale Mason, "'You Can Only Kick So Long . . .': American Indian Movement Leadership in Nebraska, 1972–1979," *Journal of the West* 23, no. 3 (July 1984): 23. BYB awareness of racism: from *NPT*, December 7, 1976. Fort Robinson occupation: from *LS*, November 16–17, 21, 1972; *OWH*, November 17, 21–22, 24, 1972; *Crawford Tribune*, November 23, 1972.

BYB and Bill Cross's roles at Wounded Knee: from Bill Cross interviews. Other sources on occupation: Calico meeting: Pete S. Catches, Sr., and Peter V. Catches, *Oceti Wakan: Sacred Fireplace* (self-published, 1997), 150–70; Dewing, *Wounded Knee II*, 49–129; Thomas Mails, *Fools Crow* (Lincoln: University of Nebraska Press, 1979), 191–93; Banks and Erdoes, *Ojibwa Warrior*, 157–209; Means, *Where White Men Fear to Tread*, 249–83; Tom Holm, *Strong Hearts, Wounded Souls: Native American Veterans of the Vietnam War* (Austin: University of Texas Press, 1996), 176–81; *Voices from Wounded Knee, 1973.*

BYB early attempts at activism: from *GJ*, March 13, 1974, March 20, 1974, May 22, 1974, July 31, 1974; Jane Morgan interview; Smith; Cross. Bloomer riot story: from interview with Clint Yellow Bird, Pine Ridge Reservation, February 21, 2004, and Cross.

Wounded Knee aftermath: from Dewing, *Wounded Knee II*, 135–55; "Report of Investigation: Oglala Sioux Tribe, General Election, 1974," Staff Report, U.S. Commission on Civil Rights, October 1974, Don L. Love Memorial Library, University of Nebraska, Lincoln. Means's troubles: from Means, *Where White Men Fear to Tread*, 338–40. Death of Coler and Williams: from Steve Hendricks, *The Unquiet Grave: The FBI and the Struggle for the Soul of Indian Country* (Thunder's Mouth Press, 2006), 207–12. Also, Dewing, *Wounded Knee II*, 157–58.

BYB's arrests: from Sheridan County court records; *GJ*, April 30, 1975, August 13, 1975. VISTA workers: from Mason, "'You Can Only Kick So Long,'" 24–25. Merrill quotation on bars: from *NPT*, December 6, 1976. Sheridan County jail food protest: from *RNS*, March 6, 1975. The poor quality of police applicants proven later in Joann Yellow Bird's 1979 civil trial: *NPT*, July 7–August 3, 1979. Abandoned Korean story: from *GJ*, December 12, 1976. *BYB* police brutality protests: from *GJ*, March 10, 1976, March 17, 1976, April 14, 1976. Interviews: Smith, Morgan, Cross.

Haceinda shootout: from testimony reported in the *NPT*, November 29 to December 9, 1976; *GJ*, May 5, 1976. Joann's difficulties: from Mason, "'You Can Only Kick So Long,'" 28. Interviews: Bill Cross, Clint Yellow Bird, Richard Yellow Bird, Charles Yellow Bird, Manderson, South Dakota, February 17, 2004. BYB's surrender: from *GJ*, July 28, 1976. Description of Sheridan Lounge riot: from testimony reported in *NPT*, July 7 to August 3, 1979; *GJ*, September 22, 1976; interviews with Bill Cross, Alvin Rawles, Gordon, Nebraska, August 2, 2005. BYB's reaction to lounge riot: from *GJ*, September 29, 1976; AP stories reprinted in *OWH:* September 22, 24, 1976.

Frank Cross reaction: from UPI story printed in *OWH*, September 30, 1976; *GJ*, September 29, 1976. BYB's allegations: from AIM press releases, September 21, 28, 30, 1976, October 30, 1976; *Crazy Horse Advocate*, December 1976. Town reaction: from *GJ*, October 6, 1976; *OWH*, October 13, 1976.

Hacienda trial: from *NPT*, November 29 to December 9, 1976; Smith interview. Monroe home invasion: from Monroe, *An Indian in White America*, 206–8; NSP case file 04-17856; *SSH*, December 21–22, 1978. Sheridan Lounge trial: *NPT* articles, July 7 to August 3, 1979. Remainder of the BYB's life: from interviews with Clint and Richard Yellow Bird, Cross.

LITTLE SKID ROW ON THE PRAIRIE

Brennan and Whiteclay: from Brennan to Commissioner of Indian Affairs Jones, January 26, 1904, letters sent to BIA, RG6508, 74. Description of Brennan: from Mails, *Fools Crow*, 69–70. Judge Westover life: from Memoriam for William H. Westover, District Court of Sixteenth Judicial District, May 23, 1927, Sheridan County Courthouse records; *Rushville Standard*, December 10, 1926. Description of Extension in 1900s: from Lockman, *The Years of Promise*, 149–50; also Emily Lewis, *Wo'wakita: Reservation Recollections* (Sioux Falls, SD: Center for Western Studies, 1980), 97. Brennan fighting bootleggers in Merriman: from *GJ*, March 11, 1904; Brennan to Commissioner, October 26, 1903, RG6508, vol. 33, 440. Mail contractor: from Brennan to Commissioner, March 13, 1903, 161–64, RG6508, vol. 33, 440. Kinkaid and Jones influence on Roosevelt: from *Omaha Daily Bee*, January 30, 1904. Settlers swarm over Extension: from *GJ*, February 19, 1904. Telegrams on Extension loss: from Brennan to Commissioner, telegram, February 5, 1904, 90; Jones to Brennan, telegram, February 6, 1904, 91. All BIA letters and telegrams, from National Archives.

Life of Dewings: from Sheridan County clerk records, census records 1885, 1910; *SCN/S*, Caroline Dewing obituary, April 4, 1974, and Tom Dewing obituary, January 29, 1953; and interview with Carrie Reeves, Whiteclay, Nebraska, December 10, 2003. Westover sale of land: from Sheridan County clerk records.

Early Whiteclay history: from interviews with Carrie Reeves, Mildred Reeves, Whiteclay, Nebraska, December 2, 2003. Description of white shellac: from interview with Ray Lamont, Gordon, Nebraska, November 10, 2003. J. W. Hanks background: from *Who's Who in Nebraska* (Lincoln: Nebraska Press Association, 1940).

Whiteclay history from the 1950s on: from interviews with Carrie Reeves, Mildred Reeves, also Margaret Talbot, Whiteclay, Nebraska, December 12, 2003; unnamed former Whiteclay grocer, Whiteclay, Nebraska, December 12, 2003; Mary Eckholt, Whiteclay, Nebraska, December 19, 2003.

Liquor ban rescinded and votes: from *SCS*, April 30, 1953; October 8, 1953;

December 10, 1953. Kelley's Cove: from *SCS*, May 5, 1953. Commission visit and crackdowns: from *SCS*, March 15, 1956, June 7, 1953.

Josie Smith information: from interviews with Carrie and Mildred Reeves, Eckholt, unnamed grocer. Also Sheridan County Court records and interview with Pat Phillips, longtime vendor in Whiteclay, Gordon, Nebraska, December 12, 2003.

Information on Jim Talbot's days as deputy sheriff: from Eckholt, Talbot, Mildred and Carries Reeves, unnamed grocer, Phillips. Also interviews with unnamed Whiteclay beer store owner, Whiteclay, Nebraska, December 17, 2003, and Gerald Big Crow, former Whiteclay bartender, Pine Ridge, South Dakota, December 13, 2003.

Death of Morgan and subsequent unrest: from *RN/S*, November 2, 1978; Sheridan County Court records; NSP case file 18770.

Clarke background and point of view: from interviews with Deanne and Vic Clarke, Whiteclay, Nebraska, June 2003, December 23, 2003. Ronnie Hard Heart background: interviews with Carol Hard Heart, Sharon Hard Heart, Pine Ridge, South Dakota, June 6, 2003; also Owen Warrior, former brother-in-law, Pine Ridge, South Dakota, June 7, 2003; Mildred Reeves, Phillips, Eckholt, Sheriff Terry Robbins, Rushville, July 2005. Wally Black Elk background: interview with Loren Black Elk, Pine Ridge, South Dakota, June 6, 2003, and Tom Poor Bear.

Quotations: "The Oglala people stood up . . . ," *LJS*, June 27, 1999; "I was here in 1972 . . . ," *RCJ*, June 27, 1999; "We're up against people . . . ," *LJS*, June 27, 1999; "We'll go after these people . . . ," *RCJ*, June 27, 1999; "We came in '72 . . . ," *RCJ*, June 28, 1999.

Description of riot from following sources: FBI file 198A-MP-52976; NSP, "Synopsis of June 26, 1999 March on Whiteclay," file E99-5424-21213, July 6, 1999; extensive coverage in *OWH, LJS, RCJ*; interviews with *LJS* photographer William Lauer, Lincoln, Nebraska, January 7, 2004; Robbins, Poor Bear, Vernon and Clyde Bellecourt, Brehmer, Means, Big Crow; Brehmer tape in author's possession. Quotations: "We're here today . . . ," *LJS*; "We're going to take that 'Welcome to Nebraska . . . , '" *RCJ*. Note: Means denies urging crowd to tear down sign. Several witnesses refute that.

THE BATTLE OF WHITECLAY

Information on the July 3, 1999, march and Billy Mills Hall speeches: from author's observations, photos, audiotapes, and notes. Also, NSP, file E99-5424-21213; NSP videotape in author's possession. Also, *LJS*, July 4, 1999; *OWH*, July 4, 1999; *RCJ*, July 4, 1999. Interviews with Poor Bear, Clyde and Vernon Bellecourt, Means, Nesbitt.

Clinton visit compiled from White House transcript of speech; *LAT*, July 8, 1999; *NYT*, July 8, 1999; *LJS*, July 8, 1999; *SCS*, July 14, 1999; *WSJ*, July 8,

1999. Taco John's photo in *Bennett County Booster*, July 14, 1999. Coolidge visit: from *NYT*, August 18, 1927; *WP*, August 18, 1927. Clinton denial of Peltier pardon: from AP, December 16, 2001.

Eviction notice: from NSP file. Johanns meeting: *OWH*, June 12, 2001.

Black Hills: *LAT*, August 19, 2001; Frank Fools Crow, Frank Kills Enemy, "We Shall Never Sell Our Sacred Black Hills," statement to congressional Sub-Committee on Interior and Insular Affairs.

Death of Ray Robinson/Aquash: from Hendricks, *The Unquiet Grave*, 345–47. Means quotation: "The people have long memories . . . ," KOTA News Web site, October 21, 2004. Means quotation on death of V. Bellecourt: told to *LJS* journalist Kevin Abourezk and featured in RezNet News Red Clout Blog, October 19, 2007.

2003 march into Whiteclay, Lincoln protest, 2004 alcohol vote: from author's notes, tapes, and observations.

ANOTHER SATURDAY NIGHT IN GORDON

Death of Dennis Cross: from *GJ*, February 5, 12, 1992; interviews with Gordon City manager Fred Hlava, Jr., 2003–4, Cross; City of Gordon transcript of March 20, 1992, community meeting.

Bank of Gordon: from interview with Will Isham, First National Bank of Gordon, vice president, February 2004; Department of Justice press release, April 15, 1996. Settlement: from *Indian Country Today*, May 19, 1997.

Remainder of chapter: from interviews with Morgan, Smith, D. Yellow Thunder, Arlene Hepner, Pat Shald, Les Hare, former wife of Pat Hare, Gibbons, Two Crow, Charlie Hinn, December 2, 2003, Rushville, Nebraska; Chuck Hinn, Gordon, Nebraska, December 2003.

Draft of Melvin Pat Hare's letter to *Penthouse* magazine, in author's possession.

SOURCES

Akens, David. *Pioneers of the Black Hills or Gordon's Stockade Party of 1874.* 1920.

Allen, Charles W., and Richard E. Jensen. *From Fort Laramie to Wounded Knee: In the West That Was.* Lincoln: University of Nebraska Press, 1997.

Anderson, Grant K. "The Black Hills Exclusion Policy: Judicial Challenges." *Nebraska History* 58, no. 1 (Spring 1977): 1–24.

Bad Heart Bull, Amos, and Helen H. Blish. *A Pictographic History of the Oglala Sioux.* Lincoln: University of Nebraska Press, 1967.

Banks, Dennis, and Richard Erdoes. *Ojibwa Warrior: Dennis Banks and the Rise of the American Indian Movement.* Norman: University of Oklahoma Press, 2004.

"Biennial Report 1899–1900." Brig. Gen. Patrick H. Barry, Adjutant General of Nebraska. 1900. Fort Robinson Museum, Crawford, Nebraska.

Biolsi, Thomas. *Organizing the Lakota: The Political Economy of the New Deal on the Pine Ridge and Rosebud Reservations.* Tucson: University of Arizona Press, 1992.

Bonney, Rachel A. "The Role of AIM Leaders in Indian Nationalism." *American Indian Quarterly* 3, no. 3 (Autumn 1977): 209–23.

Brand, Johanna. *The Life and Death of Anna Mae Aquash.* Toronto: J. Lorimer, 1978.

Bray, Kingsley M. "Spotted Tail and the Treaty of 1868." *Nebraska History* 83 (Spring 2002): 19–35.

Brown, Dee. *Bury My Heart at Wounded Knee: An Indian History of the American West.* 1971. Reprint, New York: Henry Holt, 1991.

Brown, Joseph Epps. *The Sacred Pipe: Black Elk's Account of the Seven Rites of the Oglala Sioux.* Norman: University of Oklahoma Press, 1953.

Buecker, Thomas R. *Fort Robinson and the American West: 1874–1899.* Norman: University of Oklahoma Press, 1999.

———. "History of Camp Sheridan Nebraska." *Periodical: Journal of America's Military Past* 22, no. 4 (1995): 55–73.

Burnette, Robert, and John Koster. *The Road to Wounded Knee.* New York: Bantam Books, 1974.

Carey, Fred. *Mayor Jim.* Omaha, NE: Omaha Printing Co., 1930.

Casey, Robert J. *The Black Hills and Their Incredible Characters*. Indianapolis: Bobbs-Merrill, 1949.

Catches, Pete, Sr., and Peter V. Catches. *Oceti Wakan: Sacred Fireplace*. Self-published, 1997.

Clow, Richmond L. "The Indian Reorganization Act and the Loss of Tribal Sovereignty." *Great Plains Quarterly* 7, no. 2 (Spring 1987): 125–34.

Coleman, John. "The Indian Uprising of 1890–91 Culminates in Wounded Knee." *Hay Springs News*, March 16, 23, 1928.

Coleman, William S. E. *Voices of Wounded Knee*. Lincoln: University of Nebraska Press, 2000.

Corbusier, William T. "Camp Sheridan, Nebraska." *Nebraska History* 42, no. 1 (1961): 29–53.

Crow Dog, Leonard, and Richard Erdoes. *Crow Dog: Four Generations of Sioux Medicine Men*. New York: HarperCollins, 1995.

Crow Dog, Mary, and Richard Erdoes. *Lakota Woman*. New York: HarperPerennial, 1991.

Dewing, Rolland. *Wounded Knee II*. Chadron, NE: Great Plains Network, 2000.

Dick, Everett. *Conquering the Great American Desert*. Lincoln: Nebraska State Historical Society, 1975.

Dunbar Ortiz, Roxanne. *The Great Sioux Nation: Sitting in Judgment on America*. Berkeley, CA: Moon Books, 1977.

Durhman, Leslie Francis. "Nowadays We Call It South Alliance: The Early History of a Lakota Community." Master's thesis, University of Arizona, 1997.

Edmunds, David R., ed. *The New Warriors: Native American Leaders since 1900*. Lincoln: University of Nebraska Press, 2001.

Eriksson, Erik M. "Sioux City and the Black Hills Gold Rush 1874–1877." *Iowa Journal of History and Politics* 20 (July 1922): 319–47.

Forsyth, Susan. *Representing the Massacre of American Indians at Wounded Knee, 1890–2000*. Lewiston, NY: Edwin Mellen Press, 2003.

Frazier, Ian. *On the Rez*. New York: Farrar, Straus and Giroux, 2000.

Gibbon, Guy. *The Sioux: The Dakota and Lakota Nations*. Malden, MA: Blackwell, 2003.

Gordon, Nebraska: Our First One Hundred Years. Dallas: Curtis Media Corp., 1984.

Gray, John S. *Centennial Campaign: The Sioux War of 1876*. Norman: University of Oklahoma Press, 1988.

Green, Jerry, ed. *After Wounded Knee: Correspondence of Major and Surgeon John Vance Lauderdale While Serving with the Army Occupying the Pine Ridge Indian Reservation, 1890–1891*. East Lansing: Michigan State University Press, 1996.

Greene, Jerome A. "The Sioux Land Commission of 1889: Prelude to Wounded Knee." *South Dakota History* 1, no. 1 (Winter 1970): 41–72.

Hafen, LeRoy R., ed. *Mountain Men and Fur Traders of the Far West*. Lincoln: University of Nebraska Press, 1982.

Hämäläinen, Pekka. "The Rise and Fall of Plains Indian Horse Cultures." *Journal of American History* 90, no. 3 (December 2003): 833–62.

Hendricks, Steve. *The Unquiet Grave: The FBI and the Struggle for the Soul of Indian Country*. New York: Thunder's Mouth Press, 2006.

Hittman, Michael. *Wovoka and the Ghost Dance*. Edited by Dan Lynch. Lincoln: University of Nebraska Press, 1997.

Holm, Tom. *Strong Hearts, Wounded Souls: Native American Veterans of the Vietnam War*. Austin: University of Texas Press, 1996.

Hooper, Norma Lhee. *The Land of Gone Before*. Alliance, NE: Klein Valley Books, 2003.

Huls, Don. *The Winter of 1890 (What Happened at Wounded Knee)*. Self-published, 1974.

Hutton, Harold. *Doc Middleton: Life and Legends of the Notorious Plains Outlaw*. Chicago: Swallow Press, 1974.

Hyde, George E. *Red Cloud's Folk: A History of the Oglala Sioux Indians*. 1937. Reprint, Norman: University of Oklahoma Press, 1975.

———. *A Sioux Chronicle*. Norman: University of Oklahoma Press, 1956.

———. *Spotted Tail's Folk: A History of the Brule Sioux*. Norman: University of Oklahoma Press, 1961.

Isenberg, Andrew C. *The Destruction of the Bison: An Environmental History*. New York: Cambridge University Press, 2000.

Jensen, Richard. "Big Foot's Followers at Wounded Knee." *Nebraska History Quarterly* 71, no. 4 (Winter 1990): 194–212.

Jensen, Richard, R. Eli Paul, and John E. Carter. *Eyewitness at Wounded Knee*. Lincoln: University of Nebraska Press, 1991.

Johnson, Dorothy M. *The Bloody Bozeman*. New York: McGraw-Hill, 1971.

Johnson, J. R. *Representative Nebraskans*. Lincoln, NE: Johnsen Publishing Co., 1954.

Josephy, Alvin M., Jr. *Now That the Buffalo's Gone*. Norman: University of Oklahoma Press, 1989.

Keller, Robert H., Jr. "Episcopal Reformers and Affairs at Red Cloud Agency, 1870–1876." *Nebraska History* 68, no. 3 (Fall 1987): 116–26.

Kelley, William Fitch. *Pine Ridge 1890: An Eyewitness Account of the Events Surrounding the Fighting at Wounded Knee*. Edited by Alexander Kelley and Pierre Bovis. San Francisco: P. Bovis, 1971.

Kneale, A. H. *Indian Agent*. Caldwell, ID: Caxton Publishers, 1950.

Kolbenschlag, George R. *A Whirlwind Passes: News Correspondents and the Sioux Indian Disturbances of 1890–1891*. Vermillion: University of South Dakota Press, 1990.

Kvasnicka, Robert M., and Herman J. Viola. *The Commissioners of Indian Affairs, 1824–1977*. Lincoln: University of Nebraska Press, 1979.

Larson, Robert W. *Red Cloud: Warrior Statesman of the Lakota Sioux*. Norman: University of Oklahoma Press, 1997.

Lazarus, Edward. *Black Hills / White Justice: The Sioux Nation vs. The United States, 1775 to the Present*. New York: HarperCollins, 1991.

Lewis, Emily H. *Wo'wakita: Reservation Recollections*. Sioux Falls, SD: Center for Western Studies, 1980.

Lincoln, Kenneth. *The Good Red Road: Passages into Native America*. With Al Logan Slagle. San Francisco: Harper and Row, 1987.

Lindberg, Christer. "Foreigners in Action at Wounded Knee." *Nebraska History* 71, no. 4 (Winter 1990): 170–81.

Lockman, Carl. *The Years of Promise*. Self-published, 1971.

Mails, Thomas E. *Fools Crow*. Lincoln: University of Nebraska Press, 1979.

Marley, Everett Leslie. "History of Pine Ridge Indian Reservation." Master's thesis, University of Nebraska, 1935.

Mason, W. Dale. "'You Can Only Kick So Long . . .': American Indian Movement Leadership in Nebraska 1972–1979." *Journal of the West* 23, no. 3 (July 1984): 21–31.

Matthiessen, Peter. *In the Spirit of Crazy Horse*. New York: Viking, 1983.

May, Philip A. "The Epidemiology of Alcohol Abuse among American Indians: The Mythical and Real Properties." *American Indian Culture and Research Journal* 18, no. 2 (1994): 121–43.

McGillycuddy, Julia B. *Blood on the Moon: Valentine McGillycuddy and the Sioux*. Lincoln: University of Nebraska Press, 1990.

McGregor, James H. *The Wounded Knee Massacre from the Viewpoint of the Sioux*. 1940. Reprint, Rapid City, SD: Fenwyn Press Books, 1969.

McIntosh, Charles Barron. *The Nebraska Sand Hills: The Human Landscape*. Lincoln: University of Nebraska Press, 1966.

Means, Russell. *Where White Men Fear to Tread: The Autobiography of Russell Means*. With Marvin J. Wolf. New York: St. Martin's Press, 1995.

Mills, Anson. *My Story*. Washington, DC: Self-published, 1918.

Monroe, Mark. *An Indian in White America*. Philadelphia: Temple University Press, 1994.

Mooney, James. *The Ghost-Dance Religion and the Sioux Outbreak of 1890*. 1896. Reprint, Chicago: University of Chicago Press, 1965.

Neihardt, John G. *Black Elk Speaks: Being the Life Story of a Holy Man of the Oglala Sioux*. 1932. Reprint, New York: Pocket Books, 1959.

Nurge, Ethel. *The Modern Sioux: Social Systems and Reservation Culture*. Lincoln: University of Nebraska Press, 1970.

O'Brien, Sharon. *American Indian Tribal Governments*. Norman: University of Oklahoma Press, 1989.

Olson, James C. *History of Nebraska*. Lincoln: University of Nebraska Press, 1966.

———. *Red Cloud and the Sioux Problem*. Lincoln: University of Nebraska

Press, 1965.

Parker, Watson. *Gold in the Black Hills.* Norman: University of Oklahoma Press, 1966.

Parsons, Stanley B. *The Populist Context: Rural versus Urban Power on a Great Plains Frontier.* Westport, CT: Greenwood Press, 1973.

Patrick, Jeffrey L. "To the Black Hills Gold Fields: The Letters of Samuel M. Zent, Hoosier Prospector, 1875–1876." *Indiana Magazine of History* 91, no. 3 (September 1995): 262–87.

Paul, R. Eli, ed. *Autobiography of Red Cloud: War Leader of the Oglalas.* Helena: Montana Historical Society Press, 1997.

Philp, Kenneth R. *John Collier's Crusade for Indian Reform, 1920–1954.* Tucson: University of Arizona Press, 1977.

Pickering, Kathleen Ann. *Lakota Culture, World Economy.* Lincoln: University of Nebraska Press, 2000.

Pifer, Caroline Sandoz. *A Kinkaider's Child.* Gordon, NE: Ad Pad, 1995.

Pifer, Caroline Sandoz, and Jules Sandoz, Jr. *Son of Old Jules: Memoir of Jules Sandoz Jr.* Lincoln: University of Nebraska Press, 1987.

Powers, William K. *Oglala Religion.* Lincoln: University of Nebraska Press, 1975.

Price, Catherine. *The Oglala People, 1841–1879: A Political History.* Lincoln: University of Nebraska Press, 1996.

Radabaugh, J. S. "Custer Explores the Black Hills 1874." *Military Affairs* 26, no. 4 (Winter 1962–63): 162–70.

Recollections of Sheridan County, Nebraska. Sheridan County Historical Society, 1966.

Red Shirt, Delphine. *Bead on an Anthill: A Lakota Childhood.* Lincoln: University of Nebraska Press, 1998.

Reinhardt, Akim D. *Ruling Pine Ridge: Oglala Lakota Politics from the IRA to Wounded Knee.* Lubbock: Texas Tech University Press, 2007.

Richards, Bartlett, Jr. *Bartlett Richards: Nebraska Sandhills Cattleman.* With Ruth Van Ackeren. Lincoln: Nebraska State Historical Society, 1980.

Robertson, Paul. *The Power of the Land: Identity, Ethnicity, and Class among the Oglala Lakota.* New York: Routledge, 2002.

Robinson, Charles M., III. *General Crook and the Western Frontier.* Norman: University of Oklahoma Press, 2001.

Sand Hills Archeology. Nebraska State Historical Society, 1999.

Sandoz, Mari. *The Buffalo Hunters.* 1954. Reprint, Lincoln: University of Nebraska Press, 1978.

———. *The Cattlemen: From the Rio Grande across the Far Marias.* New York: Hastings House, 1958.

———. *Crazy Horse, Strange Man of the Oglala.* New York: Hastings House, 1942.

———. *The Great Council.* Crawford, NE: Cottonwood Press, 1970.

———. *Old Jules*. Lincoln: 1935. Reprint, University of Nebraska Press, 1962.

———. *Slogum House*. Boston: Little, Brown, 1937.

———. *These Were the Sioux*. New York: Hastings House, 1961.

Shumway, Grant L., ed. *History of Western Nebraska and Its People*. Lincoln: Western Publishing and Engraving Co., 1921.

Smith, Paul Chaat, and Robert Allen Warrior. *Like a Hurricane: The Indian Movement from Alcatraz to Wounded Knee*. New York: New Press, 1996.

Smith, Rex Allen. *Moon of Popping Trees: The Tragedy at Wounded Knee and the End of the Indian Wars*. Lincoln: University of Nebraska Press, 1975.

Spindler, Will H. *Centennial Prairie*. Gordon, NE: Gordon Journal Publishing Co., 1965.

———. "Pioneers Recall Early Day Beef Issues." *Gordon Journal*, August 30, 1950.

———. *Tragedy Strikes at Wounded Knee*. Rushville, NE: News/Star, 1955.

———. *Yesterday's Trails*. Gordon, NE: Gordon Journal Publishing Co., 1961.

Standing Bear, Luther. *My People the Sioux*. Lincoln: University of Nebraska Press, 1975.

Stauffer, Helen, ed. *Letters of Mari Sandoz*. Lincoln: University of Nebraska Press, 1992.

———. *Mari Sandoz: Story Catcher of the Plains*. Lincoln: University of Nebraska Press, 1982.

Starita, Joe. *The Dull Knifes of Pine Ridge*. New York: G. P. Putnam's Sons, 1995.

Tallent, Annie D. *The Black Hills or Last Hunting Ground of the Dakotas*. Sioux Falls, SD: Brevet Press, 1974.

Tibbles, Thomas Henry. *Buckskin and Blanket Days*. 1957. Reprint, Lincoln: University of Nebraska Press, 1969.

Tuchen, Lesta V., and James D. McLaird. *The Black Hills Expedition of 1875*. Mitchell, SD: Dakota Wesleyan University Press, 1975.

Twiss, Gayla. "A Short History of Pine Ridge." *Indian Historian* 11, no. 1 (Winter 1978): 36–39.

Unrau, William E. *The White Man's Wicked Water: The Alcohol Trade and Prohibition in Indian Country, 1802–1892*. Lawrence: University Press of Kansas, 1996.

U.S. Commission on Civil Rights. "Report of Investigation: Oglala Sioux Tribe, General Election, 1974." Staff Report, U.S. Commission on Civil Rights. Washington, DC: U.S. Government Printing Office, October 1974.

Utley, Robert M. *Frontier Regulars: The United States Army and the Indian, 1886–1891*. New York: Macmillan, 1973.

Van Ackeren, Ruth, and Robert M. Howard. *Lawrence Bixby: Preserver of the Old Spade Ranch*. Caldwell, ID: Caxton Publishers, 1995.

Voices from Wounded Knee, 1973: In the Words of the Participants. Rooseveltown, NY: Akwesasne Notes, 1974.

Watson, Elmo Scott. "The Last Indian War, 1890–91: A Study of Newspaper Jingoism." *Journalism Quarterly* 20, no. 3 (September 1943): 205–19.

"What We Should Do for the Indian: Recommendations of the Friends of the Indian Held at Philadelphia January 22–23, 1919." Philadelphia: Indian Rights Association, 1919.

White, Richard. "The Winning of the West: The Expansion of the Western Sioux in the Eighteenth and Nineteenth Centuries." *Journal of American History* 65, no. 2 (September 1978): 319–43.

Who's Who in Nebraska. Lincoln: Nebraska Press Association, 1940.

Wishart, David J. *An Unspeakable Sadness: The Dispossession of the Nebraska Indians*. Lincoln: University of Nebraska Press, 1994.

Young Bear, Severt, and R. D. Theisz. *Standing in the Light: A Lakota Way of Seeing*. Lincoln: University of Nebraska Press, 1994.

INDEX

Page numbers in *italics* refer to illustrations.

Abourezk, James, 55
alcohol, 85, 192–193, 238, 292
    banning sales to Indians, 66
    bootlegging of, 258–259, 264–265
    Plains Indians' early encounters
        with, 66
    lifting ban selling to Native Ameri-
        cans, 265
    reasons for high rate of use among
        Native Americans, 277–278
    smuggling/bootlegging to Pine
        Ridge, 93–94, 300
Allen, Charley, 105–106, 109–111,
    113, 117–118, 123–125, 127,
    138, 157–158, 227
Alliance, Nebraska, 143, 167–168, 174,
    184, 189, 206, 216–217, 219,
    223, 251–253, 312
    American Indian Center, 191–193,
        251–252
    Native American community,
        191–193
    police department, 252–253
Allison, William, 80–81
American Civil Liberties Union of
    Nebraska, 240
American Horse, 42, 80, 109, 112, 115,
    136, 163–164
American Horse Creek, 42, 163, 172
American Legion Hall, Gordon,
    Nebraska, 11, 14, 19–22, 39–41,
44, 46–47, 50–51, 130, 140,
    148–150, 199, 203, 208, 218,
    222, 238, 243, 311–312
American Indian Movement, 55, 58,
    59–60, 132–133, 155–156,
    189–191, 201, 216–217, 298,
    300–302, 314
    anthem, 154
    Custer, South Dakota, courthouse
        riot, 220, 233, 237
    legacy of, 300–302, 315–316
    march on Gordon, 138–141, 222,
        280
    marches on Whiteclay, 3–10,
        279–285, 287–291
    occupation of Bureau of Indian
        Affairs, 219–229, 225, 233
    occupation of Gordon City Audi-
        torium, 141–146, 151–154,
        317–318
    occupation of Wounded Knee, 156,
        227–230, 233
Anderson, Max, 20, 22–23, 41, 51, 155,
    203–204, 208, 315
Antioch, Nebraska, 250
Apache tribe, 32
Aquash, Anna Mae. *See* Pictou-
    Aquash, Anna Mae
Arapaho tribe, 34, 68, 71–73, 80–81,
    114
Arikara tribe, 68

Arthur, Chester A., 94
Associated Press, 129–130, 139, 149, 249
Ash, Myrtle, 232
Atlantic Press, 175

Bad Heart Bull, Amos, 63–64, 67, 69, 82–83, 85, 128, 158, 165–166, 183
Bad Heart Bull, Wesley, 220
Badlands, 29–30, 43, 84, 117–118, 120, 122, 173, 215
Banks, Dennis, 4, 56, 58–61, 133, 136, 139–141, 145, 152–154, 190–191, 193–196, 197–198, 210, 220, 225, 228–230, 235–237, 279–283, 285, 288–289, 292, 300
Barnes, Robert, 246–249, 254
Battle of Little Big Horn/Greasy Grass, 82–83, 106, 115, 123, 128, 166, 220, 295
Battle of Rosebud, 82
Bayliss, Robert "Toby," 11–23, 41–42, 47, 50–53, 140, 156, 188, 197, 199, 202, 205–208, 217–220, 305, 309, 313, 315
Bayliss, Robert Sr., 15
Bayliss, Sharan, 15
Bellecourt, Clyde, 4, 7–8, 59–60, 138–139, 142, 152, 154–155, 190, 195, 220, 225, 230, 235, 237, 279–283, 285, 288–289, 300
Bellecourt, Vernon, 138–139, 142, 190, 191, 193–196, 200, 210, 213, 216–217, 220, 229, 237, 254, 296–299, 300, 302, 314
Bennett County, South Dakota, 173, 253–254, 280–281, 302
Big Foot, 105–106, 121–125, 127–128, 190, 227

Billy Jack, 220–222, 225, 319
Billy Mills Hall, 3–4, 8, 129, 132–133, 135–137, 190, 279–280, 289–291
Bird Head, Vinnie, 246
Bissonette, Pedro, 226, 235, 289
Bixby, Doyle (née Shald), 204–205, 318
Bixby, Lawrence, 204, 308
Black Bear, Chief, 74
Black Elk, Wilson "Wally" Jr., 5, 6, 277–280, 294, 296, 299, 303
Blackfoot Lakota tribe, 68
Black Hills, 9, 25–26, 28, 64, 75, 77, 81–84, 107, 136–137, 220
    expulsion of miners, 32–33, 36, 82
    President Coolidge visit, 291–292
    development into tourist destination, 292
    fight to return to Lakota Nation, 229, 295
Blish, Helen, 63–64, 183
Bordeaux, Ken, 129–130
Borman Chevrolet, 13, 19, 24, 37, 44–50, 140–141, 143, 234, 305
"boss farmers," 164–166, 171–173, 175
Bozeman Trail, 26, 71–75, 158
Brennan, John, 138, 173, 257–261
Britton, Art, 141
Brakeman, Errol, 148
Brehmer, Danny, 282
Brehmer, Gary, 282–284, 296
Bridgeport, Nebraska, 215
Broken Rope, Vincent, 52, 135, 181–182, 307
Brown, Charlene, 246–247
Brown, Dee, 138, 190, 228
Brown, Don, 246–247, 249
Brown, Dr. W. O., 50, 152, 188, 202–203, 313
Brulé Lakota tribe *or* Sicangus, 67, 73–74, 95, 108, 115

Bruning, John, 296, 298–299

Buchan, Bob, 21–22, 243

buffalo, 34, 67–69, 73, 79, 83, 85

Bull Bear, 65–67, 71, 93, 158

Bury My Heart at Wounded Knee, 52, 138, 190

Bureau of Indian Affairs, 57–58, 133, 165, 175–177, 182, 219–220, 225, 301

Calico, South Dakota, 225–227, 229

Camp, Carter, 235

Camp Sheridan, 27, 31–32, 36, 78, 80, 91–92, 225, *323*

Case, Bob, 19, 44, 46–47, 51, 132–133, 141, 143, 145–146, 152, 203, 205, 218, 233, 238, 240–243

cattle barons, 90, 98, 160–162, 166–167

Chadron Democrat, 105, 110, 117–118

Chadron, Nebraska, 16, 53, 99, 109–111, 113, 119, 143–144, 160, 179–180, 222, 224, 227, 230

Chadron State University, 38, 224, 233, 250, 313

Chambers, Ernie, 233

Chase, Cheryl, 270

Cherry County, Nebraska, 101, 147, 188, 259

Cheyenne Autumn, 175

Cheyenne River Agency/Reservation, 111–112, 121, 274

Cheyenne tribe, 34, 68, 71–73, 80–81, 114, 175

Cheyenne, Wyoming, 26, 31

Chicago Burlington & Quincy Railroad, 100, 191

Chicago & North Western Railroad, 13

Chippewa tribe. *See* Ojibwa

Chips, Wallace, 190, 195

Chivington, John, 73

Civil War, 31–32, 72–74, 78, 94, 123

"Civil War Widows," 160

Clarke, Deanna, 273–276, 281–282, 285, 296

Clarke, Vic, 273–276, 282, 296

Clear Water, Frank, 230

Cleveland, Grover, 157

Clinton, Nebraska, 96

Clinton, Bill, 6–7, 290–295

Coler, Jack, 236–237, 293

Collier, John, 175–177, 263–264

Collins, Charles, 26, 28,

Comes Last, Amelia (née Yellow Thunder), 42, 47, 51–52, 54–56, 136, 152, 164, 194, 210

Comstock, William, 160–162, 167

Coolidge, Calvin, 291–292

Coomes, Kelley, 264–266

Coomes, Mike, 283

Coon, Jack, 100–103, 115, 119–120

Crawford, Nebraska, 128, 225

Crazy Bear, Albert, 37, 42, 47

Crazy Bear, Winnie, 42

Crazy Horse Advocate, 224, 233, 255

Crazy Horse, 74, 81–84, 98, 115, 138, 158, 175, 225, 251, 289, 295

Cressey, Charles, 105–106, 118, 123–124

Cross, Bill, 222, 224, 229–230, 231, 233–234, 238–239, 245–248, 254, 306–308, 315–316

Cross, Dennis, 245–248, 306–307

Cross, Fern, 245–248

Cross, Frank, 224, 239, 249

Cross, Wayne, 251–253

Crow tribe, 34, 58, 63, 65, 67–69, 72–73, 79, 83, 85, 114, 128, 158

Crook, George/Crook Commission, 82, 106–109, 111–113, 163, 173

Crow Dog, 108, 136–137

Crow Dog, Leonard, 136–137, 139–140, 190, 225, 229, 235

Cuny, Gilbert, 269
Cuomo, Andrew, 291
Custer, George Armstrong, 26, 28, 30, 32, 79, 82, 98, 106, 123, 220
Custer, South Dakota, 220, 237
Custer's Last Stand. *See* Battle of Little Big Horn
Cutgrass, Dora, 43
Czywczynski, Jan and Jim, 228

Dahlman, Jim, 90–92, 94, 99
Dakota Territory, 29, 78–79
Davis, Angela, 229
Dawes General Allotment Act *or* Dawes Severalty Act, 107–110, 111–113, 173, 175, 283, 302
Deon, Sam, 157–158
Depression, The, 168, 174–175, 178–179, 180, 183, 191, 263–264
Des Moines Register, 148, 150
Dewing, Caroline (née Jacobs), 261–262
Dewing, Tom, 261–262, 275
Dewing, Nebraska, 262
Dull Knife, 74, 175

Eagle Fox, Annie (née Yellow Thunder), 42, 47, 51–52, 54–56, 136, 152, 194, 210, 212
Echohawk, John, 152, 154–155
Eckholt, Mary, 264, 267, 276, 282
Eckholt, Maurice, 264, 267, 282
Etzelmiller, Roger, 243, 246–247
Ellsworth, Nebraska, 100, 160, 250
Episcopal Church, 42, 78, 176
Evans, Reva, 46, 147–151, 181–182, 194, 211, 213, 217, 219, 232, 233–234, 239–240, 245, 249, 309–310
Extension, The, 7, 93–94, 257–261, 302

Exon, J. J., 142, 144, 217, 225
Eyre, Chris, 295

Federal Bureau of Investigation, 129–130, 190, 209, 226–227, 230, 235–238, 249, 293, 300–301
Fetterman, William, 74
Fetterman Massacre, 75
Fire Thunder, Cecelia, 301–302
First National Bank of Gordon, 309–310
Fisher, Charles, 180–181, 187, 189, 195, 196–200, 209–212, 216, 250, 313–314
Fisher, Charles Frank, 187, 194, 196–200, 209–211, 250, 313–314
Fools Crow, Frank, 229–230
Forsyth, James, 123–124, 127, 138
Fort C. F. Smith, 71–72
Fort Nendle, *104*, 119–120, 126
Fort Phil Kearny, 74
Fort Laramie, 66, 71–72, 75–76, 110, 157, 226
Fort Randall, 29–30, 35
Fort Robinson/Camp Robinson, 32, 63, 78, 80–81, 98, 128, 225, 233
Fort Yates, North Dakota, 236
Fremont, Elkhorn & Missouri Valley Railroad, 94–96
Frohman, Terry, 269–270
fur trappers/traders, 66, 70–71, 175

Gabriel, Roman, 55
Gardner, David, 243–244, 250
Garnier, Baptiste "Little Bat," 124–125, 127
Gall, 74
Geib, Wayne, 152

General Allotment Act. *See* Dawes
  General Allotment Act
Ghost Dance, 103–106, 115–116,
  120–122, 138, 224, 258
Ghost Dog, George, 44–45, 48, 140,
  199–200, 202–203, 313–315
Ghost Dog, Virginia, 44
Gilbert, Don, 197–198
Gildersleeve, Clive and Agnes, 190,
  226, 228
"give-aways," 165–166
Glickman, Dan, 291
gold, 26, 72–73, 76, 79, 81
GOONs. *See* Guardians of the Oglala
  Nation
Gordon, John, 25–30, 32, 35–36, 79,
  82, 95
Gordon Journal, 13, 46, 52, 140,
  147–151, 181–182, 194, 232,
  239, 242, 309
Gordon, Nebraska, 43, 61, *88–89*, 103,
  106, 129, 166–169, 179, 189,
  194, 213, 229, 249, 251, 290,
  305–312
  AIM march on, 136–141, 280
  city council, 214, 241–242
  city auditorium, *131*, 141–147,
    151, 153–154, 234, 306–308,
    317–319
  city jail, 24, 44, 141, 143
  Country Club, 315
  high school, 14, 37, 44, 187, 205,
    231, 306
  Human Relations Council,
    153–154, 231–232, 306–307
  "Indian Town," 14, 37–38,
    181–182, 224, 231–232, 316
  Memorial Hospital, 141–142,
    231–232, 239, 244, 248–249,
    254, 311, 315
  Neighborhood Center, 44–45, 132,
    134–135, 140–141, 147, 153,
    199, 229

Oglala community, 37–38, 132,
  134–135, 141–142, 151, 171,
  220–222
  origin of name, 36, 95
  police department, 45–47,
    141–143, 213, 217–218, 225,
    231–232, 238, 242–244,
    246–248, 254, 306–307, 316
  reaction to Ghost Dance, 113,
    116–117, 120
  settling of, 94–96
  volunteer fire department, 132,
    151–152
Graham, John, 300
Grant, Ulysses S., 76–77, 79, 82
Great Sioux Reservation, 75, 78, 107,
  112
Guardians of the Oglala Nation, 226,
  227, 235, 239

Haag, Ronald, 243–244
H&M Mini Store, 264, 276–278, 282,
  284, 295–296
Hacienda Motel/Restaurant/Lounge,
  229, 237–241, 243–245, 249
Haller, John, 196–197, 212–213
hang-around-the-fort Indians, 66
Hanks, J. W., 262–264
Hard Heart, Edward, 276
Hard Heart, Ronnie, 3, 5, 6, 276–281,
  294, 296, 299, 303
Hare family, 40, 154, 186–187
Hare, Charlotte, 18
Hare, Dallas Dean, 17–19, 163,
  166–168, 178–179, 185–187,
  208, 312
Hare, James, 163, 186
Hare, Jerene (née Schmidt), 14
Hare, Leslie Dean, 11, 13–23, 41,
  50–52, 132, 152, 155–156,
  178–179, 185–186, 188–189,
  194, 199, 203, 205–211,

216–217, 219, 305, 309,
312–314–315, 319–320
Hare, Melvin "Pat," 11, 13, 15–18,
50–52, 132, 152, 155–156,
178–179, 185–186, 188, 194,
199, 203, 206–211, 212,
216–217, 219, 243, 309,
312–314–315, 319–320
Hare, Miles, 18, 187, 205
Hare, Scott, 18
Hare, Vernon, 18, 309, 312
Hare, Wilma, 168
Harris, Debbie, 146
Harris, Peggy (née Shald), 204–205
Hartwig, Jeannette. *See* Thompson,
Jeannette
Has No Horse, Dawson, 320
Hayes, Rutherford, 84
Hay Springs, Nebraska, 87, 90, 96,
113, 117, 120, 169, 179
He Dog, 63, 98
Hendricks, Steve, 300
Hidatsa tribe, 68
Highland University Preparatory
School, 70
Hills, Wendall, 188
Hinn, Charles, 318
Hinn, Charlie, 311, 318
Hinn, Sam, *159*, 169–172, 311
Hlava, Fred Jr., 306–307
Hollstein, Ed, 144–145
Homestead Act, 160
Hooper, Norma Lhee, 17, 169,
178–179, 194, 205, 210–211,
312
Hooper, Dan, 205
Hooper, Pat, 169, 178
Hooper, Sandy, 169, 178
Hump, 111
Hunkpapa Lakota tribe, 68, 121–122,
274

Ibach, Max, 50–52, 130, 132–134, 137,
140, 188, 203, 209, 210–211,
218, 271–272, 313
Indian Rights Association, 108
Indian Reorganization Act, 177, 226,
229, 301
individual Indian accounts, 164–165
Irwin, Bennett, 90–92, 98–100, 160
Italian Inn, 309, 315

Jackson, Jesse, 291, 294
Jacobs, Sara, 261
Jacobs, William, 261
Jaco's Off Sale Bar, 269–272, 282
Janis, Steve, 245
Johanns, Mike, 8, 285, 294
Johnson, Andrew, 72
Johnson, Inez, 210
Johnson, Lyndon B., 275
Jones, William, 257–261
journalists, 195–196, 201, 228, 232,
249
role during/after Ghost Dance
troubles, 118–119, 121, 138,
157
role after Yellow Thunder incident,
129–130, 147–151, 217, 219,
222
role at Whiteclay riot/marches, 5,
284–285, 287
repeating false rumor of Whiteclay
deaths, 187, 297
Jumping Eagle Inn, 56, 266
Justice Department, 130, 137,
153–154, 195, 197–198, 235,
292, 306–307

Kelley's Cove, 265–266, 269
Kelley, William, 105–106, 118, 157
Kicking Bear, 114–115, 117, 121
KILI radio, 7–8, 280, 299–300

Kills Straight, Birgil, 53–56, 226
Kinkaid, Moses, 160, 260
Kinkaid Act, 160–161
Kinkaiders, 160–162, 167, 169–170
Krause brothers, 161
Kunstler, William, 235, 237, 245
Kyle, South Dakota, 43, 54, 163–166, 224, 229

Lakeside, Nebraska, 250–25
Lake Wakpamni, South Dakota, 40, 43–44, 134, 139, 317, 319
Lakota tribe, 31, 36, 79–81, 114–115, 138, 142, 175
LaMere, Frank, 296–298
Lamont, Arlene (née Crazy Bear), 37–38, 42, 44, 46–47, 50–51, 139, 145, 194, 218, 318–319
Lamont, Buddy, 230
Lamont, Ray, 37–38, 145, 194
Lane, Clarence "Sailor," 181–182, 307
Laramie loafers, 70
Last of the Mohicans, 279, 301
Laughlin, Tom, 220–221
Leech Lake Reservation, Minnesota, 58, 190–191, 195
Lennox, Dell, 49–50
Lewis and Clark expedition, 68
Lincoln, Nebraska, 132, 144, 147, 174–175, 217, 240, 298
Lincoln Journal Star, 297
Little Big Man, 81, 83–84
Los Angeles Times, 148–149
Looking Cloud, Arlo, 300–301
Looking Horse, Kelly, 318
Louis, Adrian C., 295
Lutter, Bernard "Butch," 13–14, 16–23 152, 154, 188, 202, 206–208, 243, 314
Lyman, Stanley, 133, 137, 226

Mackey, Robert, 144, 233
Mandan tribe, 68
Manderson, South Dakota, 300
Marshall, Richard, 236
Martin, South Dakota, 253–255, 302, 310
Mason, Dale, 238
Matula, Jerry, 41
McGillycuddy, Valentine, 85, 92–94, 97, 103, 110, 165
McLaughlin, Gerald, 269–270
Means, Russell, 4–5, 7, 10, 55–61, 133, 135–141, 145, 151–154, 190–191, 193–196, 198, 210–211, 220, 222–223, 225–226, 228–230, 235–237, 241, 279–283, 285, 288–292, 295, 300–302, 306
Means, Ted, 232
Merrill, Cathy, 238, 240, 250
Merriman, Nebraska, 259
Metcalf, Randy, 280–281
Middleton, Doc, 95–96
Miles, Nelson, 118–119, 121–122, 138
Miller, Larry, 269–270
Mills, Anson, 31–36, 80–81
Minneconjou Lakota tribe, 68, 106, 121–122, 138
Mirage Flats, 87, 90, 96–98, 117, 119
Missouri River, 68–70, 83–84, 107, 112
Mitchell, L. E., 217–218
mixed-blood Native Americans, 70, 93, 108, 172–173, 226, 258
Monroe, Daryl, 252–253
Monroe, Emma, 252
Monroe, Hope, 252
Monroe, Mark, 191–193, 213, 251–253
Montileaux, Martin, 236
Moran, Robert, 188–189, 196–204, 206, 211, 216–217, 225, 249–250, 253–254
Morgan, Duane, 270–271, 273
Morgan, Jane, 234, 238, 242, 316–317

Index

Morgan, Midge, 232
Moore, Bruce, 132, 141–142, 145–146,
    152
Moore, Sheila, 142
Mount Rushmore, 60, 291–292, 295
Morsett's Laundromat, 19, 23, 47

National Council of Churches, 59–60
National Urban Indian Organization,
    58–59
Native American Rights Fund, 152,
    240
Nebraska Indian Commission,
    129–130, 239–242, 245, 251
Nebraska Journalism Hall of Fame, 310
Nebraska Land and Feeding Company,
    160–162
Nebraska Liquor Control Commission,
    264–265, 268–269, 302
Nebraska National Guard, 8, 119–120,
    137
Nebraskans for Peace, 296–299
Nebraska State Journal, 106, 157
Nebraska State Patrol, 4, 9, 129,
    132–133, 137, 146, 206, 225,
    271–272, 280–281, *286*,
    287–289, 297–298
Nebraska Supreme Court, 132, 313
Nebraska Unicameral/legislature, 233,
    258, 267–268, 296
Neely, Robert, 211
Nesbitt, Tom, 8, 288–289, 296–297,
    302
Newman brothers/Ranch, 91–92, 94,
    100
New Markets Initiative, 293–294
New York Herald, 105–106, 118
New York Times, 145, 151
Niobrara River, 15, 17–18, 25, 29, 79,
    91, 94, 97, 99, 109, 174, 179
North East Panhandle Substance
    Abuse Center, 316

Northern Paiute tribe, 113
North Platte, Nebraska, 249–250, 309

Office of Indian Affairs, 31
Oglala Civil Rights Organization, 226
Oglala Lakota tribe, 52, 73, 90–91,
    128, 158, 163–166
Oglala, South Dakota, 236, 278, 281
Oglala Tribal Government/Council,
    176–177, 182, 265, 299–300,
    310
O'Gura, George, 152
Ojibwa tribe, 4, 58, 72, 190
Old Bad Heart Bull, 64
Old Jules, 90, 175
Omaha Bee, 106
Omaha Club, 162
Omaha, Nebraska, 55–56, 60, 99, 118,
    150, 160–162, 174, 298, 302
Omaha Reservation/tribe, 34, 68, 83,
    129, 259, 267
Omaha World-Herald, 149, 197
One Feather, Gerald, 54
O'Neill, Nebraska, 28, 49

Paha Sapa. *See* Black Hills
Panhandle Legal Services, 238
Paul, John, 45–47, 48–49, 51, 141,
    143–145, 153–154, 188, 200,
    205, 210, 217–218, 315
Pawnee tribe, 34, 65, 69, 73, 83, 85
Pender, Nebraska, 267–268
Penthouse, 314
Peterson, Byron, 297
Peterson, Kay Lou, 46, 205–206
Peltier, Leonard, 4, 236–237, 292–293
Phillips, Susan (née Shald), 134–135,
    139, 146, 318
*Pictographic History of the Oglala
    Sioux*, 183
Pictou-Aquash, Anna Mae, 300–302

Pine Ridge, South Dakota, 55, 96, 101,
118, 126, 128–129, 133–134,
157–158, 166, 180, 190, 298,
310
Pine Ridge Reservation/Agency,
South Dakota, 3, 9, 13, 40, 47,
56, 63, 91–94, 105, 109–110,
122, 160, 191, 215, 257–261,
303
alcohol ban, 259, 265, 299–300
alcoholism, 264, 269
banking/banks, 275, 301, 310–311
President Clinton visit, 291–294
President Coolidge visit, 291–292
dirty war, 156, 230, 234–237,
268–269, 301
early 20th century, 164–166
high school, 277, 293
hospital, 248, 264
naming of, 85
on-the-hoof beef issues, 100–103,
115, 119
poverty, 177, 290, 292
ranching on, 172–173
tribal police, 4, 284–285, *286*,
288–290
Pioneer Package Store, 283
Platte River *or* North Platte River, 66,
69, 72, 75–76
Pochon, George, 205
Ponca tribe, 34, 68, 78, 83, 235, 259
Populism, 160–162
Porcupine Singers, 135, 154, 317–318
Porcupine, South Dakota, 42, 55–56,
135, 138, 155, 189, 229, 279,
304
Poor Bear, Tom, *2*, 5, 10, 228, 236,
277–279, 288, 294, 299,
302–303, 306
Powder River Country, 71, 73–75,
82–83, 102
Pretty Cloud, Dollie, 63–64, 183
Prohibition, 171, 263

Quakers, 78

Randy's Market, 270, 273–275
Rapid City Journal, 149, 155, 280
Rapid City, South Dakota, 154–155,
175–176, 202, 244, 277, 290,
310, 314–315
Rawles, Alvin, 246–248
Red Cloud Agency, 32, 76, 78, 84–85
Red Cloud, Jack, 82
Red Cloud, 26, 40, *62*, 82–85, 93–94,
136, 251
Bozeman trail war, 71–72, 74
Dawes General Allotment Act,
106–109
early life, 64–67, 69
final years and death, 157–158
trips to Washington, 75–80, 84
Red Cloud, Oliver, 285, 288–289
Red Hawk, Jessie, 52, 135, 180–182,
187
Red Hawk, Ward, 180–181
Reeves, Howard, 264, 272, 276
Reeves, Mildred, 264, 276–278, 282,
284, 295–296
Richards, Bartlett, 98–100, 160–162,
166–167, 175, 178, 204, 308,
318
Richards, DeForest, 160
Richards, Inez, 160, 175
Robbins, Terry, 280–284, 302
Robinson, Ray, 300–301
Roosevelt, Franklin Delano, 176, 291
Roosevelt, Theodore, 7, 161–162, 166,
260, 283
Rosebud Reservation/Agency, 55,
57–58, 84–85, 108, 129,
136–137, 139, 229, 235
Rouleau, Charles, 70
Rouleau, Hubert, 69–71

Rouleau, Jesse, 70

Rouleau, John, 70

Rouleau (Sears), Susan, 69–71, 101, 126

Royer, D. F., 117

Rough Feather, 121–123, 125–126 127–128

Rucker, Harold, 41–44, 218

Rucker, James "Bucky," 41

Rushville, Nebraska, 3, 47, 50–51, 96, 113, 117–119, 137, 142, 153, 161, 168–171, 174, 179–180, 217, 219, 229, 231, 239, 251, 258–259, 262, 264–265, 267, 272–273, 285, 310–311

Rushville Volunteer Fire Department, 281, 284–285

Russell, T. H., 26, 28

Salway, Harold, 292, 300

Samuels, Jesse, 152

San Arc Lakota tribe, 68

Sandage, Bernard, 19, 21–22, 40, 155, 188, 200, 315

Sand Creek Massacre, 73

Sand Hills, 13, 17, 30, 33–34, 72, 85, 87, 90, 97, 174, 179, 183, 250, 315

early settlers' attitudes towards, 73, 91

farming, 160–162, 167

ranching, 90–92, 99–100, 160–162, 317–318

Treaty of 1868, 75, 91

Sandoz, Caroline, 178, 308

Sandoz, Emile, 161

Sandoz, James, 87, 90, 167

Sandoz, Jules, 87, 90, 96–98, 117, 119, 128, 160–161, 167–169, 174–175, 308–309

Sandoz, Mari, 87, 90, 98, 128, 167, 174–175, 178, 183, 308

Sandoz, Mary, 98

Santee tribe/reservation, 67–69, 72–73, 129

Scamahorn, John A./Scamahorn Party, 94–96, 134

Scenic, South Dakota, 236

Schmitz, Darld, 220

Scottsbluff, Nebraska, 15, 50, 253

Sears, William, 101

Seger's Cafe, 23, 41–41, 52–53

Shald's Jack and Jill, 12, 39–40, 139, 146, 229, 305

Shald family, 235, 239, 318

Shald, Ferd, 40, 171, 182, 237

Shald, Gladys (née Trueblood), 40, 134–135, 139, 146, 171, 204, 318

Shald, Mike, 40, 229, 237, 318

Shald, Pat, 39–40, 139, 146, 229, 275, 308, 318, *323*

Shelley, Mickey, 179–181, 187

Sheppard, Allen, 8–9, 288

Sheridan County, Nebraska, 3, 9, 17, 49, 56, 303

attitudes about AIM, 190

early 20th century, 163–164

fair, 103, 167, 171, 224

Historical Society, 308

jail, 231–232, 240, 248–249, 254

potato harvest, 171

settling of, 94–96, 98, 101

sheriff's department, 52, 258, 264–266

Sheridan County Star, 182, 265

Sheridan County Journal Star, 309

Sheridan County Indian Association, 249

Sheridan Hotel/Lounge, 140, 243, 245–248, 254, 271, 309

Sheridan, Philip, 32–33, 82, 123

Sherman, William Tecumseh, 26

Short, Clive, 144, 152

Short Bull (Ghost Dance leader), 114–115, 117, 121

Short Bull (uncle of Amos Bad Heart Bull), 128
Shoshone tribe, 65, 85, 114, 158, 175
Sidney, Nebraska, 26, 271
Sioux City, Iowa, 25–26, 28, 30, 36, 80
Sioux City Journal, 26, 259–260
Sioux City and Black Hills Transportation Company, 25
Sioux Nation Supermarket, 274–275
Sioux tribe. *See* Lakota
Sipp, Harold and Wayne, 185
Sitting Bull, 74, 76, 81–83, 98, 111–112, 122, 251, 289
Sixkiller, Jess, 58
Skins, 295
Slogum House, 175
smallpox, 68
Smith, Albert, 267
Smith, Jeanne, 49, 210–211
Smith, Josie, 267–268
Smith, Michael, 38–39, *39*, 48–50, 129–130, 132–135, 151–154, 156, 187–188, 194, 196–206, 209–211, 213, 217–218, 238, 241–243, 246, 248–250, 254, 309, 313–314
Smith, Roy, 263–264, 273
South Dakota Stockgrowers Association, 173
South Hills/Southhillers, 13–14, 40, 167–168, 175
Spade Ranch, 100, 160–162, 166–167, 178–179, 204–205, 213, 250, 308
Spindler, Merle, 181–182
Spotted Tail Agency, 31–32, 78
Spotted Tail, 31–32, 74–75, 77, 84, 95, 108, 136–137, 251
Spring Lake Ranch, 161
"squawmen," 70, 105
Stairs, Bill, 253
Steele, William, 235

St. Paul, Minnesota, 106, 195, 235
Standing Rock Agency/Reservation, 111–112, 121–122, 236, 279
Strasburger, Bob, 179
subagents. *See* "boss farmers"
Sullivan, Indiana, 94–95
Sun Dance, 63, 67, 69, 82, 115, 128, 165, 176–177, 319
Syrian traders, 169–170

Talbot, Jim, 238, 249, 254, 267–268, 271–272, 298
Tallent, Annie, 28
Taylor, Delores, 221–222
These Were the Sioux, 175
Thies, Donna, 264, 273–274
Thies, Randy, 264, 270, 273–274
Thompson, Jeannette (née Hartwig), 11, 14–15, 19–23, 41–42, 53, 144, 188, 206–208, 315
Thompson, John, 15
Tibbles, Thomas, 119
Trail of Broken Treaties, 219
Trial of Billy Jack, 221–222
Treaty of 1868, 33, 75–80, 107, 220, 225, 229
Treaty of 1889, 258, 283
Trueblood family, 40
Trueblood, Benjamin, 134
Trueblood, Buddy, 134
Trueblood, Jess, 235
Trueblood, Tom, 134
Trueblood, Lulu (née Sears) 126, 133–135, 204
Turner Foundation, 317–318
Turner, Ted, 317–318
Two Crow, Robert, 142–143, 317–318
Two Kettle Lakota tribe, 68

United Press/United Press International, 118, 249

United States Army/Cavalry, 30, 36,
71–75, 80–8, 85, 105–106,
118–119, 143, 191
United States Civil Rights Commis-
sion, 240
United States Marshals, 226–227, 229,
237–238
United States Supreme Court, 137,
295
University of Nebraska/University of
Nebraska-Lincoln, 63–64, 147,
296–298
University of Nebraska Press, 183
Union Pacific Railroad, 73
Unquiet Grave, 300–301

Valentine, Robert, 246–249, 254
Valentine, Nebraska, 95, 110, 119
Vietnam veterans, 142–143, 228–229,
245–246, 255, 295, 306, 317
Vietnam War, 40, 142–143, 220–221,
223, 245–246, 306
Vinton, Pat, 187
Vitalis, Wade, 271–272
VJ's Market, 275–276, 284–285, 296
Volunteers in Service to America, 238,
241–242

Wallace, George, 123
Walker, Fergus, 29, 32, 35
Walton, Robert "Curly," 179–181, 187
Washington Post, 148
Weil, Terry, 246
Western Cafe. *See* Seger's Cafe
Westover, William H., 258–261
Wheeler, Marvin, 21, 200
Wheeler, Virginia, 21, 200
Where White Men Fear to Tread, 302
whiskey ranches, 92–94, 258, 261
Whiteclay, Nebraska, *iii*, *2*, 46, 53–54,
56, 129, 132–133, 143–144, 166,

171, 180, 229, 236, 239, *256*,
273–278, 290, 292, 303
1999 riot/marches, 2–10, 279–289,
294, 300
2003 march, 296–299
Jack and Jill grocery store, 274,
283–284
origin of name, 262
source of illicit alcohol, 171–172,
262–265, 267–268
Whiteclay Nine, 289, 296
White Eye, 97–98
Williams, Ronald, 236–237, 293
Wilson, Dick, 190, 226, 235, 239
Wilson, Frank, 177
Winnebago Reservation/tribe, 129,
259, 267
Wilson, Jack. *See* Wovoka
Witcher, Eph, 29
World War I, 142, 172–173, 250
World War II, 19, 57, 142, 171,
181–182, 191, 289
Wounded Knee Legal Offense-Defense
Committee, 245, 249, 254
Wounded Knee Massacre, 4, 52, 64,
121–128, 134, 136, 138–139,
157–158, 175, 224, 227, 301
Wounded Knee occupation, 4,
227–231, 235, 279, 283, 300–301
Wounded Knee, South Dakota, 106,
138, 248, 255
Wounded Knee Trading Post, 155,
189–190, 226–228
Wovoka, 113–115
Wyoming Stock Growers Association,
99

Yankton, South Dakota, 26, 29
Yanktonai tribe, 68–69, 274
Yellow Bird Steele, Bob, 213, *214*,
215–216, 237, 244–245, 288,
300, 306–307, 309, 316

activism in Gordon, 231–234,
238–243
attack against Mark Monroe,
251–253
death of, 255
early activism, 222–225
Hacienda Motel incident, 243–244,
271
role at Wounded Knee occupation,
227–230
Sheridan Lounge incident,
245–249
Yellow Bird Steele, Charles, 215
Yellow Bird, Joann (née Cross),
222, 224–225, 230–231, 239,
243–248, 251–255, 306–307,
309, 315
Yellow Bird Steele, John, 288,
300–301
Yellow Bird Steele, Richard, 215–216,
223, 244
Yellow Bird Steele, Sarah, 215
Yellow Bird, Wesley, 224, 251
Yellow Bird, Zintkala Zi, 248, 255
Yellow Hair, Milo, 285
Yellowstone River, 69
Yellow Thunder, Amelia, 185–186, 319
Yellow Thunder, Andrew, 42, 163–166,
172
Yellow Thunder, Dennis, 43–44,
185–186, *304*, 319–320
Yellow Thunder, Jennie, 42, 163–166
Yellow Thunder, Raymond, *12*, 16,
39, 45–47, 56, 60–61, 129–130,
158, 172, 185, 205, 225, 280,
304, 317, 320
autopsies, 130, 133, 154–155, 196
assault of, 19–24, 202–204, 205,
305, 309, 312–315
childhood, 42–43, 163–164
death of, 47–48, 155, 188, 197,
208, 217–218, 232, 271, 307,
313–314
description of, 16, 142
final day, 41
marriage to Dora Cutgrass, 43
rumors about death, 53–54,
136, 140, 148–151, 155, 185,
221–222
Yellow Thunder, Russell, 44, 152,
185–186, 194, 317, 319
Young Bear, Severt, 54–56, 61, 135,
139, 154, 226, 229, 317–318
Young-Man-Afraid-of-His-Horse, 81,
106, 111

Zywiec, Ronald, 243–244, 250